Assessment of Partner Violence

Assessment of Partner Violence

A Handbook for Researchers and Practitioners

Jill H. Rathus and Eva L. Feindler

American Psychological Association

Washington, DC

Published by
American Psychological Association
750 First Street, NE
Washington, DC 20002
www.apa.org

To order	Tel: (800) 374-2721; Direct: (202) 336-5510
APA Order Department	Fax: (202) 336-5502; TDD/TTY: (202) 336-6123
P.O. Box 92984	Online: www.apa.org/books/
Washington, DC 20090-2984	E-mail: order@apa.org

In the U.K., Europe, Africa, and the Middle East, copies may be ordered from
American Psychological Association
3 Henrietta Street
Covent Garden, London
WC2E 8LU England

Typeset in New Baskerville by World Composition Services, Inc., Sterling, VA

Printer: Port City Press, Inc., Baltimore, MD
Cover Designer: NiDesign, Baltimore, MD
Technical/Production Editor: Rosemary Moulton

The opinions and statements published are the responsibility of the authors, and such opinions and statements do not necessarily represent the policies of the American Psychological Association.

Library of Congress Cataloging-in-Publication Data
Rathus, Jill H.
   Assessment of partner violence : a handbook for researchers and
practitioners / Jill H. Rathus and Eva L. Feindler.
       p. cm.
    ISBN 1-59147-005-6 (alk. paper)
1. Conjugal violence—Handbooks, manuals, etc. 2. Sexual abuse
victims—Handbooks, manuals, etc. 3. Sex crimes—Handbooks, manuals,
etc. 4. Victims of family violence—Handbooks, manuals, etc. I.
Feindler, Eva L. II. Title.

    RC560.S44R38 2004
    616.85′822—dc22   2003021812

British Library Cataloguing-in-Publication Data
A CIP record is available from the British Library.

Printed in the United States of America
First Edition

Contents

List of Measures

Chapter 7. Self-Report Measures Specific to the Assessment of Partner Abuse

Chapter 8. Self-Report Measures: Assessment of General Relationship Functioning, Anger and Hostility, and Other Correlates of Partner Abuse

Chapter 9. Analogue Methods and Behavioral Coding Devices

General Analogue Methods

Preface

This project was conceived from a conversation we first had with each other in 1995. Jill had just accepted a faculty position in the Clinical Psychology Doctoral Program at Long Island University, C.W. Post Campus, and was to serve also as cocoordinator of our program's Family Violence Specialty Concentration along with Eva. Our program's elective concentration area in family violence allows students to obtain specific training in theory, research, and clinical interventions in family violence on top of their broad training as clinical psychologists. In addition to a series of elective courses, students specializing in family violence typically gain practical and clinical experience and conduct their doctoral research in this field. We were discussing ways to enhance students' training and experience, and one issue that came up was that students setting out to design their dissertations were continually reinventing the wheel with regard to assessment instruments. Many students seemed to undertake a laborious process of sifting through the literature from scratch to find appropriate measures on such topics as partner violence, relationship adjustment, and anger. Despite the guidance students received from us as mentors, we, along with other faculty members, did not possess detailed knowledge of nearly all the standardized instruments available, especially if the topics fell well outside of our specializations within family violence (Jill with intimate partner violence and Eva with adolescents, family relationships, and anger management). Even within our areas of expertise, instruments were being created or revised rapidly and required many visits and revisits to the literature.

Thus, we came up with the idea of beginning to collect and organize, on behalf of students initiating research projects, copies of reliable and valid instruments used in the family violence field, along with related reference material pertaining to the development and psychometric evaluation of the measures as well as any critically important or classic studies using the measure. Our original discussion began with the notion of cataloguing these resources in a three-ringed binder, or perhaps a centrally located file drawer. We thought we might ask our research assistants to embark on conducting literature searches and writing authors to obtain copies of scales and planned to contribute copies of those assessments and articles of which we already had possession; thus began the task of compiling a sizable collection of widely used family violence measures.

We quickly realized that the utility of such a project could certainly reach beyond that of the graduate students in our program. Graduate students anywhere doing work in this area might benefit from such a resource, as well as professionals performing clinical work or conducting research in the family violence area. We realized that our students surely were not the only ones combing the expansive literature in search of the ideal measure for their purposes, and that access to all of the relevant information in one place could facilitate the goals of many attempting to conduct research, evaluate their treatment programs, or provide clinical or forensic assessments. Beyond the domain of psychology, we believed that a range of disciplines, including, but not limited to, psychiatry, social work, nursing, medicine, forensics, and criminology, might make use of such a compilation. Around the same time, the American Psychological Association (APA) Books put out a call for manuscripts pertaining to assessment of specific clinical domains, and the idea of rendering our student-friendly resource into a book was born.

Our original contract with APA Books specified that the book was to be a single, comprehensive volume titled *Handbook of Assessment of Family Violence* that included sections on measures pertaining to children, adults, families, and couples. However, we did not at the time realize the scope of the project we were getting into. When our initial manuscript totaled 900 pages, we renegotiated with the publisher to develop two volumes on the topic. The first was to pertain to children, adults, and families; the second exclusively to intimate partner violence. For the first volume, we also elected to invite an advanced graduate student from our program, Laura Beth Silver (who has since graduated and obtained her license), to collaborate with us on the research and writing. This first APA volume, *Assessment of Family Violence: A Handbook for Researchers and Practitioners* (Feindler, Rathus, & Silver), was published in 2003. The present volume represents the completion of the second part of this undertaking.

In reviewing the available books on related topics prior to undertaking this work, we felt ours would make a unique contribution in the following ways. First, several useful available books compile and review instruments pertaining to clinical practice or marital–family functioning. However, these books do not specialize in assessments of family violence and thus contain only a handful of instruments that would be relevant to practitioners and researchers working in the family violence field. Such books also typically lack substantial sections on assessment and measurement issues. Second, the published books directly pertaining to family violence and its assessment, though excellent, tend to contain thorough overviews of assessment issues in the field but provide only brief mention or description of the relevant measures. In our companion volumes, we sought to include a balance by devoting Part I of each book to issues in assessment ranging from clinical and research issues to reviews of psychometric principles. We then devoted Part II of each book to an extensive and detailed review of dozens of assessment tools in the field. These volumes may thus represent the only resources available that emphasize a multimethod approach to assessment by a review of interview, self-report, and analogue methods but that also describe each measure in detail, complete with sample items, administration and scoring guidelines, and related research. We also have included scale availability information to facilitate readers' ability to obtain the instruments for their own use. The books are thus aimed at a range of readers, from students just beginning their training in the field of family violence to seasoned professionals. Readers less familiar with topics such as psychometrics and modalities of assessment will find Part I of each book a useful prelude to the specific instruments reviewed in Part II; readers knowledgeable on these topics might find the chapters reviewing the clinical and research issues specific to the assessment of partner violence helpful, or might proceed directly to the review of measures in Part II. In keeping with our original "file drawer" concept, we include an index of instruments at the beginning of the book (List of Measures) that readers can scan for finding measures for their particular purposes. Because our literature review led to such a vast quantity of instruments, we could not include a detailed review of them all and still meet the page limits to which we ultimately agreed. Thus, chapter 8, on self-report measures, concludes with an appendix listing in brief many additional measures that were deemed relevant, yet in most cases beyond the scope of this volume to be reviewed in detail.

We hope that both volumes will serve their intended purpose of advancing students' training, aiding with forensic evaluations, facilitating program evaluation, enhancing assessment in clinical practice, and contributing to and stimulating research in family and partner violence.

Acknowledgments

To begin, we would like to thank each other for collaboration on this project. We did not fully realize the scope of this project when we initiated it, and it could not have been completed without each author's dedication and perseverance. We would also like to thank the student body in the Long Island University, C.W. Post Campus Clinical Psychology Doctoral Program, particularly those working with us within the family violence specialty concentration. Their quest for knowledge and commitment to conducting clinically relevant and well-designed research spurred us to develop this project. We also want to thank the multitude of families, couples, and individuals with whom we have worked throughout our clinical careers. The critical need for effective treatment programs for and quality research with those exposed to violence motivated us to see both volumes through to completion.

A special note of thanks goes to Cathy Kudlack from the Psychological Services Center at C.W. Post. She spent countless hours assisting us, at every stage. She did so with patience, tireless energy, efficiency, and a consistent smile. We are deeply indebted to her.

We greatly appreciate the contributions of several current and former clinical psychology graduate students at C.W. Post, including Anthony Anzalone, Nick Cavuoto, Pat Price, Lauren Scher, Laura Beth Silver, Miryam Sorkin, and Sharon Spitzer. These students contributed to the voluminous research needed for this book, and we cannot imagine having completed it without their help.

We also thank the numerous authors of the assessment instruments described herein. We contacted many of them requesting copies of their scales or supporting information; many went out of their way by sending us reprints and preprints or pointing us to materials over conversations by phone or e-mail. Without their devotion to the field and responsiveness to us, this book would not exist.

We feel tremendous gratitude toward the reviewers of this work, Chris Murphy as well as an anonymous reviewer. They were generous with their time, clearly devoted to their task, and provided incisive, detailed feedback that no doubt improved the quality of the book. We appreciate their excellent and ample contributions. Additionally, certain professionals in the field have knowingly or unknowingly influenced this work through their formal or informal mentoring or close professional contacts. We would like to thank these individuals, including K. Daniel O'Leary, Dina Vivian, Richard Heyman, Dan Klein, Everett Waters, Matthew Campbell, David Pelcovitz, and Amy Holtzworth-Munroe. We also thank our colleagues in the clinical psychology program at C.W. Post who have been supportive and encouraging of this undertaking, particularly the program director, Bob Keisner. Ronnie Zaglin at C.W. Post has also been consistently helpful.

We would like to thank the editorial and production staff at APA Books for their patience, flexibility, and guidance from conceptualization to the final stages of production. Their professionalism, knowledge, and feedback have greatly enhanced this work.

Jill would like to dedicate this book to her parents, Karen Shawn and Spencer Rathus, and stepparents, Keith Breiman and Lois Fichner-Rathus. Their accomplishments have been inspirational, their support and guidance invaluable.

In addition, she would like to thank her husband, Lloyd Goldsamt, and daughters, Lauren and Julia, for providing support, patience, and joy to her throughout the writing of this book (for her four-year-old twins, this book has been underway for their entire lives!). She would like to thank Gillian Goldberg Maldanado for helping her work with peace of mind. She would also like to thank Andrew Shawn as well as Alan and Barbara Goldsamt for their ongoing support and interest in this work. Finally, she would like to thank her aunt, Rita Shawn. An accomplished social worker, Rita regularly inquired about this project and sent useful resources that improved the scope of the book.

Eva would like to dedicate this volume to her mother, Joan L. Feindler, who passed away following the publication of Assessment of Family Violence. She was always an inspiration and technical support staff member for any writing project undertaken. A life-long educator, she shared the vision we had in writing these volumes to assist students in the pursuit of their clinical and career goals and to help improve family relationships.

Assessment of
Partner Violence

Introduction

Intimate partner violence is a major public health issue (Browne, 1993; Koss et al., 1994); its harmful impact on victims, its toll on child witnesses, and its associated economic costs provide challenges for professionals working in a variety of fields. The increase in shelters for victims of violence, the development of criminal justice responses encouraging the arrest of perpetrators, the increased sensitivity to the prevalence of partner violence in couples presenting for marital therapy, and increased surveillance in community samples have led to a burgeoning of identified cases. Whether determining prevalence rates, screening for program assignment, evaluating a prevention or treatment program, conducting a forensic evaluation, performing a risk assessment, or conducting controlled outcome research, the accurate assessment of partner violence is essential. In this volume we aim to provide professionals working in this field with the resources to implement multimodal, reliable, and valid assessment of partner violence and its correlates. The topic of partner violence assessment is timely given the innovations that have occurred in the field in recent years. Many scales have been adapted or revised to address concerns (e.g., the Revised Conflict Tactics Scale; Straus, Hamby, Boney-McCoy, & Sugarman, 1996), and entirely new approaches to the assessment of partner violence have emerged (e.g., the Timeline Followback Assessment, Fals-Stewart, Birchler, & Kelley, 2003; the Spousal Assault Risk Assessment Guide, Kropp & Hart, 2000). Similarly, modalities other than self-report rating scales have grown substantially in their application to the assessment of partner violence over the last decade, to include a wide range of interview and analogue assessment devices. There are thus now several dozen standardized assessment tools related to this topic. Further, many existing measures are being evaluated with a greater range of populations, and there is increasing sophistication in the field with regard to factors such as definitional issues, subtypes of violent couples and of violence perpetrators, and cultural diversity. Thus, we feel there is a present need for a practical resource handbook of this type for researchers, practitioners, and administrators.

Our intention in this volume is thus to furnish practitioners, researchers, and program evaluators with a comprehensive handbook that places information concerning assessment instruments in couple violence at their fingertips. As such, we describe and review a large variety of measurement options in the field. In this introduction, we offer an overview of the book, including its scope, its contents, its organization and format, and our criteria for the inclusion of measures.

Note that we use the terms *partner violence, couple violence, domestic violence,* and *marital violence* interchangeably throughout this book. We favor the first two terms, however, because of their specificity to couples and yet their broad applicability to partnerships other than married ones, such as same-sex, cohabitating, and dating relationships. We made the decision to use gender-neutral language rather than using the term *wife abuse,* to acknowledge the violence that occurs in same-sex couples (West, 1998a) and to acknowledge the violence that women sometimes perpetrate toward men (cf. Johnson, 1995; Vivian & Heyman, 1996). However, we are aware of the bias inherent in adapting a gender-neutral approach (see Margolin & Burman, 1993) and remain sensitive to the gender disparities in the context and impact of partner aggression (Bograd, 1998; Vivian & Langhinrichsen-Rohling, 1994; White, Smith, Koss, & Figueredo, 2000).

In addition, note that we do not equate discrete acts of physical aggression with battering. Our use of the term *battering* refers to a general pattern of violence, control, and psychological aggression, typically unidirectional; by contrast, a large portion of partner violent behavior is of lower intensity, infrequent, and often bidirectional (e.g., Johnson, 1995; Vivian & Heyman, 1996). We hope that our distinctions remain clear throughout the text as we refer to these constructs.

The scope of the present volume is limited primarily to instruments developed for or applied to the assessment of partner violence, its risk factors, its correlates, and its sequelae. We also included many measures developed for the assessment of couple interactions in general that have direct relevance to assessment of violence in couples. The companion volume to this book (Feindler, Rathus, & Silver, 2003) focuses on assessment of family violence pertaining to children (including child witnesses to domestic violence), parents, and families.

Within the parameters of couple violence/couple interactions, we have included dozens of measures, spanning five decades of research and three types of assessment methods: interview assessments, self-report/paper-and-pencil instruments, and analogue assessments. We describe measures used widely as well as measures used only in a single study, provided they meet our criteria for inclusion described below. Our hope is to provide readers with a broad sampling of measures in the field so that they can make use of specific measures we review in their clinical work or research. An additional hope is that assessors might build on the methodology described in a particular area to adapt a measure, further the development of a measure, or construct a measure of their own. Despite the exhaustive roster of measures we include and steady growth in this field, the need for new and improved instruments in couple violence remains, particularly with regard to increased cultural sensitivity (see chap. 5, this volume).

Contents

This handbook contains two major parts. Part I: Issues in the Assessment of Partner Violence provides a general overview of matters pertaining to the assessment of partner violence and contains five chapters. Part II: Assessment of Partner Violence details specific instruments that measure couple violence and contains four chapters.

Chapter 1, "Why Assess? Purposes of Assessment in Partner Violence," covers broad and specific objectives in conducting assessments of partner violence. Broad objectives include clinical evaluation (involving standard clinical practice, accountability for the provision of effective treatments, crisis management, and forensic evaluations or other professional consultations), conducting research, and program evaluation. Specific assessment objectives include obtaining a problem description and determining need for treatment, setting targets for treatment, measuring pretreatment functioning (i.e., obtaining baseline data), measuring treatment progress, measuring treatment process, measuring treatment adherence, and measuring treatment outcome.

Chapter 2, "Modalities of Assessment in Partner Violence," offers a description of specific assessment modalities and a discussion of their advantages and disadvantages. The modalities are discussed both in general terms and with regard to specific issues that arise when applying them to the assessment of couple violence. Approaches described include interviews, self-report measures/rating scales (including a specific section devoted to the Conflict Tactics Scale), analogue measures of couple interactions (including physiological and mechanical measures as well as observational coding systems), direct observation in natural settings, and archival records.

Chapter 3, "Assessment of Partner Violence in Clinical Practice," includes the following major topics: clinical issues, diagnosis in partner violence assessment, establishing rapport, and ethical and legal considerations. The clinical issues addressed include matters such as what or whom is to be the focus of assessment in partner violence, psychological abuse, the assessment of partner violence in marital treatment, who should receive treatment and in what modality, and whether there are clear aggressor and victim roles in couple violence or whether the notion of "mutual combat" more accurately captures the phenomenon. Our discussion includes such specific topics as minimization of aggression, lack of agreement between partners, and targeting violence when the couple does not view it as a problem. After discussing issues of diagnosis and strategies for establishing rapport, the chapter presents ethical considerations and relevant legal matters. Legal issues covered include risk management, subpoenas for client records, reporting requirements, forensic evaluations, and prediction of dangerousness.

Chapter 4, "Research Considerations in the Assessment of Partner Violence: Scale Development, Psychometrics, and Measuring Treatment Outcome," focuses on a number of research issues relevant to the assessment of partner violence. We first consider methods of test construction and scoring. We then provide a review of psychometric characteristics, focusing on the various types of reliability and validity. These sections provide a review for those trained in assessment but will prove most helpful for readers lacking a background in assessment or psychometrics, particularly as these readers read the relevant sections in the scale descriptions in the next chapter. The chapter also includes a discussion of measuring outcome through client-related criteria, efficiency and cost-related criteria, consumer-related criteria, and social impact measures. The final section of the chapter addresses the various problems with interpreting changes based on simple pre–post evaluation and some suggestions for managing these problems.

Chapter 5, "Research Issues and Challenges in the Assessment of Partner Violence," presents issues in conducting research in couple violence, each with its inherent challenges. These include issues of cultural diversity, problems with defining constructs, problems with selecting and defining variables to target as outcome measures in programs for partner assault, controversy over quantitative versus qualitative approaches, difficulties in establishing psychometric properties of measures, difficulties in applying sound research design, issues of "subjecting" victims to research or placing research participants at risk, and occasions when research interferes with normal administrative or clinical routines.

The second section of this volume includes direct measures of partner violence as well as measures pertaining to risk factors, correlates, and sequelae of partner violence. Subjects of assessment in these chapters include victims of violence, perpetrators of violence, or the couple as a unit. Chapters 6 through 9 review measures of interview assessment; self-report/paper-and-pencil assessment instruments specific to partner physical or psychological abuse; self-report instruments assessing general relationship functioning, anger and hostility, and other correlates of partner abuse; and analogue assessment, respectively. Chapter 8, on self-report/paper-and-pencil instruments assessing general relationship functioning, anger and hostility, and other correlates of partner abuse, concludes with an Appendix listing features of approximately 30 additional instruments. These measures were reviewed in brief within this Appendix on the basis of (a) having overly preliminary psychometric properties, (b) being peripheral enough as to be considered beyond the scope of the book for detailed review (due to space considerations) yet still of interest to the researcher or practitioner working in couple violence, or (c) our not being able to obtain the scale for review. Chapter 9, on analogue assessment, is divided into three parts: (a) basic analogue measures (i.e., those approaches used to recreate or mimic naturalistic couple interactions or serve as stimuli to elicit responses) and specialized measurement devices used in conjunction with the basic analogue measures, (b) physiological assessment, and (c) observational coding systems. Note that analogue measures take a variety of forms but all involve some type of direct behavioral observation and some type of recreation or approximation of a natural setting. Examples of analogue assessment measures are use of videotaped conflict scenarios, role-play interactions, structured discussion tasks for partners, physiological and mechanical assessment methods, and behavioral observation coding systems applied to couple interactions.

Behavioral Assessment Approach

Our orientation in this book favors a behavioral assessment approach to the measurement of family violence. Behavioral assessment, as compared with traditional assessment, emphasizes the measurement of observable rather than inferred characteristics, environmentally or contextually determined causes for events over intrapsychic factors or traits, present rather than historical events, ideographic rather than nomothetic assessment, continuous or repeated rather than one-time or pre–post evaluation, multimodal rather than single-method assessment, and the use of psychometrically sound (i.e., reliable and valid) assessment tools (Bellack & Hersen, 1998). Thus, we limit the inclusion of instruments that do not fit within the behavioral assessment tradition, such as projective measures, personality measures, and other measures that have limited or absent psychometric criteria or rely on highly inferential measurement of traitlike constructs. Instead, we feature primarily assessment tools using direct observation, analogue methods, physiological assessment, structured interviews, and behavior rating checklists.[1] Given the multidisciplinary nature of the team approach now common to the investigation and referral process in couple violence (i.e., police, judges, probation officers, case managers, etc.; see Shepard & Pence, 1999), behavioral assessment approaches offer a detailed account of the most salient variables in the family context, thereby improving communication with personnel from nonclinical fields. A more detailed discussion of the characteristics of behavioral assessment follows.

Observable Rather Than Inferred Characteristics

It is interesting to note that, in this field, the central target of assessment (partner violence) is not measured directly. That is, we do not actually witness instances of partner-directed physical aggression. Instead, we assess retrospective reports of such behaviors (e.g., number of specified abusive acts within the past year), signs or symptoms (e.g., assessments of trauma symptoms or shame), associated features (e.g., measures of psychological abuse), or risk factors (e.g., escalating negative communication patterns). In this sense, when we apply direct observation in the field of family violence, we are directly observing *in*direct indications of abuse.

In any case, a behavioral approach emphasizes assessment of observable behaviors rather than inferred attributes, with a focus on molecular behaviors rather than broad characteristics. Examples of direct observation range from monitoring specific violent acts on a checklist to laboratory-based

---

1. Note that although self-monitoring tools (e.g., a daily log of anger outbursts) fall within the domain of behavioral assessment, we do not specifically review such measures here because they tend to be highly individualized and not subject to psychometric evaluation. (For an example of such a tool, see Pence & Paymar, 1993, for a model of a self-monitoring "control log" for the assessment of forms of control over a partner.)

couple discussions in which facial expressions are coded. In these cases, a focus on molecular behaviors would mean coding and drawing conclusions about variables such as contextual violent behavior and emotions rather than traits of aggressiveness. The rubric of observable behaviors may also be considered to encompass private behaviors that are observable only to the individual, such as attitudes, beliefs, or subjective ratings of anger. Such behaviors might be assessed in an analogue paradigm wherein a target individual is given hypothetical partner behaviors as provocations of anger and the individual is asked to report his or her own affective, cognitive, or behavioral responses. These stand in contrast to inferred characteristics such as unconscious processes or structures, defense mechanisms, and needs.

Environmentally or Contextually Determined Causes for Events Over Intrapsychic Factors or Traits

A hallmark of behavioral assessment in clinical practice is functional analysis, a behavioral assessment interviewing method focused on identifying variables that elicit and maintain particular behavior patterns (Haynes & O'Brien, 1990). Thus, rather that viewing behavior as stemming primarily from internal qualities such as personality, the person–environment connection is emphasized and behaviors are viewed in context. For example, Fruzzetti, Saedi, Wilson, and Rubio (1998) have developed the Domestic Violence Interview, which assesses in detail the antecedents and consequences of violent episodes.

Also reflecting the behavioral assessment preference for contextual determinants of behavior is that behavior is often measured in the natural environment such as the home (e.g., Margolin, Burman, & John, 1989) or, similarly, in a close laboratory analogue of the natural environment such as measuring couples' conflictual interactions (i.e., providing the relational context and stimulus cues of conflict) rather than asking couples to self-report on their conflict style. Finally, consistent with this approach are self-report or interview measures of context for family violence such as marital functioning.

Present Rather Than Historical Events

Behavioral assessment emphasizes the influence of present rather than historical events. Consistent with this approach, initial inquiries as well as intervention targets are based more on proximal than early childhood factors in determining behavior (e.g., arguing with a partner leading to increased aversive arousal vs. arguing with a partner reminding one of a conflict with one's parent).

Ideographic Rather Than Nomothetic Approach

Behavioral assessment focuses on an ideographic, or individualized, approach to assessment as opposed to a nomothetic, or normative group approach. As such, behavioral assessment is often criterion-referenced as opposed to norm-referenced; that is, working to reach an individualized client goal or standard by comparing the client's level of functioning from one point in time to another rather than focusing on the client's performance compared with a normative group. In our review of assessment measures in partner violence, in fact, devices with published norms were the exception rather than the rule.

Continuous Evaluation

A behavioral assessment approach emphasizes continuous rather than one-time or two-point assessments. This may be a new concept for practitioners not familiar with the behavioral assessment approach, because typically assessment is thought of as something that occurs at the outset of treatment. Only more recently have clinicians become accustomed to the notion that assessment is used to evaluate treatment as well, typically at posttreatment. In contrast, a behavioral assessment approach advocates ongoing monitoring of behaviors targeted for change. This typically takes the form of daily, weekly, or monthly monitoring through checklists, clinical interviews, self- or other-rated scales, or some type of structured diary. However, continuous evaluation might connote the measurement of even moment-to-moment change, such as using physiological assessment or emotion ratings throughout the vicissitudes of a 15-minute interaction with a partner (e.g., Gottman et al., 1995). Particularly notable increases or decreases in measured behaviors can contribute important information to a functional analysis and provide information about the nature of change.

Multiple Sources of Data: Multimodal Assessment

Another aspect of the behavioral assessment approach is multimodal assessment, or the use of more than one instrument administered using more than one method, such as supplementing a behavioral observation assessment with a self-report measure and an interview. Use of varied modes is preferable in family violence assessment, because any single method or measure tends to yield data of limited value (see chap. 2, this volume; see also O'Leary, Vivian, & Malone, 1992). Multimodal assessment may also include the use of multiple informants, such as partner reports of a target spouse's behavior. Similarly, multimodal assessment can mean observation in multiple situations, such as observing a violent spouse in the practitioner's office and while interacting with a partner.

Use of Psychometrically Sound Assessment Tools

Finally, behavioral assessment approaches rely on the use of psychometrically sound assessment instruments. Essentially, this means that evidence supports the reliability and validity of an instrument (see chap. 4, this volume, for discussion of reliability and validity). It is not enough to demonstrate the general reliability and validity of a measure; it must be demonstrated that a measure has reliability and validity for a particular use with a particular population. As we describe assessment devices throughout this volume, we report the various types of reliability and validity that have been established for each instrument.

Organization and Format

Within each of the instrument review chapters, the measures we describe are included alphabetically by instrument name, within general category of assessment device. We devote chapters to interview methods, self-report methods (both direct measures of spousal violence and associated constructs), and analogue measures of couple interactions. Within chapters 8 (self-report of associated constructs) and 9 (analogue measures), we group instruments according to subtype of assessment device (e.g., physiological measures vs. observational coding devices).

Within subsections, we present numerous descriptions of instruments but do not include the instruments themselves. We provide the following information for each assessment device:

- *Assessment category.* This is the subcategory within which the measure fits, such as "Observational Coding Systems."
- *Title and authors.* The title of the assessment device, along with authors of the assessment device, which usually, but not always, correspond to the authors of the primary reference.
- *Description and development of assessment method.* This section provides a description of the method and describes scale development.

- *Target population.* This includes the population for whom the scale was intended, or on whom the scale was developed or evaluated. Although this section suggests past applications of the scale, it does not necessarily suggest limits on populations to whom the scale might be applied. For paper-and-pencil measures, we include the reading level of the scale here, if available.
- *Equipment needed.* Some assessment devices within the analogue assessment chapters require specific equipment for their use; these are included if specified by the authors.
- *Format.* The format section includes descriptions of any subscales, the number of items in the scale, as well as sample items.
- *Administration and scoring.* This section includes the response format (i.e., type of scaling, number of anchor points, etc.), the length of time to complete the instrument (and, when applicable, the length of time required for training in the procedure/training to expertise in the coding system), any particular instructions for the respondents, and scoring information.
- *Psychometric evaluation.* This section includes information on the scale's norms, reliability, and validity. For norms, when available, we include information on what populations the scale was normed on, means and standard deviations in various populations, or cutoffs (e.g., for "clinical" levels of the phenomenon of interest). Sometimes, the authors present extensive normative information on a variety of subpopulations in comprehensive tables in the primary article, chapter, or manual accompanying the instrument. In such cases of extensive normative data, for reasons of economy of space, we refer the reader to the relevant source.
- *Advantages.* Here we provide advantages of the particular measure described, often including a combination of those noted by the author and our own evaluation of the device's advantages.
- *Limitations.* We balance our discussion of advantages with mention of limitations inherent in the instrument.
- *Primary scale reference.* Here we provide the original source reference, which typically contains a presentation of the scale development, conceptualization, description, application, and psychometric evaluation. While these are most often journal articles, the primary scale references are, on occasion, book chapters, professionally published manuals, or unpublished manuscripts.
- *Scale availability.* Most of the time, complete interview or analogue formats or scales are not included in the primary reference. Thus,

we furnish the reader with a source for obtaining the assessment instrument itself (which usually will be accompanied by instructions for scoring). These sources typically consist of the author's direct contact information; an article, chapter, or book containing the scale; or the assessment corporation that currently owns the rights to the assessment device.

- *Related references.* Related references typically include those that contain related information on the scale's development, psychometric evaluation, or application to a couple violence population.
- *General comments and recommendations for researchers and practitioners.* This section contains a summary of our review of the scale, final comments on the instrument, or recommendations regarding its use.

Criteria for the Inclusion of Measures

We took a series of steps as we selected the many measures to be included in this volume. Note that we excluded numerous additional assessment methodologies in the field of domestic violence because they fell outside of the topical domain of this book (e.g., medical assessment approaches), fell outside of a couple violence focus, lacked psychometric support, or fell far astray of a behavioral assessment approach.

As our orientation in this book favors a behavioral assessment approach to the measurement of family violence, we primarily feature assessment tools relying on direct observation, analogue methods, physiological assessment, structured interviews, and behavior rating scales. Because we follow a behavioral orientation ourselves, we chose a more in-depth review of this approach rather than what by necessity would have been a superficial review of all available relevant assessment methodologies. While other approaches to research and assessment are certainly valid (e.g., psychodynamic, personality-based, feminist), they simply fall beyond the scope of this book. Moreover, given the multidisciplinary nature of the team approach now common to the investigation and referral process in family violence (i.e., police, judges, child protective case workers, probation officers, case managers, etc.), behavioral assessment approaches offer a detailed account of the most salient variables in the family context, thereby improving communication with personnel from nonclinical fields.

Note that despite our general intention and tendency to follow a behavioral assessment approach, we do include instruments that reflect exceptions to this tendency. Many of these consist of self-report rating scales that involve the endorsement of specific behaviors conducted within a well-defined and recent time frame (e.g., the Conflict Tactics Scale; Straus, 1979) or assess contextual stimuli rather than traitlike or intrapsychic phenomena (e.g., measures of marital functioning, such as the Dyadic Adjustment Scale; Spanier, 1976). However, we also include several instruments containing retrospective self-report items (e.g., the Propensity for Abusiveness Scale; D. G. Dutton, 1995); scales measuring traits or other nonobservable phenomena such as perceptions, automatic thoughts, or beliefs (e.g., the Inventory of Beliefs About Wife Beating; Saunders, Lynch, Grayson, & Linz, 1987); instruments based on nomothetic assessment (i.e., measures with norms for various populations, such as the State–Trait Anger Expression Inventory; Spielberger, 1988); as well as instruments designed for diagnostic purposes (e.g., Structured Clinical Interview for DSM–IV; First, Spitzer, Gibbon, & Williams, 1995a, 1995b). We included such instruments if we believed that by excluding them we would significantly limit the utility of this book or misrepresent prototypical assessment strategies in this field. However, to be included, minimum requirements of such measures were that they met at least some, if not all, characteristics of behavioral assessment measures, including meeting psychometric standards of having some degree of established reliability and validity data.[2]

We also had to make some difficult choices along the way in deciding what to and to not include. For example, a large collection of interview and self-report instruments exists to assess posttraumatic stress disorder and psychological trauma (see Foa, Cashman, Jaycox, & Perry, 1997; Kubany, Leisen, Kaplan, & Kelly, 2000; Kubany, Leisen, Kaplan, Watson et al., 2000; Wilson & Keane, 1997), which are certainly related to the contents of the present volume. However, the amount of scales available within this area was so vast that we felt reviewing them went beyond the scope of this book, and we instead decided to include only a brief sampling of these measures, particularly those especially relevant to individuals exposed to partner assault (e.g., Foa et al., 1997; Kubany, Leisen, Kaplan, Watson et al., 2000; Pelcovitz, Vanderkolk, Roth, Kaplan, Mandel, & Resnick, 1997). We refer the reader to the excellent reviews available (e.g., Wilson & Keane, 1997) for more information on this type of assessment. In addition, chapter 8 contains an

---

2. Although we attempted to provide complete descriptions and adequate psychometrics, we were at times limited by insufficient published information on a scale. We decided to include scales with incomplete information available if the scale evidenced other strengths or represented a specific area of family violence assessment not well represented by other devices.

appendix of dozens of additional measures reviewed in brief that were deemed related yet beyond our scope.

Our overall process included the following steps:

- an exhaustive literature review of measures used in the field of couple violence
- a supplementary literature review extended to the assessment of dyadic interactions (such that we included methods/scales that have not necessarily been used in the field of couple violence but that we viewed as relevant to assessment in this area)
- a categorization of what we found into "include" and "exclude" groups based on our criteria of behavioral assessment approaches, psychometric support, and other inclusion and exclusion criteria described in the previous paragraphs
- a mailing of lists of titles and authors of our selected measures to selected experts in the field for their comments and recommendations regarding any oversights on our part
- for the measures we elected to include, we wrote to authors to obtain copies of measures or information that might have been missing from the references we obtained (e.g., additional psychometric development, new adaptations of the scales)

We then reported what we were able to find, sometimes access to authors or to important information was simply not available.

Conclusion

This introduction has described the scope of this volume, its contents, and its organization and format. It also delineates our criteria for the selection of assessment devices and outlines the multistep process we undertook to arrive at our final group of measures and the information we provide on each of them. Working in the field of domestic violence in any capacity is difficult; we hope our efforts can, to some extent, facilitate such work by providing the reader with a clear and easy-to-use reference source for learning about and locating relevant assessment tools pertaining to couple violence.

Part I

Issues in the Assessment of Partner Violence

Why Assess? Purposes of Assessment in Partner Violence

Two large-scale nationally representative family violence surveys (Straus & Gelles, 1990; Straus, Gelles, & Steinmetz, 1980) have revealed that approximately 28% of married couples report at least one incident of physical aggression in their relationship. Within the year prior to the survey, 11%–12% of couples reported at least one act of physical aggression, with 3%–4% experiencing severe and repeated abuse. Despite partners reporting similar overall rates of physical aggression, women reported being the recipients of more severe assaults and suffering substantially more injuries as a result (Straus & Gelles, 1990). Estimates suggest that nearly one in three adult women will be assaulted by a male partner in their lifetime and that as many as 4 million women receive severe assaults from male partners each year (e.g., Straus & Gelles, 1990). Moreover, the number of women reporting assault by a male partner in the past year jumps to 50%–60% when considering marital clinic samples (O'Leary, Neidig, & Heyman, 1995). In essence,

> violent victimization historically has been thought about in terms of assaults occurring between nonromantic acquaintances and strangers. Yet women's greatest risk of assault is from their intimates, particularly male partners ... we know now that women are more likely to be attacked, raped, injured, or killed by current or former male partners than by any other type of assailant. (Koss et al., 1994, p. 41)

With the sweeping prevalence of partner violence, mental health and other professionals will no doubt be frequently called on to assess its presence and impact. This chapter discusses the many potential purposes for and contexts of assessments of partner violence. There are a multitude of reasons for conducting assessments in the field of couple violence, which differ little from aims of assessment in any field involving either clinical practice or research. Most broadly considered, these objectives include clinical evaluation, research, and program evaluation. Specific assessment objectives pertaining to each of these areas are also detailed in this chapter.

Clinical Evaluation

Standard Clinical Practice

The individual practitioner, regardless of the setting in which the practice is based, must conduct assessments as part of standard practice. In general, the primary foci of these assessments will include determining the presence, scope, chronicity, and nature of abuse, as well as associated features, clinical diagnoses, or sequelae that may be in need of clinical attention. This process will include measuring the degree of impairment in functioning, the client's strengths and resources, and the environmental context in which any abuse is occurring. The essential purpose of assessment for the practitioner is thus to determine the type and scope of intervention needed (e.g., individual, group, or couple-focused; short term or long term; inpatient or outpatient; the orientation or approach that best suits the client's presentation), as well as to determine if additional services and referrals are needed.

Accountability: Provision of Effective Treatments

An additional function of clinical assessment, which is rapidly becoming a facet of standard clinical practice, is assessment *during* and *following* treatment to evaluate the ongoing and ultimate effectiveness of interventions. Often, insurance reimbursement plans require specification of treatment goals and methods, and an outcome evaluation documenting the degree to which these goals were obtained. More and more, those who reimburse for services are requiring the use of standardized measures of presenting problems, symptoms, and diagnostic criteria (Hayes, Barlow, & Nelson-Gray, 1999). In addition, at the individual level, individuals who are court-mandated to treatment may require documentation of their participation in and response to treatment. At the community level, monitoring and tracking methods for domestic violence perpetrators moving through various systems and agencies are a necessary component of developing a coordinated community response to domestic violence (see Shepard & Pence,

1999). Beyond complying with third-party reimbursement mandates or legal requirements, however, clinicians ethically seek to provide effective treatments and to be willing to reconsider treatment approaches when they do not appear effective; ongoing or repeated clinical assessments allow such determinations.

Crisis Management

Often, a case involving abuse will enter treatment in some type of crisis or will enter a crisis phase during the course of treatment. The practitioner will need to have familiarity with a variety of crisis assessment and intervention strategies to respond rapidly and appropriately to the crisis. Such knowledge should include familiarity with assessments of dangerousness, risk factors for imminent danger, statutory abuse reporting and duty-to-warn requirements, suicide assessment, safety planning, and local crisis services.

Forensic Evaluations or Other Professional Consultation

The practitioner may be called on at times to conduct forensic evaluations, to serve as an expert witness, or even to serve as a consultant to the case of a professional within another discipline or who has a lesser degree of expertise in the assessment of family violence. Further, in some jurisdictions, judges seek to collaborate with mental health professionals to develop pre-sentencing service recommendations for partner violence offenders based on forensic assessments. In addition, changing demographics concerning increased dual-arrest cases involving both partners and the increasing number of female arrests for partner violence present complex considerations about perpetrator and victim distinctions and the appropriate intervention services. When conducting forensic assessments for any purpose, the practitioner will need to be well-versed not only in the various assessment strategies relevant for the particular case but also in the ethical and legal issues outlined in chapter 3.

Conducting Research

Most research depends on assessment; data collection by definition typically involves some form of measurement of the research issue at hand. The quantitative research tradition dominates the field of partner violence and is characterized by statistical analysis of data, experimental control, and efforts to operationalize and quantify constructs (Kazdin, 1998). Within this tradition, there are many ways that assessment is used in research. Assessment is used to conduct basic research related to couple violence in areas such as physiology of violent men during conflict with their partners (e.g., Meehan, Holtzworth-Munroe, & Herron, 2001). It is also used to conduct passive observational, correlational, or case control studies examining such topics as characteristics of victims or perpetrators of abuse, discrepancies in reporting between partners, correlates of certain types of abuse, and typologies of abuse or of individuals who abuse (e.g., Holtzworth-Munroe & Stuart, 1994). Assessment can be used to identify risk factors for abuse (e.g., Lawrence & Bradbury, 2001) and, therefore, to identify potential intervention targets. Similarly, assessment strategies can be used to develop or test etiological models of abuse using such statistical methodologies as path analysis (e.g., O'Leary, Malone, & Tyree, 1994). From the qualitative research tradition, assessment can focus on the phenomenological experience of individuals whose lives are affected by partner violence. Some of the classic and most influential works in the field have followed a qualitative assessment approach (e.g., R. E. Dobash & Dobash, 1979; Sonkin, Martin, & Walker, 1985).

Another avenue of research that may germinate from assessment is the study of assessment methods themselves, asking questions such as the following: Is violence more likely to be detected when relying on spontaneous reports during clinical interview, direct interview questions, or written self-reports? What are the psychometric characteristics of a particular assessment measure? Does a particular assessment strategy discriminate violent from nonviolent samples? Can the discrepancies in data collected across multiple informants and with different methodologies be of clinical relevance in our understanding of a couple?

Finally, assessment is the cornerstone of treatment outcome research. To evaluate the effectiveness of a treatment, one needs to select assessment devices. Such devices commonly include self-report measures or rating scales (e.g., a physical and psychological abuse rating scale to determine whether aggression declines following treatment). Observational/analogue measures are also useful for assessing treatment outcome (e.g., observation of couple interactions to determine whether negative communication patterns improve following an intervention). Structured or semistructured interview measures are often used for screening and diagnosis for entering a treatment study but may be used as outcome measures as well (e.g., administration of a diagnostic interview to determine whether a battered woman no longer meets diagnostic criteria for posttraumatic stress disorder [PTSD] following treatment). These various assessment approaches are discussed in a later section in this chapter. In addition to identifying efficacious treatments, assessment can be used to examine predictors of outcome with a given population or treatment (e.g., examining whether therapeutic alliance predicts reductions in aggressive behavior; see P. D. Brown & O'Leary, 2000). Investigators might apply qualitative approaches in outcome research as well, such as asking women to voice their views of helpful aspects of treatment (Nabi & Horner, 2001; J. H. Rathus et al., 2001).

Program Evaluation

Another central use for assessment in couple violence research is program evaluation. Many programs exist for the treatment of diverse aspects of intimate violence; for victims, perpetrators, and witnesses; for mandated and voluntary participants; and for physical, psychological, sexual, or other forms of abuse. These programs are typically based in settings such as state- or county-based agencies, hospitals, clinics, shelters, university-based counseling centers, or grant-funded clinics. Often, sources of funding for such programs are scarce and in need of frequent renewal. These sources may include government-sponsored grants at the federal, state, county, or city level; private corporate or foundation grants or gifts from individual donors; or state or county tax revenues. For continued financial support, it has become essential that such programs report program evaluation data to their funding sources. Understandably, funding sources have the right to know not only if programs they are supporting are working but also how they are working in relation to other possible allocations of their money. For example, if individuals arrested for spouse abuse are mandated to a psychosocial group treatment program, it is reasonable to examine the program's impact on recidivism, as well as to examine how the program stands up in terms of outcome and cost-effectiveness compared with other interventions, such as alternative psychosocial interventions, probation, or incarceration. While early couple violence program evaluation standards were such that providing data such as annual records of referral, program entry, attrition rates, and recidivism rates (often defined by reentry to the program or outside accounts of relapse such as arrest records) would suffice, there is at present a greater demand for more far-reaching and detailed outcome assessments (Hayes et al., 1999).

Program evaluation also helps in the determination of what works and what needs improvement, for internal feedback and continued program development. With use of a multimodal assessment battery, one might ascertain that certain programs within a treatment setting are meeting their intended objectives while others or not, or that a particular aspect of a program is having the intended effects while another aspect is not. For example, a multifaceted program for battered women may include a group treatment component targeting empowerment and psychoeducation and an individual component targeting PTSD symptoms. Program evaluation might reveal that one of these components is not serving its intended function.

Program evaluations target factors beyond clinical efficacy. They are concerned with the

> context, process, and content of health delivery systems. We need to ask whether a program meets a health need, covers those who need it and not others, reaches those consumers for whom it is designed, and is delivered according to plan. We need to know whether delivery of an intervention in the rough and tumble world of practice has the same outcomes as it does in highly controlled settings. (Hayes et al., 1999, p. 267)

As such, steps in program evaluation consist of conducting a needs assessment; specifying program goals and content; conducting an internal process analysis targeting what the program consists of, who receives its services, and how it functions within the broader organization; conducting a utilization review to examine appropriateness of service delivery; examining program delivery to ensure the program was delivered as specified; and assessing program outcomes in a number of domains (see section on "Measuring Treatment Outcome," chap. 4, this volume; see also Hayes et al., 1999). Several differences between program evaluation and scientific research include the following: Program evaluation clients are included in the evaluation on the basis of clinical criteria rather than scientific needs, assessments are selected on the basis of client needs rather than on scientific grounds, clients enter treatment through routine clinical channels rather than additional recruitment methods, the behaviors targeted are done so out of client need rather than study goals, and assessments are taken to assess client progress rather than to make a case to the scientific community (Hayes et al., 1999). It is clear that significant overlap exists between goals and methods of treatment outcome research and program evaluation, and, to the extent that research and clinical goals are pursued ethically, the ultimate goal of both is the developments of optimal treatment approaches for clients.

Specific Assessment Objectives

Beyond the broad objectives of clinical assessments, treatment outcome research, and program evaluation, several specific assessment goals apply to some or all of these objectives. These include obtaining a problem description and determining need for treatment, setting targets for treatment, measuring pretreatment functioning, measuring treatment progress, measuring treatment process, measuring treatment adherence, and measuring treatment outcome.

Obtaining a Problem Description and Determining Need for Treatment

A central aspect of the assessment process is to obtain a description of the presenting problem. This stage of assessment might consist of an initial screening, which would comprise a broad-based assessment to identify need for treatment. The evaluator might use comprehensive interviews along with behavioral rating scales and global symptom checklists at this time. In general, obtaining a problem description in the field of partner violence would involve addressing questions such as the following: What are the presenting symptoms/problematic behaviors? What is the extent, nature, and duration of violent behavior? What is the intensity and direction of the aggression (e.g., severe unilateral; mild bidirectional)? Are there associated forms of abusive behaviors occurring (i.e., what is the nature and extent of psychological abuse)? What is the context and impact of the abusive behavior? Are various presenting symptoms within a normative level? Are they elevated? Are they in the range of a particular population? Is the clinical picture likely to pose a risk for future danger?

Also, many, but not all clinical assessments in the field of family violence seek to establish a clinical diagnosis. Establishing a diagnosis is commonplace with individuals presenting with sequelae of abuse, who might be seeking treatment for posttraumatic stress symptoms and other functional impairments. However, assessments for perpetrators of family violence often focus more on identifying behavioral targets for change (i.e., various forms of abusive behaviors as well as skill deficits and other targets) than identifying a diagnosis. In the field of partner abuse, this trend may begin to shift somewhat as subtypes of violent individuals, based in part on diagnosis, begin to inform treatment (Holtzworth-Munroe, Meehan, Herron, Rehman, & Stuart, 2000; Holtzworth-Munroe & Stuart, 1994; Waltz, Babcock, Jacobson, & Gottman, 2000).

In addition to clinical diagnosis, obtaining a problem description involves identifying other factors that may be associated with abusive behavior, namely, historical factors and co-occurring psychological, behavioral, or contextual problems. Such factors include anger, sexist or patriarchal attitudes, depression and suicidality, jealousy, assertiveness, alcohol and drug abuse, childhood abuse history, criminal history and weapon ownership, social support, psychopathology, head injuries or other organic factors, and marital adjustment (Saunders, 1999).

Setting Targets for Treatment

Information gleaned from interviews, self-report questionnaires, or other assessment modes may suggest treatment targets such as attitudes justifying partner violence, areas of communication difficulties, problems with anger, assertiveness deficits, or trauma symptoms. Functional analysis will also yield important targets for intervention. Although partner violence is the clinical concern and the treatment priority, the component behaviors reflecting the precursor variables or sequelae will sometimes be the primary targets for intervention.

Measuring Pretreatment Functioning

Related to obtaining a problem description and identifying treatment targets is the assessment goal of measuring pretreatment functioning, or collecting baseline data. Pretreatment functioning might be assessed as part of a one-time battery and used as a basis to compare with outcome data as an indication of change resulting from treatment. Alternatively, baseline data might be assessed in a continuous manner, collecting data on one or more aspects of functioning over several days or weeks prior to the onset of treatment. For example, a client might fill out a daily questionnaire reflecting the avoidance, intrusion, and arousal symptoms of PTSD for a specified period prior to beginning a course of exposure therapy. Ongoing, as opposed to one-time assessment of pretreatment functioning, allows for an examination of stability and trends in the phenomena of interest, which permits for more accurate interpretation of change patterns across treatment (Kazdin, 1998).

Measuring Treatment Progress

It is a common misconception that assessment takes place only at the beginning and perhaps the end of treatment. Ideally, some form of assessment should be carried out during treatment, to provide ongoing feedback to both clients and treating professionals. That is, a routine part of treatment might include filling out a self-report scale, an observer-rated checklist, or a self-monitoring diary or beginning sessions with assessment questions in interview format. For example, some batterer treatment programs begin sessions with a verbal or written check-in regarding physically or psychologically aggressive behaviors over the past week (J. H. Rathus & Cavuoto, 2001). Such ongoing assessment allows the therapist to compare behaviors with baseline data and to modify aspects of treatment if appropriate. The assessor might administer a large, formal, multimodal battery at pretreatment and select a small portion of this battery to administer at regular intervals during treatment.

Those working with a population mandated for spouse abuse treatment may be required to provide ongoing indications of progress reports to judges or probation officers. A set of standardized objective assessment measures, administered across time, will serve as a valuable supplement to a subjective evaluation.

Measuring Treatment Process

Process variables pertain to the mechanisms of change in treatment. Assessing process variables is a research strategy that addresses within-session factors that relate to session-to-session changes or overall treatment outcome (Gaston, 1990). Process assessments might target such variables as therapeutic alliance, therapist self-disclosure, or client satisfaction with a particular session. Although researchers have used process research widely in treatment outcome research in general (e.g., Lambert, 1992), it has only recently been applied within the field of partner violence. For example, one promising study assessing therapeutic alliance in a treatment study of partner-assaultive men found that the bond between the male participant and therapist predicted decreased physical and psychological aggression (P. D. Brown & O'Leary, 2000). An additional study of treatment process factors found that group cohesion, homework compliance, and therapist ratings of the working alliance predicted psychological or physical abuse outcomes in group cognitive–behavioral therapy for partner-violent men (Taft, Murphy, King, Musser, & DeDeyn, 2003).

Measuring Treatment Adherence

Both treatment outcome research and program delivery are increasingly concerned with the assessment of treatment fidelity, that is, the degree to which the treatment was delivered as intended or specified by a treatment protocol. Treatment outcome research refers to this assessment target as treatment adherence and competence (Waltz, Addis, Koerner, & Jacobson, 1993), whereas program evaluation refers to this as program delivery (Hayes et al., 1999). Typically, measures of treatment adherence are developed specifically for a given treatment study (e.g., O'Leary, Heyman, & Neidig, 1999) and often involve rating systems or checklists for treatment content based on session videotapes, audiotapes, or transcripts (Kazdin, 1998). As such, they are costly, time consuming, and tend to lack standardization. However, such measures are essential for helping to determine that a specified intervention, and not other factors, lead to an observed effect.

Measuring Treatment Outcome

An essential role of assessment in clinical or research settings is to measure treatment outcome. Like pretreatment or baseline assessment, treatment outcome might be measured at one point in time (i.e., treatment termination) or, preferably, will continue for some time after treatment ends, to determine maintenance of behavior change. Continued treatment outcome assessment often takes the form of follow-up assessments at designated time periods (e.g., 6 months and 1 year). The posttreatment assessment battery might be the same or similar to that administered at pretreatment. The aim is to evaluate the overall progress in treatment across a wide variety of domains. It is helpful to share results of this posttreatment assessment with the client in terms of future treatment planning, by pointing out areas of progress and areas that still need attention. One can also maintain this information as part of overall program evaluation records, whether in one's private practice or in agency, clinic, hospital, or other settings.

Conclusion

This chapter discussed the purposes of assessment in partner violence. We first highlighted three broad purposes of assessment: clinical evaluation, research, and program evaluation. We then described a progression of more specific assessment objectives, each of which pertains to one or more of the broad assessment objectives. Assessment proves crucial not only for purposes of initial screening and obtaining a description of presenting problems but also for identifying treatment targets and obtaining measures of functioning prior to, during, and following treatment. When used optimally, assessment in clinical practice comprises a rich and ongoing part of treatment. The remainder of this volume addresses the specifics of carrying out these assessment objectives in partner violence, describing assessment modalities, discussing clinical and research issues, and presenting a range of assessment tools.

Modalities of Assessment in Partner Violence

The field of assessment of partner violence has burgeoned in the past two and a half decades since the problem of domestic abuse emerged from behind closed doors. Among other influences, this emergence was spurred by the publication of Straus, Gelles, and Steinmetz's *Behind Closed Doors: Violence in the American Family* (1980). This work compiled results of survey data revealing rates of child and partner abuse based on a nationally representative sample of approximately 2,000 American families, and it suddenly placed events once regarded as rare and private into the category of events both normative and very much in public view. Around the same period, Rebecca Emerson Dobash and Russel Dobash published *Violence Against Wives* (1979) and Lenore Walker published *The Battered Woman* (1979), both compilations of qualitative research efforts that documented the plights of battered women, similarly helping to raise awareness of a problem once regarded as a "private family matter." These works both coincided with and further propagated the shelter movement, reflecting efforts to find safe temporary housing for battered women and their children who were witnesses to violence and not uncommonly abused themselves.

The Dobash and Dobash (1979) and Walker (1979) studies presented an important counterpoint to the work of Straus et al. (1980) work in that they represented extremes in terms of assessment methodology and population studied. The former was based on in-depth qualitative reports that yielded rich portraits of women living with abuse but relied on nonrepresentative, severely abused samples and imprecise definitions of abuse. The latter was based on quantitative reports using nationally representative samples and behaviorally specific definitions, highlighting rates of male-to-female and female-to-male violence according to the Conflict Tactics Scale

(Straus, 1979). While this landmark work of Straus and colleagues focused public attention on the surprisingly high frequency of marital violence, the context and impact of violence were not emphasized, yielding little sense of the human experience of abuse behind the data. Considered together, these two approaches to assessment of experiences of domestic violence were invaluable in sparking interest in, garnering attention to, and mobilizing resources for this then-neglected problem.

In the past two and a half decades, assessment of partner violence has broadened its scope and has become increasingly sophisticated in both its psychometrics and its capturing of abusive phenomena. Many self-report instruments now delve beyond the topography of abusive behaviors to include a greater focus on context and impact (e.g., Straus et al., 1996). Further, researchers have identified the many forms and associated characteristics of partner violence and developed instruments to assess them. Moreover, family researchers in general and partner violence investigators in particular have made strides in innovative assessment modalities to include structured and semistructured interviews, physiological assessment methods, behavioral observational coding systems, and more. This chapter describes the wide range of assessment modalities available to mental health professionals and researchers working in the field of marital violence. These include interviews, paper-and-pencil self-report measures and rating scales, analogue and observational measures, and archival records.

Interviews

One of the more underdeveloped areas of assessment of partner violence in terms of structured and reliable measurement is also perhaps the most important and commonly used method of assessment: the interview. Despite the fact that nearly every initial clinical encounter involves an interview, the field of partner violence contains no "gold standard," widely used interviews.[1] This stands in sharp contrast to the general fields of child and adult psychopa-

---

1. See Neidig and Friedman (1984), Sonkin et al. (1985), Follingstad et al. (1990), and Follingstad, Hause, Rutledge, and Poleck (1992) for examples of standardized interview assessments specific to partner violence. These interviews are omitted from review in chapter 6 because of their lack of psychometric evaluation.

thology, which contain numerous psychometrically sound structured and semistructured interviews (e.g., Costello, Edelbrock, Dulcan, Kalas, & Klaric, 1984; First, Spitzer, Gibbon, & Williams, 1995a, 1995b).

Interviews are the most common form of assessment used in clinical practice. Not only are they invaluable for assessing a client's history, the meaning and context of behaviors, and phenomenological experience, but they also form the basis for building rapport. Structured and semistructured interviews also provide the basis for diagnosis of Axis I and Axis II psychopathology (e.g., First, Spitzer, Gibbon, & Williams, 1995a, 1995b; First, Spitzer, Gibbon, Williams, & Benjamin, 1994). Advantages to interviews as an assessment strategy include that they provide face-to-face contact with the client, they allow for follow-up questions and clarifications by both interviewer and interviewee (if not fully structured) that can enhance accuracy of material, and they may allow for insights or observations about the client and the phenomenon of interest that would be unlikely to arise in the absence of direct contact. Flexible formats allow the skilled interviewer to probe or highlight particular areas over others, and interview content can be broad-based or specific, depending on the needs of the situation. With a more open-ended format, the interview also allows clients to tell their story prior to imposing a structure on the assessment process, which can begin a therapeutic process while enhancing connection to the interviewer.

Data yielded from interviews are often, but not always, categorical in nature. For example, a structured interview might reveal that an individual meets diagnostic criteria for a particular disorder. However, data from the interview typically allow one to obtain dimensional information on the extent of impairment or level of symptomatology as well. Disadvantages of interviews are that they may be time and labor intensive to administer,[2] they may be subject to unreliable scoring and interpretation, or conversely, they may require substantial training to become reliable in their administration and scoring. They also may require a high level of clinical sophistication and training to administer and interpret. Additionally, if they are nonstandardized, they may be subject to inconsistent operationalization of constructs and interpretations.

---

2. Some standardized diagnostic interviews, however, have now become available in computer-administered formats.

Conducting Clinical Interviews

Interview assessment must not only occur fastidiously but also should be routinely supplemented by other assessment methods such as paper-and-pencil techniques. This is because despite the high prevalence of marital violence, it often remains underestimated or undetected. Reasons for under-estimation of spousal violence pertain primarily to underreporting by both partners (e.g., Arias & Beach, 1987). Reasons for violence remaining unde-tected include (a) the fact that most clinicians, particularly when working with couples presenting with marital problems, do not directly assess for violence, and (b) when not asked directly, the vast majority of marital clinic couples experiencing domestic violence do not spontaneously report its occurrence (Ehrensaft & Vivian, 1996; O'Leary et al., 1992). Not only do couples not spontaneously report relationship violence, but even when asked directly by interview and paper-and-pencil methods, couples are most likely to reveal violence using non face-to-face, paper-and-pencil methods (e.g., Ehrensaft & Vivian, 1996; O'Leary et al., 1992). Thus, supplementing inter-view data with other modalities may result in inconsistent reporting between methods; if this occurs, the interviewer has the opportunity to inquire about this discrepancy that may lead to important clarification (e.g., Velting, Rathus, & Asnis, 1998). Inconsistency in reporting between partners (e.g., Arias & Beach, 1987) further renders the accurate interview assessment of partner violence an elusive goal. Importantly, in addition to the problems of underdetection and underestimation, research indicates that even when aware of its presence, marital and family therapists have traditionally not focused on problems of marital violence in treatment planning (e.g., Hansen, Harway, & Cervantes, 1991).

Interview Assessment of the Couple

Because the incidence of physical aggression in couples who present for marital therapy is over 50% (e.g., Holtzworth-Munroe et al., 1992; O'Leary et al., 1992), clinicians working with couples should familiarize themselves with strategies for assessing spouse abuse. Two different approaches charac-terize conducting assessments with violent or potentially violent couples. The first approach, following a family systems or interactive perspective, involves conducting assessments with both partners present (e.g., Neidig & Friedman, 1984). The other approach, informed by a feminist perspective, involves meeting with each partner individually to conduct the assessment, and only then determining whether it is appropriate to bring them together for further assessment and possibly treatment (e.g., O'Leary, 1996). Interviewing the couple together makes intuitive sense when it is a couple that is presenting for treatment. Meeting together provides the opportunity for the couple to begin building a therapeutic relationship on equal footing, prevents the therapist from becoming the holder of secrets, and *may* help keep partners "honest" regarding reports of aggression because it might be difficult to drastically minimize events in the presence of the partner who experienced these events.

Although each approach has benefits and shortcomings, we believe, along with others (e.g., Holtzworth-Munroe, Beatty, & Anglin, 1995; O'Leary et al., 1995), that it is critical to separate partners and assess each partner directly about the presence of violence. Separate interviews are indicated because individuals may be reluctant to disclose information about abuse in front of a partner, and because a conjoint discussion involving disclosure of marital violence may increase the danger level upon leaving the therapist's office. With an abusive spouse present, partners may not feel safe in revealing crucial information and may mislead the assessor in making an informed choice regarding intervention approach. Further, because of inconsistency in reporting and the finding that husbands underreport their violence in relation to wives' reports,

> therapists should accept either spouse's report of the occurrence of violence and, given the tendency of husbands to minimize and deny their use of violence, should not ignore a wife's report of a husband's violence, even if these are not confirmed by the husband. (Holtzworth-Munroe et al., 1995, p. 319)

In separating a couple for interviews, a useful strategy is to ask the partner who is not being interviewed at the moment to fill out paper-and-pencil measures while waiting. This not only makes use of the time but allows the partner to answer self-report questions without inhibition stemming from a partner sitting nearby. Once a couple is separated, the therapist can use the individual clinical interview to assess for the presence of violence in the relationship. In bringing up the topic of physical aggression, the therapist can facilitate honest disclosure by normalizing conflict, with a statement such as "All couples experience conflict or get angry with each other at times." Rather than beginning by asking directly about *abuse* or *battering*, it is useful to broach the topic with warm-up questions, such as "How is conflict handled in your relationship?" or "How does your partner handle anger?" or "Would you say either one of you has a bad temper? Tell me about that." The therapist can then garner specific examples and probe with specific queries such as "Has there been any pushing, grabbing, shoving, or hitting?" or "Has there been any physical aggression in your relationship?" The assessor can also ask about a series of specific violent behaviors, such as those on the Conflict Tactics Scale (Straus, 1979; Straus et al., 1996) or, if the client has already completed written assessments, begin by reviewing the client's responses on self-report measures (O'Leary & Murphy, 1999). This strategy reduces the chance of eliciting defensive responses or even unintentionally minimized responses by labeling acts "abuse" or "violence" that the client may not view that way (Ehrensaft & Vivian, 1996). While such strategies are used as starting points, it is important that they lead to thorough assessments of frequency, context, impact, motivations, duration, and types of violence (O'Leary & Murphy, 1999). Note that the practitioner might also select a semistructured interview, such as the Semi-Structured Marital Interview (Vivian, 1990b; see chap. 6, this volume), to assess the presence of marital aggression.

Whether the client regards emotionally or physically aggressive behaviors as abusive or not, the interviewer must make a realistic determination of danger. The clinician may then ask for a description of a recent, prototypical, or worst-case dispute. Even if there is not clear evidence of aggression, the assessor should inquire as to whether a client feels intimidated or threatened discussing marital issues in the presence of the partner. Should a picture of violence or coercive intimidation become evident, the clinician should assess the client's safety and consider treatment other than couples therapy (O'Leary et al., 1995).

In some cases in which relationship violence has occurred, it may be appropriate to work with couples conjointly (Vivian & Heyman, 1996). This approach would be most appropriate with couples with mild, bidirectional violence, in which neither partner fears or feels coerced by the other, in which partners take responsibility for their violence (including men taking responsibility for the generally greater impact of their violence on women than vice versa), and in which both partners see the violence as a problem and express motivation to stop it (Vivian & Heyman, 1996). Assessment targets aimed at determining whether couples treatment is appropriate, consisting of both interview and paper-and-pencil data, are presented in Exhibit 2.1.

The sections below on interview assessment of battered women and interview assessment of the perpetrator provide more detailed information that can be applied to assessment of couples when partners are seen separately. Note that these sections apply primarily to moderate-to-severe, unidirectional violence, as opposed to mild bidirectional violence.

Exhibit 2.1

Assessment Strategies and Interview Questions for Determining the Appropriateness of Conjoint Treatment

1. Marital violence is rarely a presenting problem, even though it is endemic.
2. Multimodal assessment is critical.
   a. Questionnaires. Advantages include the following: (1) provide highest detection; (2) quick, can be completed outside session; (3) provide behaviorally specific definition of abuse; common definition/language for clinician and client; and (4) make it easier to broach the topic for both clinicians and client.
   b. Individual clinical interview should provide information on the following:
      i. Context of violence
      • assessment of immediate factors: (1) precipitating factors, (2) impact, (3) function (what ends are accomplished?), (4) fear, (5) safety issues, (6) extent of psychological coercion/abuse, (7) openness to discuss issues dyadically, and (8) husband's resistance to disclose/discuss violence.
      • Assessment of historical factors: (1) assessment of *past* violence, and (2) individual's *learning history* about violence, such as witnessing violence, direct personal victimization, aggressive behaviors with peers and other intimate partners, and parents' conflict management styles.
      ii. Correlates of violence
      (1) Husband: alcohol and/or drug abuse, generalized aggression, depression.
      (2) Wife: depression, posttraumatic stress disorder.
3. Integrating individual reports of violence
   a. Do they agree on presence, frequency, impact, and intent of violence?
   b. Do they disagree on what and who causes the violence?
   c. If the couple disagrees on the existence or extent of violence, will it be possible to establish a gendered treatment plan that all can agree with?
4. Different types of physically aggressive couples: integrating assessment of occurrence of violence with context and function of violence; identifying couple subgroup.

Note. From D. Vivian and R. Heyman, "Is There a Place for Conjoint Treatment of Couple Violence?", 1996, *In Session: Psychotherapy in Practice*, Vol. 2, p. 46. Copyright 1996 by Wiley Interscience. Reprinted with permission.

Interview Assessment of the Battered Woman

Assessment of the battered woman may be confounded by the fact that battered women often do not self-identify as such (Koss et al., 1994). Instead, they may present for treatment with somatic complaints, severe anxiety, fearfulness, confusion, depression, insomnia, fatigue, disturbed eating patterns, severe powerlessness and worthlessness, tension, increased startle responses, intrusive images, phobias, hostility, disrupted interpersonal relationships, apathy, and thoughts of suicide, all reactions consistent with surviving trauma (see Koss et al., 1994). Complicating matters is the fact that standard psychological tests do not factor in surviving violence and often characterize female victims as personality disordered or psychotic (Rosewater, 1985). For this reason, interviewers should routinely include screening questions about domestic violence as part of any assessment.

Once a history of partner violence has been established, interviews with battered women can provide the means to supplement information reported on self-report checklists, such as the history, range, context, impact, severity, frequency, and consequences of the violence. The interviewer should also ask about concomitant forms of abuse such as sexual violence and psychological abuse (see Sonkin et al., 1985), as many women report that such forms of abuse are as emotionally damaging or more damaging than the physical aggression (Arias & Pape, 1999; Bergen, 1998; Follingstad, Rutledge, Berg, Hause, & Polek, 1990; Jacobson, Gottman, Gortner, Berns, & Shortt, 1996; O'Leary, 1999; Vivian & Langhinrichsen-Rohling, 1994).

If it is determined that aggression is occurring, it is important to assess the woman's safety. Issues of safety include establishing escape plans, as well as securing resources, such as finances, social support, job skills, child care, and alternative housing options (e.g., M. A. Dutton, 1992a, 1992b). Thus the clinician should assess whether the woman has access to money, car keys, important documents, basic clothes for herself and her children, and at least temporary refuge, such as a friend's or relative's house or a domestic violence shelter. If the woman has not already done so, the clinician should suggest she place these essential items in a bag and store the bag away in a hidden but accessible place. The clinician should also provide the woman with phone numbers of local domestic violence hotlines and agencies as well as with information about legal resources (such as orders of protection; Koss et al., 1994). The clinician should also help the woman to assess for the level of threat to herself and her children (Koss et al., 1994). In particular, the interviewer should determine the potential risk of homicide, not only by batterers but also by female victims. Such questions might focus on

> the type and extent of the wife's violent fantasies and . . . the types of resources she has employed in the past, and, more importantly, which resources have previously failed her. These questions may identify the extent to which the female victim considers herself trapped in the violent relationship and believes that no alternatives exist besides homicide. (Holtzworth-Munroe et al., 1995, p. 320)

Finally, the woman should also be assessed for related features of abuse, such as concurrent sexual coercion, depression, suicidal ideation, posttraumatic stress symptoms, self-esteem, and alcohol/substance abuse (O'Leary & Murphy, 1999). Pregnancy and plans to separate should be noted as these are situations in which risk of aggression appears to be elevated (Browne, 1987; McFarlane, Parker, Soeken, & Bullock, 1992; Wilson & Daly, 1993).

A central goal in assessment is to help empower the abused woman (O'Leary & Murphy, 1999). First, providing education about the range of typical reactions to trauma and normalizing PTSD symptoms can provide enormous validation and allow for external rather than internal self-blaming attributions for extreme responses (M. A. Dutton, 1992a, 1992b). Second, identifying strengths and supporting effective coping strategies can reinforce such efforts while enhancing self-esteem and self-efficacy. Despite the feelings of helplessness reported by battered women, many indeed demonstrate resourcefulness and problem-solving skills (McHugh, Frieze, & Browne, 1993). Third, the clinician must be motivated to help the woman solve problems and make decisions while resisting the temptation to do so for her. One must remember that the woman is typically the best judge of when it is safe to leave an abusive relationship and that imposing one's values and preferences may recreate in the therapeutic relationship a dynamic of asymmetric control and power that mirrors what the woman experiences with her partner (Koss et al., 1994).

Interview Assessment of the Spousal Assault Perpetrator

Individual interviewing with the perpetrator of partner abuse is consistent with not only a feminist approach to spouse abuse but also with an individual approach focusing primarily on perpetrator factors such as psychopathology (e.g., personality disorders, depression, alcohol or substance abuse problems), skills deficits, and learning history (see O'Leary & Murphy, 1999). In assessing assaultive partners, the clinician should inquire as to the extent and nature of violent behavior, the level of injury resulting from the violence and overall dangerousness, the presence of weapons in the home, the extent of alcohol or substance abuse (especially as it occurs concomitant with acts of aggression), the risk of lethality, and any legal involvement related to domestic violence (e.g., arrests, probation, orders of protection). The clinician might also educate the client about the likelihood of continued violence and escalating danger, and may suggest removing any weapons or even temporarily separating during treatment (Holtzworth-Munroe et al., 1995; Saunders, 1992).

The clinician can also inquire about attitudes justifying violent behavior, family-of-origin violence (i.e., witnessed and experienced violence), patterns of violent behavior in past intimate relationships, as well as experiences associated with domestic assault such as depression, jealousy and controlling behaviors, problems with anger, stress, assertiveness deficits, and rigid sex role beliefs (e.g., Hotaling & Sugarman, 1986). Psychopathology can be assessed through structured interviews such as the Structured Clinical Interview for DSM–IV (First, Spitzer, Gibbon, & Williams, 1995a, 1995b) or through self-report measures such as the Minnesota Multiphasic Personality Inventory (Hathaway & McKinley, 1989) or the Millon Clinical Multiaxial Inventory (Millon, 1992).

As batterers have a well-documented tendency to minimize or deny their abuse (D. G. Dutton, 1986; Sonkin et al., 1985), it will be especially useful of the clinician to supplement information obtained in clinical interviews with reports or records from corroborating sources, such as partner reports (when feasible), court records, probation reports, police reports, hospital records, and previous treating clinicians. If the interview is being conducted as part of a court-referred evaluation, it is necessary to obtain informed consent including a release of information stating clearly the purposes of the evaluation and with whom the information will be shared.

Recently, there have been efforts to apply Prochaska and Di Clemente's (1984) model of stages of change to initial interviews with batterers (Daniels & Murphy, 1997; Murphy & Baxter, 1997). This model is based on the notion that individuals may be in any one of five stages with respect to addressing their problematic behaviors: precontemplation, contemplation, preparation, action, or maintenance. Miller and Rollnick (1991) suggested that matching intervention strategies to a client's stage in the change process (rather than assuming readiness to change) and moving clients to more advanced stages prior to beginning intervention, through a process known as *motivational interviewing,* substantially improve the atmosphere for therapeutic change. Motivational interviewing, applied to perpetrators of wife assault, involves first validating the clients' reluctance or ambivalence regarding being in treatment and changing their behavior, particularly when they are mandated to treatment. Next, clients are asked to discuss the ways in which their violent behavior has worked for them as well as the ways in which it has not (i.e., has caused problems or suffering for them). The motivational interviewer elicits the concerns of the client about his own behavior (rather than informing him about the problems with his behavior) and treats resistance as a sign that he or she is pushing the client beyond his readiness for change (rather than as a symptom of denial to be confronted). This process tends to lead to self-generated motivation and evades the power struggles that might emerge in a more confrontive style of interviewing.

Interviewing for Research Purposes

Whether conducting interviews in clinical or research settings, many of the same principles apply. For example, the theoretical lens through which one approaches the topic of partner abuse will influence who gets interviewed and in what format (i.e., separately or as a couple), and researchers must share identical concerns as clinicians regarding issues such as minimization of violence, interpartner inconsistency in reporting, and safety assessment and planning. Perhaps of greater concern to the researcher than to the clinician, however, is the dearth of standardized interviews developed for the assessment of partner violence. In addition, interview modes of administration have at times been applied to paper-and-pencil measures to determine optimal conditions for the disclosure of violence (e.g., Ehrensaft & Vivian, 1996; Lawrence, Heyman, & O'Leary, 1995).

Significant contributions to our current knowledge base concerning the experiences of and issues facing battered women derive from qualitative interview studies (e.g., R. E. Dobash & Dobash, 1979; Folingstad et al., 1990; Walker, 1984). Investigators conducting such studies work from the perspective that invaluable knowledge can be obtained from relatively unstructured approaches allowing participants to tell their stories in depth, often in interviews lasting hours. These interviews are often supplemented with additional information sources such as court records or structured questionnaires, coded or grouped topically, and then compiled into large qualitative studies such as the classic *Violence Against Wives: The Case Against the Patriarchy* (R. E. Dobash & Dobash, 1979) and *The Battered Woman Syndrome* (Walker, 1984).

Thus, researchers are left with several choices regarding use of interview methodology. They might select one of the few direct partner violence interviews available (see chap. 6, this volume), use standardized interviews to assess conditions associated with partner abuse such as psychopathology, develop unstructured interviews for qualitative research interests, administer paper-and-pencil questionnaires in interview format, develop their own interviews and scoring procedures, or use interviews for the purposes of rapport-building and assessing safety issues but rely primarily on self-report or analogue measures for data collection.

Self-Report Measures/Rating Scales

Self-report paper-and pencil measures comprise a critical part of a multi-modal assessment strategy in the assessment of partner-directed violence. These instruments tend to assess phenomena such as specific behaviors, personal characteristics (e.g., attitudes, preferences, beliefs, perceptions, personality characteristics), mood, and levels of psychiatric symptoms. They typically produce dimensional rather than categorical scores. Self-monitoring tools, such as daily or weekly logs of specific behaviors or events, also fall under the classification of self-report assessments. These measures are generally fashioned by clinicians for particular treatment programs or for individual clients (e.g., Pence & Paymar, 1993), and although useful behavioral assessment tools, are rarely standardized or psychometrically evaluated (one important exception is the Timeline Followback Spousal Violence Interview [Fals-Stewart et al., 2003], a valid and reliable interview strategy that relies on clients' self-monitoring of violent acts in between interview periods; see chap. 8, this volume).

Advantages and Disadvantages of Self-Report Measures and Rating Scales

Self-report paper-and-pencil measures offer the following advantages: They are confidential, easy to administer, relatively brief, and may be completed outside of sessions. They provide the highest violence detection rates, they provide behaviorally specific definitions of abuse leading to common definitions for both clinician and client, and they may facilitate introducing the topic of abuse for both the clinician and client (e.g., Vivian & Heyman, 1996). In fact, self-report measures have demonstrated superiority at detecting the presence of spousal violence over interviews (Ehrensaft & Vivian, 1996; O'Leary et al., 1992). This enhanced detection may be due to the tendency for self-report measures of violence (e.g., the Conflict Tactics Scale; Straus, 1979) to include a wide range of behaviorally specific items, in contrast to clinical interview questions, which may often ask about aggression or abuse in more general terms rather than offering a comprehensive checklist of violent acts. There may also be more reluctance to discuss acts of violence in a face-to-face format compared with the greater personal distance a paper-and-pencil instrument affords. Another advantage of self-report measures in family violence assessment is that most are quantified and yield precise, interpretable scores, lending themselves to interpretation of change and enhancing ease of communication to other professionals. Moreover, a wide variety of highly specific self-report measures related to the field of family violence has been developed to date, facilitating the ability for evaluators to assemble a comprehensive paper-and-pencil battery suitable for their assessment needs. In general, such measures are highly practical for clinical settings in that they are inexpensive, require no or minimal training, are accessible without special equipment, and are not particularly cumbersome or intrusive to clients. They are practical for research settings as well, for all of the above reasons as well as the fact that they are the least labor-intensive assessment method, able to be administered to large numbers of respondents at once.

A number of disadvantages to paper-and-pencil questionnaire measures exist as well. First, they may provide overly simplistic information. For example, self-report checklists of violent acts have been criticized for failing to provide information about context, meaning, or impact of aggressive behavior (cf. Cascardi & Vivian, 1995; Vivian & Langhinrichsen-Rohling, 1994). However, many recent self-report measures have addressed these points, such as the Revised Conflict Tactics Scale (CTS2; Straus et al., 1996). They also may be more subject to social desirability or inaccuracies in responding, in that the assessor cannot confront inconsistencies or evaluate the respondent's attitude or demeanor as the scale is filled out. Partner-violent husbands have shown tendencies to respond in a socially desirable fashion on self-report inventories (D. G. Dutton & Hemphill, 1992; Saunders, 1991). Wives in domestically violent relationships may also minimize reports of violence (both their partner's or their own) because of factors such as fear, shame, and stigma (e.g., Gelles, 1978). Responses on self-report instruments may be subject to questionable accuracy of recall or distortions in self-perception, and respondents may feel that questions are vaguely worded or force response choices that distort the nature of their intended responses.

Thus, it is important to use self-report measures with well-documented psychometric properties and to use these in the context of other forms of assessment as well as other informants when feasible. To facilitate recall as well as ensure consensus of violence definitions between assessor and respondent, it is important to use measures that ask about specific acts of violence and not just "aggression" in general:

> It is possible that some spouses denied . . . aggression during (an interview assessment) because they did not view their acts of throwing, pushing, grabbing, or slapping as aggressive. In fact, a number of spouses agreed that the acts just mentioned had occurred but insisted that they were not "aggressive." This finding clearly highlights the need for marital therapists to use self-report measures in addition to an intake interview if they are to uncover spousal aggression; moreover, it is important to

list specific tactics rather than simply asking whether any aggression has occurred. (Ehrensaft & Vivian, 1996, p. 450)

Brief History of Measuring Family Violence Using Self-Report Behavioral Rating Instruments: The Conflict Tactics Scales

Questionnaire assessment of partner violence largely surfaced with the National Family Violence Survey and Resurvey studies on family violence conducted by Murray Straus and colleagues (Straus & Gelles, 1986; Straus et al., 1980) using the Conflict Tactics Scale (CTS; Straus, 1979, 1990a), a behaviorally specific self-report instrument. In fact, the CTS has become so popular that many equate measurement of spousal aggression with use of the CTS and have little familiarity with other self-report measures in this area. Because of its central role in the field and its multiple adaptations, we discuss this scale here in addition to reviewing the CTS and several adaptations in chapter 7 (this volume).

The CTS (Straus, 1979, 1990a, 1990b; Straus & Gelles, 1990) is the most widely used, most cited, most debated, and most well-known measure in the field of partner abuse. Appropriately referred to in the plural (i.e., Conflict Tactics *Scales*), the title of this instrument now refers to not only the original CTS in both its interview and self-report formats (Straus, 1979) but also to numerous forms and adaptations of the original measure reflecting over two decades of research and commentary on the measure (see Archer, 1999). This proliferation of work has led to some confusion regarding which version and scoring method to use. The descriptions of four versions of the scale in chapter 7 offer clarifications of the intended purposes, advantages, and limitations of each.

Much controversy has arisen over the CTS for repeatedly yielding findings that women are about equally as aggressive, or even slightly more aggressive, than men (e.g., Archer, 2000, 2002; Straus, 1990a), despite widespread conviction that men are generally more aggressive than women (see O'Leary, 2000; White et al., 2000). Some of the related explanatory discourse regarding the CTS has concerned the issue of interpartner agreement. For two decades, researchers have been cautioning that reports on interpartner concordance on the CTS is low to moderate (Jouriles & O'Leary, 1985; O'Brien, John, Margolin, & Erel, 1994; O'Leary & Arias, 1988; O'Leary et al., 1992; Szinovacz, 1983), with greater agreement occurring for reports of mild than severe aggression. Archer (1999) argued, based on his meta-analysis, that male–female agreement on the CTS was moderate but higher than expected, and in fact was higher using the CTS than other measures of physical aggression. The moderate agreement Archer found, however, was significantly moderated by such variables as matched versus unmatched couples, sample (e.g., marital vs. high school dating couples), time frame and relationship reported on (i.e., current only/recent past vs. including prior relationships), with lower agreement occurring in each latter case (Archer, 1999).

Related to the issue of interpartner agreement is the utility of self-reporting on one's own violent behavior on the CTS because of the problem of underreporting. Studies have generally yielded results indicating that men tend to underreport violence compared with their partners (Edleson & Brygger, 1986; Jouriles & O'Leary, 1985; Lawrence et al., 1995; O'Leary et al., 1989; Straus & Gelles, 1990), with this discrepancy varying based on population and context of assessment (Archer, 2002; Heyman & Schlee, 1997) and widening with reports of severe aggression (Browning & Dutton, 1986; Straus & Gelles, 1990; Szinovacz, 1983).[3] Interestingly, Archer's (1999) meta-analysis indicated that both sexes systematically underreport their own acts of aggression, yet studies in which men and women came from un-matched couples yielded significantly greater rates of systematic underre-porting from men.

Scholars have also raised the issue of female underreporting of victim-ization on the CTS. Individuals might minimize victimization because of fear, shame, stigma, or different thresholds for labeling behavior abusive (e.g., Ehrensaft & Vivian, 1996) and might underreport their own violent behavior because of the same social desirability factors operating within male populations (see Archer, 1999). Even those who point to exceptions in which substantial correspondence existed between partner reports (e.g., Archer, 1999; Arias & Beach, 1987; Babcock, Waltz, Jacobson, & Gottman, 1993; Cantos, Neidig, & O'Leary, 1994; Straus et al., 1996) acknowledge the tendency to underdisclose aggression and recommend obtaining reports from both partners when possible.

---

3. It is important to note, however, that because there is typically no external criterion to validate each partner's report of violence, the possibility exists that the higher report is actually an overestimation of violence that occurred. In fact, as a result of telescoping biases (the tendency to recall events as being closer to the present than they actually were), measures such as the CTS, which rely on estimations within a given time frame, are subject to overreports of behavioral frequencies. On the other hand, a handful of studies using external criteria (D. G. Dutton, 1986; Riggs, Murphy, & O'Leary, 1989) suggest greater accuracy of victim than perpetrator reports. A negative association between ratings of social desirability and CTS scores (Sugarman & Hotaling, 1997), plus some data suggesting that recipients may actually underreport their victimization (Archer, 1999), lends additional support to the notion that individuals underreport violence perpetration.

Because of the imperfect correlation between husband and wife reports of violence, researchers have recommended using the reports of both partners, rather than relying on only one, to assess the presence of violence in a given couple (e.g., Bohannon, Dosser, & Lindley, 1995; Browning & Dutton, 1986; Szinovacz & Egley, 1995). According to Margolin (1987), accepting the report of either spouse may lead to some degree of false positives but minimizes the likelihood of missing a case of violence leading to false negatives. In contrast, using consensus reports will likely miss some positive cases but will produce more true positives, that is, a greater degree of confidence in identified cases. However, as Straus et al. (1996) pointed out, it may not only be impractical to obtain reports from both partners at times (e.g., in conducting outcome research in a treatment program for spousal assault) but may actually pose a danger to participants (e.g., a report of abuse may be received with retaliatory violence). Thus, researchers must take various factors into account when determining whether to assess one or both partners with the CTS. For circumstances warranting the use of only one partner, Heyman and Schlee (1997) calculated correction factors for such single-partner reports to enhance the accuracy of sample prevalence estimates.

Other comments about the CTS have included the fact that the original prevalence studies of partner-directed violence (i.e., the National Family Violence surveys) are based only on the report of one partner (Heyman & Schlee, 1997), the scale assesses only those violent acts committed during a conflict, the scale's high face validity renders it subject to socially desirable response sets, and the populations surveyed using the CTS were normative samples likely underrepresentative of more serious forms of couple violence (e.g., O'Leary, 2000; White et al., 2000). In fact, when studying samples selected for marital problems or physical aggression, overall effect sizes for aggression in the male-to-female direction are significantly larger than in normative or in younger-age dating samples (Archer, 2000, 2002; O'Leary, 2000). Relatedly, Johnson (1995) argued cogently that much of the controversy surrounding the Family Violence Surveys' findings of equal rates of male and female violence can be synthesized with the understanding that scholars have been debating the "true" phenomenology of what amounts to two distinct populations: a normative community sample characterized by the low level and intensity, often bidirectional "common couple violence" on the one hand, and the high intensity, typically unidirectional "patriarchal terrorism" on the other.

In addition to its use with normative/community samples, the original scale's exclusive focus on violence *topography* has been discussed as responsible for producing findings indicating equal rates of female-to-male as male-to-female violence; these findings were based on rates and forms of interpartner aggression rather than on intent of violence, meaning, context, impact, and injury (e.g., Vivian & Langhinrichsen-Rohling, 1994; White et al., 2000). Further, the CTS, like most self-report checklists of violent acts, does not take into account the clustering of violent actions during a single incident, the escalation of violence over time, the physical differences between perpetrator and target (potentially limiting the target's ability to resist or escape), threats that accompany the aggression, and perception of risk (Koss et al., 1994). As such, critics have cautioned that reports of interpartner aggression based on rating scales of this type distort the phenomenology of partner violence (R. E. Dobash & Dobash, 1984; R. P. Dobash, Dobash, Daly, & Wilson, 1992; Kurz, 1993; Saunders, 1988; White et al., 2000). For example, Nazroo (1995) reported that although the CTS yielded higher rates of all violent behaviors for women than for men, further analysis revealed that men's violent acts included more dangerous and intimidating behaviors. Archer's (2000, 2002) meta-analytic studies of individual violent acts on the CTS found greater rates of low-level violent acts committed by women but higher rates of severely violent behaviors as well as a greater likelihood of injury with acts committed by men. Additionally, research has documented that when function and contextual variables are taken into account, male-to-female violence, as compared with female-to-male violence, creates more fear (O'Leary & Curley, 1986), has a more negative psychological impact (Cascardi, Langhinrichsen, & Vivian, 1992), results in more physical injury (Berk, Berk, Loseke, & Rauma, 1983; Cantos et al., 1994; Cascardi et al., 1992; Stets & Straus, 1990), and is more likely to occur in the context of coercion and psychological abuse and less likely to occur in the context of self-defense (Browne, 1987; Cascardi & Vivian, 1995; Cascardi, Vivian, & Meyer, 1991).

Yet, the great utility of the CTS over the years has stemmed from the fact that it is highly useful for assessment of violence in large samples; the instructions can easily be changed to include violence in other than conflict situations; and without structured and direct assessment of partner violence, it will often be missed or unreported (O'Leary et al., 1992), and underdetection of physical abuse is itself a serious problem (e.g., Stark & Flitcraft, 1983). Moreover, if the purpose of the assessment is to obtain rates of behavior, or to provide screening in samples in which violence is likely to be infrequent and minor, then less interpretation/contextual information is needed, and the CTS is quite appropriate (J. C. Campbell, 2000). If the purpose is to assess function, the scale can and should be used in conjunction with appropriate supplemental assessments (Straus, 1990a, 1993). In fact, the second national family violence survey by Straus and colleagues (Straus, 1990a) contained numerous additional contextual variables that were assessed to be used in conjunction with CTS findings. In addition, Straus revised his scale and produced the CTS2 (Straus et al., 1996) to address many of the criticisms that arose over the years. The CTS2 contains items representing a broader domain of physical aggression (e.g., the addition of a sexual coercion scale), a psychological aggression scale, and items assessing impact of aggressive acts (i.e., injury). And, researchers are now starting to develop instruments that allow for more specific assessment of violent acts as they cluster together and occur over time, such as the Timeline Followback approach for assessing physical aggression (e.g., Fals-Stewart et al., 2003; see chap. 6, this volume).

Many of the instruments reviewed in chapter 7 specifically assessing partner violence may be considered descendants of the CTS; that is, they were developed in reaction to the CTS in attempts to expand or improve on it. Despite concerns about the CTS and about self-reports of partner violence in general, this assessment method has enjoyed widespread use and influence over the past two and a half decades, and a variety of such measures have proliferated.

Analogue Measures

In recent years, researchers have increasingly applied analogue measures of conflictual couple interactions in the assessment of partner violence. Such measures take a variety of forms, and all involve some type of direct behavioral observation. These approaches take place in laboratory or clinic-office settings and involve some type of re-creation or approximation of a natural setting. The goal is to assess behaviors in response to realistic stimuli, with the advantage of a controlled and standardized procedure with established scoring, coding, or other data collection approaches. Examples of analogue assessment stimuli are use of videotaped conflict scenarios, role-play interactions, or problem discussion tasks for couples. Responses to these stimuli are then coded systematically. Methods vary widely to include such assessment targets as communication or other dyadic interactions, emotions, responses to provocation, automatic thoughts, social skills, and attributions.

Physiological and mechanical assessment methods also fall within the category of analogue measures. Physiological methods assess such family violence-related variables as heart rate reactivity, blood pressure, and pulse rate, typically in response to conflict discussions or anger-eliciting stimuli. Mechanical assessment methodologies involve using some type of mechanical, usually electric device to monitor targeted behaviors. Examples include assessing variables such as agitation during conflict interactions through measurement of gross motor movement (e.g., via chair motions) or self-rated affective states while watching videos through movements on a hand-held rating dial.

Analogue assessments of couple violence allow for relatively objective observation of skills or behaviors as opposed to relying on the insight or accuracy of one's self-reports of such attributes. They may offer the next best approach to observations in naturalistic settings and may yield the best reflection of particular behaviors.

Disadvantages of analogue assessments of couple interactions include that these procedures sometimes rely on costly monitoring equipment and may involve lengthy training procedures for administration, rating, and data coding. Analogue methods are often not portable or practical outside of well-funded laboratory settings, although there are some exceptions, such as using role-play scenarios to assess assertiveness. Another concern is that the analogue situation may not provide a valid representation of what it is attempting to measure, particularly because of the obtrusive and reactive nature of many analogue assessment procedures. Not only might respondents find it uncomfortable to be videotaped or wired to monitoring equipment, as some analogue procedures require, but the assessment process itself will normally be highly salient and may alter their responses. For example, ratings of arousal during conflict may be inflated by the presence of monitoring equipment, and conflict discussions themselves might be more constrained than those occurring at home because of the demand characteristics of the setting (Vincent, Friedman, Nugent, & Messerly, 1979). However, research has generally supported the external validity of the standard couples observational paradigm, revealing that the interactions it produces are similar to interactions at home and that, if anything, they are less negative than those at home, yet still produce detectable differences between couples on a variety of processes (see Heyman, 2001). In addition, researchers typically allow for an initial period of "warmup" measurement to allow for the establishment of a stable baseline and to allow for habituation to the setting. Finally, it is important to caution that methods evoking conflictual interactions in laboratory settings might best be avoided with severely violent couples because of the potential to stimulate an aggressive argument.

The above concerns notwithstanding, it is important to note that analogue assessment has yielded invaluable data regarding dyadic interactions and revealed characteristics of violent couples that could not otherwise be accessed (e.g., Gottman et al., 1995). In clinical settings, simplified analogue measures of couple conflict can be inexpensive and relatively unobtrusive. For example, the standard couples observational paradigm can be part of a standard intake interview: The clinician can ask couples to engage in a problem-solving conversation (see Problem Solving Interaction Task, chap. 9, this volume) and observe their discussion, noting content and process such as whether the anger escalates, whether they enter repetitive negative loops, and whether they indicate after the task that the communication they displayed was typical (Heyman, 2001). Such a procedure can yield a wealth of information about communication style and the patterns of escalating interactions often seen in conflictual couples, and can richly inform treatment plans. Chapter 8 on analogue methods will cover both the laboratory analogues of conflict or other types of couple interactions and the various self-rated procedures, physiological measures, or observational coding systems that are administered in conjunction with these analogues.

Analogue Methods and Accompanying Self-Rating Procedures

The measures that fall into this category generally constitute a couple interaction task or a set of stimuli (such as recorded vignettes or written conflict scenarios) to which participants respond with ratings of emotions or thoughts (e.g., attributions, intentions, expectations) or with role-plays from which capabilities are assessed (e.g., assertiveness skills). Such assessments are designed to move a step beyond written self-report instruments toward in vivo contexts. In doing so, the aim is to surpass the ability of retrospective self-reports in capturing moment-to-moment processes and actual responses. Such measures can be particularly beneficial as supplements to standard written self-report questionnaires for areas in which respondents may have biases in reporting or a lack of insight into their behavior patterns.

Physiological Methods

Physiological assessment provides an additional dimension to the measurement of partner violence and its correlates. The rationale for targeting physiological variables in marital violence research stemmed primarily from the established connection between criminality and physiological reactivity, and between heart rate reactivity and hostility (Gottman et al., 1995). Further, autonomic nervous system assessment was originally conceptualized as offering a highly sensitive measure of anger and fear responses (Gottman & Levenson, 1986), affective states clearly central to the assessment of violent couples. While costly and feasible only for use in laboratory settings, the various modes of physiological assessment provide measures immune to the potential for misperception of self-reported-arousal (e.g., Katkin, 1985), as well as social desirability influences or reaction to demand characteristics. Used frequently within the health psychology field (e.g., relating reactivity to Type A personality), this assessment strategy was first introduced to the field of marital interaction in general (e.g., P. C. Brown & Smith, 1992; Ewart, Taylor, Kraemer, & Agras, 1991; Levenson & Gottman, 1983) and more recently to the field of family violence in particular (e.g., Gottman et al., 1995).

Physiological ratings are generally carried out by allowing participants to spend time acclimating to the laboratory setting and then affixing various ratings devices (e.g., electrodes) to the body (see Gottman et al., 1995). After this, a baseline rating is established on all of the physiological measures for a specified period of time, because the various devices might result in reactivity independent of the stimuli of interest. After this baseline assessment period, the task (e.g., problem-solving discussion) begins. Patterns of arousal are then examined, either as a function of the content of the activity (e.g., a discussion changing from calm to conflictual), a comparison between samples of interest, or as a means to identify subgroups of physiological responders. Physiological reactivity has been linked with conflict behavior, marital adjustment, and marital dissolution (e.g., Gottman & Levenson, 1992), and more recently, with physiology-based typologies of partner-violent men (Gottman et al., 1995).

Observational Coding Systems

Observational coding systems provide the opportunity for outside observers to assess affect and communication independent of clients' subjective judgments of their interaction. Whereas self-report data provide perceptions of the degree or intensity of specified behaviors or characteristics, direct observation data allow for the assessment of behavior fluctuation in an ongoing context and of behavioral processes as they unfold over time (Margolin et al., 1998). In addition, they allow for the measurement of interaction in a well-defined, rather than global, context (e.g., while discussing disagreement), while addressing characteristics and facets of interaction on which participants themselves might not be able to accurately report (Margolin et al., 1998). Such coding systems are also less subject to perceptual biases that may be especially distorted by the context of marital discord (see Heyman, 2001).

For such coding systems, couples are asked to engage in a discussion that follows a problem-solving format and typically lasts between 10 and 15 minutes. In some studies, couples have also been asked to engage in a pleasant topic conversation or simply to discuss the day's events (Gottman, 1994). Once participants are given instructions, their discussion is video-taped or audiotaped (in most cases videotaped, as coding systems tend to rate nonverbal as well as verbal interactions). Coders, trained to a criterion of reliability, then code the tapes for major variables such as problem-solving, affect, and power (Gottman, 1994), examining qualities of the interaction including verbal content, voice tone, facial expression, and body posture. Data are then analyzed on a descriptive basis (i.e., rating the frequency, duration, or intensity of specified behaviors) or in a manner focused on *process* (i.e., sequential analysis). Sequential analysis offers a more rich and complex picture of the couple interaction, providing information concerning the *reciprocity of interactions* between partners, such as the conditional probability of a complaint being countered with a cross-complaint in a sample of couples (R. L. Weiss, 1989). The researcher can then compare such interaction chains across various types of couples (e.g., does the probability of an aggressive verbal counterattack following a partner's attack differ between violent and nonviolent couples?).

Examiners often use observational coding systems in conjunction with other assessment methods. Thus, investigators might test hypotheses concerning the differences between partners or types of couples (e.g., males vs. females, maritally discordant vs. maritally discordant, physically aggressive couples), the relations between moment-to-moment interactions and more global phenomena (e.g., communication sequences in couples with a depressed spouse), or the relations between moment-to-moment interactions and other simultaneous processes (e.g., heart rate, self-reported impact of a communication).

Conducting studies based on observational coding systems involves many steps. Margolin et al. (1998) broke these steps into two categories: data collection and data coding. Steps inherent in the data collection process include (a) selecting the task and setting to optimize external validity and best match the research question, (b) breaking down the observed stream of behavior into units for coding, and (c) selecting the appropriate coding system. Steps comprising the data coding process may include (a) preparing written transcripts of spoken interactions for coding (although transcripts are normally used with microanalytic rather than molar coding systems),

(b) selecting and training coders, (c) transforming or collapsing data (again, done less often with molar coding systems), and (d) checking reliability. In essence, the researcher takes on the rather daunting task of imposing structure on inherently unstructured phenomena and attending to myriad details.

Although the equipment, data collection, and data coding procedures render use of observational coding systems more practical for use in research than clinical settings (Kerig & Lindahl, 2001), such systems nevertheless have their place in clinical work with couples (Margolin et al., 1998; see also Basco, Birchler, Kalal, Talbott, & Slater, 1991). Moreover, clinicians may benefit from familiarizing themselves with the multiple coding categories in the various systems. Such familiarity can provide the clinician with more specific communication targets for intervention and for determining progress in therapy, and may help keep the clinician focused on the *process* of, rather than mired in the *content* of, couple interactions (Notarius, Markman, & Gottman, 1981). Further, clinicians may choose to adapt aspects of these coding systems for their own use (e.g., selecting a brief subset of coding categories for targets and considering them with regard to a couple's audiotaped interaction before and after treatment). Even in informal adaptations of such systems for clinical settings, the benefit of observing couples' interactions rather than relying exclusively on self-report measures remains (Heyman, 2001).

Although one would obviously never attempt to evoke a violent interchange for the purposes of coding the escalation process, violence often (but not always—see, e.g., Jacobson et al., 1994) occurs in the context of conflict. Thus, the observation of conflictual interactions provides an excellent analogue situation for assessing the frequency and sequence of events that differentiate the disagreements of violent and nonviolent or subtypes of violent dyads. In fact, most couples indicate that they experience their interaction in the laboratory problem-solving task as a quite accurate depiction of what occurs at home (e.g., Margolin, John, & Gleberman, 1988). Because most observational coding systems were not developed for and validated with physically aggressive couples, researchers must exercise caution in drawing conclusions regarding the degree to which the conflict discussions they quantify resemble the actual conflicts of violent couples. Compared with nonviolent couples, the laboratory interactions of violent couples may stray further from their normative interactions due to fear of exposing a violent partner or the need to present in a socially desirable fashion (e.g., Follette & Alexander, 1992). On the other hand, the deficient self-control skills to limit anger arousal in such couples might render their laboratory interactions *more* similar to their interactions at home. These considerations suggest a need for ongoing validation work for use within aggressive dyads.

While observational coding methodology provides rich clinical information about couples' interactions, several problems exist in comparing research results based on this methodology across studies. The first concerns instructional variation across studies regarding the typical couples observational paradigm, a problem discussion task (Baucom & Adams, 1987) sometimes referred to as the "play-by-play interview" (Gottman, 1994). This task often begins with couples meeting at the end of a day, and then being asked to discuss the events of the day; they are then interviewed about areas of disagreement and asked to select a high-conflict area and attempt to resolve the issue, to assess problem solving; finally, they are then commonly asked to discuss things they enjoy talking about, to provide a positive conversation for observation (Gottman, 1994). However, at times couples are given other instructions or tasks (cf. Gottman, 1994; Heyman, 2001). Thus, users of this procedure must decide with care their purpose for this assessment task and provide instructions accordingly. Further, researchers must apply caution when comparing findings of observed interactions across investigations, because instructional variation in the problem-solving task could substantially affect the nature of the interaction that ensues.

Another difficulty in comparing findings across investigations concerns the lack of standardization of operationalized codes for specific variables (e.g., negativity) across systems (Heyman, Eddy, Weiss, & Vivian, 1995) plus the lack of consistency of coding schemes across modifications of the same system (Markman & Notarius, 1987). In a sense, the benefit of great flexibility and innovation in the application of these systems has created a liability in terms of generalizability.

Despite these concerns, observational coding systems nevertheless offer a unique and valuable approach in family violence assessment (see Heyman, 2001; Kerig & Lindahl, 2000, for more detailed discussion of family observational coding systems). Chapter 8 reviews measures in the above three categories: analogue measures with accompanying self-report ratings or skill responses, physiological measures, and observational coding systems.

Direct Observation in Natural Settings

Another important source of assessment data is direct observations in natural settings, such as the home or shelter. This type of observation may be of particular relevance when evaluating the quality and safety of a child's living situation who may be living with parents' marital violence. Such an assessment might target both naturalistic parent–child interactions as well as the condition of the home. For children or women living in safe homes, such observations can provide important information on adjustment or mother–child interactions following traumatic experiences, such as witnessed or experienced domestic violence and familial dissolution. Home observations of violent couple interactions have been extremely rare (see Margolin et al., 1989, for an exception) and thus are not reviewed in this volume.

Archival Records

Another source of assessment data important in the field of couple violence is the use of archival records. These are records that are used for assessment purposes after-the-fact, sometimes without any face-to-face contact or even knowing the respondents at all. This might be especially likely to occur in the context of research in areas such as sociology or criminology, in which large samples are desired and broad patterns and trends are the study targets; for example, Tolman and Weisz (1995) analyzed police reports to determine the effects of a proarrest policy on recidivism in wife assaulters in an entire county in Illinois over an 18-month period. However, clinicians working with individuals can sometimes access archival records as well and may want to include them as part of a comprehensive clinical assessment or a forensic evaluation. Archival records include such data sources as hospital or medical records, school or employment records, child protective services contacts, criminal records, or police/probation reports. Advantages to such methods include their objectivity and the often highly informative and corroborating contributions they make to self-reported data. Also, particularly when using archival records for large-scale research studies, once such records are obtained, they may be substantially less time consuming to examine or code than would data obtained from meeting with each individual represented by the records. Finally, archival records provide access to unbiased retrospective data and allow for study of trends in previous years. Potential problems with such sources of assessment data involve difficulty in obtaining access to such records; missing or ambiguous data or data not coded in a way most useful to the present purposes (e.g., a police report of a domestic violence incident lacking in detail); and having a biased or selected sample that is not under the examiner's control. Further, multiple raters of archival data lead to inaccuracies and inconsistencies, and it is not possible to determine interrater reliability. Because these measures are not standardized, we do not review them in this volume.

Conclusion

This chapter reviewed the variety of assessment modalities in the assessment of partner violence. We pointed out advantages and limitations of each modality and provided specific information regarding the use of each modality to assess partner violence. Chapters 6 through 8 review dozens of measures representing three major modalities: interviews, paper-and-pencil self-report scales, and analogue measures.

Assessment of Partner Violence in Clinical Practice

Within both clinician and research camps, approaches to the assessment of violence within intimate relationships have been sharply debated since the topic emerged from "behind closed doors" (Straus et al., 1980). The controversy has stemmed from contrasting and often conflicting theories of the etiology of marital violence (O'Leary & Murphy, 1999). For example, individual theories locate partner violence within individual psychopathology (e.g., D. G. Dutton & Browning, 1988; Hamberger & Hastings, 1988) or social learning history (e.g., O'Leary, 1988); social psychological and systems theories locate partner violence within faulty or imbalanced couple exchanges (e.g., Bersani & Chen, 1988; Neidig & Friedman, 1984); and sociohistorical and feminist theories locate partner violence within long-standing sexist social institutions and a male-dominated society that perpetuate patriarchy and condone the control and oppression of women (Bograd, 1984; Ptacek, 1988).

Focus of Assessment

Depending on the lens through which one looks, the targets for both assessment and intervention differ substantially (O'Leary & Murphy, 1999). Individual-based perspectives highlight factors such as psychopathology (e.g., personality disorders, depression, alcoholism), anger, individual skills deficits, and learning history. Much of this individual focus centers on perpetrators of spouse abuse, because research indicates that compared with victims, perpetrators vary much more from normative comparison groups on measures of personality factors and other risk markers (Hotaling

& Sugarman, 1986; Schumacher, Feldbau-Kohn, Slep, & Heyman, 2001). Systems or social exchange models target couple interactional patterns, such as communication sequences and affective escalation patterns. Finally, sociohistorical and feminist perspectives assess societal factors that maintain gender-based power imbalances, collude in male violence against women, and invalidate victims of wife abuse. On an individual scale, such perspectives focus on men's attitudes or beliefs consistent with sexism, power, and patriarchy; on gender-specific analyses of the context and impact of violence; and on victim-related variables such as posttraumatic stress disorder (PTSD), depression, and factors hindering leaving a dangerous relationship. Even the terminology used in studying marital violence has been the subject of heated debate, as feminist scholars have argued that gender-neutral terms such as *marital violence* obfuscate the fact that woman are by far the greater recipients of injury and negative psychological impact from intimate violence (Cascardi et al., 1992; Stets & Straus, 1990) and that therefore gender-sensitive terms such as *wife abuse* should be substituted (see Bograd, 1984; Margolin & Burman, 1993).

Psychological Abuse

Another issue concerns the importance of including assessment of psychological abuse, which tends to precede and occur concomitantly with physical aggression (O'Leary, 1999). Forms of psychological abuse include isolation, intimidation, threats and derogatory remarks, humiliation and degradation, economic deprivation, and excessive jealousy, suspiciousness, and monitoring (Pence, 1989; Tolman & Edleson, 1989). Such types of abuse often have severely deleterious effects, sometimes even more so than physical violence (Aguilar & Nightingale, 1994; Folingstad et al., 1990; Shields & Hanneke, 1983; Tolman & Bhosley, 1991).

Assessment of Couple Violence in Marital Treatment

Because we know that between 50% and 70% of couples seeking marital therapy will report at least one instance of physical aggression in the year prior to assessment (Cascardi et al., 1992; Holtzworth-Munroe et al., 1992; O'Leary et al., 1989; O'Leary et al., 1992), clinicians must consider the potential for the presence of violence in any couple they see. To complicate matters, most couples presenting in marital clinic settings fail to reveal violence spontaneously but must be questioned directly about its occurrence through interview or questionnaire methods (Ehrensaft, & Vivian, 1996; O'Leary et al., 1992). Commonly reported reasons for not spontaneously identifying aggression as a problem at intake include viewing violence as merely a symptom of marital discord (and thus expecting it to cease with couples therapy), seeing it as unintended and not likely to recur, or minimizing it because no injuries occurred or because the perpetrator expressed appropriate contrition (O'Leary et al., 1992). Because of the likelihood of overlooking relationship violence without direct questioning, O'Leary et al. (1992) recommended using a multimodal assessment approach, combining self-report instruments such as one of the recent modifications of the Conflict Tactics Scale (CTS; Straus, 1979; see chap. 7, this volume) with direct interview questions about the occurrence of violence. Because partners may subjectively define terms such as *abuse* or *violence*, O'Leary et al. further recommended using more neutral language or asking about specific violent acts, as on the CTS.

Minimization of Violence and Lack of Agreement Between Partners

A further complicating factor in assessment of partner violence is the minimization or denial of violence by both partners even when asked directly (Ferraro, 1983; Sonkin et al., 1985) and the low reliability between husbands' and wives' reports of marital aggression (e.g., Arias & Beach, 1987; Jouriles & O'Leary, 1985). In particular, research indicates that maritally aggressive men are especially likely to underreport the presence and impact of their violent behavior compared with their female victims, responding in a socially desirable fashion (Edleson & Brygger, 1986; Riggs et al., 1989). Studies comparing assaultive husbands' reports of violence with partner reports as well as outside means of validation of such reports (e.g., police, court, or medical records) suggest greater accuracy of victim than perpetrator reports (D. G. Dutton, 1986; Riggs et al., 1989). Thus, it becomes critically important for the practitioner or researcher to obtain reports from both partners, when possible, and to err on the side of caution by taking seriously any reports of violence by either partner.

For cases in which violence is revealed, clinicians will need to be well-versed in interview strategies to glean more detailed information on frequency, direction, context, impact, and risk of violent episodes. Furthermore, clinicians will need to be cautious regarding the potential inflammatory impact of clinical assessment of violence and be prepared to engage in safety planning when a client appears to be at risk for imminent harm

(M. A. Dutton, 1992a). Such concerns apply in research settings as well, where in some ways even greater care may be necessary to assess for danger and plan for safety, because research participation may entail limited contact with the couple. Because clients may feel coerced to minimize violence in the presence of abusive partners, and because revealing violence may result in dangerous repercussions, interviewing partners separately has become the standard approach to assessing couple violence when both partners present for treatment (cf. Holtzworth-Munroe et al., 1995; O'Leary et al., 1995).

Targeting Violence When the Couple Does Not View It as a Problem

A potential difficulty may arise when violence is uncovered during assessment but not regarded by the couple as a relevant treatment focus. Does the clinician in this case press the issue or follow the couple's lead in negating its importance?

> It has become apparent that many young men and women do not perceive single acts of slapping and shoving in anger as being significant or destructive. Indeed, many young people who report physical aggression in their marriage do not report being maritally discordant (O'Leary et al., 1989). Given these findings, it seems important to educate men and women about the insidious nature of physical aggression in relationships. Such aggression, if repeated, is associated with negative effects for husbands and wives, especially wives (depression and injury), increasing marital discord, lack of caring, poor communication, and disproportionate rates of separation and divorce (O'Leary & Vivian, 1990; O'Leary, Cascardi, & Arias, 1991). (O'Leary et al., 1992, p. 13)

As assessment in clinical settings should serve to guide treatment and enhance its outcome (Hayes, Nelson, & Jarrett, 1987), the clinician faces a dilemma when assessment reveals violence in a couple presenting for marital problems:

> It seems clear that at a minimum we cannot simply build treatments around the presenting problems as described spontaneously or in response to a minimal prompt about what the major problems are in a marriage. The evidence suggests that abused women are not often identified as victims and underidentification of physical abuse is a serious issue (Hilberman, 1980; Stark & Flitcraft, 1983). . . . Furthermore, because of the differential impact of physical aggression for men and women, the failure to address this "silent" problem in marital therapy may inadvertently reinforce the legitimization of the power differential that is likely to be intrinsic in such relationships. (O'Leary et al., 1992, p. 13)

Despite the potential benefits of addressing violence in couples present-ing for treatment, clinicians must be cautious about using therapist power and control to try to alter couples' attitudes and behaviors. When the thera-pist identifies couple violence as a problem, he or she might follow the motivational interviewing approach described in chapter 2, eliciting con-cerns of the partners themselves regarding the violent behaviors, as such an approach will likely lead to less resistance.

Who Receives Treatment and in What Modality?

Even for couples or individuals presenting with primary problems of physical or psychological aggression, the question of who receives treatment and in what modality continues to be debated (McMahon & Pence, 1996; O'Leary, 1996). Systems approaches advocating couple-focused treatment (e.g., Neidig & Freidman, 1984) have come under attack for ignoring and even reinforcing relationship power imbalances and broader societal sexism (see Bograd, 1984, 1988, 1990). By contrast, the feminist perspective delineates clear perpetrator and victim roles and maintains that gender-specific group treatment formats are needed to challenge the patriarchal attitudes of male perpetrators and to ensure the empowerment, safety, and support of victims. The psychopathology perspective focuses primarily on violence perpetrators and asserts that individual or group treatment should target the perpetrator's individual disturbances such as anger dyscontrol, beliefs justifying partner abuse, substance abuse, pathological jealousy, depression, and personality disorders. However, given the varied nature of couple violence (see below), a key question remains how to determine what type of couple or individual is appropriate for which type of treatment.

Marital Violence: Perpetrator and Victim Roles or Mutual Aggression?

Inextricably linked to the question of what treatment modality is used to target which partner is the issue of whether there are clear aggressor and victim roles in couple violence (O'Leary & Murphy, 1999). The feminist approach focuses primarily on unidirectional violence, identifying *battering* as a male phenomenon tied to gender socialization, power, and patriarchy that victimizes women (R. E. Dobash & Dobash, 1979). From this perspective, couples treatment not only places the woman in danger but also assigns shared responsibility to the woman for change, thereby implicitly blaming her for behaviors that are solely the responsibility of the man (McMahon & Pence, 1996). Similarly, the individual psychopathology approach generally identifies the perpetrator's psychological characteristics as leading to perpetrating violence against a victim. Data supporting a unilateral model of male battering and victimization of women tend to come from select samples such as shelter samples and court-mandated batterer programs and are generally based on interview assessment as opposed to survey or observational data (Vivian & Heyman, 1996). Additionally, recent scholarship identifying comparable rates of violence in same-sex couples calls into question clear gender-linked roles (Renzetti, 1997).

By contrast, sociological or psychological approaches that have studied normative populations or couples seeking treatment for marital distress have noted equivalent rates of physical aggression between husbands and wives (e.g., Straus & Gelles, 1990) and mutual verbal aggression as a strong correlate of couple violence, portraying a model that more closely resembles "mutual aggression" than wife abuse (Vivian & Heyman, 1996). In an attempt to synthesize these perspectives, Johnson (1995) distinguished "patriarchal terrorism" from "common couple violence," arguing that both types of couples exist: those with severe unilateral violence perpetrated by a controlling aggressor, and those with relatively mild, bidirectional violence resulting in low levels of injury or fear. Essentially, the splintered positions on the nature of partner violence and victimization appear to stem largely from attempts to draw global conclusions from disparate data sources. These sources encompass women from shelters and men legally mandated to treatment (often assessed using qualitative or archival methods), on the one hand, and community samples or couples seeking marital therapy (often assessed using quantitative methods), on the other.

Although the topic of treatment approaches to couple violence remains polemicized, recent discussions have identified subgroups of aggressive couples and proposed considering couple-based interventions based on variables such as violence severity, frequency, and direction (i.e., unilateral vs. bilateral); fear and power dynamics in the relationship; and acknowledgment of and acceptance of responsibility for violence by the perpetrator (O'Leary, 2002; Vivian & Heyman, 1996). Even for couples seen with a minimal level of violence, however, the clinician is still advised to address the violence directly through strategies such as "no violence" contracts, psychoeducation about the impact and possible escalation of violence, and teaching timeout and self-calming strategies (e.g., Neidig & Friedman, 1984; Vivian & Heyman, 1996). "Even minor violence must be the focus of concern because it sometimes escalates to severe violence, and can change the power dynamics of the relationship" (Saunders, 1992, p. 209). In fact, we must take care to avoid dismissing "common couple violence" (i.e., Johnson, 1995) as having minimal impact or low priority, because data suggest that even couples presenting together in marital clinics report a range of injury and other negative sequelae when violence has occurred (e.g., Cascardi et al., 1992).

Diagnosis in Partner Violence Assessment

It often becomes important to assess diagnosis when working with populations involved with family violence, because there are many diagnostic categories that have been associated with victim and perpetrator roles. (By contrast, couples with low-level, bidirectional violence have been discussed as not characterized by any particular diagnostic category or psychopathology, such as Holtzworth-Munroe and colleagues' "family-only" type of partner-violent male [Holtzworth-Munroe & Stuart, 1994; Holtzworth-Munroe et al., 2000].) Certain diagnoses may suggest assessing for abuse or may point to areas of concern and potential intervention targets in identified populations.

In cases of moderate to severe marital violence, both the batterer and battered woman are often characterized by various diagnoses of the *Diagnostic and Statistical Manual of Mental Disorders* (*DSM*). Men who assault their female partners have often been described as having elevated Axis I symptomatology, including major depression, substance abuse, and PTSD (e.g., Conner & Ackerly, 1994; Feldbau-Kohn, Heyman, & O'Leary, 1998; Hotaling & Sugarman, 1986; Kantor & Straus, 1990; Schumacher et al., 2001; Tolman & Bennet, 1990), as well as elevated Axis II symptomatology, particularly borderline, narcissistic, dependent, and antisocial (e.g., D. G. Dutton & Starzomski, 1993; Hamberger & Hastings, 1988). Note that because very few studies have actually used true diagnostic assessments (Felbau-Kohn et al., 1998, being an exception), one cannot conclude that such men meet diagnostic criteria for these disorders.

Female victims of husband assault commonly meet criteria for PTSD and other anxiety disorders, major depression, substance abuse disorders, and somatoform disorders (e.g., Cascardi, O'Leary, Lawrence, & Schlee, 1995; Houskamp & Foy, 1991; Saunders, 1992; Walker, 1991). Also, suicidality may appear alone or as part of other diagnoses such as depression or bipolar disorder. Because research has documented only one risk marker for being a victim of husband-to-wife violence—abuse in one's family of origin (specifically, witnessing parental violence [Hotaling & Sugarman, 1986] and being emotionally/verbally abused [Schumacher et al., 2000]) — clinicians must be cautioned against attributing severe disturbances in battered women to intrapersonal rather than situational causes (Koss et al., 1994).

Aside from diagnoses capturing phenomena related to the perpetration of or victimization from partner violence, until recently, there was no direct diagnostic label to describe situations of physical aggression toward a partner. Walker (1984) had identified the *battered women syndrome* to capture the emotional sequelae of women victimized by a spouse, characterized by fear of unavoidable and unpredictable physical aggression. This "diagnosis" has become admissible evidence in court in all 50 states regarding cases of spousal homicides by battered women (O'Leary & Jacobson, 1997) and has contributed greatly to the understanding of the state of mind of the battered woman. Nevertheless, the category has not been entered into the *DSM* because of its lack of reliability and validity evidence and of gender neutrality.

Noting that there was no diagnostic category in the third revised *DSM* (*DSM–III–R*; American Psychiatric Association, 1987) that adequately referred to problems of partner abuse, and that diagnoses often applied for such problems, such as intermittent explosive disorder, sadistic personality disorder, and self-defeating personality disorder, were inherently flawed, O'Leary and Jacobson (1997) argued for a new diagnostic category for the fourth edition (*DSM–IV*; American Psychiatric Association, 1994). Its defining characteristics, which incorporated aspects of the battered women syndrome, are based on a systematic review of the literature: (a) The acts of physical aggression occur in anger rather than in self-defense; (b) the acts of physical aggression usually include behaviors such as slapping, pushing, kicking, throwing objects, beating, or threatening with a weapon, and may include the use of force to obtain sexual gratification; (c) the acts of physical aggression occur more than once per year, result in physical injury requiring medical attention, or involve threats and intimidation, such that the victim is almost always fearful; and (d) the acts of physical aggression are generally unpredictable and unavoidable by the victim. Thus, *DSM–IV* contains the new V-code under Partner Relational Problem—Physical Abuse of an Adult, V61.1 (and an additional code to specify whether the focus of attention is on the victim). This addition promises to benefit not only researchers but also clients seeking services for problems of domestic violence, as *DSM–IV* diagnostic codes are necessary for receiving insurance reimbursement.

One issue that arises in the field of domestic violence is the dilemma of whether to assess and treat clients according to diagnostic presentation or according to the abusive events experienced or perpetrated. Despite a wide array of clinical presentations, treatments for both victims and perpetrators of family violence have historically tended to be generic treatment programs based on the nature of the abuse involved (e.g., Pence & Paymar, 1993). In fact, some feminist theorists have argued against disorder-based conceptualizations, contending that the assignment of clinical diagnoses risks pathologizing battered women while excusing the behavior of partner-assaultive men (D. Adams, 1988). Such scholars further contend that with the exception of PTSD, *DSM* diagnoses fail to consider etiology and environmental factors extrinsic to intrapersonal functioning, such as threat, victimization, and gender bias (Koss et al., 1994). However, more recently, others have pointed to the potential utility of disorder-specific interventions for victims and perpetrators of family violence, particularly as research continues to delineate clear diagnostic groups of both victims (Cascardi et al., 1995; Houskamp & Foy, 1991; Koss, 1990; Walker, 1991) and perpetrator subtypes (e.g., Holtzworth-Munroe et al., 2000; Holtzworth-Munroe & Stuart, 1994; Waltz et al., 2000). Addressing diagnostic/behavioral typologies might increase treatment efficiency while enhancing outcome, and thus is an area in need of empirical investigation in the coming years.

Establishing Rapport

An important aspect of the initial assessment process is the need to establish rapport with the client. The formation of a therapeutic alliance involves clarification of roles (e.g., description and expectations of a mandated treatment program or of a psychodiagnostic evaluation), agreement on goals, and establishment of a therapeutic bond (Bordin, 1979).

It is essential to establish rapport with clients during the assessment phase, as cooperation with the assessment process, retention in treatment, and even treatment outcome may depend on it (e.g., Barber, Connolly, Crits-Christoph, Gladis, & Siqueland, 2000; Brown & O'Leary, 2000). In the field of couple violence, forming a rapport can be especially difficult:

> Court-ordered clients present the added complexity of coerced assessment, including fear of legal reprisals for a negative clinical evaluation and the wish for legal exoneration from a positive clinical evaluation. Similarly, many victims have concerns about their mental health and the choices they have made to remain in an abusive relationship. They often fear negative evaluation from the clinician or insensitivity to the

complexity of their relationship, life situation, and choices. (O'Leary & Murphy, 1999, p. 25)

In essence, building a therapeutic alliance involves a collaborative agreement between client and practitioner on therapeutic tasks and goals, as well as an atmosphere of warmth and mutual respect. When working with mandated or otherwise reluctant clients, building rapport involves validating their frustration or ambivalence regarding treatment and behavior change. The interviewer can ask them to discuss the ways in which the experiences or behaviors that brought them into treatment have caused problems for them, eliciting concerns of clients about their own situations or behaviors rather than reproaching clients for their actions[1] (Daniels & Murphy, 1997; Murphy & Baxter, 1997; see section on motivational interviewing in chap. 2, this volume). Of course, the assessor must remain mindful of the tendency to present in a socially desirable manner regarding the issues being assessed. One would expect that partner-assaultive clients would not be especially forthcoming if their disclosures might substantiate criminal charges, elicit a mandate for treatment, or bring about other unwanted consequences.

O'Leary and Murphy (1999) offered a number of recommendations for maximizing the alliance with clients disinclined to treatment. First, they suggested engaging in an open-ended, empathic discussion of client concerns prior to beginning structured assessments. The assessor should then obtain consent for the assessment procedures, explain any benefits of the assessment process, and help clients to see themselves as active participants in the process. Additionally, O'Leary and Murphy emphasized being open about the assessment procedure; informing clients about the nature, length, and purpose of the assessment; answering any questions; and explaining who will have access to the assessment data and the purposes for which it will be used. Further, they recommended explaining the clinician's role regarding the legal system (e.g., courts, probation department) and clarifying the nature of contact and information shared with legal authorities. In doing so, assessors should clearly address issues of confidentiality. Finally, they urged assessors to obtain written informed consent from mandated clients about limits of confidentiality and the extent of communication the clinician will have with outside parties.

---

1. Of course, in the case of battering, one must draw a fine line between establishing a rapport with clients in the service of treatment compliance/retention and colluding with minimization or justification of abusive behavior.

When working with victims of domestic violence who have difficulty with trust and disclosure of events leading to the present assessment, it is crucial to validate their experience and their hesitancy to self-disclose. Confidentiality and its limits must be explained at the outset of the assessment process; it can be helpful to remember that such clients might not only be embarrassed about their situations and choices but also may harbor realistic concerns about whether their partners will become privy to the potentially inflammatory information they report to the assessor. Working at a slower than normal pace that does not feel intrusive to the client, and giving explicit permission to not answer questions that the client is not ready to discuss, can further put the client at ease. Giving the client a sense of control, while retaining a warm and nonjudgmental stance, can facilitate rapport in such cases. M. A. Dutton (1992a) proposed beginning structured assessment methods with open-ended interviews, allowing victims to tell their stories. In response, the interviewer should combining active listening with empathic responding (Saunders, 1999). Based on her extensive interview research with battered women, Walker (1984) cautioned that there may be a tendency for domestic violence victims to try to please the interviewer, and thereby not assert concerns about the assessment process. Walker recommended balancing a matter-of-fact attitude about the events reported with compassion for the woman's pain to attain a comfortable interaction and accurate data.

Ethical Issues

Working in family violence poses several dilemmas with regard to conducting therapeutic activities while adhering to ethical standards. For example, dilemmas that may arise include the following:

- the right to self-determination and freedom of choice versus mandating treatment (e.g., agency-based programs for perpetrators of family violence; involuntary inpatient psychiatric admission for a client determined to be a danger to self or others)
- the right to self-determination in terms of treatment goals versus imposing an agenda onto the client (e.g., in mandated programs with goal of violence cessation for violence perpetrators)
- maintaining confidentiality versus duty to warn/protect
- respecting privacy versus the obligation to assess in a potentially intrusive manner (e.g., probing questions regarding areas of discomfort for the client; contacting other pertinent individuals in client's

life to conduct a fair and thorough evaluation; asking more detailed questions once suspicions of abuse have been aroused)

In addition to these broad dilemmas, the ethical guidelines of the American Psychological Association (APA, 1997) include a number of ethical principles that pertain to issues of assessment of family violence. A list of ethical issues pertaining to the interface of these principles and family violence assessment appears in Exhibit 3.1. Although the published ethical principles by the APA are required for adherence by psychologists, evaluators from all disciplines can benefit from following them.

Legal Issues

A variety of legal issues are relevant to assessment in the field of couple violence. Although an in-depth discussion of these issues falls outside of the scope of this book, we briefly address matters of risk management, reporting requirements, forensic evaluations, and prediction of dangerousness (for further coverage of legal issues, see Ammerman & Hersen, 1999; Thyfault, 1999).

Risk Management

One way that legal issues may touch family violence professionals is in terms of lawsuits filed by clients, their families, or outside agencies. Because the outcome of assessment and treatment may have life and death consequences, risk management concerns are especially important in this field. According to a report from the Committee on Legal and Ethical Issues in the Treatment of Interpersonal Violence (American Psychological Association, 1997), good risk management practice includes obtaining consultation or supervision, adhering to ethical practice guidelines, staying current in knowledge of ethical standards as well as legal issues, and meticulously documenting actions regarding cases that pose a high risk. Such documentation involves documentation of risk assessments made, consultation or supervision sought, and an outline of decisions made and on what basis, including actions that were considered but not taken and why. Finally, comprehensive professional liability insurance is essential.

Subpoenas for Client Records

At times, practitioners working in the field of domestic violence will face subpoenas for client records or subpoena for testimony in court. This poses

Exhibit 3.1

Ethical Standards Pertaining to the Interface of APA Ethical Principles and Family Violence Assessment

The following principles are summarized from the American Psychological Association (1997):

- Psychologists should not carry out roles regarding the assessment of domestic violence cases for which they do not have specific training/expertise.
- Psychologists conducting domestic violence assessments should stay abreast of current research in this field.
- Given the limited state of knowledge regarding recidivism, future dangerousness, and so on, evaluators should qualify all statements involving prediction.
- When conducting assessments of family violence for research purposes, psychologists must ensure clients are not harmed and that they provide informed consent.
- When conducting assessments of family violence for research purposes, psychologists also take responsibility for not overgeneralizing results and ensuring that results are reported accurately.
- All mandated reporting laws must be followed when conducting family violence assessments, regardless of the purpose for or context of the assessment.
- Psychologists must notify clients clearly of their roles (e.g., forensic evaluator, therapist, research investigator) and also of when their roles change.
- Psychologists conducting family violence assessments must prevent harm when possible, work to ensure safety, and warn those in danger.
- If a psychologist encounters a family violence assessment situation for which he or she is not properly trained or knowledgeable, he or she should obtain consultation from properly trained professionals or refer the case to an expert in the relevant area.
- When making a determination of risk or danger to others, the assessor must prioritize the concern of prevention or minimization of harm when considering breaking confidentiality.
- In making contact with outside parties (such as family members or court officers) in conducting family violence evaluations, the psychologist must clarify his or her role(s) to those parties and continue to perform within that role.
- The psychologist should communicate and cooperate with outside professional parties (e.g., courts, medical institutions, domestic violence agencies) in a manner that will serve the best interests of their clients when conducting a domestic violence evaluation.
- In conducting assessments of family violence, psychologists must take care to avoid the abuse of power or the exploitation or misleading of others. Assessors must be aware of how their statements or conclusions might be used to the detriment of clients or others, and thus must remain cautious, sensitive, and objective in how they present their findings and what they disclose.
- Psychologists conducting domestic violence assessments should work toward the mitigation of causes of human suffering as well as toward policy that serves the interests of their clients and the public.
- Psychologists should use tests with which they have training in administration and interpretation of results.
- Psychologists must acknowledge the limitations of their assessment data as well as the limitations of relevant knowledge in the field.

a potential conflict between the client's right to privacy and the assessor or treating clinician's legal obligations. In this case, immediate consultation with an attorney is recommended. The APA Committee on Legal Issues also provides a booklet with guidelines for handling subpoenas (American Psychological Association, 1997).

Reporting Requirements

While it is common clinical practice to orient clients regarding informed consent to assessment/treatment and a discussion of the "duty to warn," the essential nature of such practices is highlighted in family violence assessment contexts. Any client or research participant involved in a family violence assessment must grant consent to take part in the process, following a clear explanation by the clinician/assessor of the expected nature of the interaction as well as any policies or obligations. This informed consent must include an explanation of confidentiality and under what circumstances it is upheld, as well as when it must be broken. That is, the practitioner must explain his or her duty to warn regarding threat of harm to self, threat of harm to another, or suspicion of recent or ongoing child abuse.

Practitioners conducting assessments with violent couples will need to be familiar with their state reporting requirements in terms of mandated reporting of child abuse, as well as requirements regarding the duty to warn parties who might be in danger. Although wording varies somewhat from state to state, "when a disclosure of child maltreatment occurs, *the law allows no debate*: state and federal statutes require reporting. Reporting a disclosure of abuse against elders and other adults is also permitted or mandated depending on the state" (American Psychological Association, 1997, p. 17). The APA provides guidelines on mandated reporting. With cases that are not unequivocal, reporting of abuse is most wisely carried out with the consultation of peers who are knowledgeable in this field. In addition, it may be helpful to refer clients for expert assessments in the relevant area, such as a team specializing in the assessment of the battered woman syndrome (American Psychological Association, 1997).

Because of the high prevalence of child abuse in homes in which spouse abuse is ongoing (Sudermann & Jaffe, 1999), practitioners working with violent couples will want to remain aware of child abuse potential and will inevitably encounter such cases. Many practitioners who face reporting clients to social service agencies for child abuse express concern about harming the relationship. Some may even feel it may do more harm than good to report a victim or perpetrator of spouse abuse who is engaged in and making progress in therapy. Although this may be a valid concern, it obviously does not remove the obligation to report when child abuse is suspected. However, certain strategies of reporting may mitigate its negative impact on the client's trust and connection with the practitioner. First, from the outset of treatment or even a brief assessment/evaluation, it is critical, as mentioned earlier, to begin with informed consent, where that consent includes full understanding of the practitioner's duty to break confidentiality. Second, when it is determined that a report must be made, it is advisable to avoid doing this without the client's knowledge but rather inform the client that a report has become necessary and exactly on what basis this decision was made. Then, the practitioner can explain to the client what he or she can expect to happen (i.e., usually a visit to the home by a case worker within 24 hours, etc.). The practitioner can validate the client's reactions while asking about specific concerns (e.g., is there danger from a spouse for "saying the wrong thing, " is there a fear of losing custody, etc.) and can also act in the role of advocate or problem-solving aid in helping the client to plan for and cope with these concerns. The practitioner can explain that he or she wishes to do this as collaboratively as possible, to the extent that this is possible, and that the ultimate goal is to obtain needed help for the family. Once a decision to report has been made, practitioners must remain firm and not be swayed by a client's arguments against reporting.

The issue of mandated reporting can also become delicate in instances in which practitioners must warn potential victims about individuals at risk for engaging in violent behavior. According to the state court's decision in *Tarasoff v. Regents of the University of California* (1976), mental health professionals are obligated to protect third parties from violence once a therapist reasonably ascertains that a client poses a serious threat of violence to another (Borum, 1996). This determination is especially difficult because there are no federal guidelines on reporting, there are no standard national guidelines for violence risk assessment, and violence prediction is notoriously unreliable (Borum, 1996).

Forensic Evaluations

Practitioners working in the field of domestic violence may serve as expert witnesses and testify regarding issues such as the presence and severity level of domestic abuse, the characteristics of abusive relationships, the potential causes or consequences of abuse, the state of current research knowledge in a specific area relating to domestic violence (e.g., effects of being a battered spouse in a homicide case), the likelihood of future dangerousness, or the need for treatment and particular types of treatment needed.

In the role of forensic evaluator, the assessor is careful to serve solely in the role of evaluator, meaning he or she does not also serve as treating clinician or advocate to the client. Instead, he or she

> acts in a neutral and objective manner in order to obtain information concerning a specific case or situation. In this role, the psychologist seeks to help determine whether the client sustained damages, to help evaluate various allegations, or to provide recommendations to a court concerning a disputed situation and/or future actions. (American Psychological Association, 1997, p. 11)

In doing so, the evaluator reviews all available supporting records/collateral information, remains open to multiple explanations for behaviors, pays heed to present issues of safety, and follows all laws regarding mandated reporting (see Sattler, 1997, for detailed elaboration of forensic assessment).

In conducting forensic evaluations, the therapist should be careful not to ask leading questions, and the client's privacy should be protected by interviewing him or her alone. All issues of mandated reporting and duty to warn apply to forensic evaluations, and the evaluator must attend to issues of assessing risk of harm and dangerousness.

Finally, conducting forensic evaluations in the area of domestic violence requires expertise in family violence; this means staying abreast of current research literature, attending relevant conferences, and availing oneself of other means of continuing education. It is also necessary to develop expertise in the judicial system and relevant laws.

Prediction of Dangerousness

Despite the complexity and controversy surrounding the prediction of violence, the legal system continues to seek the assistance of mental health professionals in determining potential dangerousness of clients (Borum, 1996). This task may come about in the context of evaluating a client's suitability for a particular program, determining whether to warn another party of violence risk,[2] choosing the appropriate sentence or sanction, deciding on an involuntary psychiatric commitment or otherwise evaluating

---

2. Note that any clear statement of plan or intent to harm another warrants warning the party in danger.

needed level of care, ascertaining whether discharge from a psychiatric or mandated program is warranted, determining parental fitness for retaining custody of children (see Hysjulien, Wood, & Benjamin, 1994), or making a judgment about needed services at the request of social service agencies, law enforcement workers, or the courts. Requests for such assistance are not limited to forensic mental health specialists but might be faced by mental health professionals in routine clinical practice (Borum, 1996). Thus, knowledge of the issues involved in danger prediction is beneficial for anyone involved in clinical assessment.

Of course, violence prediction is far from an exact science, largely because violence is a low-frequency and covert event. Mental health professionals make a substantial number of errors in predicting future violent behavior, predominantly of the false-positive type (Otto, 1992). However, because of factors such as improved methodology for detecting violence, greater reliance on actuarial prediction methods, and higher base rates of violence than previously believed, predictive ability has improved over the last two decades (Borum 1996; D. G. Dutton & Kropp, 2000). Review studies suggest that mental health professionals can now determine the likelihood of future violent behavior with success rates significantly higher than chance levels, and with greater than 50% accuracy in short-term predictions (Menzies & Webster, 1995; Mossman, 1994; Otto, 1992).

Certain factors lead to maximal power in predicting dangerousness, such as obtaining agreement among multiple evaluators (Werner, Rose, & Yesavage, 1990), obtaining information from the victim when possible (Whittemore & Kropp, 2002), and evaluating a series of known general risk factors for violent behavior. The risk factors may include past violence, being assigned multiple psychiatric diagnoses (particularly substance abuse disorders, along or in combination with another Axis I disorder, and personality disorders, particularly with anger, impulsiveness, and behavioral instability), past violation of community supervision, extreme minimization of spouse assault history, and consistent display of threatening/hostile mannerisms (Borum, 1996; Grann & Wedin, 2002; Limandri & Sheridan, 1995).

In considering ethical issues in the prediction of dangerousness, the clinician walks a fine line between placing potential victims in danger by erring in the direction of releasing a dangerous individual, on the one hand, and threatening the autonomy of the evaluated individual by erring in the direction of mandating services or commitment, on the other (see above section on Ethical Issues).

In general, predictions of dangerousness should be made with care and caution, including caution in making overly conclusive statements.

Conclusions should be based on review of all relevant information attained through multimodal and structured assessment. Such a battery might consist of an interview; records of past history with violence, crime, and hospitalizations; contact with other informants; and standardized paper-and-pencil measures of past violence and violence risk (e.g., Dangerous Behavior Rating Scheme, Webster & Menzies, 1993; Spouse Assault Risk Assessment Guide, Kropp & Hart, 2000; cf. Borum, 1996; D. G. Dutton & Kropp, 2000). Moreover, it is important to consider the reliability and validity data of any instruments chosen; at least a substantial part of the battery must have adequate psychometric properties that will need to be documented in any forensic reports. Also, it must be shown that any measures used are appropriate for the population to which they are applied. Limitations of instruments should be acknowledged as well. Following such precautions will help to ensure fairness to clients as well as reduce liability risk to practitioners. In all cases in which the clinician makes predictions of dangerousness, meticulous attention to risk management is essential, especially in a climate in which

> despite a long-standing controversy about the ability of mental health professionals to predict violence, the courts continue to rely on them for advice on these issues and in many cases have imposed on them a legal duty to take action when they know or should know that a patient poses a risk of serious danger to others. (Borum, 1996, p. 954)

Conclusion

Whether assessment and treatment focuses on perpetrators, victims, or couples, a therapist

> should be aware of his or her own norms and values that may influence the assessment outcome (Porter, 1986). Simply holding onto the myth that the family is universally a place of peace and security can prevent practitioners from asking directly about the occurrence of violence in the home. (Saunders, 1992, p. 210)

Despite longstanding debate over whom to target for assessment and treatment, the field of partner violence has witnessed substantial progress. That recognition of subtypes of violent couples (e.g., Holtzworth-Munroe et al., 2000; Johnson, 1995; Vivian & Heyman, 1996; Waltz et al., 2000) and mention of fear, context, and impact of aggression (e.g., O'Leary & Jacobson, 1997) have begun to inform our assessments reflects our increased understanding of and sensitivity to problems of couple violence.

Research Considerations in the Assessment of Partner Violence: Scale Development, Psychometrics, and Measuring Treatment Outcome

his chapter focuses on a number of research considerations in the assessment of family violence. We discuss scale development, psychometrics, methods of measuring treatment outcome, and ways to enhance treatment evaluation within the field of family violence.

Scale Development and Psychometrics

It is necessary to understand some basic concepts related to the development of measures for use in couple violence research to interpret the reviews of instruments provided in the remainder of this volume. As such, we discuss scale development, scoring, and psychometrics.

Methods of Scale Development

There are two general methods for developing assessment instruments: rational and empirical approaches. The rational approach consists of generating and grouping scale items on the basis of the relevant clinical literature, a priori theoretical notions of constructs, or a combination of the two. The empirical approach essentially involves grouping and retaining scale items on the basis of statistical processes involving conducting some form of factor analysis, evaluating item–scale correlations, and moving or dropping items based on maximizing internal consistency (Jackson, 1970). Both methods have been used in the development of partner violence scales. Another way to develop a scale empirically is to retain items (or assign items to particular scales) on the basis of their ability to discriminate between groups that are differentiated on the construct of interest, a procedure known as *empirical criterion keying* (Golden, Sawicki, & Franzen, 1984). Many scale developers combine both strategies, rationally generating items and then arriving at final scales on the basis of empirical methodology. Unfortunately, not all developers of instruments used in the assessment of couple violence fully describe their method of scale development; we describe scale development methods when provided.

Scoring

Another central factor in scale construction involves the scoring of the response items. One aspect of scoring is whether the scale will be scored dimensionally or categorically. Dimensional scales produce scores that occur on a continuum and represent varying degrees of the construct being assessed. Many self-report inventories are scored dimensionally; examples include inventories reflecting levels of aggressiveness or marital satisfaction. Categorical measures produce scores reflecting discrete, all-or-none membership in a particular category or set of categories and typically reflect the presence or absence of a given variable. Many observational coding systems and interviews are scored categorically; examples of categorically scored variables include clinical diagnosis or aspects of communication directed toward a partner.

An additional aspect of scoring involves scaling. Particularly in self-report inventories (but sometimes in other instrument formats as well), noncategorical individual items are rated on some type of continuous scale. The Likert-type scale is the most common of such scales and represents a range (commonly 1–5 or 1–7) of anchored choice points that reflect relative agreement or disagreement with the item. Items are then typically summed to yield total scores. The majority of partner violence instruments use Likert scales.

The Guttman scale also reflects a range of anchored choice points, but rather than a choice point reflecting a discrimination among items, the highest endorsed item by an individual subsumes all of the item choices that come below it. That is, if a respondent endorses 4 on a 7-point scale, the assumption is that Items 1 through 4 will all be true for the respondent. The Thurstone scale reflects a range of choice points, typically reflecting attitudes, that are rated by a group of judges as ranging from reflecting more to less favorable attitudes. Items are retained that reflect good agreement among judges and range evenly from one extreme of the attitude to the other (Nunnally, 1978). Forced-choice scales present the respondent with a set of choices (typically pairs) and ask the respondent to select the more favorable or applicable choice in the set. Many inventories use this format in a "yes/no" or "true/false" format.

A further consideration involving scoring of assessment devices involves whether scoring is norm-referenced or criterion-referenced. A norm-referenced approach calculates scores according to established normative scoring for a given population. An example of this type of scoring involves a construct such as marital satisfaction, measures of which yield scores that fall within the range of maritally satisfied status or clinically distressed status, based on norms from these groups. Criterion referenced scoring, in contrast, is a

> method of assessment designed to measure performance and to estimate a person's level of (or in some cases the simple presence or absence of) skill, capability, or achievement in absolute rather than relative terms. The focus is on a person's performance in certain specified content domains. (Linehan, 1980, p. 149)

An example of this type of assessment would be a role-play test to determine a person's performance in assertiveness.

Reliability and Validity

A central consideration in the development of assessment devices is the reliability and validity of the instrument (see Weathers, Keane, King, & King, 1997). Reliability refers to the precision and consistency of measurement, or the extent to which a test score consists of the true score and not measurement error (Crocker & Algina, 1986). Validity refers to the extent to which an instrument measures the construct it attempts to measure. A test cannot be valid if it is not reliable, because it cannot be said to measure a given construct adequately if it does not do so in an accurate and stable manner. As we report on assessment devices throughout this volume, we repeatedly refer to the various types of reliability and validity that have been established for each instrument. We provide definitions of the various types of reliability and validity below.

Types of Reliability

Test–Retest Reliability

Test–retest reliability refers to the degree to which a score remains stable on an instrument from Time 1 to Time 2. This stability will vary according to the target of assessment. For example, certain characteristics are expected to remain stable, such as historical factors (e.g., an individual's developmental history; reports of emotional abuse by a partner over the past year, assessed one week apart), basic capabilities in the absence of intervention (e.g., assertiveness skills), or enduring, traitlike characteristics such as intelligence and personality. Other characteristics are expected to vary substantially across time, such as mood ratings. Still other characteristics will fall somewhere in between long-term stability and substantial variability, and will vary partially on the basis of the length of time between assessment points (e.g., marital adjustment). Test–retest reliability is important for interpreting (a) the degree to which an examinee's current score is likely to reflect a true score as opposed to substantial measurement error and (b) the degree to which change in an examinee's score over time reflects change due to intervention or to life circumstances rather than to variability of the measurement instrument. Test–retest reliability is expressed as a simple correlation (i.e., from 0 to 1.0).

Interrater Agreement

Interrater agreement reflects the degree to which multiple observers agree when assigning scores using the same instrument on the same participant within the same time frame (or at the exact same time). This type of agreement is relevant in assessment situations in which subjective judgments are used, such as in observational or interview assessments. Interobserver agreement reflects the degree to which ratings reflect characteristics of the measured phenomenon rather than idiosyncratic characteristics or perceptions of particular raters. Low interrater agreement reflects high measurement error. Note that although often used interchangably, reliability and interobserver agreement are not technically equivalent. That is, the error term in a reliability score may reflect such factors as differences among observers, inconsistencies in the scoring or administration of the scale, and random fluctuations in participants' behavior or characteristics. By contrast, indices of interobserver agreement reflect only one possible source of error, that of observer differences. "In other words, a reliability coefficient reflects the relative magnitude of all error with respect to true score variability, whereas an agreement percentage reflects the absolute magnitude of just one kind of error" (Mitchell, 1979, p. 378).

Interobserver agreement is typically reported in one of four ways. For dimensional or frequency data (e.g., total scores on self-report measures), interrater agreement is normally calculated in terms of intraclass correlations (ICCs; Shrout & Fleiss, 1979) or simple Pearson correlations between raters' scores. Intraclass correlations are the preferred method as they take concordance of ranks and *levels* of ratings into account rather than being calculated solely on the basis of concordance of ranks. For categorical data (e.g., types of communication observed in an observational study), interrater agreement is normally calculated with Cohen's (1960) kappa statistic or by calculating the percentage agreement (number of agreements divided by the number of agreements plus disagreements). Kappa is the more conservative estimate of interrater agreement and is generally superior to simple percentage agreement because its calculation takes chance agreement into account. However, when category base rates are low, kappa's correction for chance may overly attenuate agreement levels (Archer, 1999). Both ICCs and kappas range from 0 to 1.0.

In couple violence, one form of interrater agreement commonly assessed is that of both partners reporting on one partner's aggression. For example, the Conflict Tactics Scale asks respondents to report on their own behavior toward their spouse as well as their spouse's behavior toward them. When both partners fill out the instrument, interpartner agreement on each partner's aggression can be calculated. When evaluating such agreement rates between spouses, however, one might apply somewhat less stringent standards in interpreting ICC or kappa values; "it is doubtful whether the same criterion should be applied to partner agreements and to ratings from trained observers and coders" (Archer, 1999, p. 1280).

Internal Consistency Reliability

Internal consistency reliability, typically measured with a statistic known as Cronbach's coefficient alpha (Cronbach, 1951), reflects the extent to which the content of a scale measures a unidimensional construct. The alpha coefficient averages the intercorrelations among scale items and ranges from 0 to 1.0. The degree to which internal consistency is desirable depends in part on the nature of the construct measured by the instrument. For example, in a measure of broad personality functioning, we would not expect internal consistency, or relatively equivalent ratings across each item on the scale. Instead, we would expect wide variability across items, reflecting differing amounts of the personality features assessed. However, within the subscales of this personality measure (e.g., Impulsivity), we would expect more uniform endorsement of characteristics, as we could describe someone as more or less impulsive. Most scales themselves endeavor, or have subscales that endeavor, to measure a single construct. Internal consistency is thus important because items on the scale measuring different constructs will only detract from measurement of the construct of interest. For tests with dichotomous response choices (e.g., true/false), the Kuder–Richardson 20 formula is used rather than Cronbach's alpha to calculate reliability.

Split-Half Reliability

Split-half reliability is a form of internal consistency reliability and measures the extent to which two halves of an instrument are intercorrelated. Internal consistency (alpha) is the intercorrelation of all possible split halves of the test.

Alternate Form Reliability

Alternate form reliability involves the preparing of an equivalent form of the test with nonoverlapping items and calculating the degree to which the two versions are correlated. Alternate form reliability reflects the degree to which the score reflects characteristics of the construct assessed and not the test item content itself. It is useful when there is concern about practice effects of taking the test, which might be particularly likely with some types of tests (e.g., tests of ability) or when the test is repeated within a short enough time frame that items are likely to be remembered.

Standard Error of Measurement

The standard error of measurement (*SEM*) is an estimate of the standard deviation of error scores of an instrument. Examination of the *SEM* allows for a direct assessment of the degree of error operating in repeated measurements using the same instrument. Thus, if changes in scores across assessment periods are larger than the *SEM*, one can conclude that the change that occurred reflects actual change in the level of the variable measured and not merely "noise" in the instrument.

Types of Validity

Construct Validity

Construct validity refers to the degree to which a test measures the particular construct it purports to measure. Various types of construct validity include convergent and discriminant validity, criterion validity, known groups validity, and factorial validity.

Convergent and Discriminant Validity. One of the central ways to establish construct validity is to determine a scale's convergent and discriminant validity. Convergent validity is the correlation of the scale with closely related or overlapping constructs with which it is expected to correlate. Discriminant validity is the lack of correlation (or a modest correlation) with measures of different constructs, with which the measure is expected to be unrelated (or modestly related). For example, a measure of family cohesion might be expected to correlate with measures of family communication and family conflict but not to a measure of job satisfaction.

A classic and rigorous technique for determining convergent and discriminant validity involves use of the multitrait, multimethod matrix (D. T. Campbell & Fiske, 1959). Using this approach, the researcher administers the instrument targeted for evaluation (e.g., a new paper-and-pencil measure of anger) along with a variety of additional instruments to a sample. These instruments would include measures tapping constructs that overlap with the target construct (e.g., other established measures of anger or closely related constructs such as hostility) as well as measures tapping constructs that differ from the target construct (e.g., measures of anxiety). In addition, the additional measures would include instruments of both the same assessment method (i.e., paper-and-pencil assessments) and at least one other assessment method (e.g., interview assessments). To support the construct validity of the instrument in question, one would then look for a correspondence in measures based primarily on trait or construct rather than based on method. Thus, one would ideally expect to find the highest correlation between the target instrument and the instrument(s) of the same construct *and* the same method (i.e., between two paper-and-pencil measures of anger). One would expect the next highest correlation to occur between the target instrument and the instrument(s) of the same construct but of differing method (i.e., between a paper-and-pencil measure of anger and an interview measure of anger). The next highest (but significantly lower) correlation should occur between the target instrument and the instrument(s) of differing constructs but the same method (i.e., between a paper-and-pencil measure of anger and a paper-and-pencil measure of anxiety), and the lowest correlation should occur between the target instrument and the instrument(s) of both differing constructs and differing methods (i.e., between a paper-and-pencil measure of anger and an interview measure of anxiety). The multitrait, multimethod approach to determining construct validity helps establish connections between theoretically overlapping constructs while ruling out connections that are simply due to method variance (i.e., similar responding based on the mode of assessment). In addition, use of assessments representing multiple traits and multiple methods provides an intelligent and comprehensive strategy for clinical assessment, independent of the quest for establishing construct validity.

Criterion-Related Validity. Criterion-related validity refers to correspondence of ratings on an instrument with a relevant specified criterion. There are two types of criterion-related validity: concurrent and predictive validity. Concurrent validity refers to correspondence on an assessment instrument with an outside criterion measure that coincides with the time of measurement. Examples include establishing the criterion-related validity of an interview assessing a recent abuse incident by corroborating the findings with court and medical records concerning that incident. Predictive validity refers to the ability of an instrument to predict an expected future outcome associated with the construct. For example, the predictive validity of an instrument administered at Time 1 designed to measure future dangerousness would be determined by its accuracy in predicting the criterion of dangerous behavior by a designated Time 2.

Known Groups Validity. Known groups validity refers to the ability of an assessment device to discriminate between groups already identified as being characterized by varying levels of the construct of interest (it is thus sometimes referred to as *discriminative* validity, not to be confused with *discriminant* validity). For example, if a measure of trauma symptoms yields significantly higher scores in a sample of abused from nonabused children, this would be evidence of the scale's known groups validity. Known groups validity may be thought of as a type of criterion validity, because it reflects a correspondence between a particular assessment measure and an established criterion (e.g., an independently determined diagnosis or condition, such as "abused" or "nonabused").

Factorial Validity. Establishing factorial validity involves the statistical technique of factor analysis. Determining validity in this manner can be done in one of two ways. The first involves conducting a factor analysis on a number of different scales, consisting of the scales of interest as well as several other scales that are theoretically related and several that are not. If the scale of interest loads on a factor with the scales with which it is expected to relate (i.e., convergent validity) and not on factors containing the scales with which it is not expected to relate (i.e., discriminant validity), then factorial validity has been supported. The second way involves examining individual item loadings. Items on the scale or subscales of interest should correlate highly with the factor score of the related construct while not correlating highly with other factors not considered to be representing the same variable.

Incremental Validity

Incremental validity refers to the extent to which an instrument contributes to the measurement of a construct. It is typically demonstrated with respect to a specified criterion, such that good incremental validity of a measure means that adding that particular measure to a battery of assessments significantly adds to the association with the criterion. For example, one might investigate whether pretreatment emotional abuse has incremental validity with respect to pretreatment physical abuse in predicting outcomes in a partner violence treatment program.

Content Validity

Content validity refers to the extent to which a measure adequately samples the content domain—that is, the universe of behaviors or attributes that make up a particular construct. For example, an instrument that measures physical abuse and includes a wide range of mild and severe acts of physical aggression might be said to have good content validity.

Face Validity

Also not technically a form of validity, face validity refers to the extent to which the purpose of the test can be detected from the item content. For example, the Conflict Tactics Scale (Straus, 1979) asks respondents to endorse the violent behaviors (e.g., push, slap, shove, punch) they have engaged in or received in the past year; this measure clearly has high face validity, as it would be obvious to respondents that violence is being assessed. In contrast, the Propensity for Abusiveness Scale (D. G. Dutton, 1995) asks respondents to report on areas such as past parental maltreatment, affective lability, and trauma symptoms; this measure has low face validity in the sense that it is not readily identifiable as a measure of potential abusiveness. High face validity is desirable to the extent that an instrument has credibility and appears relevant to the purpose of the assessment; it is undesirable to the extent that the easier it is to determine what a test is measuring, the more susceptible the test will be to both demand characteristics and response biases, such as faking good.

Measuring Treatment Outcome

Familiarity with a variety of assessment strategies is an important first step in being able to measure outcome in clinical practice. However, one also needs to know how to use such assessment tools to determine whether treatment has been effective in a clinically meaningful way. Kazdin (1998) outlined several methods to evaluate treatment outcome in research design. Although many of these methods are based on evaluating outcome in groups (or using single-case experimental designs), a number of them can be applied to measuring outcome within a clinical practice as well, whether working with groups or individuals. These variables provide additional important avenues for assessment. A selection of these methods follows.

Client-Related Criteria

Client-related criteria include evaluations based on what has been termed clinical significance (as opposed to statistical significance). That is, outcome assessment focuses not on statistical improvement alone (which may or may not reflect a notable change in the client's day-to-day functioning) but also on whether there is a meaningful clinical impact (cf. Finkelhor & Berliner, 1995; Jacobson & Traux, 1991). Areas of client-related criteria for assessing outcome, as outlined by Kazdin (1998), follow.

Does Client Fall Within the Normative Range of Functioning?

One criterion that might be applied to examine outcome in clinical practice is the evaluation of whether a client who entered treatment outside of the normal range of functioning on a measure or set of measures falls within the normative range following treatment. An example of this criterion would be a client in a group for battered women who entered treatment with scores in the depressed range on a self-report inventory of depression but who falls within the normal range following treatment. Conversely, one can evaluate whether a client's score at posttreatment departs markedly (e.g., two standard deviations) from that of dysfunctional samples.

Does Client No Longer Meet Diagnostic Criteria?

Many clients will enter treatment meeting diagnostic criteria for at least one, if not several Axis I and Axis II disorders. An indication of treatment success could include not meeting diagnostic criteria for the disorder(s) at treatment termination. An example would be a formerly physically abused woman who no longer met criteria for PTSD and major depression following a treatment program.

Does the Client (and Significant Others or Other Observers) Rate the Condition as Improved?

In addition to whether a client's scores on an assessment measure fall within the normative range or indicate no longer meeting diagnostic criteria, an essential criterion for evaluating outcome is whether the client notes subjective improvement in the area for which treatment was sought. This might include assaultive husbands who feel less angry and more able to control their extreme emotional and behavioral reactions when upset with their wives. Another important factor is whether those who come in close contact with the client (e.g., spouses, therapist) observe a change in the client's functioning. Thus, assessing improvement in a program for assaultive men might include men's subjective reports of decreased abusiveness as well as partner reports.

Is There Reasonable Breadth of Change?

An additional criteria for evaluating treatment concerns the breadth of change—that is, the extent to which client changes extend beyond a focused treatment target. For example, in a treatment targeting partner aggression, change might be reflected not only in a reduction of violence but also in improved communication and parenting skills.

Are the Treatment Changes Durable?

Naturally, it is desirable for treatment effects to last beyond the date of treatment termination. Thus, follow-up assessments might be conducted to see if treatment gains have been maintained; the longer the duration of change, the more successful the treatment. For example, in a wife abuse abatement program, it would suggest positive outcome if program participants tended to continue to refrain from both physically and emotionally abusive behavior at 1-year and 2-year follow-up evaluation periods.

Does a Large Proportion of Clients Improve?

The criterion of whether a large proportion of clients improves is best applied in group treatment settings, whether those settings emphasize clinical practice, research, or both. To arrive at this proportion, one must operationalize *treatment responder* status. Such operationalizations typically consist of one or more of the following types of criteria for improvement: (a) functioning in the normative range on a given measure, (b) achieving a specified percentage reduction in scores on a relevant measure or measures, (c) reporting zero violent behaviors within a given time frame, or (d) subjective improvement ratings. One could conclude, for example, that a particular treatment approach for abusive spouses is reasonably effective if two thirds of participants respond to treatment according to designated criteria. Alternatively, an agency or a clinic might offer two approaches to treating victims of abuse (e.g., group and individual treatment) and might note which approach leads to a greater proportion of improved clients. Even in evaluating the outcome of single clients in clinical practice, the practitioner might keep a database including improvement status for each client and evaluate the practice's treatment effectiveness over time. This is especially important because a number of biases in the clinician's judgment (Nezu & Nezu, 1989) can lead to the clinician's overestimating the proportions of clients in one's practice who respond favorably.

Efficiency and Cost-Related Criteria

Is Treatment of a Reasonable Length of Time?

What a client or practitioner regards as a reasonable length of time for treatment is of course arbitrary and variable. However, efficiency in terms of treatment length might best be evaluated in comparison to another treatment approach; that is, is the treatment, as administered within a particular time frame, as effective as the same or another treatment delivered over a longer time frame (Kazdin, 1998)?

Is Treatment Cost-Effective?

Evaluating a treatment's cost-effectiveness involves determining the intervention's cost relative to its outcome (Kazdin, 1998). In other words, to justify more costly treatments, one would need to justify more far-reaching benefits. If two treatments result in similar outcomes on relevant assessment measures, the less costly of the two would obviously be preferred.

Consumer-Related and Social Impact Criteria

Is Treatment Acceptable to Consumers?

Not only is it important to consider the actual outcomes produced by a treatment, but it is also important to consider the client's experience undergoing a particular treatment. That is, certain treatments might be more painful, uncomfortable, intrusive, inconvenient, or otherwise unpalatable to clients. The acceptability of an intervention to clients must not be overlooked when evaluating interventions, as this factor will likely relate to a client's compliance with and completion of treatment (Kazdin, 1998).

Does Treatment Affect Everyday Life or Have an Impact on Society?

A final set of assessment variables to consider in evaluating treatment outcomes in practice is whether an intervention makes an impact in the "real world" rather than simply showing change on rating scales or other subjective criteria (Kazdin, 1998). Examples of social impact measures of central importance in couple violence assessment include arrests, orders of protection issued, hospitalizations, days missed from work, emergency room visits, and suicide attempts. Many of these variables are recorded in archival databases available, with client consent, for the practitioner to examine. These dimensions might be measured in terms of temporal improvement, for example, assessing the frequency of such variables in the 6 months prior to treatment, the six months during treatment, and at a 6-month follow-up assessment after treatment. Obviously, it is important to show that treatment had an impact on these types of variables in addition to standardized assessment measures; it would do little good for a client to improve on self-report questionnaires administered in the office but to not change in a way that affects day-to-day functioning.

Problems With Pre–Post Evaluation

Although it is beneficial to evaluate one's intervention by assessing clients pre- and posttreatment, there are problems with interpreting changes based on simple pre–post evaluation. Essentially, these problems concern what is know in research methodology as *threats to internal validity* (Kazdin, 1998), which means that one cannot rule out whether factors other than the intervention itself led to the change observed. Included in the list of plausible explanations for the change *other* than the intervention include the statistical tendency for extreme scores at pretreatment to regress toward the mean; the possibility that clients matured, got wiser, or experienced some other type of internal change that led to the improvement; the possibility that factors outside of the intervention itself led to the change (e.g., a change in the marital relationship, legal status, or employment status; a television special on a related topic in domestic violence); the potential for practice with the assessment measures themselves having produced improved scores; or the chance that changes in the measurement device itself or its scoring led to changes.

In research methodology, one can account for such threats through use of group or single-case experimental designs. However, in typical practice, it is often not feasible to arrange such treatment study designs as part of the evaluation process. Yet, there are some simple strategies that the practitioner can use to enhance the interpretability of one's treatment evaluations. These include obtaining baseline data, conducting continuous assessments throughout treatment, using follow-up assessments, using a comparison group when possible, and using standardized assessment measures (Briere, 1996; Kazdin, 1998).

Obtaining baseline data involves conducting multiple assessments at baseline rather than only one at pretreatment. Ideally, this would occur regularly (i.e., weekly) for some time prior to the beginning of treatment. However, if this is not practical or possible, baseline assessments might occur once at time of initial contact, once again at time of intake, and once again on initiating treatment. The purpose is to assess the likely course of the treatment targets in the absence of any intervention (Kazdin, 1998). Thus, if the targets are stable during the baseline assessment period, change following intervention can be more readily attributed to the intervention. Likewise, if a trend is detected during the baseline phase (e.g., the problem is getting worse), a change in this trend following treatment can also more readily be attributed to the actual intervention. Note that obtaining baseline data might not always be practical; some cases will need to be evaluated and treated immediately.

Obtaining continuous assessments throughout treatment (e.g., monthly, weekly, or even daily) also strengthens the interpretability of change following intervention. For example, if the assessment data show an unstable trend (e.g., scores continually up and down throughout treatment), an improved score at posttreatment might reflect chance improvement at the posttreatment measurement period. In contrast, if the assessment data reflect a steadily improving trend during the course of treatment, or even discrete improvements corresponding with particular phases of the intervention, the likelihood that the treatment itself accounted for the change (and that the change is authentic) is increased. Obtaining continuous assessments is an especially powerful method of enhancing the conclusiveness of outcome data when paired with baseline assessment data.

Another advantage of obtaining repeated measurements is that they would help, especially in those analogue situations designed to approximate in vivo, naturalistic assessment, to desensitize the client(s) to the assessment process and thus perhaps provide a more accurate measurement of natural responding. For example, an evaluation of spouses in a problem-solving discussion to determine couples' communication strategies might yield an increasingly accurate depiction of partner interactions over repeated observations.

Follow-up assessments strengthen the ability to attribute the change to the intervention by providing assessment data for significant periods of time after treatment ends. Follow-up assessments often consist of an abbreviated assessment battery and occur at such intervals as 6 months and one year following treatment termination. Improvements remaining at follow-up assessment periods strengthen findings by demonstrating the durability of change and suggesting that gains at posttreatment are less likely to represent a random fluctuation in scores.

Whenever possible in conducting group treatment evaluation, it is desirable to use a comparison group for assessing change. Although not easy to do in nonresearch settings, showing that a comparable group not receiving the treatment fails to show similar gains on assessment measures strengthens the conclusiveness of pre–post outcome data. Possibilities for comparison groups in clinical practice include wait-list groups and groups receiving other forms of treatment. Wait-list groups consist of individuals waiting to enter treatment; depending on the practice or program, waits for treatment may range from 1 week to several months. One might then assess individuals entering the wait-list and reassess them at time of treatment entry. If one compares these results with assessments conducted with others at pretreatment and posttreatment, change following the treatment condition but not the wait-list condition helps rule out threats to interpretation such as regression to the mean, client changes, or changes due to practice effects on the assessment devices. Another possibility for a comparison group consists of clients receiving other types of treatments. Particularly in a large agency or clinic setting, various programs may exist to treat similar types of clients and problems. Thus, clients who present with similar features but who undergo different treatments may be compared; again, differential improvement in outcome observed with this approach more likely may have stemmed from intervention differences in the programs than from regression to the mean, practice with the measures, or other plausible threats to interpretation. In the absence of randomized assignment to treatment (which is rare in clinical settings), one must be cautious in interpreting comparison group approaches; if clients systematically get placed on waiting lists or in other treatment modes because of different clinical presentations, then such pretreatment client differences will likely account for the changes observed on outcome.

A final way to enhance treatment evaluation is to use standardized measures with adequate psychometric characteristics. Even if the assessment battery is administered at only two points (i.e., pre and post), using standardized, psychometrically sound measures enhances the conclusiveness of the findings. Not only are standardized measures well researched and meaningful to those interpreting them, but well-established procedures for administration and scoring help rule out the chances that changes in the measurement instrument or its scoring accounted for the change. Furthermore, sufficient test–retest reliability helps evaluate whether changes in scores from Time 1 to Time 2 are not simply due to measurement error, and sufficient interrater reliability also reduces the likelihood of idiosyncratic ratings accounting for the changes observed.

Practicalities of Multimodal Assessment

Although it may be ideal to obtain multiple, multimodal assessments before, during, and after treatment, few researchers or community practitioners have the resources to do so. Thus, small-scale assessments may be a practical alternative and are preferable to a lack of assessment altogether. Such small-scale efforts might be limited to assessments at pre- and posttreatment and include a selection of one or two brief self-report scales able to capture the central treatment targets, a well-defined behavioral rating scale to be filled out by perhaps one observer (e.g., use of the Modified Conflict Tactics Scale [Pan, Neidig, & O'Leary, 1994a] filled out by partners of clients mandated to treatment), a clinician-rated checklist, or brief global measures of functioning that sacrifice detail but provide an efficient way of noting client progress. Further, one might take a "short-hand" approach to applying resource-intensive measures, such as replacing formal observational measures with elaborate coding systems with making judgments informed by such systems on informal, office-based observations.

Conclusion

In this chapter, we discussed important research considerations in the assessment of partner violence: scale development, psychometrics, and the measurement of treatment outcome. As alluded to in the Introduction, the contents of this chapter offer a review for those trained in psychometric theory and outcome research while offering a primer for readers who lack this training. An understanding of scale development, reliability, and validity is needed to critically evaluate the instruments presented in chapters 6 through 8; knowledge of measuring treatment outcome is needed to consider the best application of these instruments toward treatment evaluation efforts.

Systematic evaluation of treatment outcome with multimodal assessment has become increasingly in demand in the last decade. The clinician might consider many variables in evaluating outcome of clinical practice, including client-related criteria, service efficiency and cost-related criteria, consumer-related criteria, and measures of social impact. Although a number of problems exist with the interpretation of pre–post evaluation of treatment, many of these can be addressed in clinical practice by obtaining multiple assessments at baseline, conducting repeated assessments over the course of treatment, conducting follow-up assessments, comparing outcome results with untreated groups or groups receiving a different treatment, and using standardized assessment instruments. The effort involved in conducting comprehensive assessments in clinical practice is surely offset by the rewards offered by the accountability, feedback, and communicability that such assessments provide.

Research Issues and Challenges in the Assessment of Partner Violence

5

In this chapter we present research issues in partner violence assessment. Many of these present challenges to the researcher that we address as well. These research issues include a dearth of attention to cultural diversity, problems with definitions of constructs, problems of selecting and defining variables to target as outcome measures in programs for partner assault, the application of quantitative versus qualitative approaches, difficulties in establishing psychometric properties of measures, concern over "subjecting" victims to research or placing research participants at risk, and occasions when research interferes with normal administrative or clinical routines.

Issues of Cultural Diversity in the Assessment of Couple Violence

The field of assessment of couple violence has suffered from a lack of attention to issues of culture and diversity, mirroring a broader problem endemic to research methodology and the training of mental health practitioners (D. W. Sue, Bingham, Porche-Burke, & Vasquez, 1999; S. Sue, 1999). Thus, one might consider an additional form of victimization in this field: that of *ethnocentric monoculturalism* (D. W. Sue et al., 1999). That is, as practices likely reflect the values and biases of majority groups, one may fail to realize "the potentially detrimental impact [this] has on racial and ethnic minorities as well as other culturally different groups in our society" (D. W. Sue et al., 1999, p. 1066). While researchers and practitioners may assume conclusions they draw from assessments they conduct reflect *etics,* or universal truths, they may in fact reflect *emics,* or truths that apply to a specific cultural group or segment of the population (Matsumoto, 1994). In one's lack of attention to the external validity (i.e., generalizability) of one's work, both in instrument development and in samples on which one uses them, one limits the ability to view those different from oneself with objectivity and may unwittingly yield damaging conclusions (Matsumoto, 1994; S. Sue, 1999).

"Cultural psychology seeks to discover systematic relationships between cultural and behavioral variables, asking whether individuals growing up in culture A tend to develop that culture's psychological qualities" (Berry, 1994, p. 120). Researchers often seek to highlight cross-cultural differences, comparing characteristics between cultures A and B (Berry, 1994). In partner violence assessment, one seeks to discover relationships between cultural and partner violence variables. For example, a researcher might study marital violence rates within a particular culture, or ask whether individuals from culture A have different attitudes toward wife abuse than those from culture B. Here we discuss central issues pertaining to sensitivity to diversity in the assessment of family violence.

Many issues warrant consideration in attempting to address culture and diversity in research. General issues include problems of defining culture, sampling issues, and measurement issues. Issues specific to partner violence assessment concern access to diverse populations engaged in partner violence and the sensitive nature of comparing practices and attitudes regarding domestic violence across cultural or ethnic groups.

Defining Culture

Definitions of culture vary widely. Although "most cross-cultural scholars agree that culture is a shared conglomeration of attitudes, values, behaviors, and beliefs, communicated from one generation to the next through language" (Matsumoto, 1994, p. 21), there is, as Matsumoto argued, no clear-cut way to delineate members of a culture. Defining culture as race is problematic, because although one might speak of Asians or African Americans, for example, members of these groups might share some characteristics but vary widely on others. For example, in reporting on cultural factors in intimate violence, Koss et al. (1994) pointed out that Hispanic Americans originate from at least 32 countries and although they share a common language and other similarities, they display significant cultural differences. Defining culture as nationality is also flawed, because great individual differences occur within populations of countries, and citizens often do not fit their nation's cultural stereotype. Additionally, further definitional complications arise when looking more broadly than culture and examining the issue of human diversity in general. Beyond race and nationality, other characteristics reflecting diversity include religion/spirituality, sexual orientation, socioeconomic status, age, disability status, and even gender. Developing a clear definition of what is meant by culture thus becomes a formidable task.

Sampling

Sample representativeness presents an issue when one recruits samples designed to represent a culture; that is, do members of the sample represent the larger population from which they are drawn? One may erroneously conclude then that findings pertain to a particular culture when in fact they represent only a limited segment of that culture. For example, in studying the psychometric properties of the Index of Spouse Abuse (Hudson & McIntosh, 1981) in a sample of African American women of lower socioeconomic status, D. W. Campbell, Campbell, King, Parker, and Ryan (1994) cautioned that results from their sample may not generalize to African American women of other social and economic groups. In general, much research on rates of partner violence in ethnic minority populations derives from clinical samples, police reports, or agencies, which tend to overrepresent minority cases (Lockhart, 1985).

Moreover, the problem of sampling occurs when one is considering the equivalence of groups one is studying. Cross-cultural research often compares cultures by sampling two or more groups and comparing them on various measures. As researchers are much more likely to rely on samples of convenience than random sampling methods (Lonner, 1994), a sample from one culture may differ systematically from that from another on variables other than cultural ones (e.g., age, education level, socioeconomic status). The conclusions therefore may reflect as much about these differences as cultural ones (Matsumoto, 1994). The problem of equivalence is especially important when one considers the danger of stereotyping racial or ethnic groups on the basis of violence proneness. Consider the fact that when variables such as age, occupational status of husband, social class, and level of acculturation are controlled, racial differences in violence rates typically disappear (West, 1998b).

Measurement

Several problems particular to the issue of measurement present themselves in cross-cultural studies (Hughes, Seidman, & Williams, 1993; Matsumoto, 1994). When applying an assessment instrument to a culture other than that on which it has been developed, a researcher faces problems of culturally based differences in meanings of constructs, meanings of test items, and item intercorrelations (i.e., factor equivalence). Language barriers pose obvious difficulties, and even when an instrument is translated, item nuances may be altered, significantly changing the intended meaning. Moreover, culture-based tendencies to respond to test items in a particular manner (i.e., response sets) are also cause for concern. For example, particular groups may have a tendency to acquiesce to a greater extent, to avoid endorsing extreme ratings, or to be less forthcoming in revealing distress or "socially undesirable" behaviors. Differences between groups due to response sets may thus be erroneously attributed to culture. Issues of task and setting equivalence can also pose difficulties. That is, the assessment situation itself may have different meanings for members of different cultural groups, which may affect responses (e.g., level of guardedness).

Access to Diverse Populations Engaged in Partner Violence

In attempting to conduct assessments of diverse populations engaged in partner violence, researchers have faced difficulties in gaining access to certain groups (Tortu, Goldsamt, & Hamid, 2002). Even large nationally representative surveys with excellent sampling methodology (e.g., Straus & Gelles, 1990; Straus et al., 1980) by necessity leave out certain segments of the population. Reports from national surveys

> are obtained through telephone surveys or in-person interviews with general probability samples of couples at home at the time interviewers call, who are willing to answer the telephone or come to the door for strangers, and who are able and willing to discuss the topic. National surveys typically do not include the very poor, those who do not speak English fluently, those whose lives are especially chaotic, military families who live on base, or individuals who are hospitalized, homeless, institutionalized, or incarcerated. . . . Single mothers, divorced and separated

women, and women in same-sex relationships are also not well-represented. (Koss et al., 1994, p. 59)

Sensitive Nature of Cultural Methodology in Partner Violence

A final cultural issue in the assessment of partner violence involves the sensitive nature of the study of diversity. Whereas some researchers have assumed common dynamics of partner violence across culture and thus adapted a color-blind approach, others have steered clear of the diversity issue for political reasons. Some members of this latter group "fear that research findings will be misinterpreted or used to reinforce negative societal stereotypes about minorities" (West, 1998b, p. 185).

Conclusions and Recommendations Regarding Cultural Issues in Partner Violence Assessment

The abovementioned problems pose significant challenges regarding sensitivity to diversity in family violence assessment. Few established measures of partner violence contain norms for diverse groups or adequately reflect diversity in their development samples. Rarely do investigators conduct cross-cultural comparative studies to obtain reliability and validity data. Seldom are standardized measures available in multiple languages that facilitate use with diverse populations. As researchers, we must begin to acquaint ourselves with these issues and tackle these problems if we are to improve competence in issues of cultural diversity as we assess partner violence.

On a positive note, the last decade has witnessed efforts to raise awareness of such issues and bring about meaningful changes in mental health research and training as well as political action and advocacy. Several special issues have appeared in journals devoted to culturally anchored methodology in general (Seidman, 1993), cultural issues in partner violence in particular (e.g., Urquiza, Wyatt, & Root, 1994), and, indeed, problems of domestic violence around the world (Walker, 1999). The 1999 National Multicultural Conference and Summit, held in Newport Beach, California and hosted by several divisions of the American Psychological Association, was the largest gathering of its kind aimed at assessing the state of the field in terms of its relevance to cultural diversity (D. W. Sue et al., 1999). The following recommendations, extracted from that conference as well as other sources, offer helpful starting points for improving cultural sensitivity in the assessment of domestic violence (Hughes et al., 1993; Matsumoto, 1994; Sandoval,

Frisby, Geisinger, Scheuneman, & Grenier, 1998; D. W. Sue et al., 1999; S. Sue, 1999; West, 1998b):

- integrate multicultural contents into domestic violence courses as well as general curriculum in graduate training programs of mental health professionals
- recruit for minority representation among faculty and students of such programs
- provide culturally sensitive support and services for students in such programs
- operationalize the meaning of multiculturism
- commit resources for obtaining multicultural competence
- encourage minority investigators to design and conduct research
- include diverse populations in human participant research
- specify the sample(s) on which tests have been developed and for whom tests are appropriate
- devote efforts to cross-validating measures (and principles derived from such measures) on diverse populations before assuming generalization
- use within-group research to examine processes within a specified cultural or ethnic group
- treat ethnicity as an independent variable rather than solely as a nuisance variable, ensuring concept, measure, and task equivalence across groups when conducting between-groups research comparing cultural communities
- conduct exploratory work such as ethnographic interviewing and focus groups to develop or adapt instruments to be culturally appropriate
- use translation and back translation to assess linguistic equivalence when applying an instrument in other languages
- include culturally relevant variables in assessments such as level of acculturation and specific racial identity
- develop new assessment methods/measures to capture nuances of the population of interest
- glean knowledge from methods including but not limited to traditional experimental strategies, such as qualitative and ethnographic assessment methods

It has been encouraging to witness recent efforts toward these ends in partner violence and trauma assessment research (e.g., D. W. Campbell et al., 1994; Cunradi, Caetano, & Schafer, 2002; Fraser, McNutt, Clark, Williams-Muhammed, & Lee, 2002; Haj-Yahia, 2002; Manson, 1997; Sugihara & Warner, 2002; Yoshihama & Horrocks, 2002), as well as burgeoning research and policy on partner violence around the world (Walker, 1999).

Problems With Definitions of Constructs Within Partner Violence

There cannot be precise measurement of a phenomenon unless one has a clear understanding of the construct to which one is referring. Yet, there is no gold standard definition of partner abuse, and variations exist in definitions across studies, measures, and intervention programs. Legal definitions (e.g., acts meeting criteria for a category of *assault*) may vary widely from entry criteria for a research study examining partner abuse (e.g., two acts of physical aggression within the past year on the CTS), which may vary still from a victim's definition (e.g., emotional abuse and isolation). Even within research, operationalizations of partner violence vary from study to study, and even the best attempts at capturing behavioral objectivity (i.e., behavior rating scales such as the CTS) may not be entirely specific or consistently interpreted. For example, in national prevalence studies, men and women appear equally violent when assessed solely with the original CTS (e.g., Straus et al., 1980), yet strong differences emerge when defining violence more broadly, incorporating context, impact, and injury (Straus & Gelles, 1990; Vivian & Langhinrichsen-Rohling, 1994). Similarly, specific items may reflect vastly different acts of aggression, ranging from mild to severe, depending on intensity and impact (Archer, 2002). For example, a "push" might result in anything from no physical harm to a head injury. Other questions arise when one considers definitions of partner violence, such as whether an aggressive act is "abuse" if occurring in the context of self-defense or if the recipient sustains no injury and is not fearful, or whether significant emotional maltreatment and control constitute partner abuse if not accompanied by physical aggression.

In 1997, O'Leary and Jacobson outlined diagnostic criteria for the newly proposed *DSM–IV* category: Partner Relational Problems With Physical Abuse. Their definition includes acts of physical aggression occurring in anger (rather than self-defense); the presence of physically aggressive acts toward a partner, such as slapping, pushing, kicking, or throwing an object; acts that occur at least once per year or that result in need for medical attention or in ongoing fear of the partner; and acts that are generally unpredictable and unavoidable. Other attempts at standardization have occurred, such as the Centers for Disease Control and Prevention's process to achieve consensus on definitions of partner violence (Saltzman, Fanslow, McMahon, & Shelley, 1999). Discussion concerning definitional issues in intimate partner violence has touched on the breadth versus specificity of definitions, whether to include physical abuse only or other dimensions such as psychological abuse, whether survey measures such as the Conflict Tactics Scale (CTS) or the National Violence Against Women Survey (Tjaden & Thoennes, 2000) are superior to those used in crime surveys, whether structured interviews should be used in high-risk population surveillance to supplement behavioral rating checklists used in general population surveillance, and whether any operational definitions adequately capture complexities of violence or victims' subjective experience (DeKeserdy, 2000; Gordon, 2000).

It is clear that we must move beyond unidimensional assessment to arrive at definitions of partner abuse that capture multiple domains of aggressive behavior and allow us to classify reliably, communicate clearly, and adequately capture the experience. Although standardization of definitions is important, it is not as essential as clear communication concerning operationalizations of abusive behavior within any given study, to make for comparable operationalizations and clear understanding of research results (J. C. Campbell, 2000).

Problems of Selecting and Defining Variables to Target as Outcome Measures in Programs for Partner Assault

Considering what variables to target as outcome measures poses difficulties in conducting outcome research in partner violence. While complete violence cessation is the stated goal of most treatment programs, violence abatement may prove an elusive assessment target for several reasons. First, for some percentage of violent couples, violence is a low-frequency event (Johnson, 1995). In fact, a relationship can be experienced as abusive in the context of little ongoing violence with a history of severe aggression, ongoing threats, or ongoing emotional abuse. Therefore, those entering treatment programs might do so with little actual physical aggression during the time of the assessment period (typically the past year), thus making it difficult to detect a change on outcome. Additionally, treatment programs are often short term (e.g., 16–32 weeks), making it difficult to know with certainty whether a lack of violence reported on postassessment represents an end to or simply a break in the violence. Similarly, mandated individuals may temporarily, at least, reduce violent behaviors corresponding to the time of beginning treatment because of the impact of arrest and increased monitoring or because of orders of protection requiring a cessation of contact. This makes it difficult, without a control group, to determine whether treatment is responsible for a change in behavior (see Dunford, 2000). However, data demonstrating that nearly one third of men reassaulted a female partner (according to partner reports) during a 15-month treatment follow-up period, that most of this recidivist physical aggression occurred within 3–6 months following entry into a domestic violence treatment program, and that the average incident rate for those who reassaulted was 4.8 suggest that there is not necessarily a period of good behavior following treatment enrollment and that one may reasonably be able to infer treatment success when violence cessation is achieved for several months or longer (Gondolf, 1997).

Another complicating factor is that unlike assessment of psychiatric symptoms, such as depression, which can be measured in terms of severity level at pretreatment, assessment of violence involves determining the frequency of discrete events. That is, with instruments such as the CTS (Straus, 1979), one obtains the number of times particular acts of aggression were perpetrated in a specified time frame prior to treatment. This time frame is typically 1 year. However, if treatment lasts less than 1 year, a posttreatment assessment of retrospective violence frequency will not span an equivalent time frame to the preassessment period. Thus, the researcher is left with the dilemma of reducing the pretreatment time frame to match treatment length and risks missing acts of aggression that occurred prior to this period, or comparing numbers of violent acts between nonequivalent time frames.

Further, many men entering treatment have already separated from the partners they have abused. They thus may accurately report nonviolence throughout treatment, but because of a lack of partner contact, rather than because of an internal change (however, because separation often precipitates offenders to assault their partners [Gondolf, 1997; Wilson & Daly, 1996], it is important not to discount the chance of reassault among partners who are living separately at time of treatment evaluation). Even when such men have entered new relationships, these young relationships are unlikely to have yet become violent (cf. Gondolf, 1997; Koss et al., 1994). Finally, the well-documented tendency for batterers to underreport their violence makes it likely that even when none of these issues apply, there will still be floor effects in measurement. Therefore, it can be helpful to assess violence throughout treatment; extend the assessment period by including periodic follow-up assessments; assess related, potentially higher frequency behaviors such as emotionally abusive acts; include an analogue measure to assess changes in capacities (see chap. 8, this volume); and use reports from other sources, such as partners of legal/criminal records, to supplement self-report data (e.g., Gondolf, 1997).

Application of Quantitative Versus Qualitative Approaches

Quantitative research is characterized by statistical analysis of data, experimental control, and efforts to operationalize and quantify constructs (Kazdin, 1998). This approach is associated with traditional empirical approaches across scientific disciplines. By contrast, qualitative research involves a greater emphasis on participants' phenomenological experiences, close contact with participants in the data collection process, and narrative accounts rather than statistical analysis of data (Taylor & Bogdan, 1998). Assessment occurs through open-ended interviews, which are characterized as much as possible in their original formats and meanings rather than reduced to numbers.

Some feminist investigators have argued that this qualitative methodology is especially applicable to the study of wife abuse, because it does not presuppose experience and does not reduce the experience of victimization to numerical data that can be interpreted out of context (Breines & Gordon, 1983; cf. Yllo, 1988). Indeed, some of the highly influential studies of spouse abuse over the past 3 decades have been qualitative in nature (e.g., Dobash & Dobash, 1979; Walker, 1984). Feminist scholars have voiced opposition to large-scale quantitative approaches, such as the Straus et al.'s (1980) national survey data reporting equal rates of male and female violence, citing the lack of inclusion of severe cases and of a methodology sensitive to impact and context as deleterious to the plight of battered women (Yllo & Bograd, 1988; cf. Murphy & O'Leary, 1994). Indeed, in contrast to ratings made on a standardized scale, the " 'human instrument' . . . can establish rapport, elicit personal information, decode interpersonal cues, perform complex pattern matching, and develop hunches or hypotheses to pursue in further questioning" (Murphy & O'Leary, 1994, p. 216).

Murphy and O'Leary (1994), however, pointed out several shortcomings of qualitative research on spouse abuse, including improper level of methodological detail (i.e., either too much or too little), lack of adequately documented conclusions, and little presentation of alternative interpretations of the results. They further pointed out that numerous quantitative studies have lent support to feminist perspectives on wife abuse (e.g., Berk et al., 1983) and suggested that researchers can benefit from an integrative approach:

> The combined rigor of qualitative methods, designed to uncover subjective perspective and social context in the creation of theories, and traditional quantitative methods, designed to evaluate the accuracy of claims through canons of deductive logic, may produce the most thorough understanding of phenomena like spouse abuse. (Murphy & O'Leary, 1994, p. 219)

Difficulties in Establishing Psychometric Properties of Measures

Although it is desirable to establish family violence assessment instruments with sound psychometric properties, several factors may make it difficult to measure reliability and validity in such instruments. An essential issue is obtaining large enough sample sizes. Large sample sizes are needed to conduct factor analysis (i.e., in obtaining factorial or construct validity), to obtain significance when attempting to discriminate groups or to determine associations among scales (i.e., to determine criterion validity, or convergent and discriminant validity), and to obtain stable calculations of reliability. However, most scale developers do not have ready access to hundreds or even dozens of domestically violent couples. To obtain large sample sizes, some scale developers rely on accessible respondents such as college students (e.g., Marshall, 1992a; J. H. Rathus & O'Leary, 1997) or "captive" respondents such women in shelters, men mandated to treatment programs, or individuals on inpatient units (e.g., Shepard & Campbell, 1992). Such populations *may* not be representative of the populations they are presumed to represent; of course, at times such samples reflect exactly the population of interest and would thus be quite appropriate for scale development purposes. Ultimately, the ability to generalize across samples depends on one's intended uses of a scale, and it becomes incumbent on both the developer of the scale and the user to carefully consider psychometric issues as they apply to samples they investigate.

Another issue pertains to obtaining reliability through use of repeated assessments (i.e., test–retest reliability), multiple raters (i.e., interrater reliability), and lengthy questionnaires (i.e., item length enhances internal consistency ratings). These strategies, although useful from a scale development perspective, may not be practical in a treatment setting. For example, one may not wish to subject an abuse victim to filling out the same set of questionnaires twice or repeat the same interview with different interviewers. Similarly, one might not wish to jeopardize a client's right to privacy by conducting an interview with two raters present to establish interrater reliability or to obtain possibly sensitive supplemental records to determine criterion-related validity. A similar issue pertains to the conflict between taking enough of a client's time to meet scale development goals, which might include filling out varying forms of the same instruments (to establish alternate forms reliability; Muskat, 1997) or filling out multiple measures of similar and dissimilar constructs (to establish convergent and discriminant validity), and protecting this time for efforts that will be of direct service to the client.

Difficulties in Applying Sound Research Design

Applying sound research design in the field of family violence is fraught with difficulties. For instance, the field contains only a handful of studies based on the assessment of randomly selected, representative samples (e.g., Schafer, Caetano, & Clark, 1998; Straus et al., 1980; Tjaden & Thoennes, 2000). In addition, it can be difficult to recruit samples through advertising or means common to other research populations. Because of issues of stigma and the tendency for family violence to occur "behind closed doors," such samples are difficult to recruit and instead are replaced with samples of convenience or captive samples such as those residing in shelters (which, again, can be perfectly appropriate if that is the population to which the researcher wishes to generalize). Thus, many research findings in the field are based on small, overly specific, or extreme samples and thus of limited external validity (i.e., generalizability).

In addition to difficulties with random selection of samples, the family violence field suffers from few studies applying random assignment to treatment conditions (Gondolf, 1997). Random assignment to treatment plus wait-list, placebo, nonspecific, or no-treatment control conditions is particularly risky in a field in which research participants may be placing others in or may themselves be in danger, or may be suffering from debilitating psychological conditions as a result of experiencing abuse. Potential remedies include offering random assignment to treatment-as-usual conditions (e.g., comparing a new treatment with community services traditionally assigned to a given population), to two plausibly effective treatment conditions that differ on a particular variable of interest rather than offer qualitatively different levels of treatment, or to a condition otherwise deemed safe on the basis of such minimal conditions as close monitoring and safety assessment and planning (e.g. Dunford, 2000; O'Leary et al., 1999). Studies that manage to recruit large or representative samples, apply random assignment to treatment, and implement other controls on the research typically come from research laboratories in well-funded university or medical center settings. The generalizability of such research may then need to be demonstrated, as such settings often differ from the local agency or clinic settings in which the majority of clients experiencing family violence receive services.

Concern Over "Subjecting" Victims to Research or Placing Research Participants at Risk

Even in nonresearch settings, assessors may harbor concerns about revictimization through lengthy, intrusive, or emotional assessment procedures. In research settings, this concern can become exacerbated with methodological requirements such as lengthy procedures and nonflexible protocols. Clinicians may feel uncomfortable administering structured interviews or questionnaire batteries or asking clients to engage in a laboratory task for behavioral observation rather than letting clients tell their stories or proceeding immediately to interventions, especially if the assessment research is not part of the normal clinical procedure but includes extra components for a research study. However, most assessment information contributes to case conceptualization and treatment planning, and most research conducted with victims is designed to enhance understanding of their experience and to inform treatment approaches. As long as assessments are carried out in a compassionate manner, there is not any a priori reason to assume they will be detrimental to clients. In fact, one study found that the majority of women reporting on their history of abuse found the experience to be a positive one (E. A. Walker, Newman, Koss, & Bernstein, 1997). Possible benefits of participating in such assessments include relief at expressing one's feelings about past abusive incidents to an accepting listener, validation of one's experiences, providing a sense of purpose or meaning in their experiences, enhancing self-awareness, and empowerment (Hutchinson, Wilson, & Wilson, 1994).

In addition, there are a number of ways to protect the rights and well-being of research participants. First, the investigator ensures that the client's responses remain confidential and anonymous and informs the client of these safeguards (Kazdin, 1998). Confidentiality refers to the fact that no material revealed in the research will be disclosed to an outside party without the explicit consent of the participant (with the necessary exceptions to confidentiality made clear; see chap. 3, this volume), and the researcher ensures written materials pertaining to the client are kept locked in a safe place. Anonymity refers to not attaching any identifying information to the research materials; instead codes are assigned to protect the identity of the participants.

Second, as part of any research, it is necessary to obtain informed consent from the client. A consent form must be signed by the participant and must include a brief description of the study purposes and procedures, a listing of the risks and benefits associated with participation in the research, and a contact person (i.e., the principal investigator) should further information or discussion be desired. Notification of the research procedures must always include the fact that clients may withdraw from the research or discontinue at any time; likewise, they may feel free not to answer a particular question. This is especially critical to convey both in words and in subtle messages conveyed through behavior, particularly because research participants may perceive a power differential between themselves and the investigator and may not feel comfortable refusing or withdrawing from the research (Kazdin, 1998). The investigator may unwittingly coerce participants to take part by presenting the assessment research protocol as a routine prerequisite for entering a treatment program. Individuals who have endured domestic violence may be especially prone to perceiving themselves of lesser status or power following their experiences of victimization (e.g., Walker, 1984).

Third, any research protocol, whether in a hospital, clinic, agency, or university setting, must be submitted to and approved by an institutional review board that will have screened the research for its potential harmfulness to the clients. Fourth, it will also be crucial, in any case, to administer assessment procedures with sensitivity, which will require a knowledge of the population that is being assessed and the issues, struggles, and common types of clinical presentation that tend to characterize the particular population of interest. Also critical is beginning the assessment process after taking the time to establish a rapport. Ideally, the assessments will begin and conclude with questions that are not as emotionally jarring for the participants. Fifth, it will be important to follow the research procedure immediately with a debriefing, which consists of not only providing more information about the purpose of the research but also gently inquiring about the impact of questions on the participants and assessing how they are feeling at present. Finally, the research assessor should be knowledgeable about local referrals for clients who need them. These might include the phone numbers of local hotlines, agencies, or shelters, as well as a list of other local resources such as practitioners and programs specializing in domestic violence, and sources of advocacy or legal representation. It is helpful to have such resources printed as handouts or pamphlets easily available to clients in need of such information. Similarly, the research assessor will need to be well versed in crisis strategies and safety planning should it become apparent in the course of the research that such interventions are needed.

Placing Research Participants at Risk

There can be a number of ways that conducting couple violence research may place participants at risk. The first has to do with conducting the assessments with a couple in such a way that issues raised during the assessment process lead to acts of aggression following the session. For example, an assessor who is studying couples' conflict escalation may interview a couple about interaction patterns during prototypical disagreements. One partner may then reveal something that causes the other to feel humiliated or enraged, which might result in aggression following the interview. This type of reaction could occur with self-report measures as well, if one partner looks over the shoulder of another and views an objectionable written response.

Contacting an abused partner for assessment information about a perpetrator may also place a research participant at risk. This strategy poses a conflict of interest between good-quality research strategies (i.e., using multiple informants and not relying on self-report of abusive behavior), on the one hand, and placing partners at risk, on the other. Risk can be reduced by contacting partners or family members after obtaining permission from the abusive individual (rather than making it a standard part of the research protocol), obtaining informed consent from the partner of the target research participant, beginning each contact with reminders that the person may withdraw at any time during the research, asking if the informant feels comfortable and safe speaking at the moment, and offering information about victim services during the contact.

A client may be placed at risk through irresponsible treatment of information, such as the researcher calling at home and leaving a message that one is calling from the "domestic abuse project," sending questionnaires with sensitive questions home, or engaging in phone interviews without being sure that the respondent is alone, feels unlikely to be interrupted, and feels safe. Common sense is needed here.

When Research Interferes With Normal Clinical Routine

There may be numerous occasions in which conducting research in couple violence interferes with normal clinical practice. This interference can pose dilemmas when staff members within a clinical setting differ in priorities (i.e., maintaining routines that have doubtlessly evolved for good reason vs. obtaining participants for research) or when an outside researcher comes into an agency or clinic setting with his or her own agenda; when research interferes with administrative routines; when a research agenda or protocol conflicts with the philosophical approach of the treatment setting; or when a research protocol poses an ethical dilemma, such as potentially placing participants at increased risk or otherwise not ensuring their well-being. Examples of research matters related to differing staff priorities or interfering with administrative practices include issues such as devoting office space to conducting research and storing research materials, arranging alterations in intake procedures and staffing responsibilities, creating additional paperwork, or administering lengthy assessment batteries. Examples of research matters that interfere with the philosophical approach of the treatment setting include issues such as paying perpetrators of family violence for research participation or introducing systemic or family-interaction research into settings that believe in individual-based etiology/responsibility for abuse perpetration. Finally, research situations that may pose ethical concerns or threaten a client's well-being include carrying out an overly extensive or intrusive assessment battery; administering treatments based on randomization, which might keep some clients on a waiting list or assign some to a potentially less effective treatment condition; or contacting partners in a manner that may place the participant in jeopardy.

Such occasions when research interferes with routine practices abound, posing additional challenges to carrying out even the most well-designed research protocols. Thus, the need for flexibility, creativity, and continual problem solving cannot be underestimated in conducting family violence research. Some specific approaches to handling potential differences that might arise follow:

- Few staff members at most family violence agencies are likely to have expertise in assessment and research methodology. Thus, arranging an orientation or workshop on assessment and research issues would be beneficial.

- Arrange a meeting with all relevant staff to present a research proposal in its early stages, which might involve an open brainstorming session. Sometimes several meetings of this type might be needed. During these meetings, it will be helpful to explain clearly the purposes of the research and its potential benefits to the agency and its clients, as well as to the field at large.

- In addition to presenting a proposal of one's own, listen carefully and take seriously the concerns of others as well as their rationales for their current policies/routines. Good listening and clear understanding is needed to be able to validate others' concerns and respond with flexible problem solving that considers these concerns while attempting to retain critical aspects of the research protocol.

- Remain open to the suggestions of others, along with an assurance that issues of safety, ethics, the well-being of clients, and the continued smooth running of the setting in question, are shared equally by the research staff.

- Offer to contribute some type of compensation for sacrifices that will be made by the agency or other setting to support the research, such as presentations of the research findings, research assistants to carry out some of the administrative burdens, volunteered hours of service, or other types of payment that would be meaningful to the agency.

- Highlight the advantages to the research protocol, such as providing an especially thorough intake that will yield comprehensive information regarding treatment, potentially bringing additional recognition or grant funding to the agency, or offering close supervision/monitoring of treatment conditions.

- Invite agency staff to participate in the process if desired. This could include training in any of the assessment methodologies.

- Help the agency to set up ongoing program evaluations. This will help them in keeping their database going plus provide data for potential grant applications.

Of course, any research protocol will go through close scrutiny by an internal review board, which will help screen for ethical or procedural concerns. However, maintaining good communication, open-mindedness, flexibility, and respect for the staff within the setting working with individuals touched by family violence will contribute to the success of initiating and carrying out a research protocol.

Conclusion

This chapter reviewed a variety of assessment research issues that challenge investigators studying partner violence. In addition to the problems presented in this chapter, researchers face many issues overlapping with those faced by practitioners and discussed in chapter 3, such as establishing rapport with research participants; determining whom should be the focus of assessment; capturing psychological abuse and other variables related to physical aggression; handling minimization of violence and inconsistent reporting between partners; determining modalities of treatment to evaluate; distinguishing between unilateral victimization and low-level, mutual violence; applying an appropriate diagnosis; adhering to ethical standards; and handling legal issues as pertinent. Thus, researchers encounter a daunting task in assessing partner violence; the information in this first section of the book and the review of instruments in the section that follows are intended to ease this task considerably.

Beyond the issues raised herein, J. C. Campbell (2000) provided additional recommendations to enhance the assessment of intimate partner violence in research contexts:

> I recommend that all scientists . . . in the field of violence against women spend time yearly in shelters or other victim services, sit in on support groups and/or spend a day in domestic violence court. I also recommend that all advocates spend time actually looking at data, listening to adolescent girls in high schools talk about their own use of violence, and interview women who have been arrested for use of violence. I recommend that all scientists in this field conduct interviews themselves with victims themselves on a periodic basis or at least regularly listen to interviews on tape. I also recommend that all advocates spend time helping to plan research studies to help with safety issues, and that researchers help service agencies plan evaluations and data systems. We can frame these activities as continuing education, mandatory training activities, in kind service, consultation, community service—whatever helps all of us actually spend time in each other's reality. Collaboration and equal partnerships are the key to establishing useful data systems that will truly benefit both the science and the service needed in the field. (pp. 723–724)

Part II

Assessment of Partner Violence

Interview Measures

This chapter reviews measures of interview assessments related to intimate partner violence. This modality of assessment is relatively underdeveloped in the field of partner violence compared with self-report and even analogue assessments. Yet the interview is a crucial assessment modality in that it is most commonly used in clinical practice, it forms the basis for establishing rapport, and it allows for assessment of a client's history and phenomenological experience. Moreover, flexible formats allow the skilled interviewer to probe or highlight particular areas depending on the needs of the situation, and the opportunity for follow-up questions and clarifications can enhance accuracy of material. We hope that including a chapter reviewing the existing standardized interview assessments of partner violence (and related topics such as relationship history) will contribute to increased use of such standardized assessments in both clinical and research contexts and will stimulate further research toward developing "gold standard" assessments of intimate partner violence.

1. Control Interview (CI; Ehrensaft)

Description and Development of Assessment Method

The CI is a semistructured interview assessing partners' perceptions of feeling controlled by a spouse. Items were written on the basis of face validity in consideration of the literature on controlling behaviors in abusive relationships. All items were then given to a group of 10 raters composed of psychologists and psychiatrists who were asked to sort them into categories.

Four items were deleted on the basis of obtaining less than 80% agreement on their classification. Retained items achieved interrater agreement of between 80% and 100%. Two additional items were deleted on the basis of significantly reducing their scale's internal consistency (alpha).

Target Population

Individuals in couple relationships.

Format

The interview contains three parts assessing different facets of a partner's controlling behaviors, including areas of control, perceptions of overall control, and perceptions of the link between a partner's aggression and controlling tendencies. The interview is available in male and female versions, which are identical except for pronouns. Sample questions from Parts I to III follow:

Part I: Questions on Four Areas of Control

Decision making

- "What happens when you try to make decisions that seem like your personal/private matters (like what you wear, how you handle something at work)? How does your spouse react?"

Relationships with others

- "Are there any people (your spouse) discourages you from spending time with? (e.g., does he/she ever tell you they are bad for you, not good enough for you in some way, or that there is something wrong with them such that they should not spend time with you?)."

Activities and time

- "What kind of freedom does your husband (or wife) give you to decide for yourself the things that you want to do, places you want to go?"

Self-image

- "Does your spouse say or do things that make you think he (or she) does not respect you? (e.g., ignoring you when you say what you think, telling you that you are stupid, making fun of you). Explain."

Part II: Overall Control Scale

- "In general, do you feel your husband (or wife) tries to control you? Please explain."
- "On a scale of 0–10, how controlled by your husband (or wife) do you feel?"

Part III: Direct Questions About Husband's (or Wife's) Aggression and Control

- "When your husband (or wife) was aggressive at that time, what do you think his (or her) motivation was?"
- "When your husband (or wife) was aggressive at that time, do you think it was because he (she) was trying to control you? Explain."

Administration and Scoring

The CI takes about 30 minutes to administer, and partners are separated during the interview. Most questions are open-ended, although several also have yes/no forced-choice response formats prior to the respondents' open-ended explanations. For each area of control in Part I to which respondents answer affirmatively, additional questions probe the general impact of experiencing such control (coded as positive, negative, or neutral) and whether disagreements over this area of control have led to violence.

Part I dimensions receive codes ranging from +2 to –2, ranging from having more control than one's spouse or complete freedom over an area to feeling significantly controlled. Detailed criteria for assigning each anchor point are provided in the primary reference. Part II is scored according to a dichotomous (yes/no) question about whether respondents feel their spouse tries to control them and a 0–10 Likert scale reflecting the degree to which participants feel controlled by their spouse. Part III is only administered to those who indicate receiving aggression from their partner and consists of two open-ended questions and two yes/no questions about motivations of control in aggression.

Psychometric Evaluation

Norms

Percentages of control responses for happy, distressed aggressive, and distressed nonaggressive couples are reported in the primary reference.

Reliability

Cronbach's alphas for each Part I dimension were as follows: decision making, $\alpha = .83$; relationships, $\alpha = .76$; activities, $\alpha = .80$; self-image, $\alpha = .75$, indicating good internal consistency. Interrater reliability was calculated on Part I through a random sample of 25% of the videotaped interviews, and fair to good rater agreement was obtained. Kappas for each rating category were as follows: +2, .94; +1, .81; 0, .53; −1, .61; and −2, .87. The kappa was .85 when the −2 and −1 codes were combined (feeling somewhat to very controlled).

Validity

Supporting convergent and discriminant validity simultaneously, the authors report, consistent with predictions, significant but moderate negative correlations with marital satisfaction for each of the four dimensions in Part I. Some evidence of convergent validity was also reported with significant or nearly significant moderate correlations between these four dimensions and the Dominance and Isolation Scale of Tolman's (1989) Psychological Maltreatment of Women Inventory. Finally, sections of the interview differentiated distressed from happy couples, distressed nonviolent from distressed violent couples, and wives' from husbands' perceptions (Ehrensaft, Langhinrichsen-Rohling, Heyman, O'Leary, & Lawrence, 1999).

Advantages

The interview offers (a) an operational definition of control in intimate relationships, (b) a direct method for assessing perceptions of feeling controlled by a partner, and (c) a method for assessing the link between control and physical aggression. The interview combines open-ended, dichotomous, and Likert-type responses, allowing for qualitative and quantitative interpretation.

Limitations

More research is needed to demonstrate the interview's construct validity, particularly with shelter or agency rather than community samples. Coding or scoring information is not specified for the open-ended questions in Part III of the interview. Although unavoidable with interviews with scoring systems coding open-ended, qualitative responses, training is needed to obtain reliable ratings.

Primary Scale Reference

Ehrensaft, Langhinrichsen-Rohling, Heyman, O'Leary, and Lawrence (1999).

Scale Availability

Miriam Ehrensaft
Columbia College of Physicians and Surgeons
Division of Child Psychiatry
722 West 168th Street, Unit 78
New York, NY 10032
E-mail: Ehrensam@child.cpmc.columbia.edu

Related Reference

Ehrensaft and Vivian (1999).

General Comments and Recommendations for Researchers and Practitioners

As coercive control has been closely tied to many theories of spouse abuse, this interview fills an important need, offering researchers and clinicians a method for defining and systematically assessing this construct. The interview is practical for clinical or research settings and appears useful for assessing perceptions of control in maritally distressed nonaggressive couples as well as aggressive couples, as it revealed significant patterns of control in both of these groups (Ehrensaft et al., 1999).

---

2. Danger Assessment Instrument (DAI; J. C. Campbell)

Description and Development of Assessment Method

The DAI is a 15-question interview asking women in battering relationships about the presence of risk factors linked with eventual homicide of battered women by their abusers or of abusers by battered women.

The DAI items were generated by examining risk factors revealed in major empirical studies of homicide of battered women by their abusers or of abusers by their battered partners.

Target Population

Victims of spouse abuse. The interview could also be used with abusive spouses self-reporting on their own risk factors.

Format

The original interview (J. C. Campbell, 1986) contains 15 questions, and an adaptation contains 2 additional questions (Stuart & Campbell, 1989). Sample questions include the following:

- "Does he ever try to choke you?"
- "Has the physical violence increased in severity during the past year and/or has a weapon or threat with weapon been used?"
- "Is there a gun in the house?"
- "Does he threaten to kill you and/or do you believe he is capable of killing you?"
- "Is he violently and constantly jealous of you? (e.g., does he say, "If I can't have you, no one can?")."
- "Has he ever threatened or tried to commit suicide?"

Administration and Scoring

The assessor begins by reading instructions, which (a) orient the interviewee to the fact that she will be answering yes or no to a list of questions containing risk factors for homicides for both batterers and battered women, and (b) include a statement that although predictions about her particular case cannot be made, the intention is for her to become aware of the danger of, and risk factors for, homicide in severe battering relationships. The interview begins by handing the respondent a calendar and asking her to indicate the approximate dates during the past year when she was beaten by her partner. Then, she is asked to rate each incident according to a 1–5 scale indicating the severity of the abusive incident (from slapping or pushing with no injuries to use of weapon/wounds from weapon). The interviewer then asks the respondent each risk factor in turn, recording yes or no responses. The DAI is scored by simply summing the total number of yes responses. According to the author, the higher the number of affirmative responses, the greater are the number of risk factors for homicide (J. C. Campbell, 1986). Following administration and scoring, the respondent is told the number of risk factors she endorsed and encouraged to ask questions about particular items. The interview takes about 10 minutes.

Psychometric Evaluation

Norms

J. C. Campbell (1995b) reported DAI means for five studies conducted on the instrument with a variety of abused populations. Among these samples, means have ranged from 5.5 to 8.7.

Reliability

Cronbach's alphas for the DAI have ranged from .60 to .86, indicating low to acceptable internal consistency (Campbell, 1995b). However, as the author points out, an instrument measuring independent risk factors would not necessarily be expected to be internally consistent. Test–retest reliability over a 1-week period was reported at .97 (J. C. Campbell, 1986), and in two later studies was reported at .89 and .94 (J. C. Campbell, 1995b).

Validity

Stuart and Campbell (1989) provided initial support for construct validity on the basis of the interview's significant correlations with self-reported severity of injury sustained and most severe degree of abuse encountered during the course of the relationship. Convergent validity was also demonstrated with significant correlations between the DAI and the Physical Abuse subscale of the Index of Spouse Abuse (Hudson & McIntosh, 1981) and with the Severe Abuse subscale of the Conflict Tactics Scale (CTS; Straus, 1979). Criterion-related validity was supported by the instrument's ability to discriminate among seven groups of women with various levels of abuse severity, with lowest scores in a nonabused sample and highest in emergency room and shelter samples (J. C. Campbell, 1995).

Advantages

The DAI is a brief, easy-to-administer and score interview that requires no particular training or skills beyond general clinical sensitivity. An efficient method of assessing a range of danger-relevant variables, it may provide the assessor with information critical in forming a treatment and safety plan.

Limitations

The measure does not have demonstrated predictive validity, although it is based on risk factors identified in the literature based on completed homicides. Because the interview is scored with a simple dimensional rating, and because the implications of a high number of affirmative responses are said to be life-threatening, the omission of a specified clinically significant level of dangerous is potentially misleading. The instrument contains the potential to incite fear or hasty reactions in the respondent if not administered within a clinical context sensitive to issues faced by battered women and not prepared to provide follow-up intervention once assessments of dangerousness have been made. However, the author stated that among the respondents,

> most of them spontaneously verbalized that the nature of the questions indicated that the researcher understood the seriousness of their situation. In addition, some stated that they felt less isolated when they learned that many women experience the same terror as they had experienced. (see Stuart & Campbell, 1989, p. 250)

Primary Scale Reference

J. C. Campbell (1986).

Scale Availability

Jacquelyn C. Campbell
Johns Hopkins University
School of Nursing
525 North Wolfe Street
Baltimore, MD 21205-2110
Phone: (410) 955-7548

The interview is also reprinted in J. C. Campbell (1995b).

Related References

J. C. Campbell (1995a, 1995b); McFarlane, Parker, Soeken, and Bullock (1992); Stuart and Campbell (1989).

General Comments and Recommendations for Researchers and Practitioners

Designed for administration by nursing staff, this instrument may serve as an economical, easy-to-administer screening for dangerousness in a variety of settings among a range of disciplines. Settings could include emergency rooms, battered women's shelters, domestic violence agencies, clinical practices treating cases involving domestic violence, or research settings. The DAI could also be administered in a paper-and-pencil format, with orienting instructions and a discussion of responses with a practitioner following completion of the scale. The instrument also serves as a method of educating the respondent regarding potential signs of danger in a battering relationship.

---

3. Distress and Abuse Classification Interviews (DACI; Heyman, Feldbau-Kohn, Ehrensaft, Langhinrichsen-Rohling, & O'Leary)

Description and Development of Assessment Method

The DACI consists of combined semistructured interviews assessing (a) current relationship distress and (b) physical aggression (victimization and perpetration). The authors aimed to develop a structured clinical interview with standardized criteria for the purpose of classifying people for the presence or absence of relationship distress and relationship aggression, to parallel the format of structured interviews in the assessment of individual psychopathology.

The marital distress diagnosis was patterned after the criteria for major depressive disorder (i.e., one key criterion is met for overall subjective state and several other related symptoms are present). Items for overall marital dissatisfaction "were based on a commonsense approach to what constitutes significant distress: overall unhappiness in the relationship, persistent thoughts of divorce, or perceived need for professional help for the relationship" (Heyman et al., 2001, p. 338). Items for key related criteria were gleaned from the scientific literature on relationship distress.

The physical abuse criteria were designed to operationalize the *Diagnostic and Statistical Manual of Mental Disorders* (4th ed., *DSM–IV*; American Psychiatric Association, 1994) diagnosis of physical abuse of adult as described by O'Leary and Jacobson (1997).

Target Population

Individuals in couple relationships.

Format

The interview is based on the format of the Structured Clinical Interview for DSM–IV Axis I Disorders—Clinical Version (SCID; First, Gibbon, Spitzer, & Williams, 1997) and contains three sections. The first section assesses relationship distress over the past month, covering subjective distress, thoughts of marital dissolution, perceived need for professional help, marked escalation of negative affect, withdrawal from interaction, distressed attributional pattern, low sense of efficacy to improve the relationship, angry or sad feelings about the partner, and apathy. The second section assesses physical aggression victimization over the past year, including physical injury and fear. The third section assesses physical aggression perpetration over the past year, also including injury and fear.

Sample questions from Sections I to III follow:

Section I: Current Relationship Distress (9 questions)

- "In the last month, have you been feeling unhappy about your relationship?"
- "In the last month, have you had thoughts of separation or divorce, or that you'd be better off without your partner?"

Section II. Physical Aggression (Victimization) (10 questions, each with follow-up probes on most serious occurrence and resulting injuries, plus one fear question)
(During the past year, has partner done this to interviewee:)

- "Thrown something at you."
- "Slapped, kicked, or bit you."
- "Some people are afraid that their partners will physically hurt them if the argue with their partners or do something their partners don't like. How much would you say you are afraid of this?"

Section III: Physical Aggression (Perpetration) (same 10 questions as victimization questions, with different pronouns, each with follow-up probes on most serious occurrence and resulting injuries, plus one fear question)
(During past year, what interviewee has done to partner:)

- "Pushed, grabbed, or shoved your partner."
- "Hit your partner with a fist or with an object."

Administration and Scoring

The DACI takes up to 15 minutes, depending on the positive endorsement of distress and aggression items and the respondent's level of descriptiveness in answering the questions. If both partners are to be given the interview, they are separated during its administration. In the relationship distress section, questions are open-ended and follow-up probes are allowed. As in the SCID, each area assessed has its own scoring criteria, printed adjacent to each question, with scores indicated adjacent to these criteria. Identical to the SCID, scores for each area are endorsed as ? (*inadequate information*),

1 (*absent or false*), 2 (*subthreshold*), and 3 (*threshold or true*). Scoring is categorical: partners receive a classification of distressed based on whether they meet a minimum of one criterion for overall dissatisfaction (unhappiness, pervasive thoughts of divorce, or perceived need for help) plus a minimum of one additional behavioral, cognitive, or affective distress symptom.

In the physical aggression sections, respondents first indicate (yes/no) whether each aggressive act occurred in the past year. For each item answered yes, respondents then describe the most serious incident in the past year and whether any injury occurred. Injury responses are then rated according to the ? 1 2 3 scale. Respondents also indicate their fear of being physically hurt by their partners on a scale ranging from *not at all* (1) to *very afraid* (3). Partners receive a classification of physical abuse (separately for victimization and perpetration) if they endorse an act of physical aggression accompanied by either injury or fear.

Psychometric Evaluation

Norms
Rates of relationship distress and physical abuse are reported in the primary reference for 74 couples of varying levels of relationship distress recruited for the study; but no actual norms are reported.

Reliability
Interrater reliability on relationship distress classification was excellent ($\kappa = .92$). High interrater reliability was obtained for abuse diagnosis: aggression toward one's partner ($\kappa = .80$), partner injury or fear ($\kappa = .85$), aggression from one's partner ($\kappa = .85$), and injury from one's partner's aggression ($\kappa = 1$).[1] Intermethod reliability was supported (interview vs. questionnaires) with concordant reports of reporting any aggression on the abuse interview and on the CTS (with added questions assessing impact): perpetration of aggression, men ($\kappa = .87$), women ($\kappa = .82$); victimization, men ($\kappa = .85$), women ($\kappa = .77$). Severe aggression, however, was less consistent when methods were compared: perpetration of aggression, men ($\kappa = .48$), women ($\kappa = .67$); victimization, men ($\kappa = .70$), women ($\kappa = .53$). Interpartner agreement was also low, with 50% agreement in reporting diagnosable levels of abuse in male-to-female cases and 17% agreement in female-to-male cases.

---

1. Kappa for fear of a partner was not reported.

Validity

The authors reported fair convergent validity between the interview of relationship distress and distress classification on the basis of the Dyadic Adjustment Scale (DAS). The relationship distress diagnosis differentiated groups in terms of self-report measures of positive affect and positive behaviors, and observational ratings of marital discussions with the Rapid Marital Interaction Coding System (Heyman & Vivian, 1993) on hostile and distress-maintaining attribution code, supporting the scale's discriminative validity.

The diagnosis of physical abuse also differentiated physically abused from nonabused wives in self-reported psychological maltreatment (i.e., dominance and isolation).

Advantages

The notion of standardized categorical classification of both distress and physical abuse offers a welcome advantage compared with typical standards for classification, that is, potentially unreliable cutoff scores on dimensional measures (e.g., the DAS; Spanier, 1976). Further, the abuse criteria include ratings of injury and fear, essential for determining impact of aggressive behaviors and for yielding a gendered understanding of couple violence (Vivian & Langhinrichsen-Rohling, 1994).

Limitations

In parallel to criticisms of standard classification criteria for psychopathology, this interview categorizes phenomena that might be best conceptualized as dimensional. In addition, more validation work is needed before accepting interview diagnostic criteria over the widely used questionnaires assessing relationship distress and abuse. In particular, more work is needed in representative samples.

Primary Scale Reference

Heyman, Feldbau-Kohn, Ehrensaft, Langhinrichsen-Rohling, and O'Leary (2001).

Scale Availability

Appendix of primary reference and

> Richard Heyman
> Department of Psychology
> University at Stony Brook
> Stony Brook, NY 11794-2500
> E-mail: richard.heyman@sunysb.edu

Related References

Heyman (1993); Pan, Ehrensaft, Heyman, O'Leary, and Schwartz (1997).

General Comments and Recommendations for Researchers and Practitioners

The authors are to be lauded for this original attempt to fashion a "gold standard" interview for establishing soundness of dimensional scale cutoff scores and to operationalize diagnostic criteria for relationship distress and physical abuse. Despite the categorization of arguably dimensional phenomena imposed by this interview, such clearly delineated clinical criteria are beneficial from the standpoint of standardization and group comparison research (in which group comparisons may be confounded by misclassified couples). The physical aggression criteria also operationalizes O'Leary and Jacobson's (1997) experimental criteria for the *DSM–IV* codes for physical abuse of adult.

While more validation work is needed, the interview offers a practical, unique assessment device for practitioners and researchers.

---

4. Domestic Violence Interview (DVI; Fruzzetti, Saedi, Wilson, & Rubio)

Description and Development of Assessment Method

The DVI is a semistructured interview that evaluates the self-reported functions of aggressive and violent behaviors in couple relationships. The interview is modeled after the traditional behavioral assessment method of functional analysis. In Saedi and Fruzzetti (2000), interviews were videotaped and interrater reliability was established by having a second rater rate a random sample of one third of the interviews.

Target Population

Males or females who have experienced violence in their relationships.

Format

The interviewer asks partners for a description of two representative relationship violence incidents. He or she then inquires about antecedents, the incident itself, and consequences of the aggression. "The DVI is to be used in conjunction with the Conflict Tactics Scale, and subjects are asked to clarify the process of aggressive episodes that they have endorsed on the CTS" (Saedi & Fruzzetti, 2000, p. 34).

Administration and Scoring

Partners are interviewed separately. The interview takes 45 to 60 minutes to administer.

Each abusive incident is rated according to each of four functional dimensions:

1. aggression/violence for the sake of self-defense or self-protection
2. aggression/violence for the sake of control
3. aggression/violence for the sake of limiting intimacy
4. aggression/violence for the sake of limiting distancing

Ratings are made on a 1–7 Likert scale (1 = *no evidence of behaviors reflecting the dimension;* 7 = *behaviors with the highest congruence with the dimension*). Ratings of 5 or greater on a dimension indicate that the dimension reflects the primary function of the violence.

The severity of each violent behavior is also rated on the basis of the order of violent acts in the CTS, as specified in the coding manual.

Psychometric Evaluation

Norms

In mixed sample of 31 community and clinic violent couples (Saedi & Fruzzetti, 2000), the percentage of females reporting each primary function of their violence was as follows: self-defense (30.5%), control (30.5%), and titrating intimacy (39%). The percentage of males reporting each violence function was as follows: self-defense (2%), control (52%), and titrating intimacy (46%).

Reliability

Interrater reliabilities were calculated with intraclass correlation coefficients (ICCs; Saedi & Fruzzetti, 2000). Reliabilities were calculated separately for male and female violence and for each function. Intraclass correlations were as follows: Self-Defense, .91(males), .97 (females); Control, .92 (males), .89 (females); Limiting Intimacy, .95 (males), .96 (females); Limiting Distance, .96 (males), .98 (females); and Overall .96 (males), .96 (females).

Validity

The authors reported that self-reported intimacy variables and communication patterns were not related to DVI codes, as expected (Saedi & Fruzzetti, 2000), bringing into question the concurrent validity of the interview. However, initial evidence of criterion validity was demonstrated in a related study, with DVI codes predictive of aggression severity (R^2 = .56) in a violent-only sample (Wilson & Fruzzetti, 2000).

Advantages

The interview allows for in-depth assessment of violent episodes and their controlling variables, following a functional assessment model. The coding categories expand the traditional conceptualization of violence functions beyond control or self-defense and include the functions of titrating intimacy (i.e., limiting intimacy or limiting distancing). The authors report excellent interrater reliability on codes of violence functions. A highly detailed manual provides a description and examples for each anchor point for every function rating.

Limitations

Because the DVI is not a fully structured interview, variability may occur in how interviewers ask questions and in the information obtained from respondents, and the interview may be subject to interviewer–experimenter expectancies. In addition, the rating categories of self-defense, control, and titration of intimacy may not capture all functions of domestic violence. Finally, further research is needed to demonstrate validity of the DVI.

Primary Scale Reference

Fruzzetti, Saedi, Wilson, and Rubio (1998).

Scale Availability

> Alan E. Fruzzetti
> Dept of Psychology 298
> University of Nevada
> Reno, NV 89557-0062

Related References

Saedi and Fruzzetti (2000); Saedi, Rubio, and Fruzzetti. (1999); Wilson and Fruzzetti (2000).

General Comments and Recommendations for Researchers and Practitioners

The DVI provides a behavior-analytic assessment of aggressive episodes, targeting the *function* of violent behaviors. This new interview, like the Semi-Structured Marital Interview (see Measure 7, this chap.), helps to fill important gaps in the standardized assessment of couple violence by combining a semistructured interview format with a functional assessment model. This information can be helpful in the clinical setting, facilitating case conceptualization and identification of treatment targets. As a research tool, the interview provides the means to go beyond assessment of topography of violent behaviors and examine critical factors such as context, process, and gender differences in partner violence. The authors are developing an additional component of the DVI that assesses the degree to which violent behaviors function to reduce negative emotions (A. E. Fruzzetti, personal communication, July 2000). The DVI, particularly with this forthcoming additional component, promises to encourage assessors to consider functions of violence other than traditional control or self-defense functions.

---

5. The Oral History Interview (Krokoff & Gottman)

Description and Development of Assessment Method

The Oral History Interview is a semistructured interview that asks respondents through a set of open-ended questions to tell the story of their courtship and marriage. The interview was developed to model the interview techniques of sociologist/reporter Studs Terkel. Lowell Krokoff (1984) pared down the interview from a 4- to 5-hour version to the present streamlined version after trial and error in administering the interview with couples.

Target Population

Married couples.

Format

The interview contains 12 questions inquiring about how a couple met, the history of their relationship, their courtship and decision to marry, difficult times in their marriage and how they got through them, and what the good times were and are currently. Couples are also asked about their philosophy of marriage (by discussing differences between a good and a bad marriage with which they are familiar) and about their parents' marriages and how they compare with their own.

Sample questions include the following:

- *Question 2.* "When you think back to the time you were dating, before you got married, what do you remember? What stands out? How long did you know each other before you got married? What do you remember of this period? What were some of the highlights? Some of the tensions? What types of things did you do together?"
- *Question 8.* "Looking back over the years, what moments stand out as the really hard times in your marriage? Why do you think you stayed together? How did you get through these difficult times?"
- *Question 11.* "Tell me about your parents' marriages. (Ask each spouse.) What was your relationship with your father like as you were growing up? What was your relationship like with your mother as you were growing up? What was their marriage like? Would you say it's very similar or different from your own marriage? How so?"

Administration and Scoring

The Oral History Interview is administered to both members of the couple together. The interview is designed in part to build rapport with a couple; the interviewer is encouraged to follow the natural course of the conversation (i.e., order of questions is not important as long as they are all covered) and to encourage elaboration on responses. Interviews are tape-recorded for coding. Characteristics of the coding dimensions are described in the coding manual and rated for their presence on a 5-point scale from *strongly agree* to *strongly disagree,* except for the family-of-origin dimensions, which are rated on a 7-point scale for happiness of the parents' marriage, quality of relationship with father, quality of relationship with mother, and similarity to the couple's marriage. The coding dimensions are as follows: Husband Fondness, Wife Fondness, Husband Negativity Toward Spouse, Wife Negativity Toward Spouse, Husband Expansiveness Versus Withdrawal, Wife Expansiveness Versus Withdrawal, Husband We-ness Versus Separateness, Wife We-ness Versus Separateness, Gender Stereotypy, Chaotic Relationships, Glorifying the Struggle, Volatile Relationships, Husband Disappointment/Disillusionment, Wife Disappointment/Disillusionment, Husband Family of Origin, and Wife Family of Origin.

Psychometric Evaluation

Norms
Not reported.

Reliability
Interrater agreement has been high, with alphas across coding categories ranging from .82 to .96.

Validity
Construct validity was demonstrated with consistent significant relationships with couples' problem-solving behavior, affect, and physiology during a conflict discussion task; the interview's predictive validity was also demonstrated in its relationship to future marital dissolution (Buehlman, Gottman, & Katz, 1992; Gottman, 1993).

Advantages
The interview has good construct and predictive validity. It is an excellent standardized tool for gathering phenomenological experiences of couples on a variety of dimensions. It is also a good format for clinical interview with violent or nonviolent couples, even if not used for research purposes.

Limitations
The interview requires a somewhat lengthy training time for coding to reliability (Buehlman and Gottman [1996] reported twice-weekly meetings over a 3-month period), as well as a substantial amount of time per interview for administering the code. It requires the presence of both partners, so it is not for use in settings treating or studying solely perpetrators or victims of spouse abuse and may not be appropriate for moderately or severely violent couples because of its potential to spark a violent conflict.

Primary Scale Reference

Buehlman and Gottman (1996).

Scale Availability

Interview, coding manual, and coding forms are included in primary reference.

Related References

Buehlman, Gottman, and Katz (1992); Gottman (1993); Krokoff (1984).

General Comments and Recommendations for Researchers and Practitioners

The Oral History Interview allows for assessment of many areas of a relationship, including love, affection, humor, nostalgia, ways of coping with marital stress, interpersonal distance, relationship chaos, engagement in gender stereotyping, disappointment, emotional constriction, philosophy of marriage, and family-of-origin dimensions. Although not developed for use with violent couples, many coding categories appear to have particular relevance for marital clinic couples presenting with marital violence, including negativity, expansiveness versus withdrawal, we-ness versus separateness, gender stereotypy, chaotic relationships, volatile relationships, and family-of-origin ratings. The interview can easily be adapted for nonmarried, cohabitating couples, makes a fine tool for research or clinical use, and is one of the very few standardized couple-specific interviews in existence.

6. Overt Aggression Scale—Modified (OAS–M; Coccaro, Harvey, Kupsaw-Lawrence, Herbert, & Bernstein)

Description and Development of Assessment Method

The OAS–M is a clinician-rated semistructured interview assessment of impulsive aggression. Items were rationally derived from the Overt Aggression Scale (Yudofsky, Silver, Jackson, Endicott, & Williams, 1986) and from the Schedule for Affective Disorders and Schizophrenia (Spitzer & Endicott, 1978) to form a scale tapping impulsive aggression features hypothesized to be modulated by central serotonergic functioning.

Target Population

Outpatients or adults with aggressive behavior patterns.

Format

The OAS–M includes scales measuring three overall categories of aggression with seven subcategories: overt aggressive behavior (verbal assault, object-directed assault, other-directed assault, and self-directed assault), irritability (subjective irritability, overt irritability), and suicidal ideation and behavior. The assessment asks respondents about aggressive events over the past week, but this time frame may be modified.

Sample items include the following:

1. *Overt aggressive behavior*
   - "verbally threatened to hit a stranger"
2. *Irritability*
   - "often shouts/loses temper"
3. *Suicidal ideation and behavior*
   - "suicide attempt with definite intent to die"

Administration and Scoring

The OAS–M is administered by an interviewer and then later scored with item weights within categories to produce a total score for aggression, irritability, and suicidality. Detailed scoring information is available from the author. Respondents are asked about the frequency of engaging in a range of behaviors falling into seven categories of aggressive behavior within the past week. Follow-up probes are allowed, including whom particular acts of aggression are directed toward, to present a fuller description of the respondent's aggressive behavior. Individual acts of aggression are rated within categories, and some degree of clarifying probes and clinical judgment may be needed to correctly classify a behavior into a category. Scoring takes place separately for each scale. Each item is rated according to the number of times the act occurred in the past week.

Psychometric Evaluation

Norms
Not reported.

Reliability
Interrater reliability between two raters on OAS–M scales was calculated with intraclass correlations and was high (ICCs ≥ .91).

Validity
Some support for construct validity was documented: In general, the theoretically related OAS–M scales were intercorrelated, and several OAS–M items were also correlated with the self-report Anger, Irritability, and Assault Questionnaire (Coccaro, Harvey, Kupsaw-Lawrence, Herbert, & Bernstein, 1991; see chap. 7, this volume, for description of this measure). The OAS–M, administered weekly, was also sensitive to a 6- to 8-week course of treatment with fluoxetine in three patients.

Advantages

This interview was developed specifically to reflect serotonin-mediated aggressive behavior and has been shown to be sensitive to change over the course of pharmacological treatment in a preliminary sample of patients. Also,

> adaptation of the OAS by assessing the various clinical anchors for each category of overt aggressive behavior separately and by adding additional items relevant to irritability and suicidality yields a semi-structured, interview-based rating that is easy to administer to outpatients and is highly reliable among raters. . . . Moreover, the ratings of OAS-M categories and sub-items with designated weights allows a more complete phenomenological assessment, which includes an estimate of the frequency and severity, respectively, of overt aggressive behavior. (Coccaro et al., 1991, p. S50)

Limitations

The scale needs further demonstration of validity; however, the authors point out that while adapted to create more construct specificity, the OAS–M closely resembles the instruments from which it was adapted, which are instruments with known psychometric properties.

Primary Scale Reference

Coccaro, Harvey, Kupsaw-Lawrence, Herbert, and Bernstein (1991).

Scale Availability

> Emil F. Coccaro
> Clinical Neuroscience Research Unit
> Department of Psychiatry
> Medical College of PA at EPPI
> 3200 Henry Avenue
> Philadelphia, PA 19129

Related Reference

Coccaro, Siever, Klar, Maurer, Cochrane, Cooper, et al. (1989).

General Comments and Recommendations for Researchers and Practitioners

This interview, along with the Anger, Irritability, and Assault Questionnaire (Coccaro et al., 1991; see chap. 7, this volume, on self-report assessments of partner violence), was developed as an outcome measure in a study to test the effectiveness of 5-HT (serotonin) uptake inhibitors in the reduction of aggressiveness in outpatients with a diagnosis of depression or personality disorder. The interview is of use in examining the neurochemical basis of impulsive aggression. The specific OAS–M subscales, such as Assault Against Others, Overt Irritability, and Suicidal Tendencies, may be useful in measuring batterer subtypes (Holtzworth-Munroe & Stuart, 1994).

7. Semi-Structured Marital Interview (SMI; Vivian)

Description and Development of Assessment Method

The SMI is a clinician-rated semistructured intake interview assessment of marital conflict including episodes of marital aggression and is based on a functional analysis conceptualization. The SMI was developed based on the Adapted Conflict Tactic Scale (ACTS; Vivian, 1990a; see chap. 7, this volume). Interview content was designed to correspond closely to content of the ACTS to allow for comparisons of interview and self-report data; however, questions were altered to allow for more expanded, detailed, and contextual responses.

Target Population

Marital clinic couples.

Format

The SMI is a 24-page interview (with spaces provided to write in client responses) with multiple sections regarding marital conflict and specific incidents of marital aggression. The main sections include a section on current marital problems and a section on marital violence. Sample items follow.

1. *Section I: Marital Conflict*

   - "Can you describe your current marital problems from your point of view, in order of importance?"

2. *Section II: Marital Aggression*
   Aggression Subsection I: Self-perpetuated

   - "During the past 12 months, have you been physically aggressive toward your partner? That is, have you thrown something at him/her, pushed, grabbed, shoved, hit, etc.?"

- (If yes) "You mentioned that you were physically aggressive toward your partner during the past 12 months. Let's talk about the *most severe* incident during the past 12 months. When did this happen? . . . Can you tell me what caused you to be physically aggressive toward him/her? . . . Can you describe what happened just before you were physically aggressive toward your partner? . . . Were you arguing? . . . What was the argument about? . . . How did things get worse and worse?"

Aggression Subsection II: Victimization

- "During the past 12 months, has your partner ever been physically aggressive toward you (that is, pushed, shoved, hit, slapped, kicked you, etc.)?" (If yes, proceed with in-depth assessment.)

Administration and Scoring

The scale is typically administered to each member of a couple individually. Several interview questions are rated according to coding systems that have been developed for specific studies (e.g., Cascardi & Vivian, 1995; Ehrensaft & Vivian, 1996). Others are rated on a Likert-type scale (e.g., Langhinrichsen Rohling & Vivian, 1994). The interview takes, on average, between 1 and 2 hours to administer, depending on the amount of sections administered and on whether or not aggression is present.

Psychometric Evaluation

Norms
Not reported.

Reliability
Interrater reliability varies depending on study and sections coded but has ranged from acceptable to excellent (e.g., Cascardi & Vivian, 1995; Ehrensaft & Vivian, 1996). Ayerle and Vivian (1996) examined interpartner agreement on the occurrence of violence in a moderately violent clinic group and a severely violent clinic group using both kappa and percentage agreement. For husband violence, past year, kappas reflected only slight to fair agreement (.18 and .31, respectively), whereas percentage agreement indicated moderate agreement (.60 and .73). Agreement about wife violence, past year, was higher, with kappas reflecting substantial to moderate agreement (.71 and .55) and percentage agreement reflecting good agreement (.86 and .79). For husband violence, prior to past year, kappas reflected fair to

moderate agreement (.37 and .55), whereas percentage agreement was somewhat higher (.68 and .80). For agreement on wife violence, prior to past year, kappas reflected fair to moderate agreement (.37 and .43), with somewhat higher percentage agreement (.67 and .72). (See Ayerle and Vivian [1996] for interpartner agreement rates on a variety of other SMI questions in four groups [clinic severely violent, clinic moderately violent, clinic nonviolent, and community nonviolent]: alcohol abuse, drug abuse, sexual dysfunction, psychiatric hospitalization, past affair, and current affair, all for both husband and wife. Using both kappa and percentage agreement, Ayerle and Vivian found that agreement rates range from poor to excellent agreement, depending on question and group.)

Validity

The scale has demonstrated reasonable correspondence with the ACTS (Vivian, 1990a), suggesting moderate convergent validity.

Advantages

The SMI provides a rich and thorough picture of marital aggression including contextual factors, assessment of impact and context, and attributions. The opportunity for therapist prompts and clarifications allows for a more comprehensive assessment of aggression than might be obtained from a measure such as the ACTS alone. The interview has enormous clinical utility, providing a systematic and structured approach to assessing an area often overlooked or glossed over by marital therapists. It also makes a useful research instrument, allowing for comparisons between spouse reports and numerous additional research questions (investigators can develop and evaluate item codes to suit particular research questions).

Limitations

The interview itself is unpublished; rather there are several published reports of its use. A single thorough coding manual has not been established for the entire interview, although coding systems for sections are presented in various studies (e.g., Cascardi & Vivian, 1995). The interview is lengthy, although independent sections can be excluded according to the needs of the assessment.

Primary Scale Reference

Vivian (1990b).

Scale Availability

> Dina Vivian
> Department of Psychology
> State University of New York at Stony Brook
> Stony Brook, NY 11794-2500

Related References

Ayerle and Vivian (1996); Cascardi and Vivian (1995); Ehrensaft and Vivian (1996); Langhinrichsen-Rohling and Vivian (1994); Vivian (1990a).

General Comments and Recommendations for Researchers and Practitioners

The SMI is the only standardized interview of its kind with published psychometric evaluation and represents an effort toward structured interviewing of marital aggression, a step in a much-needed direction in the field of family violence. The interview "provides a detailed assessment of marital aggression and investigates contextual variables such as marital problems and attributions for the aggression" (Ehrensaft & Vivian, 1996, p. 445). It assesses past aggression patterns, long-term and immediate antecedents or stressors, content of marital conflict corresponding with violent episodes, violence escalation patterns, substance abuse during violence, presence of others during conflict, consequences of violence, perceived functions of violent episodes, attributions for not spontaneously reporting marital violence, and views about the violence as a problem of abusiveness (D. Vivian, personal communication, January 21, 1999). The SMI also contains general marital intake questions concerning sexual difficulties, problems of alcohol and drug abuse, psychiatric history, affairs, demonstrations of caring, and targets for change in therapy.

---

8. Spousal Assault Risk Assessment Guide (SARA; Kropp, Hart, Webster, & Eaves)

Description and Development of Assessment Method

The SARA is a risk assessment guide designed to assess risk of violence toward an intimate partner. Because of a lack of suitable tools in the literature for violence risk assessment, the authors wished to develop this set of professional guidelines for the prediction of spousal assault. The risk factors included were based on a review of the scientific literature as well as relevant clinical and legal issues.

Target Population

Individuals with known histories of partner-assaultive behavior.

Format

The SARA includes a set of 20 risk factors for general violence risk (Factors 1–10) and risk of spousal violence (Factors 11–20) and a manual containing recommendations for spousal violence risk assessment. In addition to coding the presence of the 20 risk factors listed, the manual recommends coding any subjectively determined critical risk factors as well as an overall summary risk score.

Sample risk factors follow.

Part I: General Violence Risk

- "Past assault of family members"
- "Recent substance abuse/dependence"
- "Personality disorder with anger, impulsivity, or behavioral instability"

Part II: Risk of Spousal Assault

- "Past sexual assault/sexual jealousy"
- "Recent escalation in frequency or severity of assault"
- "Past violation of 'no contact' orders"

Administration and Scoring

Although the 20 risk factors can be administered in interview form, they can also be administered independent of client contact by review of files/records. Evaluators code the presence of each of the 20 risk factors on a 3-point scale (0 = *absent*, 1 = *possibly or partially present*, 2 = *present*). Critical items, those factors among the 20 deemed by the evaluator to be both present and strongly related to violence risk in the particular case, are coded on a 2-point scale (0 = *not critical*, 1 = *critical*). Total scores then are calculated by summing individual item ratings and range from 0 to 40. Number of factors present is also calculated, ranging from 0 to 20, and number of critical items is also summed and ranges from 0 to 20. Finally, summary risk ratings reflect evaluators' judgments of clients' risk of recidivistic spousal assault and are rated on a 3-point scale (0 = *low risk,* 1 = *moderate risk,* 2 = *high risk*).

Psychometric Evaluation

Norms
Not reported.

Reliability
The items had adequate internal consistency, with Cronbach's alphas (total scores) of .66 for Part I, .73 for Part II, and .78 for the entire scale. Total score interrater reliability was good, with ICCs of .68 for Part I, .87 for Part II, and .84 for the entire scale.

Validity
The SARA ratings significantly discriminated between offenders with and without spousal assault histories and also between recidivistic and nonrecidivistic spousal assaulters, supporting its known groups or criterion-related validity. Scale scores also evidenced good convergent and discriminant validity regarding its associations with other measures of violent/criminal behavior and risk.

Advantages
The SARA can be administered as an interview but also as a tool used without face-to-face contact, based on offender records. With promising psychometric characteristics, this tool may provide assistance to those conducting risk assessments for forensic or clinical purposes.

Limitations
The fact that some degree of clinical judgment is involved in the ratings may lead to variable predictive utility depending on the experience of the raters. Also, although concurrent validity was demonstrated, a demonstration of predictive validity would lend additional support to the scale's use as a risk assessment tool.

Primary Scale Reference

Kropp, Hart, Webster, and Eaves (1998).

Scale Availability

Spousal Assault Risk Assessment Guide: User's Manual
Published by:
Multi-Health Systems, Inc.
65 Overlea Boulevard, Suite 210
Toronto, Ontario, Canada, M4H 1P1

Related References

Kropp and Hart (2000); Kropp, Hart, Webster, and Eaves (1994, 1995).

General Comments and Recommendations for Researchers and Practitioners

The SARA guide is not a traditional interview in the sense that it can be administered in the absence of face-to-face contact with the client, based on a review of records. However, it is a promising violence risk assessment tool with good evidence of reliability and validity, developed on large and diverse samples. The method reflects an approach the authors term *structured professional judgment,* in which the scale items facilitate the reliable coding of professional judgment in predicting future risk of spouse assault.

---

9. Structured Clinical Interview for DSM–IV Axis I Disorders (SCID; First, Spitzer, Gibbon, & Williams)

Description and Development of Assessment Method

The SCID is a semistructured interview designed to diagnose Axis I disorders based on *DSM–IV* (American Psychiatric Association, 1994) categories. The interview was developed to correspond with the symptom criteria and categorization contained in the *DSM–IV*. However, it was also intended to model traditional clinical interviews, allowing the clinician to probe clients across multiple areas while entertaining and testing several diagnostic hypotheses simultaneously (Persons & Fresco, 1998).

Target Population

Outpatient or inpatient clinic samples; can be used with husbands or wives.

Format

The SCID includes modules assessing each major Axis I section in the *DSM–IV*. The general categories assessed include mood disorders, schizophrenia and other psychotic disorders, substance use disorders, anxiety disorders, somatoform disorders, eating disorders, and adjustment disorders. Disorders are assessed for current presence (criteria met for past month) and lifetime presence (ever met criteria). The interview also provides a global assessment of functioning rating and assesses demographic data, occupational history, status of current treatment, description of current problem, onset and course or exacerbation of current illness, environmental context and possible precipitants, treatment history, and medications.

Sample modules and sample module gate questions include the following:

Major depressive episode

- "In the last month, has there been a period of time when you were feeling depressed or down most of the day, nearly every day? (What was that like?) IF YES: How long did it last? (As long as two weeks?). . . . What about losing interest or pleasure in things you usually enjoyed?"

Alcohol and other substance use disorders

- "What are your drinking habits like? (How much do you drink?) How often? (What do you drink?)"
- IF NOT CURRENTLY DRINKING HEAVILY: "Was there ever a time in your life when you were drinking a lot more? (How often were you drinking?) (What were you drinking? How much? How long did that period last?)"

Posttraumatic stress disorder

- "Sometimes things happen to people that are extremely upsetting—things like being in a life-threatening situation like a major disaster, very serious accident, or fire; being physically assaulted or raped; seeing another person killed or dead, or badly hurt; or hearing about something horrible that has happened to someone you are close to. At any time during your life, have any of these things happened to you?"
- IF ANY EVENTS LISTED: "Sometimes these things keep coming back in nightmares, flashbacks, or thoughts that you can't get rid of. Has that ever happened to you?"

Administration and Scoring

General "gate" questions begin each module; when such questions are answered affirmatively, the interviewer administers the module. Otherwise, the interviewer skips to the next module. The SCID typically takes between 45 minutes and 2 hours to administer in full, depending on the amount of positive responses to gate questions (and thus the amount of modules administered). However, the Clinician Version (First, Spitzer, Gibbon, & Williams, 1995a) is somewhat shorter than the research version, excluding some detailed probes regarding diagnostic subtypes/specifiers. Interviewers are expected to have some clinical sophistication and to be familiar with classification and *DSM–IV* diagnostic criteria, as some degree of clinical judgment is required in administering/scoring the interview; the semistructured format allows for follow-up probes and clarifications. Each symptom is rated as "+" (*present*), "–" (*absent*), or "?" (*questionable*). A disorder is diagnosed if *DSM–IV* symptom criteria are met. The interview comes with a summary scoring sheet; results of the diagnostic interview are presented categorically in terms of specific diagnoses for which the interviewee meets criteria.

Psychometric Evaluation

Norms
Not reported.

Reliability
In reviews of studies evaluating the reliability of the SCID,[2] Segal and colleagues (Segal & Falk, 1998; Segal, Hersen, & Van Hasselt, 1994) reported the following: (a) Evaluations of 2-week test–retest reliability (by pairs of independent raters) in 592 participants using kappas (averaged across all modules) was .61 for current disorders and .68 for lifetime disorders in patients and .37 for current disorders and .51 for lifetime disorders in nonpatients; (b) interrater agreement using ratings of audiotaped SCIDs in 54 participants was excellent for many disorders (with kappas above .80), including schizophrenia, major depression, dysthymia, generalized anxiety disorder, panic disorder, and alcohol use disorder, and was moderate for

---

2. Reviews pertain to the SCID for *DSM–III–R* (Spitzer, Williams, Gibbon, & First, 1988).

others, including cyclothymia, posttraumatic stress disorder (PTSD), social phobia, simple phobia, bipolar disorder, and adjustment disorder, and was poor (kappas .40 or below) for obsessive compulsive disorder, agoraphobia without panic, and somatoform disorder.

Validity

The interview has established criterion validity.

Advantages

The SCID is a well-researched, highly thorough instrument for obtaining Axis I diagnoses of clinical populations and is an excellent device for obtaining differential diagnosis. Selected modules of interest may be used independently, adding to the scale's flexibility. Scoring is fairly straightforward.

Limitations

Rather weak interrater agreement in nonpatient samples. Fairly lengthy training is required in administering the interview. Provides categorical (i.e., yes/no) ratings for each diagnosis, which is useful for screening or sample description but limited in terms of data analysis and measuring change in symptom levels across therapy.

Primary Scale Reference

First, Spitzer, Gibbon, and Williams (1995a, 1995b).

Scale Availability

Michael B. First or Miriam Gibbon
Biometrics Research Department, Unit 74
New York State Psychiatric Institute
Department of Psychiatry
Columbia University
722 West 168th Street
New York, NY 10032

Related References

Cascardi, O'Leary, Lawrence, and Schlee (1995); First, Spitzer, Gibbon, and Williams (1995); Spitzer, Williams, Gibbon, and First (1988, 1992).

General Comments and Recommendations for Researchers and Practitioners

Generally considered a gold standard instrument for diagnosis of Axis I psychopathology in research studies, this interview is appropriate for diagnosing disorders associated with couple violence. Because the interview requires extensive training for reliability in administration and scoring, it is most often used in research settings. However, a Clinician Version is available that is somewhat shorter and contains only those Axis I disorders typically seen in clinical settings. The interview is available in patient (for psychiatric inpatients and outpatients) and nonpatient (for community respondents in which the presence of mental illness is not assumed) formats. A companion interview (the SCID–II) is also available for diagnosing *DSM–IV* Axis II personality disorders (Maffei et al., 1997).

---

10. Structured Interview for Disorders of Extreme Stress (SIDES; Pelcovitz, Vanderkolk, Roth, Kaplan, Mandel, & Resick)

Description and Development of Assessment Method

The SIDES is a structured clinical interview for measuring psychological alterations following exposure to extreme stress. It is designed to be administered along with the SCID PTSD module.

Target Population

Individuals exposed to extreme stress or trauma.

Format

The interview contains 48 items measuring 27 symptoms that fall within seven different categories. Categories and symptom descriptions follow (with sample items):

Regulation of affect and impulses (6 items)

- "Do you have (more) trouble letting go of things that upset you?"
- "Do you find yourself careless about making sure that you are safe?"

Attention or consciousness (2 items)

- "To what extent do you have trouble clearly remembering important things that happened to you?"
- "Do you sometimes feel so unreal that it is as if you were living in a dream, or not really there or behind a glass wall?"

Self-perception (6 items)

- "Do you have the feeling that you basically have no influence on what happens to you in your life?"
- "Do you feel set apart and very different from other people?"

Perception of perpetrator (3 items)

- "Do you sometimes think that people have the right to hurt you?"
- "Do you sometimes think that people who have hurt you are special?"

Relations with others (3 items)

- "Do you find yourself unable to trust people?"
- "Do you have difficulty working through conflicts in relationships?"

Somatization (5 items)

- "Since the trauma, have you had trouble with abdominal pain, intolerance of food?"
- "Since the trauma have you suffered from shortness of breath, chest pain?"

Systems of meaning (2 items)

- "Have you given up hope in being able to find happiness in love relationships?"
- "Do you feel that life has lost its meaning?"

Administration and Scoring

The 48 items are scored dichotomously in a yes/no format. The interviewer probes for details to get the correct rating and then arrives at a total score. Clarifying questions are provided in italics next to items. If the event took place within the past month, the interviewer indicates a severity rating for that item from 1 (*little problematic*) to 3 (*extremely problematic*).

Psychometric Evaluation

The primary reference contains percentage endorsement of each SIDES symptom by trauma type for 520 participants across five national sites.

Norms
Not reported.

Reliability
Interrater reliability on whether respondents met criteria for disorders of extreme stress was .81 using kappa. Alphas were .90 (alteration in regulation of affect and impulses), .76 (alterations in attention or consciousness), .77 (alterations in self-perception), .53 (alterations in perception of perpetrator), .77 (alterations in relations with others), .88 (somatization), .78 (alterations in systems of meaning), and .96 for the total score.

Validity
Content validity was supported by a panel of 12 experts agreeing on the final list of 27 symptoms arranged into seven categories. Experts also agreed that each subscale was a critical component of trauma, supporting the scale's face validity.

Advantages
This is a helpful instrument for investigating responses to extreme stress and identifying psychological impairment that are relevant to treatment planning. The scale offers a useful supplement to the measurement of PTSD criteria, which do not address many symptoms often seen in response to extreme trauma.

Limitations
Further validation work is needed to establish the construct validity of the scale.

Primary Scale Reference

Pelcovitz, Vanderkolk, Roth, Kaplan, Mandel, & Resick (1997)

Scale Availability

David Pelcovitz
Department of Psychiatry
North Shore University Hospital
400 Community Drive
Manhasset, NY 11030

General Comments and Recommendations for Researchers and Practitioners

The SIDES can be useful for those wishing to go beyond *DSM–IV* PTSD criteria in evaluating the impact of trauma. The interview was used in a *DSM–IV* field trial and was designed in part to test the viability of a supplemental *DSM–IV* trauma diagnosis, the category of "disorders of extreme stress." Clinicians and researchers could use the interview to assess alterations in perception, meaning, and functioning experienced by victims of partner violence.

---

11. Timeline Followback Spousal Violence Interview (TLFB–SV; Fals-Stewart, Birchler, & Kelley)

Description and Development of Assessment Method

The TLFB–SV is a calendar-based interview method designed to assess the timeline of episodes of physical aggression toward a partner. The interview was adapted from the Timeline Followback Interview method to assess substance abuse, with diary items and interview questions altered to reflect intimate partner violence. Psychometric properties were established using a sample of men and their partners from an outpatient treatment program for batterers.

Target Population

Individuals in aggressive relationships, reporting on their own or on their partner's behaviors.

Format

The TLFB–SV presents interviewees with a retrospective daily calendar spanning the number of days in the target interval. Respondents mark days of special significance (e.g., birthdays, anniversaries) on the calendar; standard U.S. holidays and days of no face-to-face contact with the partner are also noted. The interviewer provides a list of types of violent acts based on the CTS (Straus, 1990b), including a category for "other types of physical aggression not otherwise specified." Starting with the previous day, respondents enter onto the calendar days on which episodes of male-to-female and days on which female-to-male[3] aggression occurred, and what type of violent acts occurred.

For all follow-up interviews, respondents keep a weekly diary in which they monitor the violent acts that occur and on what days; this is used as a memory aid (along with any other memory aid respondents wish to use) when they return for subsequent interviews.

Administration and Scoring

The interview varies in length based on the extensiveness of violent acts reported. The TLFB–SV produces four subscales: (a) male-to-female percentage days of any violence, (b) female-to-male percentage days of any violence, (c) male-to-female percentage days of severe violence, and (d) female-to-male percentage days of severe violence.

Psychometric Evaluation

Norms
Not reported.

Reliability
The interview approach demonstrated excellent temporal stability over 2-week intervals, with ICC values ranging from .91 to 1.0 (Fals-Stewart et al., 2003).

Validity
The interview demonstrated adequate convergent and discriminant validity, correlating moderately and significantly with other measures of partner

---

3. Of course, the interview can also be used to assess violence in nonheterosexual relationships.

violence and with dyadic adjustment but not with a measure of social desirability (Fals-Stewart et al, in press).

Although female partners consistently reported more days of any type of violence than their male counterparts, partner reports were highly and significantly intercorrelated with ICCs for all of several assessment periods except for pretreatment. Thus, there was significant male–female agreement for partner reports of percentage of days of violence (Fals-Stewart, 2003).

Advantages

The TLFB–SV highlights temporal patterns of aggressive episodes and specifies the number of different days violence occurs in a given time interval. The method of calculating percentage of days violent allows for meaningful comparison across different length assessment intervals. The calendar- and diary-aided method can enhance recall of violent incidents and can thus improve accuracy of reporting as well as interpartner agreement. The instrument has excellent temporal stability and good convergent and discriminant validity.

Limitations

The TLFB–SV method can be highly labor-intensive for both the interviewer and the respondent. Respondents may neglect to fill out the weekly violence diaries in between assessment periods.

Primary Scale Reference

Fals-Stewart, Birchler, and Kelley (2003).

Scale Availability

William Fals-Stewart
Research Institute on Addictions
1021 Main Street
Buffalo, NY 14203

Related References

Fals-Stewart (2003); Fals-Stewart, O-Farrell, Freitas, McFarlin, and Rutigliano (2000); Sobell and Sobell (1996).

General Comments and Recommendations for Researchers and Practitioners

Derived from the Timeline Followback method used in the assessment of substance abuse (Sobell & Sobell, 1996), the TLFB–SV has now been applied to partner-violent samples with promising initial results (Fals-Stewart, 2003). The type of data provided by this method can provide a useful supplement to standard self-report rating scales by providing more detailed information about the nature of violent episodes between partners, specifically, about *when* aggressive episodes occurred and which aggressive acts occur within each episode. Not only can such a method enhance accuracy of recall of interpartner violence but it also can provide information about related factors, such as temporal correlates and factors predisposing partners to use of aggression.

Self-Report Measures Specific to the Assessment of Partner Abuse

This chapter reviews measures of self-report paper-and-pencil assessment instruments specific to partner physical or psychological abuse. These measures include several variants/adaptations of the Conflict Tactics Scales as well as a host of additional instruments that vary on a number of dimensions. Thus, regardless of the reader's specific purpose, he or she should be able to locate an appropriate self-report instrument measuring partner-directed physical or psychological abuse in his or her population of interest. Self-report paper-and-pencil measures of partner violence have proliferated in the past 2 decades, despite criticisms based on their being overly simplistic as abuse assessment tools, because of their many advantages for use in clinical as well as research settings. These advantages include ease of administration and scoring, brevity, standardization, provision of behaviorally specific definitions of abuse, and flexibility in administration (e.g., inside or outside of sessions, individually or in groups). Perhaps most importantly, they have proven highly sensitive to detecting violent behaviors. Thus, such measures are efficient and practical, yielding invaluable data while remaining inexpensive, requiring little or no training or equipment, and being relatively non-intrusive to clients.

12. Abuse Assessment Screen (AAS; McFarlane, Parker, Soeken, & Bullock)

Description and Development of Assessment Method

This extremely brief screening device was designed for use in prenatal care settings to assess for abuse during pregnancy; however, the instrument could be used as an abuse screening device in any setting. The scale was written for the primary reference study to evaluate experiences of abuse during pregnancy and its relation to receiving injuries and obtaining prenatal care.

Target Population

Pregnant women. Could be slightly modified for potential victims of partner violence in any setting where screening for risk of abuse is deemed important.

Format

Respondents fill out five items (and follow-up questions for items answered affirmatively) concerning abusive experiences during pregnancy and not during pregnancy and fear of the perpetrator of such experiences. Sample items follow:

- "Within the last year, have you been hit, slapped, kicked, or otherwise physically hurt by someone?"
- "If YES, by whom?"
- "Are you afraid of your partner or anyone you listed above?"

Administration and Scoring

The AAS takes about 5 minutes to complete. Response formats include yes/no ratings, indications of the nature of the relationship of abuse perpetrators (i.e., husband, ex-husband, boyfriend, stranger, other, multiple), indications of the number of times each reported abusive event category occurred, marking the area of injury on a body map, and rating each incident reported on a 1–6 abuse severity scale ranging from *threats of abuse* to *use of weapon/wound from weapon*. Affirmative answers to any of three specific abusive experience questions yield a positive score for being considered abused.

Psychometric Evaluation

Norms
The percentages in a sample of pregnant women, broken down by ethnicity, of each general category of abuse, the severity of abuse, and perpetrators of the abuse are reported in the primary reference.

Reliability
Not reported.

Validity
The authors report initial support for criterion validity in that women classified as abused according to the AAS were twice as likely to delay prenatal care and scored significantly higher on the Index of Spouse Abuse (Hudson & McIntosh, 1981).

Advantages
The AAS is a brief and convenient screening instrument that can be adapted for use (with minor wording changes) in any setting

Limitations
Reliability information is not provided. Scale items are scored categorically; there is no total score for the scale and limited potential statistical analysis with use in research settings.

Primary Scale Reference

McFarlane, Parker, Soeken, and Bullock (1992).

Scale Availability

The scale is reprinted in the primary reference.

Related References

None available.

General Comments and Recommendations for Researchers and Practitioners

The AAS provides a useful model of a brief partner abuse screening tool that could be used in a variety of health care settings by a range of professionals. Simple to use and score, the scale could be administered routinely and serve as a prelude to a more extensive interview or written assessment battery (followed by provision of education and referrals) based on scoring positive for the presence of abuse.

13. Abusive Behavior Inventory (ABI; Shepard & Campbell)

Description and Development of Assessment Method

The ABI is a 30-item[1] self-report scale assessing physical and psychological aggression directed toward a partner. The ABI was developed rationally on the basis of clinical experiences of staff members working within a domestic violence program as well as consultation with battered women. In particular, items were designed to be consistent with a variety of specific areas addressed in a feminist/psychoeducational treatment model for men who batter (Pence & Paymar, 1985). This model identifies categories of psychologically abusive acts from which items of the ABI psychological abuse subscale were drawn: emotional abuse, isolation, intimidation, threats, demands for compliance, and economic abuse. Once items were developed, the scale was administered to a sample of 100 inpatient men in a chemical dependency treatment program and 78 women partners of these men. Half of these couples reported spouse abuse and half did not. Reliability and validity evaluations were conducted within this sample, and minor changes were made in assigning items to scales based on items–scale correlations.

Target Population

Partner-violent individuals reporting on their own behavior or victims reporting on their partner's behavior. Designed to be used primarily as an outcome measure for evaluating programs for men who batter.

Format

The ABI consists of a Psychological Abuse and Physical Abuse scale. Scale items are identical for men and women except for pronouns (*her* vs. *you*).

1. *Psychological Abuse (20 items)*

   - "Gave you angry looks or stares"
   - "Put down your family and friends"
   - "Made you do something humiliating or degrading"

---

1. The authors also suggest using a 29-item version; see Limitations section.

2. *Physical Abuse (10 items)*

- "Pushed, grabbed, or shoved you"
- "Slapped, hit, or punched you"
- "Threw you around"

Administration and Scoring

The scale takes between 5 and 10 minutes to complete. Respondents fill out items using a 5-point Likert scale assessing the frequency of each behavior within the past 6 months. Frequency ratings for items, which range from *none* to *very frequently* on each subscale, are then summed. For the psychological abuse subscale, this sum is divided by 20 to obtain a mean frequency rating psychological abuse score; for the physical abuse subscale, the sum is divided by 10 to obtain a mean frequency rating physical abuse score.

Psychometric Evaluation

Norms

Mean frequency ratings for a sample of men in a chemical dependency treatment program and their partners were as follows: men's reports of psychological abuse in nonabusive relationships, 1.5 (SD = 0.45); men's reports of physical abuse in nonabusive relationships, 1.1 (SD = 0.25); men's reports of psychological abuse in abusive relationships, 2.1 (SD = 0.55); men's reports of physical abuse in abusive relationships, 1.5 (SD = 0.48); women's reports of men's psychological abuse in nonabusive relationships, 2.0 (SD = 0.70); women's reports of men's physical abuse in nonabusive relationships, 1.3 (SD = 0.65); women's reports of men's psychological abuse in abusive relationships, 2.8 (SD = 0.70); and women's reports of men's physical abuse in abusive relationships, 1.8 (SD = 0.47).

Reliability

Scale alphas were in the moderate to high range: men's reports of psychological abuse in nonabusive relationships, .79; men's reports of physical abuse in nonabusive relationships, .82; men's reports of psychological abuse in abusive relationships, .88; men's reports of physical abuse in abusive relationships, .82; women's reports of men's psychological abuse in nonabusive relationships, .92; women's reports of men's physical abuse in nonabusive relationships, .88; women's reports of men's psychological abuse in abusive relationships, .88; and women's reports of men's physical abuse in abusive relationships, .70.

The scales had small standard errors of measurement ranging from .03 to .11 (no abuse sample) and .07 to .12 (abuse sample), indicating good reliability.

Validity

Both scales of the ABI discriminated between abusive and nonabusive relationships according to both men's and women's reports, supporting the scale's criterion-related or known groups validity. The two subscales also have good factorial validity, in that the majority of the scale items correlate more highly with their own subscale than with the other subscale.

Both the physical and nonphysical abuse scales, filled out by men and women, were more strongly correlated with a clinician's assessment of abuse, clients' assessment of abuse, and arrest history related to domestic violence than they were with age and household size. Although the authors take these findings as support for the scales' convergent and discriminant validity, the scales expected to correlate with the ABI (clinician's assessment of abuse, clients' assessment of abuse, and arrest history) yielded low to moderate correlations (range = .09–.41) with each subscale. Thus, construct validity is questionable.

Advantages

The scale was able to significantly discriminate (albeit modestly) abusive from nonabusive men self-reporting on their behavior; this finding is promising in light of men's tendency to underreport their own abusive behavior. The scale is brief and simple to administer, score, and interpret.

Limitations

The development sample was a rather specific group: men receiving inpatient treatment for chemical dependency. Thus, findings regarding scale properties may not generalize beyond couples in which men share this characteristic.

In addition, the primary reference is somewhat confusing regarding scale items. On the basis of evaluation of item properties and item–scale correlations, the authors state that they dropped 1 item from the Physical Abuse scale (spanking) and moved 3 items from the Psychological Abuse to the Physical Abuse scale. Each of these 3 items involves threatened physical aggression. Dropping 1 item and moving 3 leaves 17 items on the Psychological Abuse scale and 12 items on the Physical Abuse scale, forming a 29-item scale. Yet, scoring procedures, normative data, and even the version of the ABI published in the Appendix reflect the 30-item, unrevised instrument and may be misleading.

Primary Scale Reference

Shepard and Campbell (1992).

Scale Availability

The scale is reprinted in the primary reference.

Related References

Pence and Paymar (1985).

General Comments and Recommendations for Researchers and Practitioners

The ABI was designed to assess psychological and physical aggression toward women by their partners and can be filled out by both women and their partners. The authors report that the items were developed to be consistent with a feminist approach to wife abuse, viewing abusive behaviors as functioning primarily to gain or maintain control, dominance, and power. Items are not placed in the context of conflict as in the CTS, because abuse sometimes occurs independent of disagreement.

The time frame of the scale can be modified to reflect desired assessment intervals. The primary reference is potentially misleading as it presents a version of the scale and scoring directions that differ slightly from the version of the scale the authors recommend using in their conclusion.

---

14. Conflict Tactics Scale[2] (CTS; Straus)

Description and Development of Assessment Method

The original CTS, Form N, is an 18-item self-report instrument containing a list of tactics one might use while engaged in a conflict with a partner and was used in the 1975 National Family Violence Survey. Developed for use in a face-to-face interview survey, the 18-item version of the scale has

---

2. Note that the CTS has also been used to assess conflict tactics used toward children (see Feindler, Rathus, & Silver, 2003).

become the standard used in a self-report paper-and-pencil format.[3] Form R, a 19-item[4] version of the CTS, was used in the 1985 National Family Violence Resurvey, administered over the telephone. On both scales, tactics range from calm reasoning to severe physical aggression. Respondents are asked to indicate the frequency of occurrence of each action over the past year. Specifically, they are asked to indicate how often they have carried out each action in relation to their spouse and how often their spouse carried out each action in relation to them. The instrument was developed for use in national prevalence surveys of family violence (Gelles & Straus, 1988; Straus & Gelles, 1986; Straus et al., 1980).

Items were derived theoretically based on conflict theory (Straus, 1979) and were pretested on a college student sample. Scale groupings have been supported by factor analysis (N = 2,143; Barling, O'Leary, Jouriles, Vivian, & MacEwen, 1987; Straus, 1979).

Target Population

Men or women in (or previously in) an intimate relationship. Has also been used with a variety of ethnic groups.

Format

The CTS contains three subscales: Verbal Reasoning, which contains items reflecting rational discussion and noncoercive means of resolving conflict; Verbal Aggression, which contains items reflecting verbal and symbolic acts that express hostility or emotionally hurt a partner; and Violence, which contains items reflecting use of physical force against a partner. The Violence scale may be further divided into minor and severe violence scales. The minor violence scale consists of Items k–m, and the severe violence scale consists of Items n–r (Form N) and n–s (Form R). Sample items follow:

1. *Verbal Reasoning*

    - "Discussed the issue calmly"
    - "Got information to back up your side of things"

---

3. Form A, a 15-item version, was the original self-report paper-and-pencil version of the CTS (Straus, 1974) but was not used in the national surveys. Form A contains 4 Verbal Reasoning items, 5 Verbal Aggression items, and 6 Violence items and is reprinted in Straus (1979).

4. The added item on Form R is "choked partner."

2. *Verbal Aggression*

- "Insulted or swore at partner"
- "Stomped out of the room or house or yard"
- "Did or said something to spite partner"

3. *Violence*

- "Pushed, grabbed, or shoved partner"
- "Kicked, bit, or hit with a fist"
- "Used a knife or gun"

Administration and Scoring

For each item, respondents simply circle the frequency range that reflects the number of times they or their spouse have engaged in the given behavior over the designated period of time. Most often, participants are asked about the past year, but this time period can be varied (e.g., lifetime, the past 6 months, since a relationship began, since the last assessment, etc.) based on the needs of the examiner. On Form N, frequency ratings are indicated on a 0–6 scale, with response categories of *never, once, twice, 3–5 times, 6–10 times, 11–20 times,* and *more than 20 times.* There is also a category of *don't know,* which does not receive a scaled score.[5] For each item, the respondent is also asked to indicate whether the act *ever* happened.[6] The scale takes about 5 minutes to complete.

Straus (1979, 1990b) presented a number of scoring options for the CTS:

1. For each scale, the response category code values can be summed, such that *never* = 0, *once* = 1, *twice* = 2, *3–5 times* = 3, *6–10 times* = 4, *11–20 times* = 5, and *more than 20 times* = 6. The Verbal Reasoning total can be obtained by summing Items a through c (range = 0–18) and the Verbal Aggression score by summing Items d, e, f, h, i, and j (range = 0–36). Note that Item g, "cried," is omitted from scoring

---

5. Form R contains a slight difference in response categories when administered in interview format. Rather than reading *never* as the first response choice for each act, the interviewer reads only response categories ranging from *once* to *more than 20 times,* requiring respondents to volunteer the response of *never.* This was designed to increase the rate of disclosure of sensitive behavior.

6. When administered as an interview, the respondent is asked about *ever* engaging in acts only when he or she has given a response of *no* or *don't know.*

as it does not constitute verbal aggression; "this was included in the list of actions because pre-test interviewing showed it to be a frequent response and because respondents became uneasy if there was no place to record this" (Straus, 1979, p. 80). The Violence score can be obtained by summing Items k through r (range = 0–48) on Form N, or Items k through s on Form R. A Severe Violence index can be obtained by summing Items n through r (Form N) or Items n through s (Form R; Straus, 1990b).

2. Items from each scale can be weighted as follows and then summed: For the 0–6 scale, substitute 0, 1, 2, 4, 8, 15, and 25. These weights reflect approximate midpoints of frequencies of committing each act within the past year.

3. Because the items are presented hierarchically, the Violence scale can be rated according to a Guttman scale, to produce a score reflecting the level of violence severity. With this method, each item is dichotomized to 1 or 0 indicating the presence or absence of violence, and frequency data are lost.

4. Scales can be standardized to percentages of the total score. Although providing no statistical advantage, this allows for attaining scores comparable across scales in units that have inherent meaning (e.g., "50% of the total score" has a standard meaning, as opposed to "a total of 9"). To use this method, divide the respondent's raw score (method #1) by the maximum scale score, and multiply by 100 (then round to an integer). For example, if a respondent earned a score of 9 on the Reasoning scale using a summation of unweighted category code values, the corresponding score would be 50%.

5. Scale scores can be expressed as percentile scores based on norms from the nationally representative survey sample, using raw scores (method #1) to determine percentile scores from Straus (1979).

6. The highly skewed distributions produced by the Violence scale scores may result in inaccurate statistical findings when analyzing scale data. Thus, a final option for scoring is to simply apply a dichotomous scoring system of 0 (*nonviolent*) and 1 (*violent*). This yields *rates* of violence in a population, to which nonparametric statistics can be applied. The item "ever" can be used to obtain a frequency rate reflecting the occurrence of violence over the course of the relationship.

Psychometric Evaluation

Norms
Extensive norms are presented for different subpopulations in Straus (1979, 1990b).

Reliability
Cronbach's alpha was computed for each of the three scales for husband-to-wife aggression and wife-to-husband aggression in several studies (see Straus, 1990a). Alpha scores for Reasoning ranged from .42 to .76, Verbal Aggression ranged from .62 to .88, and Violence ranged from .79 to .88.

Validity
Support for the construct validity of the CTS is moderate and is derived from a number of sources. One study (Bulcroft & Straus, 1975) found low to moderately high correlations between college-age children's reports of their parents' use of conflict tactics toward a spouse and parents' reports of their own conflict tactics toward a spouse. This study also found moderate agreement between the children's and parents' reports of incident rates of violence and strong agreement in incidence rates (percentage of sample reporting any physical violence toward a partner) between children's reports of their parents' violence and findings from the national survey sample.

The CTS also correlates with a number of variables in theoretically consistent ways, supporting its construct validity. These variables include, but are by no means limited to, intergenerational patterns of violence; risk factors such as poverty, unemployment, financial, or power discrepancies between spouses; age, stress, isolation, and heavy alcohol use; physical and mental health problems in women victims; low self-esteem in physically abused men; and high conflict (Straus, 1990a, pp. 70–71).

Factor analysis by Straus (1979) as well as other investigators (Barling et al., 1987; Hornung, Mc Cullough, & Sugimoto, 1981; Jorgensen, 1977) has also lent support to the factorial validity of the CTS by generally supporting the presence of three distinct dimensions of conflict tactics, consistent with Straus's (1979) original theoretical conceptualization. Straus (1979) and Hornung et al. (1981) identified a fourth factor representing extreme physical violence.

Agreement between partners on the CTS has ranged from strong to weak and is best summarized as moderate (see chap. 2, this volume). Additionally, violence rates obtained from the CTS are comparable with those obtained using in-depth interviews (Gelles, 1974) and reflect high rates of verbally and physically aggressive acts despite their lack of social desirability.

Advantages

The scale is brief and simple and can be administered by paper-and-pencil or interview format. Thus, the scale can be easily used as part of a research battery or as a clinical screening or treatment evaluation measure. A variety of scoring methods provide flexibility in data-analytic techniques applied to scale scores. The widespread use of the CTS and the availability of norms facilitate comparisons across studies. In addition, the reporting on behaviors of self and partner facilitates examination of interpartner agreement of aggressive behaviors.

Because the scale measures concrete acts, the likelihood of distorted responding due to idiosyncratic interpretation of items is reduced (i.e., "slap" and "kick" are less prone to variable interpretation than "aggression" or "abuse"). Although the fixed response categories may lead to loss of specificity of information compared with open-ended interviews, the checklist format tends to trigger memories of specific events that might have otherwise been forgotten (Straus, 1990a). Despite the inclusion of socially undesirable acts on the CTS, defensiveness in responding may be reduced by the fact that (a) the instructions normalize conflict in relationships and acknowledge a range of methods for handling conflict; (b) items are presented hierarchically, from least to most coercive and violent, allowing the respondent to first indicate the more socially acceptable means of resolving conflict he or she has tried; and (c) this sequence nearly legitimizes acts of aggression, because respondents are able to present violence as a last resort, having tried nearly all other available methods of resolving the conflict.

Limitations

The primary limitation of the original CTS is that it provides only topographical data on violence without consideration of impact, injury, power differentials, meaning, or context. It may thus present a misleading picture of aggression in a given sample and is not sensitive to gender differences in victimization. However, the author stresses that the scale may be used in conjunction with such measures of interest (Straus, 1990a). Additional limitations include the fact that the Reasoning scale may be a misnomer, for although it reflects civil approaches to resolving conflict, it does not include central forms of reasoning in resolving conflict such as constructively outlining all of the issues or active problem solving (Straus, 1979). This subscale offers limited utility and low internal consistency reliability. Also, the CTS does not indicate the extent to which conflict gets resolved through use of the various tactics. Also, its 1-year referent period for reporting may lead to recall error (although for the assessment of low base-rate behaviors such as specific acts of violence, a shorter time period would produce data with even greater skew). Further, the strength of the scale's brevity poses a limitation in its content validity (i.e., the adequate sampling of the universe of behaviors constituting verbal reasoning, verbal aggression, and violence). Finally, the instructions orienting respondents to acts during conflict may lead to underreporting of verbally or physically aggressive behaviors that were not provoked by conflict.

Primary Scale Reference

Straus (1979).

Scale Availability

> Measurement Research Program of the Family Research Laboratory
> University of New Hampshire
> Durham, NH 03824

Related References

Archer (1999); Gelles and Straus (1988); Straus (1990a, 1990b, 1995); Straus and Gelles (1986); Straus, Gelles, and Steinmetz (1980).

General Comments and Recommendations for Researchers and Practitioners

The CTS is the most widely used scale to measure violence within intimate relationships. Its brevity and simplicity make it an ideal measure for survey/epidemiological research, as well as a practical tool for use in clinical practice. Although the original national prevalence surveys using the CTS relied on data from married couples, the measure has been used to measure violence toward partners in cohabitating or dating relationships as well. In addition to asking respondents to report on their own or on their partner's behavior, one can obtain data on partner violence by asking adolescents to report on their parents' behavior. The scale can be easily adapted to measure the occurrence of violence in a variety of role relationships (e.g., sibling to sibling, child to parent) and may be administered using paper-and-pencil, face-to-face interview, or telephone interview formats.

Note that the Verbal Aggression scale contains two items that Straus (1979) termed *symbolic aggression*: "stomping out of the room or house or yard" and "threw or smashed or hit or kicked something." Straus classified these items as part of the Verbal Aggression scale because they reflected neither reasoning nor physical violence directed at another person, and because factor analysis supported their placement on this scale (Straus, 1979).

Despite the controversy surrounding use of this scale, it has no doubt proved valuable in (a) bringing public attention to the issue of domestic violence (e.g., Straus et al., 1980); (b) providing a forum for direct questioning about aggression in clinical settings, where otherwise it might be missed (Ehrensaft & Vivian, 1996; O'Leary et al., 1992); and (c) fueling an ongoing discussion, and resulting evolution, of measurement methods in spouse abuse (e.g., Fals-Stewart et al., 2003; Marshall, 1992a, 1992b; Straus, Hamby, Boney-McCoy, & Sugarman, 1996; Tolman, 1989; Vivian, 1990a, 1990b).

---

15. Adapted Conflict Tactics Scale (ACTS; Vivian)

Description and Development of Assessment Method

The ACTS is a 29-item self-report questionnaire expanded from the CTS (Straus, 1979) and the Modified Conflict Tactics Scale (MCTS; Neidig & Friedman, 1984; Pan, Neidig, & O'Leary, 1994a). The instrument assesses the frequency that either a spouse or his or her partner has engaged in a variety of conflict tactics in the year prior to assessment, as well as the impact, attributions of blame, and injuries resulting from aggressive acts.

The ACTS was developed based on expanding and modifying the CTS (Straus, 1979) to include functional/contextual assessment of partner violence.

Target Population

Male or female partners.

Format

Conflict tactics are measured with four scales: Communication-Based Conflict Tactics (positive, Items 1–7; negative, Items 8–10), Psychological Abuse

(Items 11–18), Mild Aggression (Items 19–22), and Severe Aggression (Items 23–29). In addition, impact on self, partner, and relationship for all three forms of aggression (psychological, mild physical, and severe physical); the degree to which respondents assign blame for these behaviors for self and partner; and injury reports of both self and partner are also assessed. Sample items from the ACTS follow:

1. *Communication Items*
   Positive:

   - "Listened to your partner's side of a problem/disagreement"
   - "Made an effort to compromise"

   Negative:

   - "Insulted or sworn at your partner"
   - "Criticized your partner in an unhelpful way"

2. *Psychological Abuse*

   - "Threatened to withhold money, have an affair, etc."
   - "Driven recklessly to frighten partner"

3. *Mild Aggression*

   - "Pushing, grabbing, or shoving"
   - "Throwing something"

4. *Severe Aggression*

   - "Kicking, biting, or hitting with a fist"
   - "Choking or strangling"

5. *Injury Ratings*

   - 1 = *no injury*
   - 2 = *superficial bruises, cuts, or abrasions (mild)*[7]
   - 3 = *nonsuperficial cuts or abrasions (moderate)*
   - 4 = *broken bones, broken teeth, or injuries to sensory organs (severe)*
   - 5 = *internal injuries or concussions (extreme)*
   - 6 = *other (please explain)*

---

7. Qualifiers such as *mild* and *moderate* following injury categories are for the scoring/categorization purposes of the test administrator only and do not appear on the ACTS.

Administration and Scoring

The instrument takes 10 to 15 minutes to complete. Items are rated using a Likert scale with 0 = *never*, 1 = *once*, 2 = *twice*, 3 = *3 to 5 times*, 4 = *6 to 10 times*, 5 = *11 to 20 times*, and 6 = *more than 20 times*. For scoring, the frequency of each conflict tactic on the 0–6 scale can be summed within each scale (e.g., to obtain a total score for any physical aggression, the scoring would range from 0 to 66, Items 19–29) or dichotomized as to the presence or absence of violence. As physical aggression items are essentially ranked in increasing order of severity (i.e., Guttman-scaled), one could also apply a value ranging from 1 to 11 to each of the violent acts in sequence. Respondents would then receive a 1–11 severity index score based on the value of the most violent act endorsed (Vivian & Langhinrichsen-Rohling, 1994).

In addition, impact ratings on self, partner, and relationship for all three forms of aggression (psychological, mild physical, and severe physical) are obtained using a 7-point Likert scale ranging from 1 (*extremely negative impact*) to 7 (*extremely positive impact*). Impact ratings can be summed across scales or considered separately for the three aggression scales. Or, as Vivian and Langhinrichsen-Rohling (1994) justified based on obtaining high correlations between impact ratings of mild and severe physical aggression, impact ratings across these two dimensions can be averaged for a single physical aggression impact rating.

The degree to which respondents assign blame for these behaviors is assessed using a 7-point Likert scale for self (1 = *I totally blame myself* to 7 = *I don't blame myself at all*) and partner (1 = *I totally blame my partner* to 7 = *I don't blame my partner at all*). Finally, injury reports of both self and partner from mildly or severely aggressive acts are rated in terms of five dichotomous (yes/no) categories. Injury categories can be described in terms of percentages of occurrence of each category of injury for the sample as a whole; injuries can be weighted and summed across injury categories to form an injury index (0 = *no injury*, 1 = *mild injury*, 5 = *moderate injury*, 10 = *severe injury*, and 15 = *extreme injury*; Cascardi et al., 1992); or injuries can be scored by assigning the respondent a 1–5 rating based on the Guttman-scaled injury list (i.e., the highest rated category can be assigned because it is presumed that each successively higher rated category reflects the occurrence of injuries in lower rated categories). Injury response choice 6, *other (please explain)*, can be coded by the examiner into one of the other five response categories or as a dichotomous code indicating the presence or absence of violence, depending on scoring approach used.

Psychometric Evaluation

Norms

Not reported.

Reliability

Alpha, calculated only on the 11 violence items, was .83 in a sample of couples seeking treatment in a marital therapy clinic. Interspousal agreement on reports of husband's physical violence in the clinic population yielded the following kappas: absence of husband's violence, $\kappa = .61$; husband's moderate violence, $\kappa = .21$; and husband's severe violence, $\kappa = .46$.

Validity

Construct validity has been supported by the scale's relationship with a number of conceptually linked variables (Boyle & Vivian, 1996; Cascardi et al., 1992; Langhinrichsen-Rohling & Vivian, 1994; Vivian & Langhinrichsen-Rohling, 1994), its sensitivity to gender differences (Vivian & Langhinrichsen-Rohling, 1994), as well as its ability to obtain high self-reported rates of aggression in a clinical sample (Ehrensaft & Vivian, 1996).

Advantages

The ACTS addresses some shortcomings of the CTS by assessing dimensions of partner aggression deemed of critical importance in interpreting topographical ratings of violence: injury and impact of violence. The measure retains a relatively simply format for administration and scoring, making it highly practical for both research and clinical use.

Limitations

The first 10 items, forming the Communication scale, appear somewhat internally inconsistent, with some items reflecting positive communication tactics and others reflecting negative communication tactics. The author has not reported data on the communication scale, and the meaning and utility of this initial scale is questionable, except perhaps as providing the respondent with the chance to present socially desirable behaviors first (see Straus, 1979). Evidence of reliability of the ACTS has been limited.

Primary Scale Reference

Vivian (1990a).

Scale Availability

> Department of Psychology
> The University at Stony Brook
> State University of New York
> Stony Brook, NY 11794-2500

Related References

Boyle and Vivian (1996); Cascardi, Langhinrichsen, and Vivian (1992); Vivian and Langhinrichsen-Rohling (1994).

General Comments and Recommendations for Researchers and Practitioners

The ACTS retains many of the advantages of the original CTS in providing a relatively brief self-report format for assessing the presence and frequency of specific acts of aggression toward a partner. In addition, the measure improves on the CTS by including "global assessments of the psychological impact of aggression/victimization on self, partner, and relationship, degree of self and partner blame, and types of injury sustained" (Vivian & Langhinrichsen-Rohling, 1994, p. 111). This adaptation of the CTS may prove especially useful for identifying a subgroup of aggressive couples, those with bidirectional, low level, low frequency, mildly negative impact, and negligible injury, for whom conjoint treatment might be most appropriate (see Vivian & Heyman, 1996).

---

16. The Modified Conflict Tactics Scale (MCTS; Pan, Neidig, & O'Leary)

Description and Development of Assessment Method

The MCTS is a 23-item version of the CTS, with additional psychological and physical aggression items and with a factor structure supporting the differentiation between mild and severe forms of physical aggression.

Six items were added to and one was deleted from the CTS to provide greater content validity, balance the number of items reflecting each conceptual domain, and reduce redundancy. Factor analysis was conducted on a large military sample ($N = 6,917$ men and 779 women) and cross-validated on a different military sample ($N = 3,596$ men and 425 women) to determine

(a) whether the conceptual distinctions of psychological aggression, mild physical aggression, and severe physical aggression would be supported, and (b) whether gender differences in factor structure would emerge. Both male and female respondents reported on their own and on their partner's behavior. As predicted, for three of the four target groups (men reporting on own behavior, men reporting on wives' behavior, and women reporting on their own behavior), three interpretable factors emerged: psychological aggression, mild physical aggression, and severe physical aggression. However, an interesting gender difference appeared: For women reporting on their husbands' behavior, only two factors emerged—psychological aggression and physical aggression—with so-designated mild and severe acts of aggression loading onto a single factor.[8] There were also slight gender differences in individual item loadings on scales (see Pan, Neidig, & O'Leary, 1994a).

Target Population

Individuals in intimate relationships.

Format

This scale contains four new psychologically aggressive acts concerning threats, withholding affection, and driving recklessly, and two new physically aggressive acts concerning physically controlling the spouse and forcing sex. These items were added both because of their prominence in interviews with couples about marital conflicts and because "they balanced the number of items conceptually related to the domains of psychologically coercive, mildly physically coercive, and severely physically coercive tactics" (Pan et al., 1994a, p. 370). An additional item (choked or strangled spouse) from the 1986 version of the scale (Form R) was retained. Finally, one item (hit or tried to hit with something) was deleted because of its overlap with another item (kicked, bit, or hit with a fist). Scales[9] and sample items follow:

1. *Psychological Aggression (Items 3–9)*

   - "Refused to give affection or sex to spouse"
   - "Threatened to leave the marriage"

---

8. Items 22 and 23, asking about threatening with or using a knife or gun, did not load on this physical aggression factor but emerged as an uninterpretable factor.
9. Item numbers not listed as falling on particular scales failed to load on particular factors.

2. *Mild Physical Aggression (Items 11–13 and 15–17)*

   - "Controlled spouse physically"
   - "Pushed, grabbed, and shoved"

3. *Severe Physical Aggression (Items 19–23)*

   - "Beat up"
   - "Used a knife or gun"

Administration and Scoring

The scale takes 5–10 minutes to complete. Respondents are asked about conflict tactics used within the past year. Responses are keyed according to a 5-point Likert scale ranging from 0 (*never*) to 4 (*more than seven times*). Scoring can be done by summing item totals for each scale or by assigning dichotomous values (1 and 0) to each item for the presence or absence of violence and obtaining sample frequency rates per act, per domain (i.e., psychological, mild physical, and severe physical abuse), or of the presence or absence of any violence.

Psychometric Evaluation

Norms
Not reported.

Reliability
For men reporting on their own behavior, Cronbach's alphas were .80 for psychological aggression, .87 for mild physical aggression, and .91 for severe physical aggression. For women reporting on their own behavior, Cronbach's alphas were .83 for psychological aggression, .90 for mild physical aggression, and .87 for severe physical aggression. For women reporting on their male partners, Cronbach's alphas were .84 for psychological aggression and .93 for severe physical aggression. For men reporting on their female partners, Cronbach's alphas were .84 for psychological aggression, .92 for mild physical aggression, and .86 for severe physical aggression.

Validity
Factor structure supports the construct validity of three distinct domains of aggression (psychological, mild physical, and severe physical) for men and women as perpetrators and men as recipients, and for two domains of aggression (psychological and physical) for women as recipients. Construct

validity was further supported by the finding that mild and severe aggression scales on the MCTS were related in theoretically consistent ways with a number of variables, including being younger, earning less, having a drug or alcohol problem, experiencing marital discord, and reporting depressive symptomatology (Pan, Neidig, & O'Leary, 1994b). Finally, most of the items are from the original scale and have received previous evidence of validation (Straus, 1979, 1990a, 1990b).

Advantages

Factor analysis of scale groupings was conducted on an extremely large sample and yielded meaningful scales concerning three dimensions of partner-directed aggression (psychological, mild physical, and severe physical) for men as victims and men and women's reports on their own behavior. Scale data also highlighted interesting gender differences in the perpetration and perception of aggression.

Limitations

Factor structure on this modification was obtained on a military sample, which may have limited generalizability.

Primary Scale Reference

Pan, Neidig, and O'Leary (1994a).

Scale Availability

> Department of Psychology
> The University at Stony Brook
> State University of New York
> Stony Brook, NY 11794-2500

Related References

Neidig and Friedman (1984); Pan Neidig, and O'Leary (1994b).

General Comments and Recommendations for Researchers and Practitioners

The finding that women reporting on their husband's aggression did not yield distinct factors for mild and severe aggression may "well be a reflection that all kinds of physical attacks from a husband are salient and similar to women" (Pan et al., 1994a, p. 379) or may suggest that marital aggression toward women commonly occurs in a variety of forms, including both mild and severe acts.

---

17. The Revised Conflict Tactics Scales (CTS2; Straus, Hamby, Boney-McCoy, & Sugarman)

Description and Development of Assessment Method

Based on the original CTS (Straus, 1979), the 39-item CTS2 includes more items, two additional scales, interspersed (rather than hierarchical) item ordering, and improved wording. Like the CTS, the instrument contains a list of tactics one might use while engaged in a conflict with a partner.

The authors revised the CTS2 based on a review of the critiques and adaptations of the original CTS, as well as examination of each item of the CTS (and items on modifications of the CTS by other authors) for ambiguity, redundancy, and universality. Items on the Injury scale are based on items included in the 1985 National Family Violence Survey. Once arriving at a revised item pool, the authors pretested the items on 97 undergraduates with solicitations for detailed comments and feedback on each item. This resulted in a 60-item pool, which were ordered according to a random numbers program, and then slightly reordered to move additional severe aggression items closer to the end of the scale. This item pool was administered to a sample of college students ($N = 317$ for all analyses). Items were retained on the basis of statistical (e.g., enhancement of internal consistency reliability) and conceptual criteria (see Straus, Hamby, Boney-McCoy, & Sugarman, 1996, for details).

Target Population

Individuals in marital, cohabiting, or dating relationships. Written for a 6th-grade reading level.

Format

The CTS2 contains five scales: Negotiation (6 items; formerly the Reasoning scale), Psychological Aggression (8 items; formerly the Verbal Aggression scale), Physical Assault (12 items; formerly the Violence scale), Injury (6 items; new scale), and Sexual Coercion (7 items; new scale). Sample items follow:

1. *Negotiation*

   Contains items reflecting attempts to discuss or otherwise noncoercively resolve conflict. The scale contains *cognitive* (reflecting attempts to settle the disagreement) and *emotional* (reflecting a positive emotional tone in the discussion) negotiation items. All items on this scale are new.

   - Cognitive negotiation: "Explained my side of a disagreement to a partner."
   - Emotional negotiation: "I showed my partner I cared even though we disagreed."

2. *Psychological Aggression*

   Contains items that reflect verbally or emotionally hurtful acts toward a partner. Four of the original six items are retained and four are new.

   - Minor psychological aggression: "Shouted or yelled at my partner."
   - Severe psychological aggression: "Destroyed something belonging to my partner."

3. *Physical Assault*

   Contains items reflecting physical aggression directed at the partner. All original violent acts are retained (some with modifications), and there a three new items.

   - Minor physical assault: "Grabbed my partner."
   - Severe physical assault: "Punched or hit my partner with something that could hurt."

4. *Sexual Coercion*

   Contains items reflecting psychologically or physically coercing partner into unwanted sexual activity.

   - Minor sexual coercion: "Insisted on sex when my partner did not want to (but did not use physical force)."
   - Severe sexual coercion: "Used force (like hitting, holding down, or using a weapon) to make my partner have sex."

5. *Injury*

Contains items reflecting various levels of injury resulting from physical assault or sexual coercion.

- Minor injury: "Felt physical pain that still hurt the next day because of a fight with my partner."
- Severe injury: "Went to a doctor because of a fight with my partner."

Administration and Scoring

When one is obtaining data from both partners, the authors recommend using the higher of the two obtained scores. Use of all 78 questions (39 items asked about both self and partner) of the scale takes about 10–15 minutes to complete. Use of only the three original scales takes 7–10 minutes. Instructions typically ask about the previous year but can be modified.

Scoring is done by summing midpoints of each response category, 1–6. Straus et al. (1996) recommend scoring 0 for *never*, 1 for *once*, 2 for *twice*, 4 for *3–5 times*, 8 for *6–10 times*, 15 for *11–20 times*, and *25 for more than 20 times*. Using this method, a chronicity variable can be obtained (i.e., frequency of occurrence of acts on a given scale within a specified time period). For responses indicating that violence occurred not in the specified time period but at some time in the past (i.e., an affirmative response to *ever*, or response category 7), score 0 if the particular time period is of primary interest. The alternative is to score a 1 (i.e., *yes*) for any affirmative response to response categories 1–7 (i.e., any violence in the relationship) to obtain overall prevalence rates of violence within a sample.

When administering the measure, it is also possible to substitute categories of *never, sometimes, frequently,* and so on for the specific numerical ranges. This is useful for comparing data across changing time frames (e.g., over the past year and then every 6 months following a treatment program). However, precision of measurement is sacrificed; this method does not allow for frequency calculations, and words such as *often* may be interpreted idiosyncratically (Straus et al., 1996).

Psychometric Evaluation

Norms
Not reported.

Reliability

Internal consistency reliability for all scales was high in a college student sample (self-report of tactics used toward partner): for Negotiation, $\alpha = .86$; for Psychological Aggression, $\alpha = .79$; for Physical Assault, $\alpha = .86$; for Sexual Coercion, $\alpha = .87$; and for Injury, $\alpha = .95$ (Straus et al., 1996).

Validity

The authors present initial construct validity of the CTS2 based on correlations between variables predicted to be, or not to be, associated (i.e., convergent and discriminant validity; D. T. Campbell & Fiske, 1959). These include a higher correlation between psychological aggression and physical assault for men than for women, a higher correlation between engaging in physical assault and causing injury for men than for women, and a high correlation between psychological aggression and physical assault for men and women (Straus et al., 1996). The authors report a low correlation, as expected, between two sets of theoretically unrelated variables: negotiation and sexual coercion, and negotiation and injury (Straus et al., 1996). Although one partner reports on the behavior of both partners, the authors recommend administering the scale to both partners and using data of each.

Advantages

The interspersed item order, while sacrificing the advantages of the hierarchical item order in the original CTS (see above), reduces response sets, enhances careful reading of each item, reduces the ability to detect which items fall on which subscale, and may yield higher prevalence rates (Dahlstrom, Brooks, & Peterson, 1990; see Straus et al., 1996). The two additional scales provide information on critical aspects of partner violence (i.e., injury and sexual coercion), and the negotiation scale (formerly the reasoning scale) contains all new items and enhanced relevance. Greater scale length improves reliability and content validity. The scale also has the advantages of more specific and clear item wording, a simplified self-report format, and distinctions between minor and severe psychologically and physically aggressive acts.

Limitations

Psychometrics to date are derived from college student sample and may have limited generalizability to clinical samples. The CTS2 does not yet have the extensive research backing of the original CTS, which has national norms and established psychometric properties. The scale is slightly longer to administer and score than the original CTS.

Primary Scale Reference

Straus, Hamby, Boney-McCoy, and Sugarman (1996).

Scale Availability

> Measurement Research Program
> Family Research Laboratory
> University of New Hampshire
> Durham, NH 03824

Related References

Holtzworth-Munroe, Meehan, Herron, Rehman, and Stuart (2000).

General Comments and Recommendations for Researchers and Practitioners

The CTS2 contains the following changes: (a) It provides two new scales, an injury scale and a sexual coercion scale; (b) it adds items to each scale to increase content validity and reliability (by increasing the number of observations); (c) it improves item wording (i.e., *my partner* replaces *him/her,* unclear items were reworded or replaced); (d) it improves the operationalization of minor and severe violence levels; (e) it extends the distinction between minor and severe to the scales of psychological aggression, sexual coercion, and injury; (f) it contains a format that enhances clarity of the questions in its paper-and-pencil format (rather than two columns of response categories, one for the participant's acts toward the partner and one for the partner's acts, each question is stated twice, first in reference to the participant's behavior and then for the partner's behavior); and (g) it contains an interspersed order of items (Straus et al., 1996).

---

18. Emotional Abuse Scale (EAS; Murphy & Hoover)

Description and Development of Assessment Method

The EAS is a 4-factor scale assessing emotional abuse in dating relationships. An initial 34-item set representing a 4-factor model of abuse (i.e., Hostile Withdrawal, Dominance/Intimidation, Denigration, and Restrictive Engulfment) based on extensive literature reviews and appropriateness to dating relationships was constructed and administered to college students in dating relationships. Items were discarded on the basis of low response frequency, low item–scale correlations, or item–scale correlations with a poor ability to discriminate among scales. Additional items were generated based on the first author's (Murphy's) clinical experience with domestic abuse as well as discussions with students in dating relationships about the four types of behavior included in the model. The scale was administered to 157 female college students in dating relationships reporting on their own and on their partners' behavior, along with other scales to evaluate convergent and discriminant validity. A principal-components analysis was conducted to confirm the 4-factor model on these female students' reports of only their partners' behaviors. Results generally supported the 4-factor model, and items were thus retained as originally rationally assigned.

Target Population

Female college students in dating relationships. Could also be used with male or female respondents in any intimate relationship.

Format

This 54-item scale contains four subscales assessing Hostile Withdrawal (coldly and punitively withdrawing from the partner during conflict), Dominance/Intimidation (using verbal aggression, threats, and property damage to coercively dominate a partner), Denigration (attacking the partner's self-esteem in ways designed to humiliate and degrade), and Restrictive Engulfment (tracking and monitoring the partner's whereabouts and restricting activities potentially threatening to the relationship). Sample items follow:

1. *Hostile Withdrawal (9 items)*

   - "Sulked or refused to talk about the issue"
   - "Acted cold or distant when angry"

2. *Dominance/Intimidation (15 items)*

   - "Threatened to throw something at partner"
   - "Intentionally destroyed belongings"

3. *Denigration (17 items)*

   - "Said that partner would never amount to anything"
   - "Called partner worthless"

4. *Restrictive Engulfment (13 items)*

- "Asked where she/he had been or who she/he had been with in a suspicious manner"
- "Tried to make partner feel guilty for not spending time together"

Administration and Scoring

The scale takes about 10–15 minutes to complete. Respondents are asked to indicate how often both they and their partner engaged in each behavior over the previous 4-month period on the following 7-point frequency scale: *never, once, twice, 3–5 times, 6–10 times, 11–20 times,* and *more than 20 times.* Items are summed to arrive at scale scores and a total score.

Psychometric Evaluation

Norms
Not reported.

Reliability
Coefficient alphas for reports of abusive behaviors by self and partner, respectively, were .88 and .91 (Hostile Withdrawal), .83 and .91 (Dominance/Intimidation), .89 and .92 (Denigration), and .84 and .85 (Restrictive Engulfment).

Validity
Convergent validity was supported by the following findings: All of the scales of abuse by self and partner were significantly correlated with physical aggression perpetrated by self and partner, respectively (with particularly strong associations between the Dominance/Intimidation and Denigration scales with physical aggression); the Restrictive Engulfment (abuse by self) scale was significantly correlated with scales measuring anxious/insecure attachment (proximity seeking, separation protest, and feared loss); and all scales assessing abuse by self were significantly correlated with domineering, vindictive, and intrusive interpersonal behavior. Discriminant validity was supported by the lack of any abuse by self scales' correlations with overly nurturant, exploitable, nonassertive, and socially avoidant interpersonal behavior, indicating that emotionally abusive behavior related to controlling (i.e., domineering, vindictive, and intrusive) rather than passive interpersonal behavior styles.

Discriminant validity was also somewhat supported by the scales' modest or nonsignificant correlations with social desirability: For reports of abuse by self, all four scales were modestly but significantly correlated with social desirability characterized by impression management (deliberate public presentations of inflated self-descriptions), and the Restrictive Engulfment scale was modestly but significantly correlated with social desirability characterized by self-deception (i.e., honest but inflated descriptions of the self). For reports of abuse by partner, only the Hostile Withdrawal scale was correlated with social desirability, with modest but significant correlations with impression management and self-deception.

Advantages

The multifactorial model assesses a broad domain of emotional abuse. Yet, unlike some scales of emotional abuse, the EAS contains no items pertaining directly to emotionally abusive aspects of physical abuse (e.g., blaming partner for physical violence) and thus is appropriate for use in relationships in which there is no physical aggression. The scale evidences good initial psychometric properties.

Limitations

The four rationally derived scales were only partially supported by factor analysis, and the scale development and validation sample excluded males.

Primary Scale Reference

Murphy and Hoover (1999).

Scale Availability

Christopher M. Murphy
Department of Psychology
University of Maryland Baltimore County
1000 Hilltop Circle
Baltimore, MD 21250

Related References

Murphy and Cascardi (1999).

General Comments and Recommendations for Researchers and Practitioners

The scale permits further work in an area characterized by little research, namely, emotional abuse in dating relationships. Such work may allow for further understanding of developmental processes associated with relation-ship violence and for detection of couples at risk for physical aggression (Murphy & Hoover, 1999). The authors report that further work is under way to explore the scale's factor structure with male participants. This scale is highly practical for both research and clinical settings.

19. Index of Spouse Abuse (ISA; Hudson & McIntosh)

Description and Development of Assessment Method

This 30-item scale measures the severity of physical and nonphysical abuse a woman has received from a partner. The scale was administered to 398 graduate and undergraduate students. A principal-components analysis with varimax rotation was conducted to confirm the two hypothesized dimensions of spouse abuse (physical and nonphysical). Several items were assigned on an a priori basis the designation of physical or nonphysical abuse items; others, for which the distinction was not as clear, would be assigned on the basis of factor loadings. Items from a marital satisfaction measure were included in the analysis in an attempt to confirm, through factor loadings, that the ISA was not merely measuring marital discord. The analysis pro-duced three rotated factors with eigenvalues greater than 1, with all of the marital satisfaction items loading most highly, and none of the ISA items loading most highly, on the first factor. The predesignated items loaded on distinct factors of physical and nonphysical abuse, and the remaining items were assigned to these scales on the basis of factor loadings (with the exception of Items 11 and 19, which loaded slightly higher on physical abuse but were classified as nonphysical abuse item based on item content not reflecting physical aggression).

Next, a sample of 188 graduate and undergraduate students and faculty members rated each item for perceived severity (see Hudson & McIntosh, 1981, for details of this procedure) for weighting purposes. Finally, the scale was administered to women recruited from social agencies, 64 of whom were victims of partner abuse (largely residing in shelters) and 43 of whom were not victims of partner abuse, for determining the reliability and validity of the ISA as well as cutoff scores for abusiveness on each scale.

Target Population

Individuals in intimate relationships, particularly known abusive relationships.

Format

Respondents fill out a 1–5 Likert scale ranging from *never* to *very frequently*. Sample scale items follow:

1. *Physical Abuse (11 items)*

   - "My partner punches me with his fists."
   - "My partner becomes surly and angry if I tell him he is drinking too much."
   - "My partner frightens me."

2. *Nonphysical Abuse (19 items)*

   - "My partner belittles me."
   - "My partner has no respect for my feelings."
   - "My partner feels that I should not work or go to school."

Administration and Scoring

The ISA takes about 5 minutes to complete and yields two total scores: a physical abuse severity score and a nonphysical abuse severity score. Each of these scales ranges from 1 to 100, with higher scores representing greater levels of abusiveness. Items are weighted according to severity; a weighted scoring procedure is detailed in the primary reference. Clinical cutoffs that minimize the number of false positives and false negatives were found to be a score of 10 on the physical abuse scale and 25 on the nonphysical abuse scale.

Psychometric Evaluation

Norms

Mean physical and nonphysical abuse scale scores in a sample of abused women were 45.2 and 58.9, respectively. In contrast, mean physical and nonphysical abuse scale scores in nonabused women were 3.8 and 8.3, respectively.

Reliability

Internal consistency of each of the two subscales was high: In a sample of 398 students, alphas were .90 for the physical and .91 for the nonphysical abuse scales. In a sample of 107 women recruited from social agencies, alphas were .94 and .97, respectively. The standard error of measurement was reported as 3.68 for the physical abuse subscale and 3.30 for the nonphysical abuse subscale, indicating little measurement error.

Validity

Known groups validity was examined by comparing scores on the ISA between 64 abused and 43 nonabused women; the scales strongly discriminated these two groups. Convergent validity was demonstrated with high correlations between the two ISA scales and abuse status, and moderate correlations between ISA scales and measures of self-esteem, marital problems, sexual relationship problems, and symptoms such as fearfulness, anxiety, and unhappiness. Discriminant validity was demonstrated with low correlations between ISA scales and measures of difficulties at work and in relationships with one's family and friends independent of the marital relationship, constructs predicted to have little relation with spouse abuse.

Advantages

The ISA has strong psychometric characteristics. Its items have objective weighting criteria that enhance the discrimination between acts of more severe and less severe abuse based on scale scores. It provides relatively thorough assessment of psychological abuse. The ISA is also one of the rare instruments that has psychometric data available on a population of color (see D. W. Campbell et al., 1994; Kaslow et al., 1998; Kaslow et al., 2002).

Limitations

As the abused women were largely from shelters, the scale's properties may have restricted generalizability to severely abused women. Further, because many items were assigned to scales on the basis of factor loadings, about half of the items on the physical abuse subscale do not directly assess acts of physical aggression. Thus, despite the scale's ability to discriminate between abused and nonabused women, the actual construct measured with this scale is not entirely clear. Item content on this subscale seems to reflect bullying, control, and intimidation, in addition to violence. The content validity of the scale as a measure of physical abuse is highly limited, with only a handful of violent acts sampled. Also, the weighted scoring procedure detailed in the primary reference is rather complex.

Primary Scale Reference

Hudson and McIntosh (1981).

Scale Availability

The scale is reprinted in the primary reference. Professionally printed copies of the scale, computerized scoring packages, and related measures by the same author are available through:

Walmyr Publishing Co.
P.O. Box 24779
Tempe, AZ 85285-4779
Phone: (602) 897-1040, Fax: (602) 897-8168
E-mail: walmyr@Indirect.com

Related References

D. W. Campbell, Campbell, King, Parker, and Ryan (1994); Kaslow, Thompson, Meadows, Jacobs, Chance, Gibb, Bornstein, Hollins, Rashid, and Phillips (1998); Kaslow, Thompson, Okun, Price, Young, Bender, Wyckoff, Twomey, Goldin, and Parker (2002).

General Comments and Recommendations for Researchers and Practitioners

The ISA is a psychometrically sound instrument that is brief and easy for respondents to fill out, although somewhat cumbersome to score. A relative weakness of the ISA may also be thought of as a relative strength: Its lack of unambiguous measurement of physical violence on the physical abuse subscale makes it a rather comprehensive scale for measuring psychological forms of abuse, an aspect that is less well-developed on some of the other violence scales (such as the CTS [Straus, 1979] or the Severity of Violence Against Women Scales [Marshall, 1992a]). The response format geared toward female respondents only limits the scale's use to settings in which only the woman's report is needed and precludes interpartner comparisons.

---

20. Measure of Wife Abuse (MWA; Rodenburg & Fantuzzo)

Description and Development of Assessment Method

The MWA is a 60-item self-report scale measuring the frequency and severity of physical, sexual, psychological, and verbal abuse from a partner. The initial item pool was constructed from three sources: behaviors listed in restraining orders filed by women receiving treatment in a domestic abuse program, clinical case reports, and directors of battered women's shelters. Two raters (with 96% interrater agreement) then eliminated items on the basis of bizarre or unlikely content. Five raters then sorted the remaining items into categories of physical, psychological, and verbal abuse, eliminating items that did not attain 80% interrater agreement. Four professionals in the field of domestic violence then sorted the items into a maximum of five categories, labeling each and determining the 10 items that were most representative of each. Then, based on interrater agreement and items chosen to best represent their categories, 15 items were selected for each of four final abuse scales: physical, sexual, psychological, and verbal. The items were also worded to be gender-neutral.

Items were administered to 164 women in physically abusive relationships recruited from a shelter, an outpatient clinic, and newspaper ads. A confirmatory multiple-group factor analysis was used to examine item correlations with scales. Most items loaded most heavily, and exclusively, on the expected factors.

Target Population

Individuals in current abusive intimate relationships or individuals not currently in relationships reporting on abuse from a past relationship.

Format

The physical abuse subscale depicts direct acts, rather than threats, of physical aggression, ranging in severity from "pushed" to "shot with a gun." The sexual abuse subscale depicts varied graphic acts of sexual aggression that include rape as well as other degrading and terrorizing sexual acts. The psychological abuse subscale contains items related to isolating, dominating, harassing, and stalking. The verbal abuse subscale contains items consisting of verbal insults, degradations, and threats. Sample items follow:

1. *Physical Abuse*

   - "Your partner shook you"
   - "Your partner whipped you"

2. *Sexual Abuse*

   - "Your partner raped you"
   - "Your partner held you down and cut your pubic hair"

3. *Psychological Abuse*

- "Your partner kidnapped your children"
- "Your partner imprisoned you in the house"

4. *Verbal Abuse*

- "Your partner told you that no one would ever want you"
- "Your partner told you that you were stupid"

Administration and Scoring

Instructions ask respondents to indicate abuse received over the past 6 months (or the last 6 months of a relationship which has ended), rating both the frequency ("write in the number of times your partner did these actions to you") and impact, on a 4-point Likert scale from 1 = *this never hurt or upset me* to 4 = *this often hurt or upset me*. The scale takes between 10 and 15 minutes to complete.

Scores can be calculated in three ways: summing the frequency counts for each scale, summing the severity ratings for each scale, and summing the frequency-by-severity scores. The authors report scale development information based on severity ratings.

Psychometric Evaluation

Norms
Not reported.

Reliability
Alpha coefficients for the scales were as follows: physical abuse, .81; sexual abuse, .73; psychological abuse, .94; verbal abuse, .83; total MWA, .93, indicating good to excellent internal consistency.

Validity
Initial convergent validity was demonstrated with significant correlations between the MWA subscales and the verbal aggression and violence subscales of the CTS (Straus, 1979), as well as between total scores on the MWA and the CTS. Also, the factor structure of the MWA was supported in a sample of abused women.

Advantages

The inclusion of the sexual abuse subscale enhances the breadth of this wife abuse measure relative to most other abuse measures. The scale is comprehensive and includes many extremely abusive items that have been omitted from other scales and would prove useful when assessment of severe experiences of aggression is of interest.

Limitations

The scale is longer than many of the other wife abuse scales, and its graphic items and inclusion of several rarely occurring abusive events (e.g., "your partner forced you to have sex with animals") may induce a defensive response set. Additional validation work is needed to examine this measure's criterion and construct validity, in particular its relation to social desirability. Although the different scoring procedures provide useful information (i.e., frequency and impact ratings), the three scoring procedures may become cumbersome. Moreover, with open-ended ratings of frequency, the possibility of obtaining highly skewed distributions of scores exists.

Primary Scale Reference

Rodenburg and Fantuzzo (1993).

Scale Availability

The scale is reprinted in the primary reference.

Related References

None available.

General Comments and Recommendations for Researchers and Practitioners

The items on the MWA, overall, depict more severe acts of abuse than other measures, making the scale much more appropriate for use with known samples of abused women rather than population-based or even marital clinic samples. The somewhat graphic nature of the items may elicit a response bias; they also might prove disturbing to answer. The gender-neutral wording makes the scale usable for same-sex couples without needing to reword items. The inclusion of a sexual abuse subscale offers the assessment of an important aspect of partner abuse that is typically omitted from scales of this nature.

21. Past Feelings and Acts of Violence Scale (PFAV; Plutchik & van Praag)

Description and Development of Assessment Method

The PVAV is a brief self-report scale designed to measure violence risk. The items lend themselves to use in the assessment of batterer subtypes, and in particular capture features of the antisocial subtype (Holtzworth-Munroe & Stuart, 1994).

The scale was developed from the 36-item Feelings and Acts of Violence Scale (FAV; Plutchik, Climent, & Ervin, 1976). The 12 items with the highest item–total correlations as well as the most normal distributions were selected to comprise the PFAV. Validity data were gathered by administering the PFAV to psychiatric patients and college students.

Target Population

Male and female psychiatric inpatients and college students. Also well-suited for use with clinic or domestic violence agency samples of domestic violence perpetrators.

Format

This 12-item scale is a unitary scale assessing anger, use of violence, injuries caused as a result of violence, the use and possession of weapons, and history of being arrested.

Sample items:

- "Do you find that you get angry for no reason at all?"
- "Are weapons easily accessible to you?"

Sample items for classifying respondent as violent:

- "Have you ever hit or attacked a member of your family?"
- "Have you ever been arrested for a violent crime such as armed robbery or assault?"

Administration and Scoring

The scale takes less than 5 minutes to complete. The PFAV contains nine items filled out on a 4-point scale from *never* to *very often,* two items on a 4-point scale from *never* to *more than twice,* and one dichotomous item rated as *yes* or *no*. To score the measure, the 4-point scale items are weighted as 0, 1, 2, or 3; the dichotomous item is rated as 0 or 1. Items are then summed to arrive at a total score.

Psychometric Evaluation

Norms
A cutoff score of 5 correctly classifies violent and nonviolent patients approximately 71% of the time, whereas a cutoff score of 4 correctly classifies violent and nonviolent normal comparison group samples approximately 75% of the time.

Reliability
Coefficient alpha was .77 in a sample consisting of 100 psychiatric patients.

Validity
Construct validity was supported by the following findings: (a) In approximately two thirds of cases, there was agreement between classification on the PFAV as violent and hospital records reporting violence in 157 psychiatric inpatients; (b) there was a significantly higher proportion of psychiatric patients classified as violent on the PFAV than normals (i.e., a sample of 84 college students), and psychiatric patients also obtained significantly higher overall scores on the PFAV; scale items discriminated between violent patients and nonviolent normals.

Advantages
This is a brief, easy-to-administer and score instrument that assesses variables of importance in a variety of clinical and research contexts.

Limitations
Further psychometric work is needed, relating to test–retest reliability and convergent and discriminant, as well as criterion and predictive validity. In the validation work, the authors' selection of items to classify respondents as "violent" seems arbitrary; for example, they exclude a clear act of violence in their classification ("have you ever caused injury in a fight [for example, bruises, bleeding, or broken bones]?") and only count violence toward a member of the family as violent if the respondent also reports violence outside of the family. However, a researcher or clinician might develop his or her own criteria for violence classification and still find utility in the item content.

Primary Scale Reference

Plutchik and van Praag (1990).

Scale Availability

The primary reference contains the scale.

Related References

Plutchik, Climent, and Ervin (1976).

General Comments and Recommendations for Researchers and Practitioners

The authors acknowledge the inherent difficulties in predicting when a given individual might become violent but clarify their intention in developing the PFAV:

> it should be possible to say that individuals with a certain profile of characteristics have a certain probability of violent behaviors over a certain time period. From this point of view, a test for measuring violence risk is designed to identify a profile of characteristics that have a certain probability of being associated with violent acts over time. (Plutchik & van Praag, 1990, p. 454)

Although this measure was not developed for the domestic violence field, the scale might prove useful in this capacity for research on batterer subtypes (Holtzworth-Munroe & Stuart, 1994) and for identifying individuals in clinical samples who may have increased capacity for dangerousness.

---

22. Profile of Psychological Abuse and Fear of Abuse Scale (PPA and FAS; Sackett & Saunders)

Description and Development of Assessment Method

The PPA is a self-report scale measuring four types of psychological abuse from a partner. The supplemental FAS assesses fear of abuse from the partner.

Forty-two items for the PPA were constructed on the basis of the authors' clinical experience and literature on tactics of abusive men as well as the experiences of battered women to capture a broad array of psychologically abusive behaviors. Seven items were then deleted on the basis of ambiguous wording. Items were administered to 60 women who had sought help from a domestic violence agency, 30 of whom were currently residing in shelters and 30 of whom were seeking domestic violence counseling but not living in shelters. A principal-components analysis with varimax rotation on the remaining 35 items yielded five interpretable factors. However, one 6-item factor was eliminated because it contained behaviors that were not clearly abusive. To improve reliability of scales, 8 additional items were eliminated, leaving 21 items and four scales. A second factor analysis confirmed the factor structure, and thus this 21-item, 4-scale version was retained.

For the FAS, 14 items were written for the present study and administered to the same sample. Items were deleted based on item analysis and on selecting items that best captured the emotional impact of abuse from a partner, leaving 6 items.

Target Population

Individuals in abusive relationships.

Format

The PPA contains 21 items across four scales. The supplemental FAS is a unidimensional scale containing 6 items. Scales and sample items follow:

1. *Jealous Control (8 items)*

   - "How often does your partner ask for detailed reports of your hourly activities?"
   - "How often does your partner check up on you throughout the day?"

2. *Ignore (5 items)*

   - "How often does your partner complain or ridicule you if you are upset or ask for emotional support?"
   - "How often does your partner ignore you when you begin a conversation?"

3. *Ridicule Traits (5 items)*

   - "How often does your partner suggest you are crazy or stupid?"
   - "How often does your partner make fun of your triumphs, discourage your plans, or minimize your successes?"

4. *Criticize Behavior (3 items)*

- "How often does your partner inspect your work and make overly critical comments?"
- "How often does your partner request that everything be done in a precise way or it will be unacceptable to him?"

5. *Supplemental FAS (6 items)*

- "How often do you do things your partner wants you to do because you feel afraid?"
- "How often do you fear that your partner will hit you if you don't comply with his wishes?"

Administration and Scoring

For both the PPA and the FAS, respondents are asked to indicate the frequency of each item over the course of the current relationship on a 1–7 Likert scale (1 = *never*, 2 = *less than once*, 3 = *once a month*, 4 = *two to three times a month*, 5 = *once a week*, 6 = *two to three times a week*, 7 = *daily*). The scale takes about 5 to 10 minutes to complete. Items are summed to produce scale scores.

Psychometric Evaluation

Norms

Means and standard deviations for each scale for shelter-residing battered women and non-shelter-residing battered women are presented in the primary reference.

Reliability

Alpha coefficients for the scales were as follows: Jealous Control = .85, Ignore = .80, Ridicule Traits = .79, and Criticize Behavior = .75, indicating good internal consistency. Coefficient alpha for the FAS = .86.

Validity

Criterion validity of the PPA was supported by the finding that the shelter-dwelling battered women, who reported experiencing more severe physical abuse, reported greater levels of ridicule traits and jealous control than the non-shelter-dwelling battered women. Convergent validity was generally supported by relationships in expected directions between PPA scales and measures of psychological abuse severity, depression, amount of violence, low self-esteem, and fear of abuse.

Advantages

This brief, easy-to-administer scale allows for examination of the presence and differential impact of various forms of psychological abuse. The supplemental FAS offers measurement of a construct essential for determining abused clients' affective states and potential risk of danger, as well as for determining appropriateness of conjoint treatment approaches.

Limitations

The scale development sample was small and made up entirely of help-seeking clients; thus normative data, factor structure, and validity and reliability for nonabused women are not known.

Primary Scale Reference

Sackett and Saunders (1999).

Scale Availability

> Daniel G. Saunders
> University of Michigan
> School of Social Work
> 1080 University Avenue
> Ann Arbor, MI 48109

Scale items are also reprinted in the primary reference.

General Comments and Recommendations for Researchers and Practitioners

Assessing an aspect of abusive relationships that has received growing attention in the past decade, the factor structure of the PPA resembles that found in other measures of psychologically abusive behavior, such as Murphy and Hoover's (1999) Emotional Abuse Scale and Tolman's (1989) Psychological Maltreatment of Women Inventory (both reviewed in this chapter), suggesting the existence of fairly robust clusters of such behavior. The FAS assesses a critical area in the assessment of partner abuse and with further psychometric evaluation, could become an invaluable clinical screening tool.

23. Psychological Maltreatment of Women Inventory (PMWI; Tolman)

Description and Development of Assessment Method

The PMWI is a 58-item scale measuring psychologically abusive behaviors toward women in intimate relationships. A 14-item version is also available (see General Comments section below).

Items were derived from the nonphysical abuse scale of the Index of Spouse Abuse (Hudson & McIntosh, 1981), from the psychological and verbal aggression items on the CTS (Straus, 1979), and from the clinical literature as well as the author's clinical observations. The scale was then administered at time of intake to a sample of 407 men who batter and 207 battered women entering a domestic violence program. Exploratory principal-components analyses with varimax rotation were conducted separately for men and women, yielding a 2-factor solution with similar item loadings for men and women. Many items loaded highly on both the Dominance–Isolation and the Emotional–Verbal factors, and the factors are highly correlated (r = .73 for men and .74 for women), suggesting only moderate multidimensionality within the construct of psychological maltreatment of a partner.

Target Population

The PMWI was designed for individuals in intimate relationships. Respondents fill out in reference to behaviors they have used toward their partner. Respondents can also fill out in reference to behaviors they have experienced from their partner. Two versions contain slightly different wording for self or partner reports. Pilot testing indicated that the items were easily understood by partner-assaultive men.

Format

The PMWI contains two subscales. The Dominance–Isolation scale reflects monitoring and restricting a partner's movements, isolating a partner from social contacts and resources, and demanding subservience from a partner. The Emotional–Verbal scale reflects use of verbally attacking or demeaning behavior, as well as emotionally withholding behavior toward a partner. Sample items from each scale follow:

1. *Dominance–Isolation (20 items)*[10]

   - "Monitored partner's time and whereabouts"
   - "Did not allow socializing with friends"
   - "Acted jealous of other men"

2. *Emotional–Verbal* (28 items)

   - "Yelled and screamed"
   - "Treated partner like she was stupid"
   - "Gave partner silent treatment"

Administration and Scoring

The scale can be completed in 10 to 15 minutes. Respondents indicate how often each of 58 items occurred within the past 6 months on a 5-point Likert scale ranging from *never* to *very frequently*. Scales are scored by summing item ratings.

Psychometric Evaluation

Norms

For the Dominance–Isolation scale, mean scores were 43.3 (SD = 15.8) for men and 70.7 (SD = 13.5) for women. For the Emotional–Verbal scale, mean scores were 51.7 (SD = 15.7) for men and 79.4 (SD = 17.9) for women. Mean ratings and percentage of the sample who endorsed each item for men and women in the scale development sample are provided in the primary reference.

Reliability

Alpha coefficients for women in the development sample were .95 for the Dominance–Isolation scale and .93 for the Emotional–Verbal scale; for men they were .91 for Dominance–Isolation and .93 for Emotional–Verbal, suggesting high internal consistency reliability for both men and women.

---

10. Factor analysis indicated that 20 items loaded > .4 on Dominance–Isolation and 28 items loaded > .4 on Emotional–Verbal abuse. Ten items loaded < .4 on both factors.

Interpartner reliability was examined for 28 couples from the scale development sample. Men's and women's scores were significantly correlated on the Dominance–Isolation scale ($r = .48$, $p = .007$) and were not significantly correlated on the Emotional–Verbal scale ($r = .30$, $p = .265$). The overall low degree of interpartner agreement was consistent with past research of low agreement between partners on ratings of abuse (e.g., O'Leary & Arias, 1988).

Validity

Factor analysis supported the factor validity of the two scales. Individuals who work with battered women and men who batter provided feedback that the items adequately represented the domain of psychologically abusive behaviors in intimate relationships, supporting the content validity of the scale. Further, all items had at least a 29% endorsement rate in the scale development sample of battered women (range = 29%–98%), indicating that these items were well within the domain of experiences of battered women, lending further support to content validity (Tolman, 1989).

Convergent validity was supported by both subscales' significant correlations with established measures of psychological abuse (yielding the highest correlations), physical abuse, marital discord, and general psychiatric symptoms in a sample of 100 battered and nonbattered women. Discriminant validity was supported by the scales' lack of significant correlations with demographic variables in the same sample (Tolman, 1999).

Finally, criterion validity was supported by both scales' ability to discriminate among three groups. Physically abused women scored significantly higher than relationship-distressed nonabused women and relationship-satisfied women, and relationship-distressed nonabused women scored significantly higher than relationship-satisfied women (Tolman, 1999).

Advantages

The PMWI is easily administered and scored. As it is worded for both male and female respondents, it allows for female partner reports of received psychological maltreatment, which is important given the tendency for men to underreport abusive behavior (e.g., O'Leary & Arias, 1988).

Limitations

The development sample of men who batter yielded low item endorsement rates (ranging from 4% to 91%, with 17 items endorsed by 25% or fewer men) and low item means for those items that were endorsed (all in the *never* to *sometimes* range). Thus, for men reporting on their own behavior, the scale may produce a restricted range and a tendency toward floor effects and thus may be limited in its ability to discriminate groups or to show change in pre–post evaluations.

Primary Scale Reference

Tolman (1989).

Scale Availability

> Richard M. Tolman
> University of Michigan
> School of Social Work
> 1080 South University
> Room 3680
> Ann Arbor, MI 48109-1106

Scale items also appear in the primary reference and in Tolman (1999).

Related References

Cascardi, O'Leary, Lawrence, and Schlee, (1995); D. G. Dutton and Starzomski (1993); O'Leary, Heyman, and Neidig (1999); Tolman (1999).

General Comments and Recommendations for Researchers and Practitioners

The PMWI measures psychological aggression, a critical aspect of partner abuse that can have more deleterious effects than physical aggression (Follingstad et al., 1990) and may remain or increase following treatment if not targeted directly (Edleson & Brygger, 1986; Gondolf & Russel, 1986). Although many of the behaviors measured in the PMWI may occur in nonviolent but discordant couples, such behaviors may be particularly damaging and frightening in the context of a physically aggressive relationship (Walker, 1979). The scale does not include items assessing maltreatment that involves any physical component (e.g., forcing sex acts) or threats of physical aggression, making it a useful and nonredundant supplement to other scales measuring such forms of maltreatment. Although the scale has low interpartner reliability, the availability of a female-respondent form enables the examiner to compare men's data with partner data. The PMWI offers utility in both clinical and research settings because of its administration ease, its male and female respondent versions, and its comprehensive assessment of the construct of psychological maltreatment in relationships.

Note that Tolman (1999) has also developed a short version of the PMWI (with seven items on each scale), selecting items that significantly discriminated between battered women and relationship-distressed non-abused women to capture items most "likely to be the aspects of psychological maltreatment most distinct from general relationship distress" (p. 29). This brief scale has excellent internal consistency reliability and good initial evidence of construct validity.

24. Severity of Violence Against Men Scales[11] (SVAMS; Marshall)

Description and Development of Assessment Method

This 16-item scale provides the counterpart to the Severity of Violence Against Women Scale (SWAWS; see below) and assesses the occurrence of eight dimensions of aggression from a female toward a male partner. Items were rationally derived based on the family violence literature. A pool of items was then administered to two samples of men: college students (n = 570) and community men (n = 115). With both samples, the items were rated on 10-point scales for severity. For the college student sample, severity ratings were based on respondents' judgments as to the degree each of 49 acts would be serious, aggressive, abusive, threatening, and violent, if done to a man by a woman. Three items related to sexual violence were dropped based on respondents' feedback that these items would vary substantially by gender in terms of meaning. For the community sample, severity ratings were based on only respondents' judgments as to the degree each of the remaining 46 acts would be serious, aggressive, and abusive, if done to a man by a woman.

For the college student sample, each of the five severity ratings per act was then averaged to form a global severity rating for each item within each sample. Global severity scores were factor analyzed in this sample. An 8-factor

---

11. An alternative form of the scale, called the Severity of Violence Against Men Scale—Students (SVAW–S) contains somewhat different item ordering and impact ratings and should be used with high school or college student samples. This version is also in the primary reference.

solution was chosen that accounted for 78% of the variance. Thus, conceptually justified factors were chosen and tested by (a) calculating internal consistency reliability in each factor, which proved high; (b) testing for significance of mean differences in severity ratings between factors, which yielded seven significantly different severity levels; and (c) calculating correlations of severity scores to determine whether within-dimension correlations would be higher than between-dimensions correlations. Except for moderate violence, all of the within-dimension mean correlations were higher than the between-dimensions correlations, supporting the constructs suggested by each dimension.

Replication of these procedures in the community sample yielded similar patterns for factors, mean severity scores across dimensions, alphas, significant mean differences in severity ratings between factors, and intercorrelations among factors.

Target Population

Clinic or community samples, or college or high school students.

Format

The scale assesses eight dimensions of threats of violence or actual violent behavior. Dimensions of violence and sample items follow:

1. *Threats of Mild Violence*
   "Shook a fist at him"
2. *Threats of Moderate Violence*
   "Threatened to destroy property"
3. *Threats of Serious Violence*
   "Threatened him with a weapon"
4. *Mild Violence*
   "Held him down, pinning him in place"
5. *Minor Violence*
   "Pulled his hair"
6. *Moderate Violence*
   "Slapped him with the palm of her hand"
7. *Serious Violence*
   "Choked him"
8. *Sexual Violence*
   "Made him have sexual intercourse against his will"

Administration and Scoring

Respondents rate the frequency with which they have received each of 46 aggressive acts from their partner during the past year. Items are rated on 1 to 4 scale from *never* to *many* times. The scale takes approximately 15 minutes to complete. To score, frequency responses are multiplied by item weights, and then summed for a total score within each dimension.

Psychometric Evaluation

Norms

Normative impact ratings per aggression dimension and per item, for both student and community samples, are published in the primary reference.

Reliability

In the student sample, alpha coefficients of severity ratings ranged from .93 to .95 across the nine dimensions. Alphas had the identical range (.93 to .95) in the community sample.

Validity

Initial construct validity is supported by the scale development procedures, which provide empirical support for dimensions through item impact ratings, factor analysis, and scale intercorrelations.

Advantages

Like the SVAWS, the SVAMS makes the distinction between threatened and completed aggressive acts. Although the scale's length could be decreased by eliminating redundancy of similar items, the large number of highly specific acts allows for thorough and objective assessment of violent acts. The fine discriminations between scales allow for conducting many types of comparisons in group research (e.g., differences in impact between threatened and actual acts of aggression). The scale contains normative ratings for each item; violent acts are presented hierarchically in order of severity based on men's reports.

Limitations

Because item weightings are based on normative severity ratings, scores may not reflect the subjective impact of violent acts for a given man. Injury and context of violent acts are also not provided by the measure. The response format (e.g., "many times," etc.) is open to subjective interpretation and does not assess actual frequency rates. In addition, more evidence of convergent and discriminant validity is needed for the scale in general, with more evidence needed of the incremental validity of the various dimensions of violence.

Primary Scale Reference

Marshall (1992b).

Scale Availability

In primary reference.

Related References

Marshall (1992a).

General Comments and Recommendations for Researchers and Practitioners

The central purpose in developing the SVAMS was to develop a normative behavioral assessment of female violence toward male partners; the author provides item weightings for scoring two populations (community and student). Used in conjunction with its "sister" scale, the Severity of Violence Against Women Scales (Marshall, 1992a), the SVAMS lends itself to gender-based comparisons of rates and severity of acts of violence and can be useful in the assessment of couples by giving each member of the couple the gender-specific scale. The measurement of topography of violent acts without measurement of function, impact on the individual respondent (as opposed to hypothetical impact, which weighted scoring system reflects), and injury in the SVAMS make this scale vulnerable to some of the same criticisms (e.g., Saunders, 1988; Vivian & Langhinrichsen-Rohling, 1994) of the original CTS (Straus, 1979) concerning the potential for misrepresentation of female violence against men. It is interesting, however, that although the male and female versions of this scale contain the same items, the acts received lower severity ratings when evaluated as being perpetrated by a woman toward a man than by a man toward a woman; thus, item weightings differ between the two scales to reflect this differing severity level. As with the SVAWS, because the SVAMS was developed using third-person ratings rather than subjective perceptions of violence that might happen or actually has happened to oneself, the author concludes that this provides a more objective normative assessment of the severity of the acts. Naturally, however, some degree of subjectivity must enter into even hypothetical ratings of the victimization of others. The SVAMS contains only items that reflect physical threats or actions and does not include items assessing emotional abuse that may accompany physically aggressive acts. The scale is available in both community and student population versions. For research, the author recommends use of the normed-weighting scoring procedure, for clinical use, subjective impact ratings of items might be obtained.

25. Severity of Violence Against Women Scales[12] (SVAWS; Marshall)

Description and Development of Assessment Method

This 46-item scale assesses the occurrence of, and provides normative severity ratings for, nine dimensions of aggression from a male toward a female partner. Items were rationally derived based on the family violence literature. A pool of 49 items was then administered to two samples of women: college students (n = 707) and community women (n = 208). With both samples, the items were rated on 10-point scales for severity. For the college student sample, severity ratings were based on respondents' judgments as to the degree each act would be serious, aggressive, abusive, threatening, violent, would cause physical harm, and would cause psychological/emotional harm, if done to a woman by a man. For the community sample, severity ratings were based on only respondents' judgments as to the degree each act would be serious, aggressive, abusive, would cause physical harm, and would cause psychological/emotional harm, if done to a woman by a man. Each of these ratings per act was then averaged to form a global severity rating for each item within each sample. Three items related to sexual violence were dropped on the basis of respondents' feedback.

Severity scores were factor analyzed in the college student sample. Although four factors yielded eigenvalues greater than 1, a 9-factor solution was arrived at because

> in striving for a comprehensive and sensitive scale, it was desirable that several severity levels for threats and physical violence be represented because of the possibility that minor, moderate, and serious threats (or

---

12. An alternative form of the scale, called the Severity of Violence Against Women Scale—Students (SVAW–S), contains somewhat different item ordering and impact ratings and should be used with high school or college student samples. This version is also in the primary reference.

minor, moderate, and serious violence) may have different effects on relevant variables. (Marshall, 1992a, p. 107)

Thus, conceptually justified factors were chosen and tested by (a) calculating internal consistency reliability in each factor, which proved high; (b) testing for significance of mean differences in severity ratings between factors, which yielded a majority of significant differences; and (c) calculating correlations to determine if correlations were higher within dimensions than between them. Except for symbolic violence, which had the same mean within-dimension correlation as its correlation between the dimensions, all dimensions had higher within- than between-dimension correlations. Replication of these procedures in the community sample yielded similar patterns for factors, mean severity scores across dimensions, alphas, significant mean differences in severity ratings between factors, and intercorrelations among factors.

Target Population

Shelter populations, clinic or community women, or college or high school students.

Format

The scale assesses nine dimensions of threats of violence or actual violent behavior. Dimensions of violence and sample items follow:

1. *Symbolic Violence*
   "Threw, smashed, or broke an object"
2. *Threats of Mild Violence*
   "Shook a fist at her"
3. *Threats of Moderate Violence*
   "Threatened to destroy property"
4. *Threats of Serious Violence*
   "Threatened her with a weapon"
5. *Mild Violence*
   "Held her down, pinning her in place"
6. *Minor Violence*
   "Pulled her hair"
7. *Moderate Violence*
   "Slapped her with the palm of his hand"
8. *Serious Violence*
   "Kicked her"

9. *Sexual Violence*
   "Physically forced her to have sex"

Administration and Scoring

The scale takes approximately 15 minutes to complete. Respondents rate the frequency with which they have received each of 46 aggressive acts from their partner during the past year. Items are rated on 1 to 4 scale from *never* to *many times*. To score, frequency responses are multiplied by item weights and then summed for a total score within each dimension.

Psychometric Evaluation

Norms
Normative impact ratings per aggression dimension and per item, for both student and community samples, are published in the primary reference.

Reliability
In the student sample, alpha coefficients of severity ratings ranged from .92 to .96 across the nine dimensions. Alphas ranged from .89 to .96 in the community sample, indicating excellent internal consistency in both samples.

Validity
Initial construct validity is supported by the scale development procedures, which provide empirical support for dimensions through item impact ratings, factor analysis, and scale intercorrelations.

Advantages
The SVAWS makes the distinction between threatened and completed acts of aggression. Although the scale's efficiency could be increased by eliminating items with statistical overlap, the wide range of acts makes the scale comprehensive and reduces problems of idiosyncratic interpretation of individual items. Fine discriminations between scales allow for comparisons of women who have experienced distinct forms of aggression or between threatened and actual violence. Acts of violence are presented hierarchically in empirically determined order of severity, based on women's reports. Thus the scale's normative ratings for each item increase the interpretability of scores and make the scale a sound selection for research use.

Limitations

For clinical use, item weightings based on normative severity scores may not reflect the experiences of a given woman. Even the normative sample based severity ratings on hypothetical acts occurring from a man toward a woman rather than on their own experience of the acts. In fact, despite the empirically derived normative impact ratings producing more meaningful scores than a measure in which item severity is determined by the author (such as the CTS; Straus, 1979), the scale still does not provide assessment of actual impact, injury, or context of violent acts for women filling out the scale. Also, the response format (e.g., "many times," etc.) is open to subjective interpretation and does not allow for calculation of frequency rates.

In addition, more evidence of convergent and discriminant validity is needed. Further, evidence of incremental validity of the many dimensions of violence is needed, particularly because the author chose a 9-factor solution comprising five factors with eigenvalues < 1 (with the total variance accounted for by these five factors ranging from between 1.6% and 0.7%).

Primary Scale Reference

Marshall (1992a).

Scale Availability

In primary reference.

Related References

Marshall (1992b, 1996, 1999).

General Comments and Recommendations for Researchers and Practitioners

The SVAWS contains only items that reflect some degree of physical threat and thus excludes verbal/emotional abuse items common to other violence scales. It is available in two versions: community and student populations. The central purpose was to develop a normative behavioral assessment of male violence toward female partners, and the availability of normative data on two populations (community and student) grants the measure wide applicability. The scale, used in conjunction with its "brother" scale, the Severity of Violence Against Men Scales (Marshall, 1992b), lends itself to gender-based comparisons of rates and severity of acts of violence. The author recommends use of normed-weighting procedure for scoring in research use but suggests the possibility of obtaining an individual's subjective impact ratings of items in clinical use (Marshall, 1992a).

26. Survey of Consequences to Aggression in Relationships (SCAR; Riggs & Caulfield)

Description and Development of Assessment Method

The SCAR is a brief self-report instrument assessing expected consequences of behaving aggressively toward a partner. The scale was developed based on an earlier scale (Breslin, Riggs, O'Leary, & Arias, 1990) and revised to include a more streamlined set of consequences and more specifically defined aggressive acts. The 15 consequences listed in the scale were subjected to a principal-components factor analysis with oblique rotation. Five components with eigenvalues greater than 1 were extracted and form the five general categories of consequences.

Target Population

Developed for use with college males in dating relationships. Could also be used within any couple relationship.

Format

The SCAR contains 15 specific consequences of three violent acts toward an intimate partner: shoving, slapping, and punching. These 15 consequences fall within five general categories: breakup of the relationship, winning the argument, partner retaliation, partner upset, and perpetrator guilt. Sample items follow:

1. *Perpetrator Guilty* (3 items)
   "You apologize"
2. *Relationship Interrupted* (3 items)
   "Partner breaks up"
3. *Perpetrator Wins* (3 items)
   "You get your way"
4. *Partner Retaliates* (3 items)
   "Partner hits you"

5. *Partner Upset* (3 items)
   "Partner becomes depressed"

Administration and Scoring

The scale takes between 10 and 15 minutes to complete. Respondents are asked to indicate which consequences they believe would occur should they engage in one of the specified aggressive acts during an argument. Respondents may check as many consequences as they wish. The consequences checked are then summed across the three violent acts to yield a single score for each of the 15 consequences ranging from 0 to 3.

Psychometric Evaluation

Norms
Not reported.

Reliability
Not specifically reported, but factor loadings support the unidimensionality of each scale.

Validity
The scale differentiated between expectations of violent and nonviolent men; specifically, violent men were more likely to expect that aggression would lead to winning an argument, and nonviolent men were more likely to expect that violence would lead to interruption or dissolution of the relationship. In addition, there was a trend for violent men to expect to feel less guilty for an aggressive behavior. The item distribution across the five categories is supported by factor analysis

Advantages
The SCAR is a brief measure that is simple to score and taps into cognitive factors that may predict or maintain aggressive behavior toward a partner.

Limitations
Expected consequences endorsed may be confounded by actual experience with consequences (and thus the scale may be tapping into experience rather than outcome expectations). Only two scales significantly discriminated violent from nonviolent men.

Primary Scale Reference

Riggs and Caulfield (1997).

Scale Availability

David S. Riggs
National Center for PTSD (116B-2)
Boston Dept. of Veterans Administration Medical Center
150 South Huntington Avenue
Boston, MA 02130

Related References

Breslin, Riggs, O'Leary, and Arias (1990).

General Comments and Recommendations for Researchers and Practitioners

This scale measures the cognitive dimension of expectations regarding violent acts toward a partner. Although developed for college students in dating relationships, the scale can be used with adult spouses. The scale can also be adapted to assess expected consequences to a greater range of aggressive acts.

---

27. Women's Experiences With Battering Scale (WEB; Smith, Earp, & DeVellis)

Description and Development of Assessment Method

The WEB is a 10-item scale assessing women's experiences with feeling controlled, vulnerable, and fearful in the context of an abusive relationship. The authors conducted focus groups with battered women to generate items, which were then administered to known groups of battered and nonbattered women. Items were refined and deleted based on ability to differentiate these known groups, resulting in 40 items. A factor analysis of these items yielded a single-factor solution accounting for nearly 74% of the variance. The 10 items with the highest factor loadings on this strong factor were retained to construct the final scale.

Target Population

Victims of intimate partner violence.

Format

The WEB contains 10 items reflecting along a single dimension the subjective experiences of battered women. Sample items follow:

- "He makes me feel unsafe even in my own home"
- "I feel owned and controlled by him"
- "He can scare me without laying a hand on me"

Administration and Scoring

The scale takes only several minutes to complete. Respondents are asked to indicate the degree to which they agree with each statements along a 6-point Likert scale. Total score is determined by summing scale items, with six items reverse-scored, to produce a single score ranging from 10 to 60.

Psychometric Evaluation

Norms
Not reported.

Reliability
Cronbach's alpha for a battered women sample was .93, supporting the scale's internal consistency.

Validity
Scale items differentiated between identified groups of battered and nonbattered women, supporting its known groups or criterion validity. Convergent validity was demonstrated with significant associations in the expected directions with the following variables: physical abuse, psychological abuse, belief in a just world, self-esteem, marital satisfaction, locus of control, depression, anxiety, injury, perceived health status, and physician visits. Discriminant validity was indicated by the lack of association between the WEB and social desirability.

Advantages
The WEB is a brief, reliable, and valid scale for assessing the experiences of battered women.

Limitations
The scale would not be applicable to individuals in relationships with infrequent, low-intensity violence. Further, because the scale has only been evaluated using large group data, its use for individual diagnosis or evaluation remains unknown.

Primary Scale Reference

Smith, Earp, and DeVellis (1995).

Scale Availability

Printed in the primary reference.

General Comments and Recommendations for Researchers and Practitioners

The WEB helps meet the expressed need for instruments that address the experiential, rather than the behavioral, features of battering, in particular, the meaning and consequences of battering for victims (R. P. Dobash et al., 1992). Its strong psychometric properties and brevity make it an excellent potential tool for clinical and research use in populations who have been subject to battering.

Self-Report Measures: Assessment of General Relationship Functioning, Anger and Hostility, and Other Correlates of Partner Abuse

This chapter reviews self-report paper-and-pencil instruments that assess general relationship functioning, anger and hostility, and other correlates of partner abuse. The other correlates of partner abuse include such constructs as beliefs about wife abuse, posttraumatic stress symptoms, propensity for abusiveness, rape myths acceptance, readiness to change partner violence, and spouse-specific dependency. We included this set of self-report paper-and-pencil measures in a separate chapter because they serve a different purpose than those measures designed for specific assessment of physical or psychological aggression, as included in the previous chapter. The chapter concludes with an Appendix listing features of approximately 30 additional instruments. These measures were described in brief in the appendix because they were deemed relevant to this volume yet (a) were considered enough beyond the scope of the book to qualify for detailed review (due to space considerations), (b) had overly preliminary psychometric properties, or (c) we were not able to obtain the scale or descriptive information on the scale. Constructs included among these instruments related to partner violence include those such as attachment, depression, family-of-origin violence, jealousy, personality/psychopathology, psychopathy, and substance abuse. References are included so that interested readers can avail themselves of these instruments.

28. Dyadic Adjustment Scale (DAS; Spanier)

Description and Development of Assessment Method

The DAS is a widely used self-report measure used to assess the degree of relationship satisfaction for individuals in marital or cohabitating relationships. The DAS was developed on samples of married ($n = 218$) and divorced ($n = 94$) individuals. Factor analysis revealed a 4-factor solution. The factors are labeled Dyadic Satisfaction, Dyadic Cohesion, Dyadic Consensus, and Affectional Expression. This 4-factor solution has been controversial, with some researchers (Sharpley & Rogers, 1985) questioning its consistency across samples.

Target Population

Any man or woman in a marital or similarly committed relationship, including dating relationships and same-sex relationships.

Format

The DAS contains 32 items that are answered in either a yes/no format (2 items) or using one of seven different scales written for individual or groups of items. The measure contains four subscales: dyadic satisfaction, dyadic cohesion, dyadic consensus, and affectional expression. Sample items follow (note that items are paraphrased here; each of the following items is answered using a different scale):

1. *Dyadic Satisfaction (10 items)*

   - "In general, how often do you think that things between you and your partner are going well?"
   - "Do you confide in your mate?"

2. *Dyadic Cohesion (5 items)*

   - "Do you and your mate engage in outside interests together?"

3. *Dyadic Consensus (13 items)*

   - "Please indicate the extent of agreement or disagreement between you and your partner on matters of recreation."
   - "Please indicate the extent of agreement or disagreement between you and your partner on ways of dealing with parent or in-laws."

4. *Affectional Expression (4 items)*

- "Has not showing love caused differences of opinions or problems in your relationship during the past few weeks?"

Administration and Scoring

The measure is completed individually and takes approximately 10 minutes. Total and factor scores are derived by summing the responses to the appropriate set of items. Scores range from 0 to 151.

Psychometric Evaluation

Norms

The mean total score was 114.8 (SD = 17.8) for a sample of 218 married individuals (mean age = 35.1 years, mean length of marriage = 13.2 years). The mean total score was 70.7 (SD = 23.8) for a sample of 94 divorced individuals (mean age = 30.4 years, mean length of marriage = 8.5 years). Scores below 97 provide a sensitive indicator of marital distress (Eddy, Heyman, & Weiss, 1991).

Reliability

Internal consistency for the total scale is high (α = .96). The dyadic satisfaction subscale has an alpha of .94. The dyadic cohesion subscale has an alpha of .81. The dyadic consensus subscale has an alpha of .90. The affectional expression subscale has an alpha of .73. Test–retest reliability was .87 over a 2-week interval (Carey, Spector, Lantinga, & Krauss, 1993).

Validity

The DAS has discriminated between married and divorced couples as well as between happy and discordant marital couples (Spanier, 1976) and was sensitive to change following a course of behavioral marital therapy (Baucom & Lester, 1986), supporting its criterion-related validity. The measure correlates with other measures of marital satisfaction, such as the Locke–Wallace Marital Adjustment Scale, indicating convergent validity. Content validity was supported by judges' ratings (Spanier, 1976).

Advantages

The utility of the DAS across a wide variety of clinical and nonclinical populations makes this measure an excellent clinical resource and research tool. Items are more contemporary than those of older measures, such as the Marital Adjustment Test. Examination of subscales can provide information on the separate components of marital adjustment.

Limitations

Multiple scaling approaches throughout the instrument may be confusing to some respondents. Research on the scale has found problems with the validity of the dyadic satisfaction and affectional expression subscales as well as with some individual items, and the scale has often been evaluated on only separated/divorced individuals as opposed to distressed and nondistressed couples (Busby, Christensen, Crane, & Larson, 1995).

Primary Scale Reference

Spanier (1976).

Scale Availability

Multi-Health Systems, Inc.
908 Niagra Falls Blvd.
North Tonawanda, NY 14120-2060
(716) 842-0308

The scale is also reprinted in the primary reference.

Related References

Busby, Christensen, Crane, and Larson (1995); Eddy, Heyman, and Weiss (1991); Sabourin, Lussier, Laplante, and Wright (1990); Sharpley and Rogers (1985); Spanier and Filsinger (1983).

General Comments and Recommendations for Researchers and Practitioners

With widespread use in research studies (including many studies of marital violence) and marital clinic settings, the DAS is a classic and dependable instrument for a variety of uses in diverse settings. The scale has been criticized for redundant items and questionable factorial validity (Busby et al., 1995) and has evoked controversy over whether dyadic adjustment is best considered a unidimensional or multidimensional construct (e.g., Sabourin et al., 1990). To address some of these concerns, Busby and colleagues (Busby et al., 1995) have developed a reliable and valid short version of the scale (Revised DAS, or RDAS). This revised version contains 14 items representing three domains of marital adjustment (consensus, satisfaction, and cohesion) and is reprinted in the primary reference (Busby et al., 1995).

---

29. Managing Affect and Differences Scale (MADS; Arellano & Markman)

Description and Development of Assessment Method

The MADS is a self-report measure that assesses communication skills used by couples during conflict. Scales and items for the MADS were based on the empirical literature regarding positive and negative communication skills. The scale was developed across two studies. The first study recruited 31 opposite-sex couples and included items only assessing perceptions of one's own communication skills. For the second study, 36 same-sex couples were recruited for cross-validation in a different population, and the authors added one additional scale (withdrawal) and added items assessing respondents' partners' skills, as well as additional items assessing relationship satisfaction. In these studies, scales were correlated with a variety of other measures including observational coding data to assess validity.

Target Population

Couples.

Format

The MADS contains 109 items on 12 scales. Scale names and sample items follow:

> *Leveling (telling one's partner what one is feeling clearly and constructively; 11 items)*

- "I help my partner to understand what I am saying."

> *Emotional Expressivity (the degree of comfort with emotional expression; 10 items)*

- "My partner tells me when he/she is pleased."

> *Validation (expressing value in partner's perspective; 18 items)*

- "I verbally communicate to my partner that I understand and value his/her position."

Love and Affection (love and affection expressed toward one's partner; 10 items)

• "My partner feels comfort with expression of affection."

Editing (controlling one's reactions to a partner's message; 14 items)

• "My partner tries to phrase things positively."

Negative Escalation (a pattern of following negative messages with another negative message; 6 items)

• "When we argue, I lose my temper easily."

Negativity (expression of negative feelings; 14 items)

• "We often disagree and quarrel with each other."

Feedback (paraphrasing or clarifying a partner's message; 7 items)

• "My partner summarizes what I say to make sure he/she understands my position."

Stop Actions (stopping an escalating discussion and agreeing to discuss another time; 4 items)

• "When conflicts get out of hand, I usually try to stop them and ask if we can set up another time for discussion."

Focusing (discussing only one issue at a time; 5 items)

• "When we drift off topic, my partner tries to get us on track."

Withdrawal (physically or emotionally withdrawing from discussions for fear of conflict; 6 items)

• "When problems arise, I often leave the room."

Communication Over Time (improvements in communication over time; 4 items)

• "My partner understands me better than in the past."

Administration and Scoring

The measure takes about 15 minutes to complete. Respondents rate each item on a 5-point scale ranging from *strongly disagree* to *strongly agree*. Items are simply summed to produce a total score for each subscale.

Psychometric Evaluation

Norms

Means and standard deviations for each of the scales for both distressed and nondistressed couples are reported in the primary reference.

Reliability

Cronbach's alphas on the 12 scales ranged from .64 to .90 in the opposite-sex sample and .67 to .92 in the same-sex sample, indicating moderate to excellent internal consistency.

Validity

Distressed couples reported using more negative communication strategies and fewer positive communication strategies than nondistressed couples, supporting the scale's discriminative validity. Communication and conflict management skills were generally correlated in the expected directions with marital satisfaction, problem intensity, and relationship efficacy (the degree to which couples feel confident they can solve relationship conflicts), lending support to the scale's concurrent validity with established self-report measures. In addition, seven scales were related to verbal aggression for same-sex couples (love and affection, editing, validation, feedback, and focusing were negatively related; negativity and negative escalation were positively related), and two scales were related to verbal aggression for opposite-sex couples (validation was negatively related and negativity was positively related). Further, two scales (stop actions and focusing) were negatively related to physical aggression for same-sex couples, and none was related to physical aggression for opposite-sex couples. Thus, findings related to verbal and physical aggression offer some support for concurrent validity in the same-sex but not the opposite-sex population. Finally, scales on the MADS were generally not related to observational coding data, indicating a lack of concurrent validity based on observational methods.

Advantages

The MADS allows for assessment of participants' perceptions of their communication skills in specific areas of communication that have been linked to marital satisfaction. The authors present validation data on same-sex as well as opposite-sex couples.

Limitations

Validity of the measure was not supported by observational methods.

Primary Scale Reference

Arellano and Markman (1995).

Scale Availability

> Charleanea M. Arellano
> Department of Psychology
> C-137 Clark Building
> Colorado State University
> Fort Collins, CO 80523

Related References

None available.

General Comments and Recommendations
for Researchers and Practitioners

The MADS can be used both as a screening device to identify a couple's specific areas of communication and conflict management skill strengths and deficits and as a measure to monitor improvement in these skills. It offers measurement of a variety of specific communication areas that might be of interest in studying conflict management styles in aggressive couples, such as negative escalation and withdrawal. The scale is one of the only scales in the literature to report development data based on same-sex as well as heterosexual couples. Although the scale did not relate to observational coding data of communication styles, the scale is still of use in offering assessment of couples' own perceptions of their communication behaviors.

---

30. Marital Adjustment Test (MAT; Locke & Wallace)

Description and Development of Assessment Method

The MAT is a brief self-report measure for assessing general marital satisfaction. The authors intended to consolidate the many items tapping marital adjustment that were contained in various other scales measuring this construct into one brief, nonredundant instrument. First, items were selected from previous measures. The number of items was then narrowed by selecting those that "(1) had the highest level of discrimination in the original studies, (2) did not duplicate other included items, and (3) would cover the important areas of marital adjustment . . . as judged by the authors" (Locke & Wallace, 1959, p. 252). This left 15 items, which constituted the final MAT. The reliability and validity of these items were then tested by applying them to a new sample.

Target Population

Men or women in marital or cohabitating relationships.

Format

The MAT contains 15 items assessing perceived level of agreement on various matters, feelings about being married, and general marital happiness. Responses are given using several different scaling formats. Sample items follow:

- "State the extent of agreement or disagreement between you and your mate on demonstrations of affection."
- "Do you and your mate engage in outside interests together?"
- "Do you ever wish you had not married?"

Administration and Scoring

The measure takes less than 5 minutes to complete. Some items are rated using a Likert-type format and other items are rated categorically, with different amounts of points assigned to different responses. Scoring is conducted by summing scale items according to the scoring key provided with the scale, with possible scores ranging from 2 to 158.

Psychometric Evaluation

Norms

Mean scores in community samples are typically around 120. In samples of couples who define themselves as happy, the mean score is approximately 130, whereas clinically distressed couples typically have mean scores in the 70s. In research studies, cutoff scores of 100 are typically used to differentiate maritally distressed and nondistressed couples.

Reliability

Split-half reliability calculated using the Spearman–Brown formula was .90 in the original development sample (Locke & Wallace, 1959), indicating high internal consistency.

Validity

Numerous marital therapy outcome measures are correlated with the MAT, and the scale is sensitive to changes in marital therapy, supporting its construct validity (O'Leary, 1987). Criterion-related validity was supported by the scale's ability to differentiate well-adjusted from maladjusted couples (Locke & Wallace, 1959), and the scale has repeatedly been demonstrated to be sensitive to change resulting from marital therapy.

Advantages

The MAT is brief enough to be administered and interpreted prior to an initial interaction with a patient/client.

Limitations

The measure is considered by some to be "dated," and its scoring has been criticized as being sexist because scores are decreased if husbands compromise in conflicts rather than wives.

Primary Scale Reference

Locke and Wallace (1959).

Scale Availability

The scale and scoring criteria are reprinted in the primary reference.

Related References

Heyman, O'Leary, and Jouriles (1995).

General Comments and Recommendations for Researchers and Practitioners

The most widely used measure of marital satisfaction, the MAT is brief, easy to administer and score, and highly practical for both clinical and research settings. The scale has been used in numerous studies of partner violence (e.g., Heyman et al., 1995).

---

31. Anger, Irritability, and Assault Questionnaire (AIAQ; Coccaro, Harvey, Kupsaw-Lawrence, Herbert, & Bernstein)

Description and Development of Assessment Method

The AIAQ is a 42-item self-report scale to measure impulsive aggression in outpatients. Items were derived from the Buss–Durkee Hostility Inventory

(BDHI; Buss & Durkee, 1957) and the Affective Lability Scale (ALS; Harvey, Greenberg, & Serper, 1989) to form a scale tapping behavior irritability, physical assaultiveness, and unpredictable dysregulation of anger, all impulsive aggression features hypothesized to be modulated by central serotonergic functioning.

Target Population

Outpatients.

Format

Items are rated on a 4-point Likert scale ranging from *very characteristic* to *very uncharacteristic*. Each item is further rated for time frame; respondents rate degree to which each item characterizes them over the past week, past month, their adulthood (age 18), their adolescence (ages 12–18), and their childhood (ages 6–10). A version of the AIAQ with past-week ratings only is available.

The AIAQ contains the following subscales: irritability, labile anger, and assault (which is further subdivided into direct assault, verbal assault, and indirect assault). Sample items follow:

1. *Irritability*

   • "I have been kind of grouchy."

2. *Labile Anger*

   • "It's very common for me to be extremely angry about something and then to suddenly feel like my normal self."

3. *Direct Assault*

   • "I get into fights about as often as the next person."

4. *Verbal Assault*

   • "I can't help getting into arguments when people disagree with me."

5. *Indirect Assault*

   • "I can be so angry that I will pick up the nearest thing and break it."

Administration and Scoring

This self-rated scale takes about 15 minutes to complete. The AIAQ is scored by summing item ratings for each scale, separately for each time frame.

Psychometric Evaluation

Norms

Not reported.

Reliability

Test–retest reliability within 2 weeks was calculated using intraclass correlation coefficients (ICCs), a conservative method of calculating rating stability. ICCs were calculated for ratings of aggression concerning the past week, past month, and adulthood. For patients, ICCs ranged from .53 to .93. For controls, ICCs ranged from .66 to .98.

Validity

Coccaro, Harvey, Kupsaw-Lawrence, Herbert, and Bernstein (1991) reported significant correlations between the AIAQ and the BDHI and the ALS, which have demonstrated construct validity. All three AIAQ scales (Labile Anger, Irritability, and Assault) were intercorrelated for patients for all three time periods rated, but only the Labile Anger and Irritability scales were correlated across three time periods for nonpatients. The Irritability and Labile Anger scales correlated significantly with clinicians' ratings of alcohol use. The scale also discriminated between psychiatric patient and nonpatient populations.

Advantages

Because the AIAQ inquires about impulsive aggressive behavior within highly specific time frames, it allows for capturing the variation of aggressive behaviors over time (e.g., from adolescence to adulthood). Test–retest reliabilities indicate the stability of the AIAQ subscales "over the time interval generally used in psychopharmacological trials (i.e., 1–2 weeks)" (Coccaro et al., 1991, p. S50). In addition, the scale was created from the BDHI and the ALS to create a more specific measure for the constructs of irritability and assaultiveness.

Limitations

Construct validity is based in part on correlations with the scales from which items were taken. The authors caution that the AIAQ may not be fully applicable to a female population, because the relationship between 5-HT (serotonin) function and aggressive behavior in women has received little research attention.

Primary Scale Reference

Coccaro, Harvey, Kupsaw-Lawrence, Herbert, and Bernstein (1991).

Scale Availability

> Emil F. Coccaro
> Clinical Neuroscience Research Unit
> Department of Psychiatry
> Medical College of PA at EPPI
> 3200 Henry Avenue
> Philadelphia, PA 19129

Related References

Coccaro, Siever, Klar, Maurer, Cochrane, Cooper, et al. (1989).

General Comments and Recommendations for Researchers and Practitioners

The scale, along with the Overt Aggression Scale—Modified (Coccaro et al., 1991; see chap. 6, this volume, on interview assessments of partner violence), was developed as an outcome measure in a study to test the effectiveness of 5-HT (serotonin) uptake inhibitors in the reduction of aggressiveness in outpatients with a diagnosis of depression or personality disorder. The scale is of use in examining the neurochemical basis of impulsive aggression. Specific subscales, such as labile anger and direct assault, may be useful in measuring batterer subtypes (Holtzworth-Munroe & Stuart, 1994).

---

32. Buss–Durkee Hostility Inventory (BDHI; Buss & Durkee)

Description and Development of Assessment Method

The BDHI consists of 75 true–false items, 66 of which assess various aspects of hostility and 9 of which measure guilt. An initial pool of 105 items was developed by the authors and included items adapted from other measures.

Subscales were determined a priori, and items were selected to represent each scale. These items were administered to 85 male and 74 female college students. Criteria for item retention were that (a) the item must be endorsed as true by 15%–85% of the sample and (b) the item must have an item–total correlation of at least .40 for both the male and female sample. By using both of these criteria, 60 of the initial items were retained. An additional 34 items were added by rewriting old items and authoring new items. This revised, 94-item measure was administered to a second sample of 62 male and 58 female college students. Items were retained if they met the original item–total correlation criteria of at least .40 in both samples, and if between 15% and 85% of respondents in either sample endorsed the item as true. This procedure yielded the 75 items (66 hostility items and 9 guilt items) in the final instrument.

A factor analysis using scale scores as variables was conducted on a sample of 85 male and 88 female college students. For male students, the resentment and suspicion subscales constitute one factor, whereas assault, indirect hostility, irritability, and verbal hostility constitute a second factor. For female students, the first factor includes the resentment, suspicion, and guilt subscales, whereas the second factor includes assault, indirect hostility, irritability, verbal hostility, and negativism.

Target Population

Developed with male and female college students in 1957 but extensively used since then with many other populations, including maritally violent men.

Format

The BDHI contains eight subscales, including assault, indirect hostility, irritability, negativism, resentment, suspicion, verbal hostility, and guilt. Sample items for each subscale follow:

1. *Assault (10 items)*

   • "Once in a while I cannot control my urge to harm others."
   • "I seldom strike back, even if someone hits me first."

2. *Indirect Hostility (9 items)*

   • "I never get mad enough to throw things."
   • "I sometimes spread gossip about people I don't like."

3. *Irritability (11 items)*

   • "I am irritated a great deal more than people are aware of."
   • "If someone doesn't treat me right, I don't let it annoy me."

4. *Negativism (5 items)*

   • "When someone is bossy, I do the opposite of what he/she asks."

5. *Resentment (8 items)*

   • "I don't seem to get what's coming to me."
   • "I don't know any people that I downright hate."

6. *Suspicion (10 items)*

   • "I know that people tend to talk about me behind my back."
   • "I have no enemies who really wish to harm me."

7. *Verbal Hostility (13 items)*

   • "When people yell at me, I yell back."
   • "I would rather concede a point than get into an argument about it."

8. *Guilt (9 items)*

   • "Failure gives me a feeling of remorse."
   • "It depresses me that I did not do more for my parents."

Administration and Scoring

Respondents endorse each item as either true or false. Scores for each subscale are derived by summing the number of true responses (several items are reverse-scored). A total hostility score is derived by summing true responses to all of the test items (after accounting for reverse-scored items). The measure takes approximately 15 minutes to complete.

Psychometric Evaluation

Norms

Norms are based on results from the original sample of 85 male and 88 female college students. For the total hostility scale (the sum of all seven hostility subscales, not including the guilt subscale), the mean for men was 30.87 (*SD* = 10.24) and for women was 27.74 (*SD* = 8.75). For the assault subscale, the mean for men was 5.07 (*SD* = 2.48) and for women was 3.27

(SD = 2.31). For the indirect hostility subscale, the mean for men was 4.47 (SD = 2.23) and for women was 5.17 (SD = 1.96). For the irritability subscale, the mean for men was 5.94 (SD = 2.65) and for women was 6.14 (SD = 2.78). For the negativism subscale, the mean for men was 2.19 (SD = 1.34) and for women was 2.30 (SD = 1.20). For the resentment subscale, the mean for men was 2.26 (SD = 1.89) and for women was 1.78 (SD = 1.63). For the suspicion subscale, the mean for men was 3.33 (SD = 2.07) and for women was 2.26 (SD = 1.81). For the verbal hostility subscale, the mean for men was 7.61 (SD = 2.74) and for women was 6.82 (SD = 2.59). For the guilt subscale, the mean for men was 5.34 (SD = 1.88) and for women was 4.41 (SD = 2.31).

Reliability

Reliability data are not presented by the authors. However, each item must have a minimum item–total correlation of .40 to be included in the instrument. Others, however, suggest that reliability of the subscales is poor (Biaggio, Supplee, & Curtis, 1981).

Validity

The scale has a moderate correlation with social desirability of .27 for college men and .30 for college women, using a method in which scores are correlated with ratings of the social desirability of each item by a separate but similar group of respondents. The BDHI has discriminated violent from nonviolent prisoners (Gunn & Gristwood, 1975) and has discriminated domestically assaultive men from controls on its Assault, Indirect Aggression, Irritability, Resentment, and Suspicion scales (Maiuro, Cahn, Vitaliano, Wagner, & Zegree, 1988). Biaggio and colleagues (Biaggio, 1980; Biaggio et al., 1981) suggest that the instrument has poor predictive validity.

Advantages

The different dimensions of hostility are logical and provide a broad picture of its different components, which may be particularly useful in clinical assessment.

Limitations

It is unlikely that the BDHI is measuring a unitary concept of hostility; more likely the scale is measuring several partially overlapping components of hostility. The poor reliability data and moderate correlation with social desirability limit the utility of this instrument as well.

Primary Scale Reference

Buss and Durkee (1957).

Scale Availability

Arnold H. Buss
Department of Psychology
330 Mezes Hall
University of Texas
Austin, TX 78712

Related References

Biaggio (1980); Biaggio Supplee, and Curtis (1981); Buss and Perry (1992); Eckhardt, Barbour, and Stuart (1997); Maiuro, Cahn, Vitaliano, Wagner, and Zegree (1988); O'Sullivan and Jemelka (1993).

General Comments and Recommendations for Researchers and Practitioners

The BDHI is the most commonly used measure in research on hostility in maritally violent men (Eckhardt et al., 1997). A newer version of the BDHI, the Aggression Questionnaire, has recently been developed with four subscales—anger, hostility, verbal aggression, and physical aggression (Buss & Perry, 1992)—with strong initial psychometric properties and clear relevance for the assessment of marital violence.

---

33. Hostile Automatic Thoughts Scale (HAT; Snyder, Crowson, Houston, Kurylo, & Poirer)

Description and Development of Assessment Method

The HAT is a brief self-report measure assessing hostile automatic thoughts. A group of 100 male and female college students were asked to vividly recall an experience of feeling hostile toward another person and to write at least five thoughts they had in these situations. Seventy-five items were retained after the authors reduced the item set based on redundancy or ambiguity. These items were then administered, along with other measures, to 309 undergraduates. Positive cognitions were interspersed in the item pool to reduce response sets. A principal-components analysis with varimax rotation was performed, leading to three interpretable factors with eigenvalues > 1 comprising a total of 30 items accounting for 31% of the variance. Psychometric properties were also examined on these 30 items. The 30 items were then readministered, along with other measures, to a second sample of 235 college students. The purpose was to cross-validate the findings of the first study in a second sample through confirmatory factor analysis and additional evaluation of reliability. Results from the second study closely corresponded with findings from the first in terms of factor structures, internal consistency reliability, and relationships with other measures; thus the 30 items and scale assignments were retained.

Target Population

Male and female college students. Could be used with other populations (e.g., adults in dating, cohabiting, or marital abusive or nonabusive relationships; or adults not currently in intimate relationships).

Format

The HAT contains 30 items on three scales. Scale names and sample items follow:

1. *Physical Aggression (11 items)*

   • "I hate this person so much I could kill him/her!"
   • "I want to beat the hell out of this person!"

2. *Derogation of Others (10 items)*

   • "What an idiot!"
   • "Why doesn't this person just shut up?"

3. *Revenge (9 items)*

   • "I just want to hurt this person as bad as he/she hurt me."
   • "I'll show this person!"

Administration and Scoring

The measure takes about 5 minutes to complete. Respondents rate each item on a 5-point Likert-type scale indicating the frequency with which the thought occurred within the last week (1 = *not at all,* 2 = *sometimes,*

3 = *moderately often,* 4 = *often,* and 5 = *all the time).* Items are summed to produce a score for each subscale and a total score.

Psychometric Evaluation

Norms

In Study 1 in the primary reference, the total scale mean from a sample of undergraduate introductory psychology students was 59.41 (SD = 17.17). The mean for males was 59.79 (SD = 17.25) and for females was 58.64 (SD = 17.05); these did not significantly differ. In Study 2, also conducted on undergraduate introductory psychology students, the total scale mean was 58.02 (SD = 19.15). The mean for males was 63.09 (SD = 22.50) and significantly higher than that for females, which was 52.86 (SD = 13.23), $t(233)$ = 13.11, $p < .001$.

Reliability

Cronbach's alphas on the three scales was .92 (physical aggression), .88 (derogation of others), and .91 (revenge). Cronbach's alpha on the total HAT scale was .94, and split-half reliability (based on odd/even items) was .95, indicating very good internal consistency.

Validity

Convergent validity was supported by the scale's moderate positive correlations with other indices of hostility and modest but significant correlations with measures of other negative affect states (i.e., depression and anxiety). Discriminant validity was supported by the scale's lack of relationship with a measure of positive thoughts about one's self and daily functioning, which the authors expected to be unrelated to hostility.

Advantages

The scale is highly flexible and could easily be adapted for a variety of specific clinical or research uses. It is also brief and easy to score and has promising initial psychometric properties.

Limitations

Scale development was conducted on college students with nonspecific thought referents; the scale thus needs further work to evaluate its utility for use within intimate relationships.

Primary Scale Reference

Snyder, Crowson, Houston, Kurylo, and Poirer (1997).

Scale Availability

> C. R. Snyder
> Graduate Training Program in Clinical Psychology
> Department of Psychology
> Fraser Hall
> University of Kansas
> Lawrence, KS 66045-2462

General Comments and Recommendations for Researchers and Practitioners

The HAT taps cognitive aspects of interpersonal interactions that might prove important in clinical work or research with partner abuse. Although not yet applied to violent relationships, the HAT could be used as a screening device to identify potentially violent reactions to conflict or as an outcome measure in an anger management program or other program related to the treatment of domestic abuse. The instructions could be modified to extend the use of the scale to more transient (e.g., automatic thoughts in the last few minutes) or more traitlike (automatic thoughts most of the time) situations, and also to be more situation specific (reporting such thoughts in response to one's partner, or to one's partner in given real or hypothetical situations).

---

34. Multidimensional Anger Inventory (MAI; Siegel)

Description and Development of Assessment Method

The MAI is a self-report measure covering a range of anger dimensions. The items were rationally constructed to cover each subscale. Some items were adapted from existing measures, whereas others were written by the author. The instrument was given to a sample of 74 male and 124 female college students who received experimental credit for their participation. It was also given to a total of 288 men who ranged in age from 40 to 62 years old and who had been working in a particular job setting (either a high-noise or low-noise factory) for at least 10 years.

Two separate principal-components analyses were conducted. One included only items from the mode of expression subscale, whereas the second included all remaining items. The mode of expression items yielded two factors: anger-in (withholding angry feelings) and anger-out (verbal/ physical aggression). The remaining items yielded a 3-factor solution: anger arousal (frequency, duration, and magnitude items), anger-eliciting situations, and hostile outlook.

Target Population

A wide range of populations, including college students, blue-collar men, maritally violent men, nonclinical community populations, and incarcerated men.

Format

The MAI contains 38 self-descriptive items distributed across the following six subscales: frequency, duration, magnitude, mode of expression, hostile outlook, and range of anger-arousing situations. Sample items follow:

1. *Frequency (5 items)*
   "I tend to get angry more frequently than most people."
2. *Duration (2 items)*
   "When I get angry, I stay angry for hours."
3. *Magnitude (4 items)*
   "I often feel angrier than I think I should."
4. *Mode of Expression (12 items)*
   "When I hide my anger from others, I forget about it pretty quickly."
   "When I am angry with someone, I take it out on whoever is around."
5. *Hostile Outlook (6 items)*
   "People talk about me behind my back."
6. *Range of Anger-Arousing Situations (9 items)*
   "I get angry when I am delayed."
   "I get angry when I am not given credit for something I have done."

Administration and Scoring

Participants rate each item on the basis of how well it describes them, using a 5-point Likert scale ranging from *completely undescriptive of you* (1) to *completely descriptive of you* (5). Items are summed to yield individual subscale or total measure scores. Several items are reverse-scored. The measure takes approximately 10 minutes to complete.

Psychometric Evaluation

Norms
The only reported means are for the total scale. The factory sample had a mean total score of 71.18, whereas the college sample had a mean total score of 68.45, a significant difference.

Reliability
Test–retest reliabilities across 3–4 weeks range from .50 to .75 (Siegel, 1985, 1986). The overall alpha levels were .84 for the college sample and .89 for the factory sample, with subscale alpha coefficients ranging from .51 to .83, indicating moderate to good internal consistency.

Validity
The relevant MAI subscales demonstrate weak correlations with some other measures of anger and hostility (e.g., the BDHI) and stronger correlations with others (e.g., the Novaco Anger Scale). A variety of studies by other researchers (Eckhardt et al., 1997) reveal an inconsistent pattern of results, making it difficult to adequately determine the validity of the MAI.

Advantages
The instrument assesses anger through respondents' self-descriptions on several dimensions, which provide a complementary perspective to more behavioral assessments.

Limitations
The MAI focuses on how frequently anger occurs (by assessing how self-descriptive the statements are) rather than the intensity of angry feelings in specific situations.

Primary Scale Reference

Siegel (1986).

Scale Availability

Judith M. Siegal
Division of Behavioral Sciences and Health Education
UCLA School of Public Health
Los Angeles, CA 90024

Related References

Boyle and Vivian (1996); D. G. Dutton and Starzomski (1994); Eckhardt, Barbour, and Stuart (1997); Siegel (1985).

General Comments and Recommendations for Researchers and Practitioners

The MAI assesses anger as a multidimensional construct consisting of six dimensions: frequency, duration, magnitude, mode of expression, hostile outlook, and range of anger-eliciting situations. It has been used in studies of maritally violent men.

---

35. Novaco Anger Scale (NAS; Novaco)

Description and Development of Assessment Method

The NAS consists of 90 items describing potentially anger-provoking situations. An 80-item version has also been published (Novaco, 1977). Items were developed intuitively by the author following interviews with college students about things that make them angry. Items were administered to a sample of 138 male and 138 female undergraduate students who received experimental credit for their participation. A principal-components analysis revealed one underlying scale for both males and females.

Target Population

College students and outpatient and general population samples, as well as maritally violent populations.

Format

The scale contains no subscales. Sample items follow:

- "You are walking along, minding your own business, when someone comes rushing past, knocking you out of his way."
- "You are trying to concentrate, and a person near you is tapping his foot."
- "Acts of prejudice against a minority or ethnic group."

Administration and Scoring

Respondents rate the degree to which the incident described by each item would "anger or provoke you" on a 5-point Likert scale ranging from *not at all* (1) to *very much* (5). A single summary score is derived by adding individual item scores. Administration time is approximately 15 minutes.

Psychometric Evaluation

Norms

In the initial study, the 90-item version had a mean of 299.8 (SD = 39.2) for males and 308.3 (SD = 45.3) for females. Significant differences between gender have been found on 36 of the 90 items. In general, males rated physical content items higher than females; females rated items describing unjust situations higher than males. In a later study, the 80-item version (Novaco, 1977) had a mean of 241.4 (SD = 42.85) for undergraduates.

Reliability

A preliminary study by the author found the scale to be highly internally consistent, with Cronbach alphas of .94 for males and .96 for females. In another study, test–retest reliability was only .17 (Biaggio et al., 1981).

Validity

The NAS was not significantly correlated with either self-ratings of anger provocation or reactions to imagined or role-played situations (Biaggio et al., 1981), suggesting weak criterion validity. Convergent validity with established measures of anger and hostility has varied widely (mean r = .24). The instrument has been shown to discriminate between participants with and without anger control problems, supporting its known groups validity. No correlation was found between the NAS and the Crowne–Marlowe Scale, a measure of social desirability (Crowne & Marlowe, 1960).

Advantages

The NAS measures predisposition to anger rather than behaviorally angry responses to real or analog situations, thus making it a useful screening instrument for potentially at-risk populations.

Limitations

The instrument does not contain any items relating directly to intimate partners. It has low test–retest reliability and limited validity.

Primary Scale Reference

Novaco (1975).

Scale Availability

In primary reference.

Related References

Biaggio, Supplee, and Curtis (1981); Eckhardt, Barbour, and Stuart (1997); Lohr, Hamberger, and Bonge (1988); Novaco (1977).

General Comments and Recommendations for Researchers and Practitioners

The NAS has been used with several studies of maritally violent men and assesses the degree to which respondents find particular situations anger arousing.

> Thus, high scores could indicate that (a) the individual experiences at least mild anger to a wide range of these situations, or (b) the individual experiences intense levels of anger to relatively few anger-provoking situations . . . and may provide useful data on antecedent or activating situations associated with anger arousal as opposed to data on anger intensity, duration, or manner of anger expression. (Eckhardt et al., 1997, p. 346)

---

36. State–Trait Anger Expression Inventory (STAXI; Spielberger)

Description and Development of Assessment Method

The STAXI consists of 44 items, which measure experiential, expressive, transitory, and trait aspects of anger. The scales were derived through factor analysis.

Target Population

Adult clients, including maritally violent individuals (also norms for college students and adolescents).

Format

The STAXI contains five subscales that assess State Anger, Trait Anger, and Anger Expression (consisting of Anger In, Anger Out, and Anger Control). State Anger assesses transitory experiences of anger, Trait Anger assesses the tendency to respond to a variety of situations with anger, Anger Expression/ Anger In assesses the extent to which respondents experience but inhibit their angry feelings, Anger Expression/Anger Out assesses the extent to which anger is expressed outwardly, and Anger Expression/Anger Control assesses the extent to which respondents effectively control and reduce their anger. Sample items for each subscale follow:

1. *State Anger (10 items)*
   How I feel right now:
   "I feel like yelling at somebody."
2. *Trait Anger (10 items)*
   How I generally feel:
   "I have a fiery temper."
3. *Anger Expression (24 items)*
   Anger In
   When angry or furious . . .
   "I boil inside, but I don't show it."
   Anger Out
   When angry or furious . . .
   "I express my anger."
   Anger Control
   When angry or furious . . .
   "I calm down faster than most other people."

Administration and Scoring

The STAXI takes between 10 and 15 minutes to complete and is written at a fifth-grade reading level. Responses are on a 4-point Likert scale ranging from *not at all* to *very much so* (State Anger) and *almost never* to *almost always* (Trait Anger and Anger Expression). Respondents fill out items that are duplicated directly onto the scoring sheet. Subscale items are then summed and converted to standardized scores.

Psychometric Evaluation

Norms
See primary scale reference.

Reliability

The STAXI subscales have excellent internal consistency, with alphas of .80 and higher.

Validity

Convergent validity has been supported through significant correlations with other measures of anger and hostility (Deffenbacher et al., 1996; Spielberger, 1988).

Advantages

The STAXI has strong psychometric properties and encompasses a broad and unique model of anger.

Limitations

The instrument has a somewhat complicated scoring system.

Primary Scale Reference

Spielberger (1988).

Scale Availability

Psychological Assessment Resources, Inc.
P.O. Box 998
Odessa, FL 33556
(800) 331-TEST
http://www.parinc.com

or

Sigma Assessment Systems, Inc.
1110 Military Street
P.O. Box 610984
Port Huron, MI 48061-0984
Fax: (800) 361-9411

Related References

Boyle and Vivian (1996); Deffenbacher, Oetting, Thwaites, Lynch, Baker, Stark, et al. (1996); Eckhardt, Barbour, and Stuart (1997); Spielberger and Sydeman (1994).

General Comments and Recommendations for Researchers and Practitioners

The STAXI is a strong scale for use in clinical or research settings and is useful as both a screening tool and an outcome measure. It is based on a unique model of anger that distinguishes between anger, hostility, and aggression; between state and trait aspects of anger; and between the experience and expression of anger. Although selected subscales have been used with maritally violent populations (Boyle & Vivian, 1996; see Eckhardt et al., 1997, for brief review), no study to date with this population has used the scale in its entirety.

37. Distressing Event Questionnaire (DEQ; Kubany, Leisen, Kaplan, & Kelly)

Description and Development of Assessment Method

The DEQ is a brief self-report scale for assessing posttraumatic stress disorder (PTSD) according to *DSM–IV* criteria. Items for the DEQ were written to correspond to *DSM–IV* Criteria A through F. Additional items were included to assess trauma-related guilt, anger, and unresolved grief. Six PTSD experts then rated for instructions, content validity, and response formats. Final items were administered to a variety of samples (war combat veterans and four samples of treatment-seeking women survivors of various types of abuse: incest, rape, partner abuse, and women with histories of prostitution and substance and sexual abuse) to assess reliability and validity.

Target Population

Male and female victims of diverse causes of trauma. Has psychometric data available on women with histories of partner abuse.

Format

Respondents fill out each item, corresponding to the six *DSM–IV* criteria for the diagnosis of PTSD, as well as the additional questions pertaining to guilt, anger, and unresolved grief.

Administration and Scoring

The Flesch reading level of the scale is Grade 7.3. The scale should take several minutes to complete. Cutoff scores of 18 or higher were optimal for classifying women as meeting or not meeting diagnostic criteria for PTSD. A computerized scoring system is also available from the authors.

Psychometric Evaluation

Norms

Available for several different populations in the primary reference.

Reliability

For the samples of women, internal consistency reliability was good, with alphas ranging from .80 to .91 for Criterion B symptoms, .84 to .91 for Criterion C symptoms, .83 to .85 for Criterion D symptoms, and .94 to .95 for the entire scale. In a sample of battered women, test–retest reliability across a 1- to 3-week period was .83 for the total score.

Validity

The DEQ demonstrated good convergent validity with other PTSD instruments and indices of depression, self-esteem, social avoidance and distress, and trauma-related guilt. Discriminative validity was demonstrated with the lack of association with social desirability.

Advantages

The scale has good psychometric properties, is easy to use in clinical and research settings, and is one of the rare scales of its type developed on samples of female abuse survivors who were also ethnically diverse (see Kubany, Leisen, Kaplan, & Kelly, 2000, for a review).

Limitations

Caution must be used in applying this instrument exclusively to obtain a diagnosis of PTSD.

Primary Scale Reference

Kubany, Leisen, Kaplan, and Kelly (2000).

Scale Availability

Edward S. Kubany
National Center for PTSD
Pacific Islands Division
Department of Veteran's Affairs
VAM and ROC
1132 Bishop Street, Suite 307
Honolulu, HI 96813

Related References

Kubany, Leisen, Kaplan, Watson, et al. (2000).

General Comments and Recommendations for Researchers and Practitioners

Several different versions of the instructions are available for clinicians aware of the traumatic event the respondent experienced to make the scale appropriate for different populations. In addition, a version is available when the clinician is unaware of the event experienced, such as for general surveys or emergency room screenings. Depending on one's desired use of the scale, one can use cutoff scores or examine the pattern and severity of specific PTSD symptoms or symptom clusters. Because of their association with failure to recover from PTSD, the scale also includes items assessing trauma-related guilt, anger, and unresolved grief.

The authors recommend use of this instrument in conjunction with the Traumatic Life Events Questionnaire (TLEQ; Kubany, Leisen, Kaplan, Watson, et al., 2000, which measures a broad range of traumatic events.

---

38. Interpersonal Jealousy Scale (IJS; Mathes & Severa)

Description and Development of Assessment Method

The IJS is a 28-item self-report measure assessing jealousy in a romantic relationship. Items were written to reflect jealous content; psychometrics were evaluated on college student samples.

Target Population

Individuals in intimate relationships.

Format

The 28-item scale consists of descriptions of brief potentially jealousy-inducing situations. Sample items follow:

- "If ____ went out with same-sex friends, I would feel compelled to know what he/she did."

- "I don't think it would bother me if _____ flirted with someone of the opposite sex." (reverse-scored).
- "I feel possessive toward _____."

Administration and Scoring

The scale takes about 5–10 minutes to complete. Items are rated on a 9-point scale from *absolutely true, agree completely* to *absolutely false, disagree completely.* Seven items are reverse-scored. Total scores are obtained by summing items.

Psychometric Evaluation

Norms

The mean total scores were 139.3 (*SD* = 35.7) for men and 127.0 (*SD* = 36.0) for women (Mathes, Phillips, Skowran, & Dick, 1982).

Reliability

Internal consistency reliability (coefficient alpha) was .92 across the 28 items.

Validity

The scale was significantly positively correlated with romantic love and dependency, and with insecurity in women, and had a low correlation with social desirability, supporting the scale's convergent and discriminant validity (Mathes & Severa, 1981). The scale also demonstrated concurrent validity with significant correlations with behavioral measures of threat and possessiveness (Mathes et al., 1982). More recently, the scale has demonstrated additional evidence of concurrent validity as it differentiated assaultive from nonassaultive husbands (e.g., D. Dutton, vanGinkel, & Landolt, 1996).

Advantages

The scale has strong validation data and is brief and simple to score.

Limitations

The 9-point response scale has confusing anchor discriminations (i.e., respondents must make distinctions between *absolutely true, definitely true, true,* and *slightly true*) and should be reduced to a 5- or 7-point scale.

Primary Scale Reference

Mathes and Severa (1981).

Scale Availability

Eugene W. Mathes
Psychology Department
Western Illinois University
Macomb, IL 61455

Related References

D. Dutton, vanGinkel, and Landolt (1996); Mathes, Phillips, Skowran, and Dick (1982); Meehan, Holtzworth-Munroe, & Herron (2001).

General Comments and Recommendations for Researchers and Practitioners

This measure assesses a central construct linked with abusive and controlling relationships and has demonstrated concurrent validity within an assaultive population. Developed on students, some items would need revision for use with adults/married partners (e.g., wording involving getting help with one's homework). Items would also have to be reworded for use with same-sex couples. Finally, the Likert scale should be modified to include fewer than nine response options. The instrument has recently been used in the study of physically aggressive relationships (Meehan et al., 2001).

---

39. Inventory of Beliefs About Wife Beating (IBWB; Saunders, Lynch, Grayson, & Linz)

Description and Development of Assessment Method

The IBWB is a 36-item measure of beliefs and attitudes about husband-to-wife violence. First, 119 items were constructed based on the wife abuse literature and clinical exposure to battered women and their partners. Items were eliminated on the basis of low inter-item correlations or "if they were ambiguous or required knowledge of facts" (Saunders, Lynch, Grayson, & Linz, 1987, p. 42), leaving 41 items. The scale was then administered to 675 students and factor analyzed using first varimax and then oblique rotation. This yielded 12 unrotated factors. These 12 factors were combined into five reliable subscales comprising 36 items based on item-scale loadings and the elimination of factors with poor reliabilities. Construct and known groups validity studies were then carried out with a variety of samples.

Target Population

Partner-violent men.

Format

The five subscales are Wife Beating Is Justified, reflecting beliefs that a husband has the right to beat his wife or that certain actions on the wife's part justify violence; Wives Gain From Beatings, reflecting the view that wives in some way can foresee the violence, desire it, or get attain desired sympathy and attention from it; Help Should Be Given, reflecting the belief that individuals, the law, and social service agencies should assist victims of domestic violence; Offender Should Be Punished, reflecting the extent of consequences the assaulter should face for wife beating; and Offender Is Responsible, reflecting the view that battering is the fault of the husband. Sample items follow:

1. *Wife Beating Is Justified (12 items)*

   • "Even when women lie to their husbands they do not deserve to get a beating." (reverse-scored)

2. *Wives Gain From Beatings (7 items)*

   • "Wives try to get beaten by their husbands to get sympathy from others."

3. *Help Should Be Given (5 items)*

   • "Social agencies should do more to help battered women."

4. *Offender Should Be Punished (5 items)*

   • "The best way to deal with wife beating is to arrest the husband."

5. *Offender Is Responsible (4 items, including 2 repeated from Offender Should Be Punished)*

   • "Cases of wife beating are the fault of the husband."

Administration and Scoring

Respondents fill out 36 items on a 7-point Likert scale ranging from *strongly disagree* to *strongly agree*. The scale takes about 10 minutes to complete. Scoring is done by reversing designated items and then summing items from each subscale.

Psychometric Evaluation

Norms

The primary reference contains means and standard deviations for batterer, student, and female advocate for battered women samples. However, norms from the general population are lacking.

Reliability

Internal consistency reliabilities of the scales range from good to moderate: Wife Beating Is Justified, .86; Wives Gain From Beatings, .77; Help Should Be Given, .67; Offender Should Be Punished, .61; and Offender Is Responsible, .62.

Validity

The authors conducted several validity studies that were reported in the scale development paper. In support of construct validity, the scales were correlated in predicted ways with rape myth acceptance, attitudes about sex roles, hostility toward women, propensity toward violence, and, as predicted, were generally not related to personality. Gender discriminated all but the Offender Is Responsible scales, and scales had little to no relationship with measures of social desirability. The authors demonstrated known groups validity by comparing scores on the IBWB among three samples: advocates for battered women, college students, and men who batter. The groups differed in the expected directions on all subscales, with batterers scoring higher than advocates on beliefs that wife beating is justified and that wives gain from abuse, and advocates scoring higher than batterers on beliefs that help should be given to victims, offenders should be punished, and offenders are responsible for violence. Students' scores fell in between those of the other two groups on each subscale, as the authors predicted.

Advantages

Advantages of the IBWB include strong validation data, the range of populations in which validation studies were carried out, and ease of scoring and administration.

Limitations

Three of the five scales have five or fewer items and correspondingly lower reliabilities (range = .61–.67) than the other two scales. Norms on the general population are not available.

Primary Scale Reference

Saunders, Lynch, Grayson, and Linz (1987).

Scale Availability

Scale is contained in primary reference.

Related References

None available.

General Comments and Recommendations for Researchers and Practitioners

Although designed primarily to examine attitudes related to the perpetration of wife abuse in violent husbands, the scale can also be used with other populations, such as students, men and women in dating relationships, people working with men who batter; and those working in the various social service agencies and institutions with which battered women come in contact. The IBWB

> can help us understand more fully social responses to the plight of battered women. . . . Finally, it can contribute to a greater understanding of the cultural origins of women abuse, which can subsequently improve methods for preventing this serious and widespread problem. (Saunders et al., 1987, p. 53)

---

40. Negative Intentions Questionnaire (NIQ; Holtzworth-Munroe & Hutchinson)

Description and Development of Assessment Method

The NIQ is a measure assessing men's negative attributions of wives' behaviors. The scale was designed to be used in conjunction with Holtzworth-Munroe and Anglin's (1991) Problematic Marital Situations Vignettes (described in chap. 9, this volume), which pose a series of hypothetical provocative marital stimuli, but the scale could be used with other situations, real or hypothetical.

The scale was modeled after the Responsibility Attribution Question-naire (RAQ; Fincham & Bradbury, 1992), an instrument that assesses attributions in maritally distressed couples. The NIQ was designed to capture attributions that might be especially relevant for maritally violent men.

Target Population

Maritally violent men, but could also be used with maritally violent women, and nonviolent individuals.

Format

In response to a series of hypothetical problematic marital situation vignettes, respondents rate their attributions regarding their wives' possible negative intentions. Respondents rate each of the following five negative intentions for each vignette:

> *She was trying to . . . :*
> "make me angry"
> "hurt my feelings"
> "put me down"
> "get something for herself"
> "pick a fight"

Administration and Scoring

Hypothetical marital vignettes are presented on a tape recorder. Respondents are asked to imagine that each scenario is happening in their own relationship. They then rate the degree to which they agree or disagree (on a 6-point scale) that their partner had acted with each specific negative intention. Husbands are also asked to rate the valence of their wife's last behavior in each vignette on a 1–13 scale, where 1 = *very negative* and 13 = *very positive,* to examine the perceived impact of each situation. The length of time to complete the scale obviously depends on the number of stimulus scenarios presented, but the time to complete each set of negative intention ratings is about 1 minute. Scoring is conducted by averaging respondents' ratings on the scales to form a composite measure of wives' negative intentions for each scenario. This score ranges from 1 to 6, with higher scores reflecting more negative attributions regarding wives' intentions.

Psychometric Evaluation

Norms

The primary reference presents means and standard deviations for violent, distressed nonviolent, and nondistressed nonviolent groups of men for each problematic marital situation.

Reliability

Composite scores had high internal consistency reliability with a Cronbach's alpha of .95.

Validity

Convergent validity was supported with a correlation of .71 between to NIQ and the measure of responsibility attributions used in the primary reference, the RAQ. Criterion validity was supported by the scale's ability to discriminate maritally violent from both distressed nonviolent and nondistressed nonviolent men such that maritally violent men were more likely than those in the comparison groups to attribute negative intent to the wife's actions.

Advantages

The measure is brief and easy to administer and score. It could easily be adapted for use with a variety of scenarios presented in a variety of formats (including actual rather than hypothetical partner behaviors) and for use with female partners.

Limitations

The study sample of violent men was recruited from a domestic violence treatment program, and thus criterion validity of the NIQ may not be applicable to other groups of violent men.

Primary Scale Reference

Holtzworth-Munroe and Hutchinson (1993).

Scale Availability

Amy Holtzworth-Munroe
Department of Psychology
Indiana University
Bloomington, IN 47405

Related References

Fincham and Bradbury (1992).

General Comments and Recommendations for Researchers and Practitioners

The NIQ is practical for use in both clinical and research settings and can be flexibly applied to a range of stimulus situations. This work offers a useful mechanism for studying cognitive attributional processes that might play key roles in violence escalation and justification.

41. Personal and Relationships Profile (PRP; Straus, Hamby, Boney-McCoy, & Sugarman[1])

Description and Development of Assessment Method

The PRP is a comprehensive pencil-and-paper measure assessing risk factors and etiological factors in partner abuse. Constructs included were based on those identified in the literature to be theoretically or empirically related to partner assault. Scale development was initiated by a theoretical analysis of each construct to be measured to identify domains of the construct. The authors created item pools based on reviews of existing measures and their clinical and research expertise. Item sets were revised according to discussion among the research team and in some cases pilot-testing of items for difficulty and clarity. Revised item sets were administered to student samples (Ns ranging from 200 to 400). Items were included based on item analysis (highest item–total scores), factor analysis (highest factor loadings), or in some cases, content analysis (choosing items with lower coefficients to adequately sample the domain). Scale development is ongoing (see Straus, Hamby, Boney-McCoy, & Sugarman, 1999).

---

1. These authors designed the PRP and authored some of the scales. Others authored or coauthored specific scales; these are E. DeVoe, T. Dietz, G. Kaufman-Kantor, E. M. Kinard, V. Mouradian, S. Ross, S. Stith, L.Williams, and C. Yodanis.

Target Population

Adults in abusive relationships, particularly perpetrators of partner assault. Could also be used to assess general or at-risk populations, such as community samples or maritally distressed couples.

Format

The PRP assesses both intrapsychic and interpersonal variables across 21 scales (plus a social desirability response bias scale). "The substantive scales measure constructs for which there is an empirical or theoretical basis to expect a link to physically assaulting a partner" (Straus & Mouradian, 1999, p. 4). Scales and sample items follow:

Personal or Intrapsychic Scales:
1. *Antisocial personality (9 items)*
   "I often do things that are against the law."
2. *Borderline personality (9 items)*
   "My mood is always changing."
3. *Criminal history (8 items)*
   "Before age 15, I physically attacked someone with the idea of seriously hurting them."
4. *Depression (8 items)*
   "I am so sad, sometimes I wonder why I bother to go on living."
5. *Gender hostility (10 items)*
   "Women treat men badly."
6. *Neglect history (8 items)*
   "My parents did not comfort me when I was upset."
7. *Posttraumatic stress disorder (8 items)*
   "I am easily startled."
8. *Social desirability response bias (13 items)*
   "I sometimes feel resentful when I don't get my way." (reverse-scored)
9. *Social integration (10 items)*
   "I share my thoughts with a family member."
10. *Stressful conditions (9 items)*
    "People at work or school don't get along with me."
11. *Substance abuse (8 items)*
    "I have been treated for a drug problem."

12. *Sexual abuse history (8 items)*
    "Before I was 18, an adult in my family made me look at or touch their private parts (sex organs) or looked at or touched mine."
13. *Violence approval (10 items)*
    "I can think of a situation when I would approve of a husband slapping a wife's face."
14. *Violent socialization (8 items)*
    "My mother or father told me to hit back if someone hit or insulted me."

Relationship Scales:
15. *Anger management (9 items)*
    "I feel my blood rising when I start to get mad at my partner." (reverse-scored)
16. *Communication problems (8 items)*
    "When my partner says something mean, I usually say something mean back."
17. *Conflict (9 items)*
    "My partner and I disagree about when to have sex."
18. *Dominance (9 items)*
    "I have a right to know everything my partner does."
19. *Jealousy (8 items)*
    "I would hate it if my partner confided in someone besides me."
20. *Negative attribution (4 items)*
    "My partner does things just to annoy me."
21. *Relationship commitment (6 items)*
    "I have considered leaving my partner." (reverse-scored)
22. *Relationship distress (8 items)*
    "My partner and I have a very good relationship." (reverse-scored)

Administration and Scoring

The PRP takes an average of 32 minutes to complete and requires a sixth-grade reading ability as measured by the Flesch-Kincaid Grade Level score. Respondents complete a 4-point Likert scale with 1 = *strongly disagree*, 2 = *disagree*, 3 = *agree*, and 4 = *strongly agree*. Individual scales are then summed for total scale scores after reversing items worded in the reverse direction. Straus and Mouradian (1999) provide adjustment coefficients and a formula for adjusting items based on Social Desirability scale scores. Scores can be plotted on a single profile form.

Psychometric Evaluation

Discussion of specific psychometric data for each scale can be found in Straus and Mouradian (1999).

Norms

Scale means and standard deviations for student and offender populations are presented in Straus and Mouradian (1999). The authors suggest using scores one standard deviation above the student means as indicating a characteristic of clinical concern.

Reliability

Internal consistency reliability was reported for student and offender samples. The brief table below, from Straus and Mouradian (1999, p. 9), reports the percentage of scales falling within each Cronbach's alpha range:

Alpha	Students	Offenders
≤ .59	—	13%
.60 to .69	27%	40%
.70 to .79	41%	40%
.80 to .87	32%	7%
Mean α	.74	.69

Reported alphas suggest an overall adequate level of internal consistency reliability for scales of the PRP.

Validity

Known groups validity was evaluated by comparing scale means between male and female college students, and between male students and incarcerated offender populations. For gender comparisons, male students significantly differed from female students on 18 or 21 scales predominantly in ways consistent with previous research on gender differences.

For student versus offender comparisons, only 12 substantive scales were compared, because the offender population was given an earlier version of the PRP containing fewer scales. Eleven of the 12 scales (all but Substance Abuse) indicate a higher degree of problems for the offenders than for male college students, suggesting that the scale adequately discriminates between these two groups. However, when using a more conservative p value to adjust for familywise error, the Antisocial Personality scale failed to discriminate students from the offenders, calling into question the validity of this scale.

Across samples, approximately 90% of the scales were either moderately or strongly correlated with the Social Desirability scale, reflecting rather weak discriminant validity with this construct and suggesting that social desirability must be controlled for when interpreting scale scores. Finally, in the student sample, there were modest correlations between PRP scales and a history of partner assault, evidencing relatively weak criterion validity. All of the offenders had a history of partner assault, and thus this association could not be tested within this sample.

Advantages

By measuring a wide array of partner-assault-related constructs using one set of instructions and uniform response format and scale norming, the PRP maximizes the amount of information one can obtain in a limited time frame while allowing for comparison across scales. The PRP is thus an efficient and exhaustive measure of etiological factors and correlates of partner assault and will be of interest to clinicians and researchers alike.

Limitations

Item pool inclusion and psychometric evaluation of the PRP were based on development with college student and incarcerated domestic violence offender samples. Thus, the scale's performance with more diverse populations is not yet known. The Antisocial scale weakly discriminated college students from incarcerated domestic violence offenders and is thus of questionable validity. Further research is needed to evaluate test–retest reliability, demonstrate construct validity of individual scales, and establish clinical cutoff points for scale scores. Finally, the authors caution that the scales of the PRP are intended only for initial screening for further in-depth consideration and not for formal diagnosis.

Primary Scale Reference

Straus, Hamby, Boney-McCoy, and Sugarman (1999).

Scale Availability

Murray A. Straus
Family Research Laboratory
University of New Hampshire
Durham, NH 03824
E-mail: mas2@christa.unh.edu
Web site: http://www.unh.edu/frl

Related References

Straus and Mouradian (1999); Straus and Ramirez (1999).

General Comments and Recommendations for Researchers and Practitioners

The PRP was developed for the purpose of screening, treatment planning, and etiological research and can be used in treatment, research, or applied forensic settings. Clinicians and researchers often wish to assess many factors associated with relationship aggression but face the dilemma of sacrificing comprehensiveness for feasibility. "Researchers often deal with the length problem by developing ad hoc and unvalidated short forms, and clinicians deal with it by not using these tests. The PRP can be thought of as a set of tested and validated short forms" (Straus & Mouradian, 1999, p. 5). Providing a profile of scores on 22 constructs related to partner assault, the scale proves thorough and efficient for a variety of applications. The instrument addresses both characteristics and background of the target individual and characteristics of the relationship, and particular scales could be used as treatment outcome measures. Note that the scale does not include direct indices of physical or psychological abuse and thus should be used in conjunction with this type of measure (e.g., the Revised Conflict Tactics Scale; Straus et al., 1996). The authors report that the scale remains under development; they intend to reduce the number of scales based on their empirical relationships to partner violence and on results of psychometric analysis with additional samples. Despite the preliminary form of the device, the PRP is the only multiconstruct instrument designed for use with perpetrators of partner violence and offers a novel approach to comprehensive assessment of individual and relationship variables with this population.

42. Posttraumatic Diagnostic Scale (PTDS; Foa, Cashman, Jaycox, & Perry)

Description and Development of Assessment Method

The PTDS is a 42-item self-report scale for screening and assessing PTSD. The scale was developed by generating an initial item pool of 10 categories of traumatic situations, questions about the most distressing situation, the *DSM–IV* PTSD symptoms, the duration of these symptoms, and inquiries about a wide range of impairments. The questions were then reviewed by

15 PTSD experts, leading to the final version consisting of 11 specific categories and 1 residual category.

Target Population

Male and female victims of diverse causes of trauma.

Format

The scale begins with a checklist of 12 traumatic events that respondents might have experienced or witnessed. Respondents then indicate which event has disturbed them the most in the past month and are asked to briefly describe the event in the provided space. The remaining questions refer to this event. Criterion A questions include 4 yes/no questions about injury to self or others and how the individual felt at the time of the event. Individuals then complete 17 PTSD symptom items covering reexperiencing, avoidance, and arousal. Respondents rate the frequency of each symptom in the past month on a 4-point scale (0 = *not at all or only one time*, 3 = *five or more times per week/almost always*). To assess Criterion F, 9 additional yes/no items assess impairment across a range of areas. Sample items follow:

- "Experiencing dreams or nightmares about the traumatic event"
- "Trying not to think about, talk about, or have feelings about the traumatic event"
- "Feeling irritable or having fits of anger"

Administration and Scoring

The scale takes about 5 minutes to complete. The reading level is between 7th and 11th grade. To meet the diagnosis of PTSD, it is required that responses must include the following: presence of physical injury or threat to life; feeling helpless or terrified during the event; ratings of 1 or higher on at least one reexperiencing symptom, three avoidance symptoms, and two arousal symptoms, symptoms spanning at least 1 month, and impairment in at least one area of functioning. One can also obtain a severity score by summing the 17 symptom items.

Psychometric Evaluation

Norms

Norms on each symptom scale for respondents with and without PTSD are presented in the primary reference.

Reliability

Alphas were .92 (total symptom severity), .78 (reexperiencing), .84 (avoidance), and .84 (arousal), reflecting the scale's good internal consistency. The scale evidenced good temporal stability, with test–retest reliability on diagnoses, using kappa, of .74 over 2–3 weeks. Test–retest reliabilities for total scores were .83 (total symptoms), .77 (reexperiencing), .81 (avoidance), and .85 (arousal).

Validity

The scale evidenced good convergent validity with high associations with the Structured Clinical Interview for *DSM–IV* diagnoses of PTSD (Spitzer, Williams, Gibbons, & First, 1992) and scales assessing trauma-related psychopathology.

Advantages

With its complete correspondence to all six *DSM–IV* criteria for PTSD, the PTDS offers both severity scores and diagnostic ability in a self-report format.

Limitations

Diagnoses obtained should be considered preliminary or used primarily for screening, because true diagnoses are best obtained with evaluation by a trained clinician using a semistructured approach.

Primary Scale Reference

Foa, Cashman, Jaycox, and Perry (1997).

Scale Availability

Edna Foa
Center for the Treatment and Study of Anxiety
Medical College of PA Division
Allegheny University of Health Sciences
3200 Henry Ave
Philadelphia, PA 19129
E-mail: Foa@AUHS.edu

General Comments and Recommendations for Researchers and Practitioners

Because the development sample included assault victims (as opposed to solely combat veterans, as is characteristic of many scales assessing PTSD symptoms; Foa et al., 1997), this instrument should be appropriate for use with victims of partner violence. However, further testing with this population is warranted. The scale offers a reliable and valid instrument not only for use in obtaining a dimensional severity score but also as a diagnostic tool.

43. Propensity for Abusiveness Scale (PAS; Dutton)

Description and Development of Assessment Method

The PAS is a 29-item self-report scale that assesses several variables that have been linked with abusiveness toward a partner. Thus, the measure purportedly provides a composite abusive personality.

Items were derived from scales the author found were correlated with physical aggression but less subject to social desirability reporting bias than direct indices of aggression. These scales included assessments of borderline personality organization, trauma symptoms, attachment style, parental rejection, and anger (see D. G. Dutton, 1995). Scales were then administered to a sample comprising assaultive and nonassaultive men, and additional assessments were administered to a subgroup of their female partners. The scale was then constructed by choosing subscales correlating most highly with partner reports of the men's psychologically abusive behavior (yielding a 29-item scale), calculating item–total correlations, conducting factor analysis with the pool of items, and correlating the PAS with a set of criterion variables.

Target Population

Assaultive and nonassaultive men, heterosexual and gay men, alcoholics and nonalcoholics, and the following nationalities: Euro Canadian, Chinese Canadian, Iranian Canadian, Indo Canadian, and Aboriginal Peoples.

Format

Factor analysis yielded three scales: Recalled Negative Parental Treatment, Affective Lability, and Trauma Symptoms. However, the measure is considered to be one construct of abusiveness propensity. Sample items follow:

- "I can make myself angry about something in the past just by thinking about it."
- "I feel empty inside."
- "I worry that I will be hurt if I allow myself to become too close to others."
- "As a child I was physically punished or scolded in the presence of others."

(Experienced in the last 2 months:)
- "Restless sleep"
- "Feeling tense all the time"

Administration and Scoring

The scale takes about 10 minutes to complete. Items 1–2 are rated on a 1–5 Likert scale ranging from *not at all like me* to *very much like me,* Items 13–21 are rated on a 0–3 Likert scale ranging from *never* to *very often,* and Items 23–29 are rated on a 1–4 Likert scale ranging from *never occurred* to *always occurred.* Items are simply summed to yield a total score.

Psychometric Evaluation

Norms
The mean PAS score in the sample of assaultive men was 59.2 (*SD* = 17.1); the mean in the control sample was 44.7 (*SD* = 11.7).

Reliability
Cronbach's alpha for the PAS is .92, indicating excellent internal consistency.

Validity
Validity was supported by the scale's significantly higher score within the assaultive than the control sample, and by significant correlations with men's female partners' reports of victimization on the Dominance/Isolation scale (*r* = .51) and the Emotional/Verbal Abuse scale (*r* = .47) of the Psychological Maltreatment of Women Inventory (PMWI; Tolman, 1989), as well as the Conflict Tactics Scale (CTS; Straus, 1979). Furthermore, using discriminant function analysis, the PAS correctly classified 82.2% of respondents into high-abuse and low-abuse categories (based on the criteria of one standard deviation above and below the mean) on the PMWI. These findings were upheld in a cross-validation sample (D. G. Dutton, 1995).

Advantages

The scale items are written to be less subject to socially desirable responding in that they contain no explicit mention of abusive behavior. The scale correlates strongly with female partners' reports of their husbands' abusiveness, providing promising concurrent validity.

Limitations

More validation work needs to be done regarding the predictive validity of the measure, particularly in samples not presenting for abuse.

Primary Scale Reference

D. G. Dutton (1995).

Scale Availability

Scale published in primary reference.

Related References

None available.

General Comments and Recommendations for Researchers and Practitioners

The author's intention was to devise an instrument that would not be subject to reactivity, because wife assaulters tend to minimize acts of violence on self-report measures (e.g., Browning & Dutton, 1986). On the basis of item content, the scale may be particularly useful in identifying the borderline-dysphoric subtype of partner-assaultive male (Holtzworth-Munroe & Stuart, 1994).

---

44. Rape Myths Acceptance Scale (RMA; Burt)

Description and Development of Assessment Method

The RMA is a self-report instrument measuring acceptance of rape myths that can be used alone or in combination with five companion scales on related attitudes. Items were rationally and empirically derived based on feminist theory, social–psychological theory, sex-role stereotyping research, and the author's professional experience. The primary scale, Rape Myths

Acceptance, was derived in conjunction with five related scales for testing the scale's relation with theoretically related variables. Items were developed to form a large item pool, which was administered by interview format to adults in randomly selected households in Minnesota. Variables were retained primarily based on regression analysis conducted to test the author's theoretical model (see Burt, 1980).

Target Population

Men or women, within or not within a marital, cohabitating, or dating relationship.

Format

The complete instrument contains six scales, with between 7 and 19 items per scale. Scale descriptions and sample items follow:

1. *Rape Myth Acceptance,* or belief in a number of victim-blaming attitudes toward rape victims

   - "A woman who goes to the home or apartment of a man on the first date implies that she is willing to have sex."
   - "Any female can get raped." (reverse-scored)

2. *Sexual Conservatism,* or conservative values concerning the appropriateness of various sexual encounters/relationships

   - "People should not have oral sex."
   - "I would have no respect for a woman who engages in sexual relationships without any emotional involvement."

3. *Adversarial Sexual Beliefs,* or beliefs that men and women in relationships are sly, manipulative, and exploitive

   - "Men are only out for one thing."
   - "Women are usually sweet until they've caught a man, but then they let their true self show."

4. *Acceptance of Interpersonal Violence,* or the belief in the legitimacy of using violent force or coercion to get one's way in an intimate relationship

   - "Being roughed up is sexually stimulating to many women."
   - "A man is never justified in hitting his wife." (reverse-scored)

5. *Sex-Role Stereotyping,* or beliefs that men and women should live according to traditionally defined sex roles

- "It is acceptable for a woman to have a career, but marriage and family should come first."
- "A wife should never contradict her husband in public."

6. *Sex-Role Satisfaction,* or the extent of one's satisfaction with sexual and gender-role performance and with general self-esteem

- "How satisfied are you with your attractiveness to the opposite sex?"
- "How satisfied are you with the amount of money you earn?"

Administration and Scoring

The scale takes 15–20 minutes to complete. Most items are rated on a 1–7 Likert scale ranging from *strongly disagree* to *strongly agree.* Two items asking about percentages are rated on a 1–7 scale from *almost none* to *almost all,* six items asking about likelihood of believing statements are rated on a 1–7 scale from *never* to *always,* and the Sex Role Satisfaction items are rated on a 1–7 scale from *very dissatisfied* to *very satisfied.*

Psychometric Evaluation

Norms
Not reported.

Reliability
Cronbach's alphas were as follows: Rape Myth Acceptance = .88; Sexual Conservatism = .81; Adversarial Sexual Beliefs = .80; Acceptance of Interpersonal Violence = .59; Sex Role Stereotyping = .80; and Sex Role Satisfaction = .78.

Validity
For both men and women, the Rape Myths Acceptance Scale correlated in theoretically consistent ways with a number of variables, including acceptance of interpersonal violence, sex role stereotyping, adversarial sexual beliefs, and education.

Advantages
Subscales can be used independently. The scales assess attitudinal constructs relevant to sexual coercion/sexual violence in intimate relationships.

Limitations

The Acceptance of Interpersonal Violence scale has low internal consistency. Limited scale validity is based primarily on a "bootstrapping" method; that is, reporting correlations among scales developed for the study and without known construct validity.

Primary Scale Reference

Burt (1980).

Scale Availability

Martha R. Burt
The Urban Institute
2100 M Street, N.W.
Washington, DC 20037

Related References

None available.

General Comments and Recommendations for Researchers and Practitioners

Based on both feminist theory of rape and social–psychological research on attitudes toward victims, this measure provides an assessment of "victim-distancing" attitudes in rape (Burt, 1980). The author's intent was to develop a scale of rape myth acceptance. However, any of the scales may be used alone for the purposes of the assessor, and the six scales used in conjunction with one another provide a comprehensive assessment of traditional sex role values and victim-blaming attitudes toward sexual coerciveness and sexual assault.

---

45. Safe at Home Instrument for Assessing Readiness to Change Intimate Partner Violence (SHI–IPV; Begun, Murphy, Bolt, Weinstein, Strodhoff, Short, & Shelley)

Description and Development of Assessment Method

The SHI–IPV instrument is a 24-item self-report scale designed to assess individuals' readiness to change intimate partner violence, based on Prochaska and DiClemente's (1983) transtheoretical model of stages of change.

Items were developed by asking four experienced batterer group program leaders trained in the model to submit lists of statements they had heard from program participants reflecting each stage of change. The authors then edited the resultant 108 items for language clarity, simplified them for reading level, deleted redundant items, and split complex thoughts into multiple statements, resulting in a final set of 35 items. An initial exploratory factor analysis yielded a three-factor solution consistent with three stages from the transtheoretical model of behavior change: Precontemplation, Contemplation, and Preparation/Action (Preparation and Action loaded on one factor, despite being distinct scales in the model; the Maintenance stage was not represented in the factor analysis). These factors were supported by confirmatory factor analyses. The scale authors report development data on the 24 items that attained the highest factor loadings on each scale.

Target Population

Partner-violent men or women in heterosexual or same-sex relationships.

Format

The instrument contains three scales with eight items each: Precontemplation, which reflects unawareness or denial of having a problem; Contemplation, which reflects recognizing one has a problem and desiring to change it; and Preparation/Action, which reflects preparing to take action as well as actually taking action to address the problem. Sample items follow:

Precontemplation

- "It's her fault I act this way when we disagree."
- "It's no big deal if I lose my temper."

Contemplation

- "I need to change before it's too late."
- "I have a problem with losing control."

Preparation/Action

- "I have a plan for what to do when I'm upset."
- "I know the early cues for when I'm losing control."

Administration and Scoring

Completing the scale should take approximately 5 minutes. Respondents rate their agreement with each statement along a 5-point scale. Scale scores are then summed to produce a scores for each factor.

Psychometric Evaluation

Reliability

Cronbach's alphas were as follows: Precontemplation = .59, Contemplation = .91, and Preparation/Action = .79.

Validity

Partial support for concurrent validity was demonstrated with a variety of associations with related constructs (see original reference for descriptions of these relationships). Discriminant validity was demonstrated with a lack of association between any of the three scales and social desirability.

Advantages

A brief, user-friendly scale, the SHI–IPV makes a significant contribution to the partner violence assessment literature by focusing on the *process* of change.

Limitations

Factor analysis in men at intake for batterers interventions programs confirmed only three of the five stages of change in the transtheoretical model; these may not generalize to other populations. However, these may be the three most important stages in the model. The scale would benefit from additional evaluation work to evaluate its factor structure in other populations.

Primary Scale Reference

Begun, Murphy, Bolt, Weinstein, Strodhoff, Short, & Shelley (2003).

Scale Availability

> Audrey Begun
> University of Wisconsin–Milwaukee
> School of Social Welfare
> P. O. Box 786
> Milwaukee, WI 53201-0786
> E-mail: begun@csd.uwm.edu

Related References

Daniels and Murphy (1997); Prochaska, Velicer, Rossi, Goldstein, Marcus, Rakowski, et al. (1994).

General Comments and Recommendations for Researchers and Practitioners

Applied to a variety of health-related behaviors (Prochaska et al., 1994), the stages of change model provides information about the change process during treatment. In particular, the assessment of readiness to change has implications for matching intervention approach to readiness stage to enhance outcome and reduce attrition. More recently, this approach had begun to be applied to the problem of partner violence (Daniels & Murphy, 1997). The SHI–IPV represents an exciting advance in self-report assessment of partner violence: a focus on change process rather than symptom level or behavioral events. With acceptable preliminary psychometric properties derived from development in a large sample of partner-violent men at intake, the instrument is appropriate for use in evaluation of batterers treatment programs. Note that an edition of the scale has been translated into Spanish (Begun et al., 2003).

---

46. Sex Role Egalitarianism Scale (SRES; Beere, King, Beere, & King)

Description and Development of Assessment Method

The SRES is a 95-item paper-and-pencil scale to measure egalitarian sex role attitudes.[2] Two parallel forms of the 95-item scale are available. Five

---

2. A short form is also available with 25 items. This was constructed by selecting the 5 items on each scale with the highest item–total correlations. This form is available from Sigma Assessment Systems, Inc. as well.

domains in which sex role egalitarianism manifests itself were specified. An initial pool of 524 items reflecting the five domains was constructed. Graduate student judges sorted items into each of the five domains. Any item that was not classified with 100% agreement was dropped. Approximately 40 items were then selected from each domain and then administered to over 500 mostly young adults living in central Michigan. The authors then examined item–total correlations and, because of high internal consistency reliability, decided to construct two parallel forms of the scale. Items that reduced the internal consistency of their domain were eliminated, and additional items with low item–total correlations were then eliminated to yield an equal number of items (i.e., 38) per domain. These items were then matched for content and then alternately assigned to Forms B and K.

Target Population

Men or women, within or not within a marital, cohabitating, or dating relationship.

Format

The scale covers five role categories with 19 items representing each domain. These domains are as follows.

1. *Marital roles,* or beliefs about the role equality of partners in marriage
2. *Parental roles,* or beliefs about the role equality of male and female partners as parents
3. *Employment roles,* or beliefs about the role equality of males and females in the workforce
4. *Social–interpersonal–heterosexual roles,* or beliefs about the role equality of males and females in terms of social roles and sexuality
5. *Educational roles,* or beliefs about the role equality of males and females in educational settings

Sample items:

- "A wife should be the one to decide on a couple's social activities."
- "Male managers are more valuable to an organization than female managers."
- "Men and women are equally qualified for law enforcement jobs."

Administration and Scoring

The scale takes approximately 25 minutes to complete and has a reading level of Grade 6 or 7. Items are rated on a 5-point Likert scale from *strongly disagree* to *strongly agree*. Scoring takes about 5 minutes and is done by summing scores for each of the five scales and then plotting the scores on a separate sheet to derive a profile.

Psychometric Evaluation

Norms
Available in the test manual.

Reliability
Cronbach's alpha for all 95 items was .97 on each form and averaged .87 over all five domains across the two forms. Three- to 4-week test–retest reliability averaged .85 over the domains. Alternate forms reliability (i.e., Pearson correlation between Forms B and K) was .93 (Beere, King, Beere, & King, 1984). Alpha was .89 for the 25-item version of the scale (Stith, 1986).

Validity
Convergent and discriminant validity has been demonstrated through the scale's relationships with other measures, and construct validity has been supported through group differences on the SRES (Beere et al., 1984).

Advantages
Assesses attitudes about nontraditional sex role behavior of both men and women. The scale is thorough in addressing attitudes across five domains and can be used for research or for evaluating interventions targeting sex role attitudes.

Limitations
The scale is lengthy for use in clinical practice, although the 25-item short form may be substituted.

Primary Scale Reference

Beere, King, Beere, and King (1984).

Scale Availability

Sigma Assessment Systems, Inc.
1110 Military Street
P.O. Box 610984
Port Huron, MI 48061-0984
(800) 265-1285

Related References

Crossman, Stith, and Bender (1990).

General Comments and Recommendations for Researchers and Practitioners

Useful for studying group and individual differences in attitudes toward the equality of men and women, the SRES allows for measurement of a construct associated with sociocultural analyses of violence toward women (Coleman & Straus, 1986; R. E. Dobash & Dobash, 1979). More traditional (nonegalitarian) sex role attitudes have been found to relate to both attitudes supporting marital violence (Crossman et al., 1990; Finn, 1986) and the use of relationship violence (Coleman & Straus, 1986; Crossman et al., 1990), although the link between sex role attitudes and relationship violence has not held up across studies (Hotaling & Sugarman, 1986).

---

47. Spouse-Specific Assertion and Aggression Scale (SSAA; O'Leary & Curley)

Description and Development of Assessment Method

The SSAA is a 29-item self-report instrument to assess assertion and verbal aggression specific to one's relationship with an intimate partner. An initial item pool was constructed from a variety of sources, including many taken from the Buss–Durkee Hostility Inventory (Buss & Durkee, 1957), and reworded to reflect behaviors directed specifically toward one's partner; eight graduate student judges then rated this item pool to classify items as assertive, aggressive, or neither. Items were discarded on the basis of rater disagreement, resulting in a 29-item scale with interrater reliability of item classification of .86. An exploratory factor analysis was performed on 72 couples (consisting of violent, discordant nonviolent, and maritally satisfied couples), yielding a two-factor solution confirming the authors' a priori notions of an assertiveness and aggressiveness factor.

Target Population

Violent or nonviolent couples.

Format

The 17 assertion items reflect communicating openly and directly with one's partner, particularly in the context of anticipated disapproval or objection, and the 12 aggression items reflect verbal aggression or hostile actions toward one's partner that do not include physical violence. Sample items follow:

Spouse-Specific Assertion (17 items)

- "Saying 'no' to my mate when I would like to say 'no' is easy for me to do."
- "I do not have difficulty telling my mate my true feelings."

Spouse-Specific Aggression (12 items)

- "I often make threats to my mate that I don't really intend to carry out."
- "I often say nasty things to my mate, especially when I'm angrily discussing something with him/her."

Administration and Scoring

Scale items are rated on a 7-point Likert scale from −3 (*extremely unlike me*) to +3 (*extremely like me*); the scale takes about 10 minutes to complete. For scoring, items are simply summed from each scale.

Psychometric Evaluation

Norms
Means for men and women in violent, discordant nonviolent, and maritally satisfied couples on both spouse-specific assertiveness and spouse-specific aggressiveness are reported in the original article.

Reliability
Cronbach's alpha for assertion was .87 and for aggression was .82 (O'Leary & Curley, 1986), indicating good internal consistency.

Validity
Initial validity of the SSAA scale was supported in the following ways:

(a) reliable assignment of items to assertion and aggression categories, by eight clinical graduate students; (b) factor analysis which confirmed the a priori notions about placement of items on the assertion and aggression scales; (c) differentiation of maritally discordant and satisfactorily married couples on measures of spouse-specific assertion and spouse-specific aggression. (O'Leary & Curley, 1986, p. 287)

Advantages

Advantages of the scale include its specific measurement of assertiveness within intimate relationships, in contrast to available scales measuring general assertiveness (e.g., the Rathus Assertiveness Schedule; S. A. Rathus, 1973). In addition, the presence of verbal aggression items within the same scale allow for distinctions to be made between assertive and aggressive behavior. Furthermore, norms are available for violent, discordant nonviolent, and maritally satisfied couples.

Limitations

More validation work is needed, particularly pertaining to the relationship between the spouse-specific aggression subscale and its relation to other scales of verbal aggression, such as the verbal aggression scale on the CTS (Straus, 1979) or its adaptations, or the emotional/verbal abuse scale on the PMWI (Tolman, 1989).

Primary Scale Reference

O'Leary and Curley (1986).

Scale Availability

K. Daniel O'Leary
Department of Psychology
SUNY at Stony Brook
Stony Brook, NY 11794-2500

Related References

Boyle and Vivian (1996); Rosenbaum and O'Leary (1981).

General Comments and Recommendations for Researchers and Practitioners

The SSAA is an easy-to-administer scale well suited for both clinical or research settings. The scale was an initial effort in the marital violence field that was followed by other, similar efforts toward measuring general constructs as they are manifest specifically within one's primary intimate relationship (see, e.g., Boyle & Vivian, 1996, regarding anger and assertion; Holtzworth-Munroe, Stuart, & Hutchinson, 1997, regarding attachment and dependency; J. H. Rathus & O'Leary, 1997, regarding dependency). The scale contains several items that might be construed as measuring passive-aggressive behavior (e.g., "I will often break a 'rule' my mate has made just to spite him/her," "I often take my time 'just to show' my mate, when he/she tries to boss me around"). Although these items loaded on the aggressiveness factor, further analysis might examine the extent to which these items form a conceptually distinct scale, as passive-aggressiveness may relate to a lack of assertiveness and may be an additional variable of interest in the study of marital aggression.

---

48. Spouse-Specific Dependency Scale (SSDS; J. H. Rathus & O'Leary)

Description and Development of Assessment Method

The SSDS consists of gender-specific, 30-item scales for assessing emotional dependency in the primary intimate relationship. Scale development followed both a rational and an empirical approach. First, 129 items were selected from a variety of preexisting measures of general interpersonal dependency and reworded into relationship-specific statements. Forty additional items were generated on the basis of the dependency literature, creating a pool of 178 items. Items were then assigned to 15 rational scales reflecting semantic similarity. Several items were rewritten or eliminated at this point to reduce redundancy and enhance clarity.

Items were then administered to 196 male and female undergraduates in dating relationships, and a principal-components analysis with varimax rotation was performed on the 15 scales separately for each gender. This yielded four principal components with eigenvalues greater than 1 for men and 3 for women. New factor scales were then computed by combining scales that loaded most heavily on each component. Internal consistency was maximized by computing a correlation matrix between scales and items and reassigning each of the 159 items to the factor scale with which it correlated most highly. An abbreviated item set was then obtained by first selecting a criteria of a minimum factor scale correlation of .5 (this led to the loss of all but one item for one of the factor scales for males; thus, this scale was dropped leaving three scales), and then ranking items according to their correlation with each factor scale and retaining the 10 items on each scale with the highest item–scale correlations.

Target Population

Violent or nonviolent couples, or individuals reporting on the primary relationship.

Format

Men and women fill out gender-specific scales. For both men and women, the three subscales on the SSDS are Anxious Attachment, Exclusive Dependency, and Emotional Dependency. Anxious attachment involves a sensitivity to separation from one's partner, fear of abandonment, and preoccupation with the partner. Exclusive dependency reflects a narrow focus on one's partner to the exclusion of other social supports and interests. Emotional dependency reflects the extent to which one relies on one's primary relationship for emotional support, desires contact and intimacy from one's partner, and derives self-esteem and identity through one's partner. Sample items follow:

Men's Version:

1. *Anxious Attachment (10 items)*

   - "I feel most secure when my partner is at my side."
   - "I like to be sure my partner is in close reach in case something unpleasant happens to me."

2. *Exclusive Dependency (10 items)*

   - "I talk about personal things with others, not just my partner." (reverse-scored)
   - "If I lost my partner, I don't know to whom I would turn."

3. *Emotional Dependency (10 items)*

   - "I can't enjoy what I'm doing when I don't feel my partner really cares about me."
   - "Being in this relationship makes me feel like a whole person."

Women's Version:

1. *Anxious Attachment (10 items)*

   - "I often think about the danger of losing my partner."
   - "I am very sensitive to signs of rejection from my partner."

2. *Exclusive Dependency (10 items)*

- "I have interests and hobbies that I engage in without my partner." (reverse-scored)
- "If my partner were to go out with friends one evening, I would probably find myself with nothing to do."

3. *Emotional Dependency (10 items)*

- "I like my partner to be protective and sympathetic."
- "Without my partner, the demands of life would seem like too much to handle."

Administration and Scoring

Respondents endorse items on a 6-point Likert scale ranging from *disagree strongly* (1) to *agree strongly* (6). Thus, each scale yields a score ranging from 10 to 60. The measure takes less than 10 minutes to complete. Scales are scored by simply summing items that compose the scale (several items are reverse-scored); the three scales can also be summed for a total spouse-specific dependency score. Higher scores indicate greater levels of dependency on a partner.

Psychometric Evaluation

Norms
Not reported.

Reliability
Internal consistency reliabilities for the Anxious Attachment, Exclusive Dependency, and Emotional Dependency scales for men are .89, .89, and .84, respectively, and for women are .88, .84, and .86, respectively. Total scale alphas are .93 for men and .93 for women.

Validity
The internal consistency scale development approach supports the three distinct aspects of the spouse-specific dependency construct (i.e., factorial validity). The SSDS has moderate interscale correlations (range = .46 to .65 for men, .60 to .68 for women), suggesting that the subscales measure distinct yet closely related constructs. In addition, the scale has discriminated among distressed violent, distressed nonviolent, and nondistressed nonviolent husbands (Holtzworth-Munroe et al., 1997; Murphy, Meyer, & O'Leary, 1994).

Advantages

The SSDS is the only scale to measure dependency specific to one's primary intimate relationship. It is a brief, easy-to-score measure with gender-specific scales, useful for clinical practice or research. Subscales can be used independently to capture specific constructs of interest, such as anxious attachment.

Limitations

Further work is needed on the scale's reliability (test–retest) and convergent and discriminant validity. In particular, a useful research direction might determine the relationship between the SSDS and measures of general interpersonal dependency, relationship satisfaction, self-esteem, depression, social support, and introversion. Further, normative data are needed in community and clinic samples.

Primary Scale Reference

J. H. Rathus and O'Leary (1997).

Scale Availability

Primary reference

or

Jill H. Rathus
Department of Psychology
Clinical Psychology Program
Long Island University/C.W. Post Campus
Brookville, NY 11548

Related References

Holtzworth-Munroe, Stuart, and Hutchinson (1997); Murphy, Meyer, and O'Leary (1994).

General Comments and Recommendations for Researchers and Practitioners

The SSDS measures a set of closely related constructs that appear to be important in the study of marital violence (e.g., Murphy et al., 1994). It is interesting that the gender-specific scales have low item overlap yet high conceptual similarity, suggesting that relationship dependency contains similar components for both men and women in relationships. Correlates of these components for men and women, however, have yet to be studied and may well yield gender differences. The SSDS might prove useful as a treatment outcome measure as well as a tool for examining processes potentially related to relationship dependency such as rejection sensitivity, the development of depression in the context of relationship discord, and coercive control strategies.

49. Thoughts About Relationships Questionnaire (TARQ; Chase, Treboux, O'Leary, & Strassberg)

Description and Development of Assessment Method

The TARQ measures the justification of aggression toward partners or same-sex peers in response to hypothetical vignettes describing provocative situations. The instrument was developed for use in the primary reference study; pilot data revealed the three themes of betrayal, nonsupport, and public embarrassment to be particularly evocative of conflict across the four types of age-mate relationships assessed.

Target Population

High-risk adolescents with current or past dating partners. Could be adapted for use with adults.

Format

The TARQ contains 12 vignettes, each representing one of three themes: betrayal, nonsupport (not backing up the respondent in a difficult situation), and public embarrassment. Each of the vignettes is read aloud to the respondent. Three vignettes each (one of each theme) correspond to four types of relationships: current/most recent dating partner, past dating partner, same-sex liked peer, and same-sex disliked peer, for a total of 12 vignette–relationship combinations. A sample vignette follows:

> You walk into a party and see *partner's name* talking to his/her ex-partner, and *partner's name* has his/her arm on his/her ex's shoulder. It appears that *partner's name* is having a good time. It just happens that *partner's name* looks over at you, smiles, and turns back to his/her ex, at which point they walk away from the group to a corner and continue speaking.

Administration and Scoring

The TARQ takes about 40 minutes to complete and has a Flesch–Kincaid reading level of 6.0. For each vignette, respondents first indicate whether they have been in a similar situation (yes/no). They then rate a 4-point Likert scale indicating the degree to which they believe four categories of responses would be justified or "OK": complaining without yelling, a strong verbal response (e.g., swearing or saying something spiteful), a somewhat physical response (e.g., slapping or physically restraining the person), or a very physical response (e.g., punch, beat up). The acts of mild and severe aggression provided as examples are from the CTS. Scale points are 0 = *definitely not OK*, 1 = *maybe OK*, 2 = *probably OK*, and 3 = *definitely OK*. Items are then scored for each vignette, and scale scores are computed by taking the mean scores across the three vignettes for each of the four relationships assessed.

Psychometric Evaluation

Norms
Not reported.

Reliability
Cronbach's alpha across the relationship types ranged from .74 to .89 (males) and .80 to .96 (females).

Validity
Initial evidence of concurrent validity was demonstrated with significant or near-significant correlations between aggression toward an age-mate and ratings of justification of aggression toward that age-mate.

Advantages
This is a simply administered scale allowing for assessment of justification of aggression across four types of relationships. The scale could easily be adapted for use with other types of relationships (e.g., married or cohabitating couples).

Limitations
The measure has yet to be evaluated with an adult population. Because all responses are based on only three vignettes, content validity or aggression justification may be limited.

Primary Scale Reference

Chase, Treboux, O'Leary, and Strassberg (1998).

Scale Availability

> Kenneth A. Chase
> Harvard Families and Addiction Program (116B1)
> Harvard Medical School Department of Psychiatry
> at the VAMC
> 940 Belmont Street, Bldg. 5, C138
> Brockton, MA 02301

General Comments and Recommendations for Researchers and Practitioners

The TARQ is an easy-to-administer measure assessing justification of aggression toward four different age-mate relationships. Although not yet used with adult samples, the measure could be easily adopted for various adult relationships (e.g., assessing justification for aggression toward spouses, dating relationships, same-sex friends). The scale allows for interesting comparisons for aggression justification across various relationship contexts (e.g., partner specific, intimate relationship specific) and might yield different correlates across different subtypes of aggressive populations (Holtzworth-Munroe & Stuart, 1994). Clinically, the measure might tap into relevant aggression-supporting belief systems.

Appendix 8.1

This Appendix lists in brief additional measures that were deemed relevant but are beyond the scope of this volume.

Category	Scale Name	Reference	Description	Comments
Alcoholism	Michigan Alcoholism Screening Test (MAST)	Selzer (1971)	A widely used measure of drinking problems, including assessment of the social, psychological, and physical consequences of alcohol abuse.	The MAST has high test–retest reliability and good criterion validity and has been used in several studies of battering husbands (Heyman, O'Leary, & Jouriles, 1995).
Attachment	Adult Attachment Scale (AAS)	Collins and Read (1990)	An 18-item self-report measure of attachment containing three scales: Anxiety Over Abandonment, Avoidance of Dependency, and Comfort With Closeness.	This widely used brief instrument has adequate psychometric properties and has been used in studies of wife batterers (e.g., Waltz, Babcock, Jacobson, & Gottman, 2000).

continued

Category	Scale Name	Reference	Description	Comments
Attachment	Attachment Questionnaire (AQ)	West, Sheldon, and Reiffer (1987)	A 75-item scale measuring pathological attachment patterns: compulsive self-reliance, compulsive caregiving, compulsive care-seeking, and angry withdrawal.	Used to classify pathological attachment patterns in adults, this instrument has discriminated subtypes of maritally violent men (e.g., Waltz et al., 2000).
Attachment	Relationship Styles Questionnaire (RSQ)	Griffen and Bartholomew (1994)	A 30-item self-report scale assessing four attachment patterns in adult relationships: Secure, Fearful, Preoccupied, and Dismissing.	The scale contains items derived from other attachment scales, and the authors have demonstrated convergent validity between the pencil-and-paper and interview methods of administration.
Attachment	Continuing Emotional Involvement Scale (CEI)	D. G. Dutton and Painter (1993)	A 20-item scale assessing continued emotional involvement following relationship separation or dissolution.	Items reflect bereavement related to separation and an ongoing obsession with the partner. The scale has good internal consistency.

Attitudes	London Family Court Clinic Questionnaire on Violence in Intimate Relationships (QVIR)	Jaffe, Sudermann, Reitzel, and Killip (1992)	A 48-item self-report measure of knowledge or attitudes about wife assault, sex roles, and dating violence, and of behavioral intentions in violence-related situations.	In addition to Likert-rated attitude items, the QVIR includes a set of hypothetical situations in which respondents rate how they would respond. Limited psychometrics reported.
Attributions	Relationship Attribution Questionnaire (RAQ)	Fincham and Bradbury (1992)	Four hypothetical partner behaviors are each rated on a 6-point Likert scale for causality (locus, stability, globality) and responsibility (intentionality, motivation, responsibility).	Validity and reliability of the RAQ have been demonstrated. The measure has been used to assess negative attributions and their correlates in both maritally aggressive husbands and victimized women.
Borderline personality	Self-Report Instrument for Borderline Personality Organization (BPO)	Oldham et al. (1985)	A 30-item self-report scale measuring three aspects of borderline personality organization: identity diffusion, primitive defenses, and reality testing.	The scale has adequate internal consistency and has been shown to relate to violence severity, psychological abusiveness, and jealousy in violent relationships (e.g., D. Dutton, vanGinkel, & Landolt, 1996).

continued

Category	Scale Name	Reference	Description	Comments
Borderline personality features	Life Problems Inventory (LPI)	Rathus and Miller (2002)	A 60-item scale measuring four aspects of borderline personality: confusion about self, impulsivity, emotional dysregulation, and interpersonal chaos.	Developed on an adolescent population, this scale has promising psychometric properties and has been recently adapted for use with batterers (J. H. Rathus & Cavuoto, 2001).
Date rape/ sexual coercion	Attitudes Toward Forcible Date Rape (ATFDR)	Fischer and Chen (1994)	A self-report scale measuring attitudes toward date rape through the presentation of six dating scenarios	This scale is a brief, unidimensional measure with evidence of reliability and validity.
Depression	Beck Depression Inventory (BDI)	Beck, Ward, Mendelson, Mock, and Erbaugh (1961)	A widely used 21-item self-report scale measuring depression.	Easy to score and with good reliability and validity, this scale is useful for assessing depression in battered women or aggressive husbands.

Dominance	Dominance Scale (DS)	Hamby (1996)	A self-report scale measuring three aspects of dominance over an intimate partner: Authority, Restrictiveness, and Disparagement.	Developed on a college student sample, this measure has promising initial construct validity with all three scales significantly associated with psychological aggression toward a partner.
Drug abuse	Drug Abuse Screening Test (DAST)	Skinner (1982)	A 21-item screening measure for brief assessment of drug use; positive screening indicators can be followed by in-depth diagnostic assessment.	This simple-to-use instrument has good reliability and is a useful part of an assessment battery in assessments of partner violence. The instrument has discriminated subgroups of violent husbands (Holtzworth-Munroe, Meehan, Herron, Rehman, & Stuart, 2000).

continued

Category	Scale Name	Reference	Description	Comments
Family-of-origin violence	Family of Origin Violence Questionnaire (FOVQ)	Holtzworth-Munroe, Meehan, Herron, Rehman, and Stuart (2000).	A self-report 15-item scale measuring witnessed parental violence and 23 items measuring parental abusive and neglectful behaviors experienced as a child.	With items adapted from other violence measures, this measure has adequate internal consistency yet needs additional validation work.
Fear of spouse	Fear Scale	O'Leary and Curley (1986)	A brief 11-item instrument asking women to rate overall fear of their partners and fear that their partners will engage in a range of specific threatening or abusive behaviors.	This scale measures an important construct in partner abuse and displays moderate internal consistency (O'Leary, Heyman, & Neidig, 1999). The scale needs more validation research.
Grief	Grief Response Assessment (GRA)	Varvaro (1990)	A 10-item scale assessing the degree of detachment from the relationship with an abusive partner.	The brief scale assesses the grief response following leaving a battering relationship. The scale's psychometric properties have not been evaluated.

Hostility toward women	Hostility Toward Women Scale (HTW)	Check (1988)	A 30-item scale assessing adversarial–hostile attitudes toward women.	The instrument has demonstrated psychometric properties and has been used to compare subgroups of maritally violent men (e.g., Holtzworth-Munroe et al., 2000).
Marital dissolution	Marital Status Inventory (MSI)	R. L. Weiss and Cerreto (1980)	A 14-item true–false scale assessing steps taken toward marital dissolution (e.g., taken steps to obtain a divorce).	The MSI is a useful measure of one's determination to end one's marriage; this scale is valid and reliable as an indicator of marital stability (e.g., Heyman et al., 1995).

continued

Category	Scale Name	Reference	Description	Comments
Personality/ psycho- pathology	Millon Clinical Multi- axial Inventory–II (MCMI-II)	Millon (1992)	A 175-item inventory measuring Axis I clinical syndromes, Axis II per- sonality patterns, and response styles on 25 scales.	Although complex to score (computer scoring program is available), this instrument has sound psychometric properties and has been used in several studies of assaultive husbands.
Personality/ psycho- pathology	Minnesota Multiphasic Personality Inventory (MMPI)	Hathaway and McKinley (1989)	A 566-item self-report instrument containing 10 clinical scales, 4 validity scales, and several research scales.	The scale has good evi- dence of reliability and validity and has been used in the assessment of partner violence (e.g., Greene, Coles, & Johnson, 1994).
Personality/ psycho- pathology	Personality Research Form (PRF)	Jackson (1974)	A self-report measure containing twenty-two 16-item scales measur- ing a range of personal- ity traits, including aggression.	The PRF has good evi- dence of reliability and validity and has been used in studies of as- saultive husbands (e.g., Heyman et al., 1995).

Pregnancy	Pregnancy Risk Assessment Monitoring System (PRAMS)	M. M. Adams et al. (1991)	A 67-item survey assessing maternal health behaviors during pregnancy.	Used in population-based surveillance, the PRAMS assesses physical violence and has provided risk factors for violence during pregnancy.
Psychopathy	Hare Psychopathy Self-Report Checklist–Revised	Hare (1985)	A 29-item checklist assessing characteristics of psychopathy.	Devised for assessing psychopathy in criminal populations, this scale has documented psychometric properties and has been used in batterer research.
Self-esteem	Rosenberg Self-Esteem Scale (SES)	Rosenberg (1979)	A 10-item scale measuring the construct of self-esteem in a brief paper-and-pencil format.	The SES has been shown to be internally consistent and to have convergent validity, and has been used in studies of spouse abuse (e.g., Murphy, Meyer, & O'Leary, 1994).

continued

Category	Scale Name	Reference	Description	Comments
Social desirability	Marlowe–Crowne Social Desirability Scale (MC)	Crowne and Marlowe (1960)	A 33-item scale for assessing socially desirable responding.	This scale is used frequently in conjunction with self-report measures of marital violence to attempt to adjust for under-reporting (D. G. Dutton & Hemphill, 1992; Saunders, 1991).
Trauma	Impact of Event Scale (IES) Impact of Event Scale—Revised (IES–R)	Horowitz, Wilner, and Alvarez (1980); D. S. Weiss and Marmar (1997)	A 15-item scale for assessing symptoms of posttraumatic stress disorder (PTSD).	The IES has been used widely in studying impact of trauma (e.g., rape) on survivors and has been used in studies of battered women (e.g., Houskamp & Foy, 1991). The revised 22-item scale corresponds to DSM–IV PTSD diagnostic criteria and has good psychometric properties.

Trauma	Trauma Symptom Checklist (TSC–33)	Briere and Runtz (1989)	A 33-item self-report scale assessing symptoms of PTSD.	Although designed primarily for use with survivors of sexual abuse, the TSC–33 can be used for trauma symptoms resulting from other types of trauma (e.g., violence) as well. The scale has been used with adults involved in violent relationships.
Vicarious traumatization	Traumatic Stress Institute Belief Scale (TSI Belief Scale)	Pearlman (in press)	A 79-item scale assessing disrupted cognitive schemas in areas of safety, trust, intimacy, esteem, and power.	This scale measures aspects of the relatively new construct of vicarious traumatization, or the deleterious effects on therapists of working with traumatized clients.
Wife abuse	Wife Abuse Inventory (WSI)	Lewis (1985)	A 34-item self-report scale developed to serve as a screening device for identifying battered women. Has good internal consistency and discriminates between abused and nonabused women.	Few items assess actual abuse; some reflect marital adjustment and others reflect husband characteristics; thus the nature of the construct is unclear.

continued

Category	Scale Name	Reference	Description	Comments
Wife abuse	Battered Woman Scale (BWS)	Schwartz and Mattley (1993)	A 7-item self-report measure of self-concept in female victims of battering, designed for use with women who have left battering relationships.	The items are adapted from the Personal Attributes Questionnaire (PAQ; Spence, Helmreich, & Stapp, 1974) based on relevance to experiences of battered women. No psychometric data are reported, and the scale appears too brief to sample content domain; measurement of self-concept might best be attained with use of original PAQ.

9

Analogue Methods and Behavioral Coding Devices

This chapter reviews analogue assessment of couple interactions or couple conflict. We divide this chapter into three parts: (a) basic analogue approaches (used for the purpose of recreating or mimicking naturalistic couple interactions or serving as realistic stimuli related to partner interactions to elicit interpretable responses), (b) physiological assessment, and (c) observational coding systems. To qualify for inclusion in our chapter on analogue measures, the assessment device could take a variety of forms but had to involve some type of direct behavioral observation, and some type of re-creation or approximation of a natural setting or stimulus context. We included a range of analogue assessments such as use of videotaped conflict scenarios, role-play interactions, structured discussion tasks for partners, physiological and mechanical assessment methods, and behavioral observation coding systems applied to couple interactions.

Note that in this chapter we introduce a section new to our review of assessment devices: "Equipment Needed." This is because analogue assessment of couple interactions or couple conflict typically requires special equipment that serves as stimuli (such as videotaped couple conflicts) for obtaining responses that are then coded in some way, or that serves as the measuring device itself (such as emotion rating dials or physiological monitoring equipment). Further, for the section describing physiological assessments, we omit the psychometric evaluation section. This is because it was deemed not necessary in the case of such devices. Reliability is not reported for such types of measurement devices and is a less relevant consideration since such measures are highly precise. Validity of such measurement devices also tends not to be reported and is also less of a consideration in the sense that the measures are direct assessments of a physiological phenomenon (e.g., blood pressure), the methods for which have been well-established in the medical/bio-technology fields; this is in contrast to operationally defining a psychological construct (e.g., psychological aggression), which may have greater flexibility and thus more of a need for demonstration of the appropriateness of the assessment approach. On the other hand, criterion validity of physiological assessment devices as measurements indicative of relationship distress or as correlates of abuse would certainly be of interest. While not reported directly as validity of these physiological measures in the original references, their relationships with other constructs of interest are discussed in the descriptions of the assessment method herein.

50. Articulated Thoughts in Simulated Situations Paradigm (ATSS; Eckhardt, Barbour, & Davison)[1]

Description and Development of Assessment Method

The ATSS is a think-aloud cognitive assessment task, in which raters code cognitive biases and distortions produced in respondents' open-ended verbal reporting of thoughts while listening to anger-arousing audiotapes. Assessment stimuli were produced by simply tape recording instructions and scenarios. The coding system was devised on the basis of literature review, clinical experience, and taped response content.

Target Population

Maritally violent, maritally distressed nonviolent, and maritally satisfied nonviolent husbands.

Equipment Needed

Two tape recorders: one for playing audiotaped scenarios and one for recording participants' articulated thoughts.

---

1. Although Davison, Robins, and Johnson (1983) authored the original paradigm, Eckhardt, Barbour, and Davison (1998) applied the paradigm to a sample of maritally violent husbands.

Format

Three scenarios were used, two of which were intended to arouse anger. The first, a control condition, involved the husband and his wife interacting with another couple and the husband becoming annoyed at the other couple, but not his own wife. The second involved an overheard conversation between the wife and her friend in which the wife expressed doubt about the marital relationship and spoke negatively about the husband, and captured themes of wife abandonment and ridicule of the husband. The third involved the husband arriving home early to find his wife talking and laughing with a male acquaintance in an interaction containing flirtatious overtones, and captured the theme of sexual jealousy.

Participants listen to a sequence of audiotaped scenarios and imagine that they are involved in each interaction. Then, on hearing a tone, participants speak into a microphone, articulating their thoughts and feelings.

Administration and Scoring

The control tape was always presented first as a warm-up device, and the other two scenarios were presented in counterbalanced order. Each scenario was divided into eight 30-second segments for the purpose of attaining respondents' thoughts.

Tapes of articulated thoughts were transcribed and coded by coders trained for 30 hours with the ATSS coding manual and basic study of cognitive theories of emotion. Ratings were made across four categories: irrational beliefs, cognitive biases, hostile attributional biases, and anger control strategies. For irrational beliefs and cognitive biases, raters indicated on a 5-point scale the degree to which each occurred in each segment, with 0 = *not present at all* and 4 = *extremely present*. Summary scores were obtained by summing the average ratings across the eight segments of each scenario. Hostile attributional bias and anger control statements were rated by summing the total number of each type of statement across each scenario.

Psychometric Evaluation

Norms
Not reported.

Reliability

Interrater agreement on articulated thoughts was computed in the following four categories using Pearson correlations: irrational beliefs ($r = .85$), cognitive biases ($r = .84$), hostile attributional biases ($r = .92$), and anger-control statements ($r = .94$).

Validity

The authors administered a self-rated state anger scale (the State–Trait Anger Expression Inventory; Spielberger, 1988) before and immediately after the procedure and found that men in all three groups experienced significant increases in anger following the procedure; this served as a manipulation check. Construct, concurrent, and predictive validity have been demonstrated extensively with the ATSS paradigm and are reviewed in Davison, Navarre, and Vogel (1995) and in Davison, Vogel, and Coffman (1997). Furthermore, Eckhardt and colleagues (Eckhardt, Barbour, & Davison, 1998; Eckhardt & Kassinove, 1998) provided evidence for the paradigm's criterion validity with maritally violent men; however, support for criterion validity in this population was weak in another study by the same research group (Barbour, Eckhardt, Davison, & Kassinove, 1998).

Advantages

Rather than relying on post hoc notions of thinking processes, as would be assessed using pencil-and-paper methods of measuring cognitions, this paradigm allows accessibility to cognitive activity concurrent with emotionally evocative stimuli. With short scenarios and immediate reporting of thoughts, access of cognitions in short-term memory is maximized, whereas distortions due to retrospective reports of typical thought sequences is minimized. In addition, responses are open-ended rather than constricting the respondent to select from forced choices that may not represent their cognitions. Finally, the method can be used concurrently with physiological assessment methods (Davison et al., 1997).

Limitations

The procedure does not prevent respondents from withholding responses or responding in a socially desirable fashion. Responses to scenarios may not reflect responses to actual arguments with partners.

Primary Scale Reference

Eckhardt, Barbour, and Davison (1998).

Scale Availability[2]

Christopher I. Eckhardt
Department of Psychology
Southern Methodist University
Dallas, TX 75275

Related References

Barbour, Eckhardt, Davison, and Kassinove (1998); Davison, Navarre, and Vogel (1995); Davison, Robins, and Johnson (1983); Davison, Vogel, and Coffman (1997); Eckhardt and Kassinove (1998).

General Comments and Recommendations for Researchers and Practitioners

The ATSS is a useful and relatively simple device for assessing participants' thoughts during presentation of affect-laden stimuli. Thus, in presence of affective arousal, access to cognitive contents may be enhanced. Although the authors specify coding criteria, coding schemes could be modified to fit the needs of the investigator. Further, the ATSS method allows for selecting situations of relevance (i.e., choosing among the established scenarios or developing one's own) to one's theoretical interest and establishing tight experimental control in assessing cognitions (Davison et al., 1995). Finally, the procedure could be simplified (i.e., used without formal coding of responses) and adapted for use in a clinical setting.

---

51. Problematic Marital Situations Vignettes (Holtzworth-Munroe & Anglin)

Description and Development of Assessment Method

Audiotaped vignettes describing provocative marital scenarios serve as stimuli for attaining verbal responses or self-rated attributions regarding the conflicts. Forty-eight vignettes were developed based on a literature review of problematic situations for distressed and violent couples, interviews with

---

2. Coding manual is also available through Christopher I. Eckhardt.

distressed nonviolent and violent samples, and practitioners working in the marital distress/marital violence areas. They were then piloted on a sample of male participants consisting of undergraduates, community, and clinic males. To be retained, situations were required to meet the criteria of being considered realistic, important, and difficult or uncomfortable by the raters and had to evoke a wide range of responses.

Target Population

Maritally violent husbands.

Format

Twenty-two brief vignettes are presented to respondents via an audiotaped recording of a man's voice. The conflict situations each describe potentially negative wife behaviors, as told from the man's viewpoint, and represent a range of themes, including the wife rejecting, challenging/embarrassing, teasing, invoking jealousy, and making demands of the husband.

Sample vignettes include the following:

"You are at a social gathering and you notice that for the past half hour your wife has been talking and laughing with the same attractive man. He seems to be flirting with her." (Jealousy theme)

"You are interested in sex and let your partner know this. She isn't very interested, but agrees to have sex. You begin to start things, making romantic moves. After a little while, you notice that she isn't very responsive; she doesn't seem to be very 'turned on' or interested in what you are doing." (Rejection theme)

"You had promised your partner that you'd do a certain job around the house no later than last week. But you forgot all about it. Now, you are in the middle of watching an important and interesting program on TV; you are really enjoying it. She comes in and reminds you of the job; she says, 'You didn't do what you promised. When are you going to do it?' You tell her you'll do it after the program is over. She says, 'Sure— I'll believe it when I see it.' " (Demands theme)

Administration and Scoring

Each vignette is told in well under a minute (each constitutes a short paragraph), so the length of administration depends on how many are administered, how many times they are administered, and what the respondent is asked to do following each vignette. Respondents listen to one tape-recorded conflict situation at a time, the tape is paused, and they then indicate some response.

In one study, maritally violent, maritally distressed nonviolent, and nonviolent nondistressed husbands listened to the entire set of vignettes twice, in a procedure lasting over 2 hours (Holtzworth-Munroe & Anglin, 1991). Following each vignette in the first set, participants were asked, "What would you say or do in this situation?" Following each vignette in the second set, participants were instructed, "You have already told us what you *would* say or do in this situation. Now we want to know what you think would be the *best* thing to say or do in this situation?" The purpose was to assess social skills deficits in maritally violent husbands (specifically, the ability to generate competent responses). Men's responses were audiotaped and then coded using a coding manual with responses rated on a 5-point scale ranging from *incompetent* to *competent* (the coding manual contained well-defined attributes of responses at the various scale points for each vignette). Competent ratings were assigned for responses involving reasonable negotiation and appropriate expression of feelings, and incompetent ratings were assigned for responses involving threats, put-downs, or hostility.

In another study, nine of the problematic marital vignettes were administered to maritally violent, maritally distressed nonviolent, and nonviolent nondistressed husbands (Holtzworth-Munroe & Hutchinson, 1993). After listening to each, husbands rated their attributions concerning the degree to which they thought the wives were responsible for the conflict and the degree to which they believed the wives were acting intentionally negatively. Attributions were assessed using the Responsibility Attribution Questionnaire (RAQ; Fincham & Bradbury, 1992) and the Negative Intentions Questionnaire (NIQ; Holtzworth-Munroe & Hutchinson, 1993; reviewed in chap. 8, this volume). Husbands were also asked to rate the valence of the wife's last behavior in each vignette on a 1–13 scale, where 1 = *very negative* and 13 = *very positive*. Thus, group differences could be examined for the influence of the perceived impact of each situation.

Psychometric Evaluation

Norms
Not reported.

Reliability
Cohen's kappa across rater pairs for the response competency ratings (Holtzworth-Munroe & Anglin, 1991) averaged .73 (proportional weighting)

for the question of what participants "would do" in each situation, and .77 (proportional weighting) for the question of "what is the best thing to do," indicating acceptable interrater reliability.

Validity

The scale development process supported the construct validity of the vignettes, because (a) they were derived from the marital distress/marital violence literatures and clinical interviews, and (b) those retained were rated by a diverse sample of males as realistic, of moderate importance, and difficult or uncomfortable to handle. Further, retained vignettes elicited multiple responses.

Advantages

The use of Problematic Marital Situations Vignettes provides a set of standardized, empirically derived stimuli to which husbands can respond. This eliminates ambiguity in detecting group differences, because husband behaviors in an in vivo couple interaction may be influenced by group differences in the types of situations discussed or in wife behaviors. In addition, various additional assessment methods could be used in conjunction with the vignettes (e.g., coding of social skills, attribution ratings).

Limitations

Men's reports of what they would hypothetically do may not predict their actual behavior.

Primary Scale Reference

Holtzworth-Munroe and Anglin (1991).

Scale Availability

> Amy Holtzworth-Munroe
> Department of Psychology
> Indiana University
> Bloomington, IN 47405

Related References

Fincham and Bradbury (1992); Holtzworth-Munroe and Hutchinson (1993).

General Comments and Recommendations for Researchers and Practitioners

The vignettes offer a useful measure for examining the social skills or attributions of maritally violent husbands, as well as for examining which particular *types* of situations inhibit social competency or elicit negative cognitions. The vignettes are flexible in the assessments conducted in conjunction with them and may be used in smaller sets depending on need. They may be used in a variety of settings, including as a research tool or as a clinical outcome measure.

52. Problem Solving Interaction Task (Gottman)

Description and Development of Assessment Method

The basis for much of the analogue assessment research, this method, also referred to as the Play-by-Play Interview, involves asking clients to discuss an area of relationship conflict while being videotaped, audiotaped, or observed. First, both maritally distressed and nondistressed couples were interviewed, to derive a list of problem areas rated as conflict-inducing by both groups. Couples then completed a problem inventory, which required them to rate a list of specific problem areas in terms of severity and duration of each problem in their own marriages. An interview followed, to help couples narrow their focus to a particular conflict area that had been a major source of disagreement for both partners; each couple was then instructed to attempt to resolve the selected disagreement. This method was found to produce comparable communication samples that could be contrasted between groups.

Target Population

Clinic couples (nonclinic, community couples are often included as comparison groups when the problem-solving discussion is used in research contexts).

Format

Face-to-face discussion in laboratory or clinic office.

Administration and Scoring

Clients are asked to select a salient interpersonal issue in their relationship (often following completion of a problem inventory targeting areas of disagreement) and then given instructions. Instructions may direct the couple to try to come to a resolution about the disagreement or to discuss the disagreement just as they would at home (variants on instructions include asking couples to discuss events of the day or to have an enjoyable conversation about a pleasurable matter). Once the couple selects a topic, the videotaping or audiotaping begins. Clients are typically left in a room to discuss the conflict by themselves and are told the length of time they will be engaging in the discussion (typically about 15 minutes but ranging from 10 to 60 minutes depending on the study). Although the procedure itself varies from study to study (and likewise from clinical context to clinical context), scoring possibilities for this procedure are virtually infinite, ranging from a vast array of observational coding systems, physiological measures, or post hoc subjective ratings by participants to idiosyncratic appraisals by the clinician. The discussion has been conceptualized as occurring in three phases targeted for observation: the agenda-building phase, the disagreement phase, and the negotiation phase (Notarius et al., 1981).

Psychometric Evaluation

Norms
Not reported.

Reliability and Validity
This depends on the measurement system applied to the couple interaction task.

Advantages
The Problem Solving Interaction Task can be used in a wide range of contexts (from the practitioner's office to a structured research setting) and is the basis for the application of many interaction-based assessment strategies. The procedure allows for a live sample of interaction in a particular context (e.g., solving a problem), and thus reduces the potential for biased or overly general self-reported evaluations of communication or affect. The procedure makes it possible to study interaction components sequentially, globally (e.g., base rates of particular behaviors), or in relation to couples' self-perceptions. This method has been important for studying communication and affective variables in couples with marital violence,

supplying information on interactional differences in violent and nonviolent spouses and on subtypes of aggressive couples.

Limitations

Because much information is gleaned from a single, brief, sample of couple behavior, caution must be applied in generalizing from this interaction to conclusions about a couple's global interaction patterns. Furthermore, this procedure may be subject to reactivity based on awareness of observation or on intrusive adjunctive assessment methods (e.g., electrodes attached to assess heart rate reactivity during the interaction). Because this procedure has been administered with many variations (i.e., length of time, instructions, setting), it is difficult to compare findings across studies.

A potential limitation in using this procedure with violent couples should be noted. Differences found between violent and nonviolent couples, or within subgroups of violent couples, are commonly interpreted as due to differences in the behavior, affect, or physiology of the populations being compared. However, as noted by Cordova, Jacobson, Gottman, Rushe, and Cox (1993), an alternative interpretation is that the *nature of the problems* that these populations generate differs and that *attributes of the problem selected* (i.e., more severe), rather than *attributes of the groups* themselves, account for findings of group differences. This confound can be addressed with research aimed at coding chosen problems for variables such as type and difficulty level, or by assigning groups to discuss the same problems. Gottman and Levenson (1986) noted the similar issue that the same interaction task may induce conflict in certain subgroups of couples but not others; Gottman (1979) thus empirically derived tasks that produced conflict in both distressed and nondistressed partners.

Primary Scale Reference

Gottman (1979).

Scale Availability

This task is described in the primary and related references.

Related References

Gottman (1994); Gottman, Jacobson, Rushe, Shortt, Babcock, La Taillade, and Waltz (1995); Gottman, Notarius, Gonso, and Markman (1976); Gottman, Notarius, Markman, Bank, Yoppi, and Rubin (1976).

General Comments and Recommendations for Researchers and Practitioners

An enormously popular paradigm for the study of marital interaction, use of behavior samples from this play-by-play interview is limited only by the investigator's imagination. The procedure can also be used by the clinician as a behavioral assessment task without the application of formalized coding systems or physiological measures. Following the task, couples can also be asked to comment on their experiences during the live interaction (e.g., affect, beliefs, attributions, perceptions, arousal level) or to view a videotape of the interaction and rate it on various attributes (e.g., Levenson & Gottman, 1983). The clinician can also tape record the task and use it in session for didactic discussion concerning communication and for gauging improvement over time.

---

53. Rating Dial Procedure (Levenson & Gottman)

Description and Development of Assessment Method

This assessment device consists of a rating dial on which partners independently rate their own affect while viewing a videotape of a laboratory-based conflictual marital interaction with their spouse. This procedure was developed to improve on the Talk Table procedure (reviewed later in this chapter) and to obtain a valid procedure for assessing affect during marital interaction. The authors validated the procedure by testing whether couples actually relived their emotional experience of the conflictual interaction during the videotaped recall procedure by comparing physiological measures during both the actual discussion and the viewing of the videotaped playback of the discussion (Gottman & Levenson, 1985).

Target Population

Clinic couples.

Equipment Needed

Video equipment, rating dial connected to a computer programmed to record continuous data points and to synchronize affect ratings with videotape recordings (for description of the equipment, see Gottman & Levenson, 1985; Levenson & Gottman, 1983).

Format

Partners independently view a videotaped recording of their interactions with a spouse and provide continuous ratings of their affect during the interaction using a rating dial. The rating dial is manipulated over a 180° arc spanning a 9-point scale from *very negative* to *very positive*, with 90° indicating a neutral rating.

Administration and Scoring

The length of this procedure is equal to double the length of the conflict discussion a couple engages in, because each partner rates his or her affect while viewing a videotape playback of a conflict interaction in which they have just engaged. Partners are instructed to rate how they felt during the actual interaction, as opposed to how they feel about viewing themselves on tape. They are further told that they may adjust the dial continuously to correspond with their moment-to-moment affect states. Rating dial data were recorded by dividing the continuous ratings into 10-second blocks and processed in three ways: (a) averaging for each participant the dial position across the ninety 10-second blocks within the 15-minute interactions viewed, (b) computing z-score time series for both spouses during the interaction segments for use in spectral time series analysis, and (c) classifying each 10-second block as positive (z-score = +1.5), negative (z-score = −1.5), or neutral (all scores in between) to create categorical data (Gottman & Levenson, 1985).

Psychometric Evaluation

Norms
Not reported.

Reliability
There were significant correlations between husband and wife ratings of affect on videotaped recall of interactions, indicating interpartner agreement.

Validity
Rating dial recordings of affect discriminated high- from low-conflict discussions, correlated with self-reported marital satisfaction, and corresponded with observer ratings of affect. Moreover, the validity of the procedure was supported by close simultaneous associations between various physiological

measures of affect obtained during the interaction procedure and the recall procedure. According to Gottman and Levenson (1985, p. 157), participants "appear to sweat, change their heart rate, and change their pulse transmission times at nearly the same time points when viewing the videotape of the interaction as they did when they were in the original interaction," suggesting a "reliving" of the interaction session.

Advantages

The Rating Dial Procedure offers a valid technique for attaining moment-to-moment affect ratings during interaction with a partner. The procedure yields continuous data and does not intrude on the marital interaction. Various ways to process the data allow for flexibility in data analysis.

Limitations

The procedure is impractical for clinical settings.

Primary Scale Reference

Levenson and Gottman (1983).

Scale Availability

This method is described in detail in the primary and related references.

Related References

Gottman and Levenson (1985, 1992).

General Comments and Recommendations for Researchers and Practitioners

The Rating Dial Procedure allows for partners to continuously rate their own experience of affect over the course of an interaction while viewing a video recall of that interaction. The procedure has strong validity data, even when the video recall ratings took place several days after the original interaction (Gottman & Levenson, 1985). In research settings, this procedure provides an excellent strategy for assessing ongoing affective patterns in the communication interactions of violent couples.

54. Role Play Test of Assertion Scale
(RPT; Morrison, VanHasselt, & Bellack)

Description and Development of Assessment Method

Participants are administered assertiveness scenarios and must role-play responses. Responses are videotaped and coded. The scenarios and coding categories are based on previous social skills literature.

Target Population

Violent, distressed nonviolent, and nondistressed nonviolent husbands and wives.

Format

Twelve scenarios include eight interactions with a nonspouse and four with a spouse. Half of the scenarios prompted the participant to respond by assertively asking for something and half by assertively declining a request or demand. Male and female confederates participated in each role-play scene and presented standardized prompts for each scene.

Administration and Scoring

Participants were videotaped and their performance in each assertion role-play was coded. Husbands and wives were coded separately, and husband–wife pairs were summed. Behavioral rating categories[3] were as follows:

Eye contact	Defined by length of eye contact following a prompt
Response duration	Time of participant response
Speech disturbances	Number of pauses, stutters, "ums," and so on
Disapproval	Communication of disapproval/dislike
Requests	Communication of request
Compliance	Communication of compliance with demands
Praise/appreciation	Communication of gratitude or approval
Smiles	Number of smiles during response
Global assertiveness	Rated on a 1-to-5 scale

---

3. Categories are taken from "Assessment of Assertion and Problem-Solving Skills in Wife Abusers and Their Spouses," by R. L. Morrison, V. B. Van Hasselt, and A. S. Bellack, 1987, *Journal of Family Violence, 2,* p. 232.

Psychometric Evaluation

Norms
Not reported.

Reliability
Interrater reliabilities, based on percentage agreement for each category, ranged from 79% to 97%.

Validity
Various components of assertion discriminated abusive couples from control groups (Morrison, Van Hasselt, & Bellack, 1987), lending support to the role-play test's criterion validity. Abusive husbands had more speech disturbances than maritally discordant husbands and engaged in less praise/appreciation than maritally satisfied husbands. Women in physically abusive relationships had more speech disturbances than maritally discordant wives and were more compliant than maritally satisfied wives.

Advantages
The RPT allows for standardized presentation of assertiveness stimuli and provides actual behavioral samples rather than relying on self-report of assertive behavior.

Limitations
With confederates participating in role-plays and the application of a coding system for scoring, this method is not practical for nonresearch settings. Assertiveness skills during role-plays may not generalize to behavior with partner.

Primary Scale Reference

Morrison, Van Hasselt, and Bellack (1987).

Scale Availability

Randall L. Morrison	or Vincent Van Hasselt
or Alan Bellack	Department of Psychiatry
Department of Psychiatry	and Human Behavior
Medical College of Pennsylvania	University of California
at EPPI	Irvine Medical Center
Philadelphia, PA 19129	Irvine, CA 92664

General Comments and Recommendations for Researchers and Practitioners

In Morrison et al. (1987), only the category of speech disturbances on the assertiveness role-play task discriminated violent from distressed nonviolent husbands. Thus, future use of assertiveness role-plays in the assessment of couple violence might involve a revised set of role-plays and rating categories.

---

55. Talk Table (Gottman, Notarius, Markman, Bank, Yoppi, & Rubin)

Description and Development of Assessment Method

The Talk Table refers to a table with rating buttons on both sides that allow partners to code the intended impact and the actual intent of messages during conflict interactions. The Talk Table was developed as part of a study aiming to discriminate distressed from nondistressed couples in terms of perceptions in ongoing marital interactions.

Target Population

Clinic couples.

Equipment Needed

Sloped table with electronically wired buttons.

Format

The Talk Table is a table sloped on both sides with two rows of five buttons on each side. On either side, five buttons represent intent ratings by the speaker, and five represent impact ratings by the listener. Button labels include ratings of super negative, negative, neutral, positive, and super positive. A switch located on the side of the table allows partners to illuminate a light on the side of the speaker. Partners seated on opposite sides of the table can see each other but cannot see each other's ratings.

Administration and Scoring

The device allows only one person to speak at a time. After the partner in the speaker role completes an utterance, the speaker codes the *intent* of the message, and the listener codes the *impact* of the message before responding. Then, the listener assumes the speaker role, and so on, with partners alternating in this fashion throughout the task. Couples are allowed a few minutes to practice, and then structured tasks begin. The level of coding in this task is the "floor switch," meaning the beginning of one partner's utterance to the beginning of the next partner's utterance, regardless of the number of sentences or thoughts. Gottman and colleagues (Gottman, Notarius, Markman, et al., 1976) compared distressed and nondistressed couples with impact/intent ratings with this device, using three low-conflict and two high-conflict tasks. Low-conflict tasks involved ranking lists of preferences on topics such as favorite dog breeds, jointly developing stories in response to TAT (Thematic Apperception Test) cards, and another ranking task involving rating nutritional value in various food items or rating items for their survival value on a trip to the moon. High-conflict tasks involved agreeing on the responsible partner in each of a set of conflict vignettes and discussing and attempting to resolve a current, salient marital problem. Impact and intent discrepancies were compared between groups; although distressed and nondistressed spouses reported the same *intent* of their communications, distressed spouses reported more negative *impact* of those communications.

Psychometric Evaluation

Norms
Not reported.

Reliability
Not reported.

Validity
Talk Table impact ratings correlated with marital satisfaction (Gottman, Notarius, Markman, et al., 1976), discriminated clinic from nonclinic couples (Gottman, Notarius, Markman, et al., 1976), and, in a study of couples planning to marry, predicted relationship satisfaction 2.5 years later for both men and women (Markman, 1977, as cited in Gottman, 1979).

Advantages
The Talk Table procedure offers a relatively low-cost method of rating cognitive aspects (i.e., perceptions) of a couple's communication. Further, compared with observer-rated findings, this method of couples rating their own behavior led to stronger discriminations between distressed and nondistressed couples.

Limitations

The Talk Table procedure is highly intrusive and does not yield continuous data. It is also impractical for conventional clinical settings and is costly and time consuming compared with general self-report measures of communication impact.

Primary Scale Reference

Gottman, Notarius, Markman, Bank, Yoppi, and Rubin (1976).

Scale Availability

The device is described in detail in the primary references.

Related References

Markman and Floyd (1980); Schacter and O'Leary (1985).

General Comments and Recommendations for Researchers and Practitioners

The Talk Table, which has also been called a Communication Box (Markman & Floyd, 1980), provides a unique self-report measure of moment-to-moment intentions and impacts during partner conflict interactions. The procedure can also be used to rate other dimensions, such as satisfaction with a particular marital exchange. As in Gottman, Notarius, Markman, et al. (1976), the procedure can be used in conjunction with observer ratings of behavior.

---

56. Videotaped Conflict Situations (D. G. Dutton & Browning)

Description and Development of Assessment Method

D. G. Dutton and Browning's (1988) conflict situations consist of videotaped depictions of heated marital conflict that participants view and then respond to on a variety of measures. The taped conflict scenes were piloted on "a small number of married men in their late twenties to provide an estimate of the arousal-producing properties of the tapes as well as a rough check on the power and intimacy change manipulation" (Dutton & Browning, 1988, p. 171).

Target Population

Maritally violent husbands. Could be administered to any individuals in intimate relationships.

Equipment Needed

VCR with monitor.

Format

Six conflict scenes were developed, with a set of three depicting a male-dominant interaction and another set of three depicting a female-dominant interaction. In each of these two sets, one of each of the following levels of attempted intimacy change was depicted: abandonment, engulfment, and neutral. Each scene depicted the same man and woman and was filmed using professional actors in a home (rather than laboratory) setting to increase realism. Scene content was as follows:

- *Abandonment:* In this scene the woman expressed a desire for greater autonomy, including spending more time with her friends and joining a consciousness-raising group.
- *Engulfment:* In this scene the woman urged the man to more openly share his thoughts and feelings and spend more time talking with her.
- *Neutral Condition:* This scene depicted the couple arguing over where to spend their vacation, a topic chosen deliberately to be unrelated to the control of intimacy.

Administration and Scoring

Participants were presented with a sequence of three videotaped segments counterbalanced for order across participants (either male-dominant or female-dominant, based on random assignment) and were asked to imagine themselves in the man's position. Dominance was defined as a higher amount of talking, more interruptions of the partner, and getting one's way in the argument. Thus, both level of power (male or female having greater power) and intimacy conditions were manipulated. Self-reports of affective arousal (using 10 adjectives from the compilation by Russel & Mehrabian, 1977) and behavioral response likelihood (i.e., the degree to which participants rated themselves as likely to engage in constructive reasoning, verbal aggression, or physical aggression in the same situation;

Novaco, 1975) were then recorded in response to each conflict scene. Each scene lasted between 5 and 7 minutes.

Psychometric Evaluation

Norms
Not reported.

Reliability
This depends on the rating instrument used in response to videotape stimuli. Reliability for anger and behavioral response probability ratings used in the primary reference were not reported.

Validity
The conflict scenarios evidenced criterion validity by differentiating physically aggressive men from control groups of verbally aggressive and nonaggressive men. Physically aggressive men reported the most anger in response to the abandonment scene, rated their behavioral response probabilities as likely to include the least constructive reasoning and the most verbal and physical aggression in response to the scenarios (with strongest differences for the abandonment scenario), and rated the abandonment issue as most relevant to their own relationships.

Advantages
Videotaped conflict situations provide emotional stimuli that is standardized across men (as opposed to strategies based on laboratory conflict discussions with wives, in which wife behavior differences could have an impact on group differences in husbands' responses). The method also allowed for an experimental research design with manipulation of variables of interest, which would not have been possible had men reported on actual conflict discussions with their own partners.

Limitations
The scale development information provided is vague. The research using the procedure did not control for level of marital distress; thus, conclusions on the basis of marital violence are limited.

Primary Scale Reference
D. G. Dutton and Browning (1988).

Scale Availability

Donald G. Dutton
Department of Psychology
2136 West Mall
University of British Columbia
Vancouver, British Columbia, Canada V6T 124

General Comments and Recommendations
for Researchers and Practitioners

Used comparing physically aggressive, verbally aggressive, and nonaggressive husbands, this Videotaped Conflict Situations procedure contributed to the literature indicating the recognition of abandonment themes as of strong clinical relevance in physically aggressive husbands. Future researchers could use such a strategy to examine reactivity to other relationship themes; the procedure could be administered to either partner. The videotapes could also serve as standardized stimuli for assessment of physiological responding, because most research in this area has used in vivo couple interactions. Although the in vivo method likely evokes greater emotional responsiveness, partner differences may obfuscate findings of group differences or subtypes of aggressive couples.

57. Blood Pressure Reactivity (Ewart, Taylor, Kramer, & Agras)

Description and Development of Assessment Method

Blood Pressure Reactivity measures are administered to assess changes in cardiovascular responding during a problem-solving discussion.

Target Population

Couples with conflictual interactions.

Equipment Needed

A sphygmomanometer that records Korotkoff sounds using an electric microphone that is positioned over the brachial artery; blood pressure cuff.

Administration and Scoring

Baseline clinic blood pressure is assessed in visits scheduled prior to the interaction task. Then couples are asked to attempt to resolve a problem that is a current source of conflict for 10 minutes. Participants are given 5 minutes to adjust to the attached blood pressure cuff with discussion of pleasant or neutral topics. Couples are not asked to begin the problem discussion until a baseline reading is established. This is defined as whichever of the following came first: three consecutive readings with relatively consistent readings (without an increasing trend over 1-minute intervals) or 8 minutes. Blood pressure then continues to be assessed at 1-minute intervals throughout the discussion, and then for another 5 minutes following the discussion as couples are directed to return to pleasant or neutral topics.

Advantages
This measure provides an objective measure of cardiovascular responsivity to conflict. It is less invasive than several other physiological indices that require blood samples or the attachment of electrodes.

Limitations
This measure is not practical for purely clinical setting. For research setting, it requires technician and appropriate equipment. It is also costly and time consuming and is best used in conjunction with an observational coding system to link cardiovascular responding to changes in communication.

Primary Reference

Ewart, Taylor, Kraemer, and Agras (1991).

Availability

Technical Resources, Inc.
200 Spring Rd., Suite 202
Oak Brook, IL 60521-1847
Tel: (630) 574-0200

or

Bio-Technical Resources, Inc.
Manitowoc, WI
http://www.biotechresources.com
Tel: (920) 684-5518

General Comments and Recommendations for Researchers and Practitioners

Although impractical for most settings other than research laboratories, this assessment method is one of the more simple measures of heart rate reactivity for the scientist or practitioner interested in obtaining physiological data. In Ewart et al. (1991), systolic and diastolic blood pressure increases were linked to a change from the neutral topics to the problem-solving focus for both wives and husbands, increasing hostility in women and increasing speech rate in men. Using a similar methodology, P. C. Brown and Smith (1992) found greater systolic blood pressure increases in husbands attempting to control or influence their wives compared with husbands simply discussing a problem with their wives. In addition, this cardiovascular reactivity paralleled concomitant increases in anger and hostility. Taken together, these findings implicate blood pressure reactivity as linked to variables of strong relevance to marital violence, namely, anger, hostility, and interpersonal control.

---

58. Cardiac Interbeat Interval (IBI; Gottman, Jacobson, Rushe, Shortt, Babcock, La Taillade, & Waltz)

Description and Development of Assessment Method

Electrocardiogram (ECG) equipment is used to monitor time between spikes (R-waves), capturing rate of heart beat.

Target Population

Can be used with various populations; reported for use with violent couples during conflict discussions.

Equipment Needed

ECG equipment.

Administration and Scoring

Electrodes are attached to the participant's chest by adhesive and conductive paste. A digital computer monitors the interbeat interval and reports average

IBIs across 1-second periods. Electrodes remain attached through the duration of a problem-solving discussion (e.g., 15 minutes while discussing an area of relationship disagreement).

Advantages

This method provides an objective measure of heart rate rather than relying on participants' self-report of arousal. It is an excellent research assessment tool for studying physiological arousal during disagreement.

Limitations

It is not practical for purely clinical settings. For research settings, this procedure requires costly equipment and may be cumbersome for research participants.

Primary Reference

Gottman, Jacobson, Rushe, Shortt, Babcock, La Taillade, and Waltz (1995).

Availability

Medical or laboratory supply companies.

Related References

Jacobson, Gottman, Waltz, Rushe, Babcock, and Holtzworth-Munroe (1994); Meehan, Holtzworth-Munroe, and Herron (2001).

General Comments and Recommendations for Researchers and Practitioners

Because of its costliness (laboratory space, ECG equipment, and trained personnel are needed) and the complexity of its use (e.g., as compared with a paper-and-pencil measure of physiological reactivity), this assessment method remains impractical for most settings other than well-funded research laboratories. However, for the scientist or practitioner particularly interested in physiological data, this procedure offers a relatively straightforward assessment of heart rate reactivity.

59. Endocrine Function Assessment (Kiecolt-Glaser, Newton, Cacioppo, MacCallum, Glaser, & Malarkey)

Description and Development of Assessment Method

This is a measure of endocrine function as attained through repeated blood samples.

Target Population

Couples during interactive tasks.

Equipment Needed

Blood-draw equipment and laboratory facilities.

Format

Hormones are assessed through blood samples.

Administration and Scoring (Include Length of Time)

A heparin well is inserted into the client's arm to allow for repeated blood draws with minimal discomfort. After a baseline period, clients engage in interactions designed to elicit varied reactivity (e.g., conflict discussion, discussion of relationship history, or mental arithmetic tasks). Data can be collected immediately before, during, and immediately after a particular task, or at regular intervals throughout a specified time period (e.g., hourly throughout the day, as in Kiecolt-Glaser et al., 1996). Kiecolt-Glaser et al. (1996) analyzed the values of six hormones—the three major stress hormones: epinephrine (EPI), norepinephrine (NEPI), and cortisol, and the related hormones ACTH, growth hormone, and prolactin.

Advantages

This procedure allows for objective assessment of the link between marital functioning and physiological reactivity. It can take repeated measures across varied situations or stressors.

Limitations

This method is highly intrusive to participants, costly, and requires a laboratory setting. It is practical only in research settings.

Primary Reference

Kiecolt-Glaser, Newton, Cacioppo, MacCallum, Glaser, and Malarkey (1996).

Availability

Medical or laboratory supply companies.

Related References

Kiecolt-Glaser, Malarkey, Chee, Newton, Cacioppo, Mao, and Glaser (1993); Kuhn (1989); Malarkey, Kiecolt-Glaser, Pearl, and Glaser (1994).

General Comments and Recommendations for Researchers and Practitioners

Because interpersonal stress has been shown to affect hormonal functioning (e.g., elevations in epinephrine, norepinephrine, and cortisol), assessing endocrine function offers an objective measure of physiological reactivity in relation to marital conflict. Although to date this method has been used only in the study of endocrine reactivity to conflict behaviors among nonviolent husbands and wives, the approach could be applied to study physiological responding in couples reporting physical aggression. Particular uses might include measuring husband versus wife reactivity in violent and nonviolent couples, or linking endocrine functioning with other measures in validating subtypes of aggression perpetrators (see Gottman et al., 1995).

---

60. General Somatic Activity Level (ACT; Gottman, Jacobson, Rushe, Shortt, Babcock, La Taillade, & Waltz)

Description and Development of Assessment Method

The ACT measures general activity level by detecting barely perceptible movements in a base on which participants' chairs are mounted (platform's movements are not detectible to individuals sitting in chair). Such movements reflect muscular activity and offer an unobtrusive measure of heart rate changes (i.e., sympathetic nervous system [SNS] activation).

Target Population

Can be used with various populations; reported here for use with violent couples during conflict discussions.

Equipment Needed

A 10-channel Coulbourn polygraph, LSI 11/23 microcomputer, chair mounted to flexible platform wired to produce current to polygraph in relation to movements.

Administration and Scoring

Participants sit in chairs mounted on a slightly flexible base wired to detect all movements; the base's movements are not detectible to the participant. The computer averages the current indicated by the polygraph across 1-second intervals. Measurement occurs throughout a problem-solving discussion; increased movement reflects higher muscular activity and thus SNS activation.

Advantages
The ACT provides an objective measure of SNS arousal that is highly sensitive to movements and nonobtrusive to participants. It can be measured continuously.

Limitations
This method is not practical for most clinical settings. It requires polygraph and microcomputer equipment along with a specially wired flexible platform.

Primary Reference

Gottman, Jacobson, Rushe, Shortt, Babcock, La Taillade, and Waltz (1995).

Availability

Medical or laboratory supply companies.

General Comments and Recommendations for Researchers and Practitioners

Like the physiological measures discussed earlier, the ACT device is impractical for most settings other than well-funded research laboratories. However, as an objective measure of SNS arousal, the ACT allows for validation of other measures of heart rate (e.g., cardiac interbeat interval, above) and offers the least obtrusive measure of SNS activity.

61. Pulse Transmission Time to Finger and Finger Pulse Amplitude (PTT–F and FPA; Gottman, Jacobson, Rushe, Shortt, Babcock, La Taillade, & Waltz)

Description and Development of Assessment Method

PTT–F records the transmission time from the heart beat (R-wave of the ECG) to the pulse wave in the finger and is used as a measure of SNS activation. FPA enhances the measurement of SNS activation by measuring changes in peripheral blood flow by determining blood flow to finger as it corresponds to heart beats across time.

Target Population

Various populations; reported here for use with violent couples during conflict discussions.

Equipment Needed

Photoplethysmograph, computer.

Administration and Scoring

A photoplethysmograph (a device in which a light-sensitive resistor records the volume of light shone through the finger, indicating blood volume in finger per heart beat) attached to the participant's middle finger of the nondominant hand provides both the PTT–F and the FPA ratings. For PTT–F, a computer times intervals between each ECG spike and finger pulse wave and reports average pulse velocity per 1-second interval. The photoplethysmograph remains attached for the duration of a problem-solving discussion. Faster PTT–F indicates higher SNS activation.

For FPA, relative blood volume in the finger is recorded by the computer following each heart beat (as indicated by taking the valley-to-peak amplitude for each finger pulse signal) and reported as average finger pulse amplitude per 1-second interval. Reduced blood flow in the finger suggests increased SNS activation, as under conditions of activation, blood flow decreases in peripheral blood vessels as it increases in central blood vessels.

Advantages

The PTT–F provides an objective measure of SNS arousal as opposed to relying on participants' self-report. It can be measured continuously during an interaction (as opposed to blood pressure). The PTT–F is considered an excellent research assessment tool for studying sympathetic arousal, as it is sensitive to both the strength of the heart contraction and the degree to which the arteries are open or closed.

The FPA adds an additional, specific measure of SNS activation by indicating changes in peripheral blood flow. "The inclusion of the FPA measure advanced the goal of the comprehensiveness of physiological measurement, as it is more sensitive to changes in alpha-sympathetic stimulation, whereas PTT is more sensitive to beta-sympathetic influences" (Gottman et al., 1995, p. 231).

Limitations

This method is not practical for most practitioners. It requires costly equipment and trained personnel.

Primary Reference

Gottman, Jacobson, Rushe, Shortt, Babcock, La Taillade, and Waltz (1995).

Availability

Medical or laboratory supply companies.

Related References

Jacobson, Gottman, Waltz, Rushe, Babcock, and Holtzworth-Munroe (1994).

General Comments and Recommendations for Researchers and Practitioners

Because of its costliness (laboratory space, photoplethysmograph device, computer equipment, and trained personnel are needed) and complexity, this assessment method remains impractical for most settings other than well-funded research laboratories. However, for readers interested in physiological measurement of SNS activity, the PTT–F and FPA offer the advantage over blood pressure assessment of continuous measurement and sensitivity to arterial constriction.

62. Skin Conductance Level (SCL; Gottman, Jacobson, Rushe, Shortt, Babcock, La Taillade, & Waltz)

Description and Development of Assessment Method

The SCL provides a measure of changes in the level of sweat in the palm of the participant's hand. These glands are reactive to emotional changes and produce increased sweat as a result of SNS activation.

Target Population

Can be used with various populations; reported here for use with violent couples during conflict discussions.

Equipment Needed

Electrodes and computer equipment.

Administration and Scoring

Electrodes are attached to the participant's first and third fingers (of non-dominant hand), and a low voltage passed between them averages the electrodermal activity across 1-second intervals. Measurement occurs throughout a problem-solving discussion. Increased skin conductance indicates higher SNS activation.

Advantages

The SCL provides an objective measure of SNS arousal preferable to self-report of internal arousal. The eccrine sweat glands (those found on the palms) respond to SNS arousal independent of adrenaline circulation or temperature, and so provide an independent measure of SNS activity. Finally, skin conductance can be measured continuously.

Limitations

This method is not practical for most clinical settings. It requires laboratory equipment and trained personnel.

Primary Reference

Gottman, Jacobson, Rushe, Shortt, Babcock, La Taillade, and Waltz (1995).

Availability

Medical or laboratory supply companies.

General Comments and Recommendations for Researchers and Practitioners

Like the ECG equipment and the photoplethysmograph device described earlier, SCL equipment is somewhat costly to attain and use, and so is similarly impractical for most settings other than well-funded research laboratories. However, as an objective measure of SNS arousal, the SCL provides a measure independent of adrenaline circulation (as opposed to measures of heart rate or blood flow).

---

63. Couples Interaction Scoring System (CISS; Notarius, Markman, & Gottman)

Description and Development of Assessment Method

The CISS is an observational coding system designed to study content, affect, and context of these ratings in marital conflict discussions. The CISS was developed as part of a large study comparing distressed and nondistressed couples on conflict resolution behavior (see Gottman, 1979). The coding scheme was based in part on existing coding systems (e.g., the Marital Interaction Coding System; Hops, Wills, Patterson, & Weiss, 1972) and in part on a series of iterations based on the experience of coders applying the system. The intention was to develop a system that would prove exhaustive, able to capture the richness of intimate dyadic communication, and be replicable/teachable (Notarius, Markman, & Gottman, 1981). Eight summary codes were derived based on 28 content codes.

Target Population

Couples.

Equipment Needed

Two remote-controlled video cameras, microphones.

Format

Couples are videotaped during a 10–15-minute problem-solving discussion. Raters then assign each unit of analysis one of eight summary codes, each of which is further assigned one of three affect codes (based on facial expression, voice tone, and body movement) of positive, neutral, or negative. The eight summary codes reflect a reduction of 28 verbal content codes. These summary content codes are as follows:

1. expressing feelings or attitudes about a problem
2. mind reading feelings, attitudes, opinions, or behaviors
3. expressing agreement with a partner
4. expressing disagreement with a partner
5. problem solving or exchanging information
6. talking about the communication process (i.e., metacommunication)
7. summarizing other
8. summarizing self

One can also code the listener's nonverbal behavior (Gottman, 1979; Gottman, Markman, & Notarius, 1977).

Administration and Scoring

Codes are applied to three aspects of communication: content of the message (coded on the basis of the speaker's verbal message), affect (coded on the basis of the speaker's nonverbal behavior including voice tone, facial expression, gestures, and body position), and context (coded on the basis of the listener's nonverbal behaviors). The unit of analysis is the *thought unit,* or a phrase, sentence, or speech fragment that is grammatical and separated by periods, commas, ands, buts, or pauses. Recorded interactions are transcribed and coders place slashes after each thought unit to code verbal behavior; nonverbal behavior is coded directly from viewing video sequences. Coder training takes between 30 and 40 hours for content codes and somewhat less time for mastery of nonverbal behavior codes.

Psychometric Evaluation

Norms
Not reported.

Reliability

For content codes, Gottman (1979) reported mean Cohen's kappas on observer agreement as .91. For nonverbal codes, kappas averaged .76.

Validity

Verbal content codes in combination with nonverbal codes strongly discriminate distressed from nondistressed couples (Gottman, 1979).

Advantages

The CISS allows for coding interactions of both verbal and nonverbal messages (i.e., content and observed affect), which allows for more accurate capturing of emotional states. Such emotional states provide crucial information in determining the meaning of a communication. The code has identified key interactional sequences in distressed and nondistressed couples, including cross-complaining, validation sequences, mind-reading sequences, metacommunication sequences, negative and positive reciprocity, and hidden agendas.

Limitations

A large amount of training is needed, as well as a large amount of time for coding (up to 24 hours per hour of videotape for beginning coders), making the system costly and time consuming. While eight summary codes facilitate coding, they of course limit specificity.

Primary Scale Reference

Notarius, Markman, and Gottman (1981).

Scale Availability

John M. Gottman
Department of Psychology
University of Washington
Seattle, WA 98195

Related References

Gottman (1979); Markman and Notarius (1987).

General Comments and Recommendations for Researchers and Practitioners

The CISS was designed specifically to disentangle affect from behavior in couple interactions. Because the system allows for independent coding of verbal and nonverbal communication, two codes are assigned for every unit of interaction (or three codes, if the listener's nonverbal behavior is coded). The CISS codes aspects of communication skills relevant to marital satisfaction. The time-consuming nature of learning and applying the system makes it impractical for use as part of a standard couple assessment battery. Even without using the actual system, however, the clinician can benefit from familiarity with the various interaction patterns picked up by the code for informally assessing partners' emotional communication:

> We act as participant-observers during marital therapy sessions to identify the specific interactional patterns operative in our client couples. The study of interactional sequences with CISS has provided us with a language system necessary for identifying these sequences and for communication with couples about their interactional styles. (Notarius et al., 1981, p. 127)

64. Rapid Couples Interaction Scoring System (R-CISS; Krokoff, Gottman, & Hass)

Description and Development of Assessment Method

The R-CISS is an observational coding system designed to study in a relatively rapid fashion the manner in which couples solve marital disputes. The R-CISS was developed by selecting positive and negative items from five marital interaction coding systems: the Marital Interaction Coding System (Hops, Wils, Patterson, & Weiss, 1972), the Interpersonal Marital Communication System (Ting-Toomey, 1983), the Marital and Family Interaction Coding System (Olson, 1981), the Coding Scheme for Interpersonal Conflict (Raush, Barry, Hertel, & Swain, 1974), and the CISS (Notarius et al., 1981). Items from these systems were then sorted into four central tasks of conflict resolution: agenda-building codes, problem-solving codes, emotional repair and maintenance codes, and context of message reception codes (focused on the listener). Redundancies were eliminated in code definitions, and sequential patterns of interaction were added from the research literature. For the 22-code version of the R-CISS, those codes were retained that maximally discriminated distressed from nondistressed couples.

Target Population

Couples.

Equipment Needed

Two remote-controlled video cameras, microphones, training videotape, training manual.

Format

The system is applied to couples' videotaped problem-solving interactions during a discussion lasting between 10 and 15 minutes. The long version of the R-CISS contains 65 codes, and a maximally discriminative version, most commonly used and discussed here, contains 22 codes. The codes (from Gottman, 1996) are as follows:

Codes	Negative	Positive
Agenda building (own views)	Complain Criticize Negative relationship issue problem talk	Neutral or positive problem description Task-oriented relationship information
Agenda building (response)	Yes-but Defensive (protect self)	Assent
Emotional repair and maintenance	Put down Escalate negative affect	Humor/laugh
	Other negative	*Other positive*
Listener codes	Absence of backchannels[a] Absence of facial movement Negative facial expression Avoidant listener gaze Pattern	Backchannels Facial movement Positive facial expression Connected listener gaze pattern Responsive facial movement

Note. Neutral codes are also applied if no positive or negative codes apply to a turn.

After initial coding, the data are summarized into the following categories: (a) complain/ criticize, (b) defensiveness, (c) contempt, (d) stonewalling, (e) positive presentation of issues, (f) assent, (g) humor, and (h) positive listener.

[a]Backchannels refer to vocalizations by the listening spouse such as "Mmm-hmm."

Administration and Scoring

The unit of analysis in the R-CISS is the speaker turn, or the entirety of one partner's utterance before the other partner begins speaking. The R-CISS uses a detection system (in which coder checks all codes that apply during a given turn) rather than a categorical system (in which the coder decides on one code that best fits the interaction unit. Coding output is presented in one of two formats: speaker and listener cumulative point graphs (graphs based on points accumulated per code for each interaction or two-turn unit, allowing for a visual scan of a conversation) and proportions of each scale for the entire interaction (taking the total score and dividing by the number of turns). Codes are made on the basis of couples' videotaped problem discussions and verbatim transcripts of these discussions.

Psychometric Evaluation

Norms
Not reported.

Reliability
There was an overall 76% agreement rate between coders, ranging from .61 to .90 across codes.

Validity
The maximally discriminative version of the R-CISS discriminates distressed from nondistressed couples (Krokoff, Gottman, & Hass, 1989) as well as conflict avoiders and conflict engagers (Gottman, 1994), is predictive of marital dissolution (Gottman & Levenson, 1992), and correlates with couples' recollections of their relationship history (Buehlman et al., 1992).

Advantages
The R-CISS incorporates codes from several other systems and is designed to offer a relatively rapid system for learning and administration that discriminates among couples. The system allows for observation of both speaker behavior and context in which this behavior is received by the listener.

Limitations
Although less time consuming than some of the other coding systems, the R-CISS remains impractical for standard clinical settings because coder training to reliability and lengthy administration time are still required.

Primary Scale Reference

Krokoff, Gottman, and Hass (1989).

Scale Availability

> John M. Gottman
> Department of Psychology
> University of Washington
> Seattle, WA 98195

or

> Lowell J. Krokoff
> Dept of Child and Family Studies
> University of Wisconsin
> 1430 Linden Drive
> Madison, WI 53705

Related References

Gottman (1994, 1996).

General Comments and Recommendations for Researchers and Practitioners

The R-CISS was designed to provide a more rapid system for coding couple interactions. The code encompasses both content and affective components, and the 22 codes contained in the short version (discussed here) have been shown to maximally discriminate distressed from nondistressed dyads.

---

65. Interaction Coding System (ICS/Kategoriensystem fur partnershaftliche Interaktion, KPI; Hahlweg, Reisner, Kohli, Vollmer, Schindler, & Revenstorf)

Description and Development of Assessment Method

Hahlweg and colleagues developed this behavioral coding system to capture the marital and family communications emphasized in most behavioral communication skills programs. Raters apply verbal content and nonverbal codes to couples' (or families') videotaped interactions. The category descriptions are derived from standard couples communication skills programs and from aspects of other coding systems, including the Marital Interaction Coding System (Hops et al., 1972) and the Couples Interaction Scoring System (Gottman, 1979).

Target Population

Maritally distressed couples. Also applied to additional populations, examining the relationship between family interaction and psychopathology.

Equipment Needed

Two remote-controlled video cameras, microphones.

Format

The coding system is applied to couples' interactions during a videotaped problem-solving discussion, usually lasting between 10 and 15 minutes. The ICS contains the following 12 coding categories: self-disclosure, positive solution, acceptance of the other, agreement, problem description, meta-communication, rest category (when does not fit into other categories or when inaudible), listening, criticize, negative solution, justification, and disagreement.

Administration and Scoring

Scoring involves breaking a couple's verbal interaction into coding units, composed of discrete verbal responses based on uniform content (this may vary in length from words to sentences). Trained raters apply codes to each coding unit from the 12 categories, as well as nonverbal codes of negative, neutral, and positive, based on facial and body cues. For sequential analysis of the data, codes may be reduced to either four or six summary codes.

Psychometric Evaluation

Norms
Not reported.

Reliability
Interrater reliability has been satisfactory for coding categories across studies, with kappas tending to fall above .80.

Validity

The coding system is sensitive to change following behavioral marital therapy (Hahlweg, Revenstorf, & Schindler, 1984) and discriminates between maritally distressed and nondistressed couples (Hahlweg et al., 1984).

Advantages

The ICS is an excellent research tool, with a coding system that is reasonably easy to learn.

Limitations

It is less practical for clinical than for research settings because videotape equipment is needed as well as training in the coding system.

Primary Scale Reference

Hahlweg, Reisner, Kohli, Vollmer, Schindler, and Revenstorf (1984).

Scale Availability

> Kurt Hahlweg
> Institute for Psychology
> Technische Universitat
> Braunschweig, Germany

Related References

Hahlweg, Revenstorf, and Schindler (1984).

General Comments and Recommendations for Researchers and Practitioners

Although not developed specifically for use in assessing characteristics of violent couples, communication skill deficits have been found to characterize aggressive couples, and many marital violence treatment programs teach the communication skills the ICS assesses. Thus, the coding device might be used as a diagnostic tool or as a treatment outcome measure with violent partners. For use in research, the ICS provides data that can be analyzed in terms of frequency of codes or sequential analysis.

66. Interactional Dimensions Coding System (IDCS; Julien, Markman, & Lindahl)

Description and Development of Assessment Method

The IDCS is a global observational measure of couple interactions. Dimensions were selected on theoretical and empirical grounds. Core interactional dimensions that are consistent with most theories of family distress and that have guided the development of other interactional coding systems were included. Codes were also included that had been shown to discriminate functional from dysfunctional familial interaction patterns (Julien, Markman, & Lindahl, 1989).

Target Population

Individuals in intimate relationships.

Equipment Needed

Two remote-controlled video cameras, microphones.

Format

The IDCS contains five negative dimensions (conflict, dominance, withdrawal, denial, and negative affect), four positive dimensions (communication skills, support/validation, problem-solving, and positive affect), and two dyadic dimensions (negative and positive escalation).

Administration and Scoring

The unit of observation for the IDCS is obtained by dividing the interaction into three equal segments (based on number of thought units), except for the two dyadic dimensions, which use the complete interaction. Observers base coding decisions on both affect and content cues. Observers rate the dimensions according to a 9-point scale. Observers watch the first segment, rate one partner along each of the first nine dimensions, and then the other partner, watching again if necessary. The second and third segments are rated using the same procedure. The rater then rates partners again, using the total interaction as coding unit. Finally, on the two dyadic dimensions, the observer rates the couple based on the entire interaction. Raters indicate whether partners are *low* (1–3), *moderate* (4–6), or *high* (7–9) on the given dimension, based on the intensity, frequency, and duration of behavioral cues. Coding time is about 6 hours per hour of interaction, which is notably shorter than many microanalytic coding systems such as the CISS. Graduate and undergraduate coders received about 25 hours of training.

Psychometric Evaluation

Norms
Not reported.

Reliability
Pearson correlations between coders' ratings on separate individual dimensions ranged from .27 to .66 for male partners and from .05 to .71 for female partners. For the individual dimensions combined, correlations were .70 for male and .74 for female partners. For the dyadic dimensions combined, coders' ratings on couple interactions were .64 for positive escalation, .49 for negative escalation, and .61 for the combined dyadic dimensions.

Validity
Concurrent validity was assessed by comparing IDCS with CISS codes, ratings of the communication impact by partners themselves, and measures of marital quality. Most IDCS negative dimensions were associated in the expected direction with CISS negative affect; positive IDCS dimensions were not related to CISS positive affect. In general, IDCS-rated communication was not associated with spouses' self-reported impact of that communication.

Additionally, concurrent and predictive validity were assessed by comparing the dyadic dimensions to current and later marital satisfaction ratings. Codes were associated with males' but not females' reports of marital quality and showed some predictive power in forecasting later relationship satisfaction.

Advantages
The coding device's global codes and larger coding units reduce training and coding time. The system codes specific aspects of positive marital communication.

Limitations
There is limited evidence of interrater reliability, which likely attenuated the also modest validity findings. The research sample consisted of mostly happily married couples, which would likely result in limited variance on behavioral dimensions and thus reduce the interrater correlations.

Primary Scale Reference

Julien, Markman, and Lindahl (1989).

Scale Availability

Daniel Julien
Department de Psychologie
Universite du Quebec a Montreal CP 8888, Succursale "A"
Montreal, Quebec, Canada H3C 3P8

or

Howard J. Markman
University of Denver
Center for Marital and Family Studies
2450 S. Vine
Denver, CO 80210

General Comments and Recommendations for Researchers and Practitioners

This system was designed to provide a more economical coding procedure, to provide measurement of relevant negative and positive communication dimensions ignored by other systems, and to predict specific relationship outcomes (such as divorce; Julien et al., 1989). The system measures facilitative communication skills captured in most theories of marital functioning but that are rarely directly measured (Julien et al., 1989). More work is needed, ideally with more heterogeneous samples, to provide evidence of interrater agreement and validity.

---

67. Marital Interaction Coding System (MICS; Hops, Wills, Patterson, & Weiss)

Description and Development of Assessment Method

The MICS is a widely used and widely adapted behavioral observational coding system used to analyze verbal and nonverbal communication behavior during videotaped problem discussions. The coding system was based on tape-recorded narrations of home observations of couples' interactions. It was an outgrowth of the Family Interaction Coding System (Patterson, Ray, Shaw, & Cobb, 1969) and was based on the behavioral marital therapy approach, which holds problem-solving skills as central to marital adjustment.

Target Population

Couples.

Equipment Needed

Two remote-controlled video cameras, microphones.

Format

The original codes are the following: agree, approve, accept responsibility, assent, attention, command, compliance, complain, criticize, compromise, disagree, deny responsibility, excuse, humor, interrupt, mind reading, noncompliance, normative, no response, negative solution, not tracking, problem description, positive physical contact, paraphrase/reflection, positive solution, put down, question, smile/laugh, talk, and turn off (R. L. Weiss & Perry, 1979).

Administration and Scoring

The MICS contains approximately 30 codes (minor revisions of the system have had slight code variations) for classifying couple behavior. After assigning specific codes to speaker utterances (in either 15-second or 30-second intervals), they are collapsed into global categories. Established on an a priori basis and formed using rational item groupings, these summary categories have varied from simple classifications of positive and negative to a six-category classifications into problem solving, verbal positive, nonverbal positive, verbal negative, nonverbal negative, and neutral.

Psychometric Evaluation

Norms
Not reported.

Reliability

The mean weighted Cohen's kappa across all codes as rated by two independent observers was .60 (Gottman, 1994), indicating good inter-rater reliability. High interobserver agreement of the MICS has been demonstrated across numerous additional studies as well (e.g., Birchler, Weiss, & Vincent, 1975; Wieder & Weiss, 1980; cf. Heyman, Weiss, & Eddy, 1995).

Validity

A number of MICS codes have been shown to differentiate distressed from nondistressed couples in a variety of frequency analysis and sequential analysis studies (Gottman, 1994). Global codes of positivity and negativity also predicted concurrent marital satisfaction as well as change in marital satisfaction (Gottman & Krokoff, 1989). MICS scores have also been shown to relate to couples' self-descriptions of their laboratory interactions, their relationship cognitions, and their home interactions (R. L. Weiss & Summers, 1983).

Advantages

The most commonly used couples coding system, the MICS has been widely evaluated. The coding system accounts for verbal and nonverbal behaviors (although such codes cannot be applied simultaneously to the speaker). The system allows for rating listener nonverbal codes concurrently with speaker verbal codes.

Limitations

Husband and wife codes are combined when classifying nonverbal behavior; thus, the degree of nonverbal responding emitted by either partner while in the speaker or listener role cannot be determined. Global categories do not indicate specific aspects of behaviors or emotions (e.g., nonverbal negative may reflect a range of different affect states. The MICS does not independently code verbal and nonverbal behavior in a partner's single utterance. Also, several variations of the original MICS scoring categories exist, making it difficult to pinpoint psychometric properties of the system or to compare findings across studies.

Primary Scale Reference

Hops, Wills, Patterson, and Weiss (1972).

Scale Availability

ASIS/NAPS
C/O Microfiche Publications
305 E. 46th Street
New York, NY 10017

Related References

Gottman and Krokoff (1989); Heyman, Weiss, and Eddy (1995); Oregon Marital Studies Center (1975); R. L. Weiss and Summers (1983).

General Comments and Recommendations for Researchers and Practitioners

The MICS and its variants are among the most widely used couple interactional scoring systems. Although not originally developed for use with violent couples, the system (in its adapted forms) has recently been used in this capacity (e.g., Heyman, Brown, Feldbau-Kohn, & O'Leary, 1999). Descriptions of various adaptations of the original coding system follow.

---

68. Marital Interaction Coding System (MICS–III; R. L. Weiss & Summers)

Description and Development of Assessment Method

Adapted from the MICS, the MICS–III is a behavioral observational coding system used to analyze couple verbal and nonverbal interactions during problem discussions. The coding system was adapted from earlier versions of the MICS and was designed to improve the system for analytic purposes by assigning only one code to each coding unit.

Target Population

Couples.

Equipment Needed

Two remote-controlled video cameras, microphones.

Format

The MICS–III contains 30 codes for coding couple interaction. The codes can be collapsed into three global categories of positive behaviors (includes codes such as agree, assent, smile/laugh, and positive physical contact), problem solution behaviors (includes codes such as accept responsibility, compromise, and positive solution), and negative behaviors (includes codes such as criticize, deny responsibility, no response, and put down). They have also been categorized into aversive behaviors (e.g., criticize, disagree), facilitative behaviors (e.g., agree, assent, compromise, positive solution), and neutral behaviors (e.g., normative, problem description, question; Cordova et al., 1993).

Administration and Scoring

Couples are asked to select a marital problem and attempt to resolve the issue much as they would at home. Couples are permitted to continue their discussion for 10 minutes and are videotaped.

Coding units are in the form of *dyadic behavioral units* (DBU), which take both partners' behaviors into account and are defined by the length of time that both partners are engaged in a particular behavior without changing it. The moment one partner changes a behavior (e.g., from smiling to frowning), the next DBU begins and is coded anew for both partners.

The MICS–III contains four groups of codes: *behavior codes,* which capture specific behaviors (e.g., positive solution); *state codes,* which define the context for the behavior codes (e.g., while making eye contact), *modifier codes,* which describe the manner in which a behavior occurred (e.g., as a question); and *nonverbal affect carrier codes,* which capture the nonverbal behavior accompanying a verbal message. If the state, modifier, or affect carrier codes occur in the absence of a behavior code, they are assigned as primary codes for that segment, but if they occur in conjunction with a behavior code, they are considered supplemental and not considered discrete behaviors on their own.

The MICS–III requires 2–3 months of weekly training and practice to code reliably (R. L. Weiss & Summers, 1983).

Psychometric Evaluation

Norms
Not reported.

Reliability

In a study of violent, distressed nonviolent, and happily married couples, kappas for summary codes ranged from .60 to .79; the overall kappa (based on all codes) was .62 (Cordova et al., 1993). In a study of college dating couples, percentage agreement across all codes ranged from 74% to 100%, with a mean percentage agreement of 84.37% (Follette & Alexander, 1992).

Validity

Codes from the MICS–III discriminated violent from distressed nonviolent and happily married couples using both frequency analysis and sequential analysis (Cordova et al., 1993). In addition, MICS–III codes were related to concurrent relationship variables in dating couples, such that more dissatisfied couples emitted more negative communication behaviors and physical aggression was related to male communication patterns (Follette & Alexander, 1992).

Advantages

The MICS–III codes place a somewhat greater emphasis on emotions than the original MICS. Because singular rather than multiple codes are applied to each coding unit, the system is more amenable to sequential analysis than the original MICS.

Limitations

There is a large investment of time and money needed in training, coding, video equipment, and data analysis.

Primary Scale Reference

R. L. Weiss and Summers (1983).

Scale Availability

> Robert L. Weiss
> Oregon Marital Studies Program
> Department of Psychology
> Straub Hall
> University of Oregon
> Eugene, OR 97403

Related References

Cordova, Jacobson, Gottman, Rushe, and Cox (1993).

General Comments and Recommendations for Researchers and Practitioners

Rather than treating verbal and nonverbal behavior codes equally for coding purposes, the MICS–III uses modifier codes to lend additional specificity to verbal behavior codes. It has been used to assess communication in dating relationships and demonstrated a relationship between physical aggression in dating relationships and negative communication strategies in the male partner (Follette & Alexander, 1992). The MICS–III codes have also demonstrated a greater tendency to engage in negative reciprocity (i.e., following a partner's negative behavior with continued negative behavior) in maritally distressed violent compared with distressed nonviolent couples, and a higher proportion of aversive communication behavior in maritally distressed violent compared with distressed nonviolent husbands (Cordova et al., 1993).

---

69. Marital Interaction Coding System— Global (MICS–G; R. L. Weiss & Tolman)

Description and Development of Assessment Method

The MICS–G is a behavioral observational coding system used to analyze couple interactions during problem discussions. Based on the MICS (described above), the MICS–G uses entire interaction sequences rather than moment-to-moment behaviors as the unit of analysis. The coding system was adapted from earlier versions of the MICS and designed to improve the system for analytic purposes by assigning only one code to each coding unit.

Target Population

Couples.

Equipment Needed

Two remote-controlled video cameras, microphones.

Format

The MICS–G contains six global rating categories: Conflict, Problem Solving, Validation, Invalidation, Facilitation, and Withdrawal. Rather than rating specific codes and collapsing these into summary codes, the MICS–G uses several behavioral exemplars for each global category and units of analysis are directly assigned to a category. Examples from the Invalidation category are disagreement, deny responsibility, change subjects, consistent interruption, turn off behaviors, and domineering behaviors; examples from the Facilitation category are positive mind read, paraphrase, humor, positive physical, smile/laugh, open posture, and warm voice tone.

Administration and Scoring

Training in the coding system was conducted in 10 hours for coders with no experience in observational coding systems for couples (R. L. Weiss & Tolman, 1990). The coding system is used in conjunction with 10–15-minute videotaped problem discussions in which couples are instructed to attempt to resolve a relationship conflict, much as they would discuss it at home. In R. L. Weiss and Tolman (1990), couples' discussions were divided into two 3-minute segments and re-recorded on separate tapes for the purposes of coding. Each category is scored along a 6-point scale from 0 (*none*) to 5 (*very high*), taking into account both frequency and intensity of behaviors. Raters considered affect and content in assigning categories (e.g., warm voice tone would reflect affect whereas paraphrasing would reflect content). While viewing tapes, raters mark category-relevant cues on rating sheets containing each category and its behavioral example; these tallies later assist in their ratings.

Psychometric Evaluation

Norms
Not reported.

Reliability
Intraclass correlation coefficients ranged from .49 to .82 across categories for coding of husband data and from .53 to .78 for wife data, indicating acceptable interrater agreement.

Validity
Moderate convergent validity was demonstrated with the corresponding MICS categories, whereas a high level of discriminant validity was demonstrated among rating categories. Category ratings on the MICS–G were also

related to marital satisfaction and, with the exception of the Problem Solving category, were able to discriminate distressed from nondistressed couples.

Advantages
The MICS–G requires substantially less training and coding time than the MICS or the MICS–III. The coding system takes into account behavior and affect.

Limitations
Because the MICS–G does not assign specific codes, it cannot be used for sequential analysis of couple interactions.

Primary Scale Reference

R. L. Weiss and Tolman (1990).

Scale Availability

> Robert L. Weiss
> Oregon Marital Studies Program
> Department of Psychology
> Straub Hall
> University of Oregon
> Eugene, OR 97403

General Comments and Recommendations for Researchers and Practitioners

The MICS–G includes judgments of affect in addition to specific communication behaviors and shows promise as a cost-effective alternative to the MICS or MICS–III. Because it cannot be used for sequential analysis, the authors themselves question the cost-effectiveness of using such a measure to identify distressed couples when self-report measures can do the same. However, they do recommend its use for assessing rates of particular behaviors, evaluating behavior changes following treatment, and providing a measure for convergent validity in developing new measures of marital functioning.

70. Rapid Marital Interaction Coding System (RMICS; Heyman & Vivian)

Description and Development of Assessment Method

The RMICS is an observational coding system adapted from the MICS–IV (Heyman et al., 1995). The authors developed the RMICS following a series of steps, including factor analyzing MICS data of 1,088 couples and dividing one factor and adding dimensions (including two codes from the KPI; Hahlweg et al., 1984), to enhance the system's breadth and content validity.

Target Population

Distressed and nondistressed couples, violent couples.

Equipment Needed

Two remote-controlled video cameras, microphones.

Format

Couples are directed to resolve a conflict in a 10–15-minute laboratory discussion while being videotaped. The RMICS contains 11 codes: psychological abuse, distress maintaining attribution, hostility, dysphoric affect, withdrawal, relationship enhancing attribution, acceptance, self-disclosure–neutral or positive, humor, constructive problem discussion/solution, and other.

Administration and Scoring

The RMICS requires 12–16 hours of training time. Once trained, a 15-minute tape can be coded in 20–25 minutes. Speaker turns (i.e., speaker's entire utterance falling in between the partner's previous and next utterance) serve as the unit of analysis. Codes are assigned in hierarchical order, such that partners receive the highest code on the hierarchy if emitting multiple codes within a given turn. The hierarchy goes, in order of highest to lowest, from negative to positive to neutral codes, following research substantiating the relative importance of these code valences in explaining marital distress (R. L. Weiss & Heyman, 1997). Raters code turns longer than 30 seconds in 30-second intervals.

Psychometric Evaluation

Norms
Not reported.

Reliability
Interrater reliability for the RMICS is very good, with kappas ranging from .50 to .86 across codes (Heyman et al., 1999).

Validity
The coding system discriminates between distressed and nondistressed couples, and certain codes were predictive of dropout and continued aggression in husbands (Heyman et al., 1999).

Advantages
The RMICS offers a coding system that captures microanalytic constructs and yet is faster to learn and to code than other microanalytic systems, because it is coded at the level of category rather than at the level of specific codes that are then collapsed into categories.

Limitations
Because 11 global codes replace previous systems' greater number of specific codes, a certain degree of content specificity is sacrificed.

Primary Scale Reference

Heyman and Vivian (1997a).

Scale Availability

Richard Heyman
Department of Psychology
University of Stony Brook
State University of New York
Stony Brook, NY 11794-2500

Related References

Heyman, Eddy, and Weiss, and Vivian (1995); Heyman and Vivian (1997b).

General Comments and Recommendations for Researchers and Practitioners

The RMICS was designed to capture advantages of both microanalytic and global coding systems. It contains a code specific to family violence (psychological abuse) and also contains the acceptance code, reflecting a burgeoning topic in the field of couple distress (Christensen & Jacobson, 1996). Coders are also trained to takes into account stylistic differences in couples when assigning codes. The system has been used to predict treatment response of violent couples (Heyman et al., 1999).

71. Specific Affect Coding System (SPAFF; Gottman)

Description and Development of Assessment Method

The SPAFF is an observational coding system designed to study affective processes in marital conflict situations. Expanded from the affect portion of the CISS and influenced by Ekman and Friesen's (1978) Facial Action Coding System (FACS), Gottman developed the SPAFF to provide enriched coding capability for capturing couples' emotions. The 16-code version was developed after viewing videotapes of violent couples' interactions and noting the presence of emotions not captured by the 10-code version.

Target Population

Couples.

Equipment Needed

Two remote-controlled video cameras, microphones, computer-assisted video coding station, computer program providing automated timing information, training manual.

Format

Raters code affects of speaker and listener based on the judgment of combined data from verbal content, voice tone, facial expression, body movement, and gestures. The SPAFF is available in a 10-code and a newer 16-code version. The 10-code version global ratings are neutral, humor, affection/ caring, interest/curiosity, joy, anger, disgust/scorn/contempt, whining/ defensiveness, sadness, and fear. Gottman (1996) expanded to the 16-code version in part as a result of coding interactions of violent couples, noticing emotional expressions present in these couples that were not captured in the briefer version of the SPAFF. The 16-code version global ratings are disgust, contempt, belligerence, domineering, anger, fear, defensiveness, whining, sadness, stonewalling, neutral, interest, affection/caring, humor, delight/excitement/surprise, and validation.

Administration and Scoring

Coders rate affects of husbands and wives separately from videotaped recordings of a problem-solving interaction. Each onset of a new affect is coded. Episodes, defined as the time between the onset of one behavior code and the next, are also counted.

Psychometric Evaluation

Norms
Not reported.

Reliability
Gottman (1996) reported interobserver agreement using Cohen's kappas on the 16-code version as ranging from .75 to .95, with a mean kappa of .86.

Validity
Select SPAFF codes differentiated regulated from dysregulated (classified according to the R-CISS as having increasingly positive vs. increasingly negative utterances, respectively, during a problem-solving interaction) couples during conflict interaction tasks (Gottman, 1994) and discriminated conflict engagers from conflict avoiders (Gottman, 1994). In addition, emotional aggression codes (contempt and belligerence) discriminated violent from distressed nonviolent couples (Jacobson et al., 1994), and Type I (those whose heart rates decreased during conflict discussions) from Type II husbands (those whose heart rates increased during conflict; Gottman et al., 1995).

Advantages
The SPAFF is an objective measure of couple interactions focusing exclusively on affect and offers much more detailed coding of emotions than does the CISS. It allows the researcher to test hypotheses related to the relationship between specific observed emotions and marital conflict behaviors, the relationship between observer ratings and subjective experience

of emotions, and differences in affective expression between groups (e.g., violent and nonviolent couples).

Limitations

Because it is highly costly in training time and administration methods, the SPAFF is most practical for well-funded research settings. Another coding system may be needed in conjunction with the SPAFF if identification of verbal content/interactional sequences is desired, because the SPAFF is limited to coding of affect.

Primary Scale Reference

Gottman (1996).

Scale Availability

> John M. Gottman
> Department of Psychology
> University of Washington
> Seattle, WA 98195

Related References

Gottman (1994); Gottman, Jacobson, Rushe, Shortt, Babcock, La Taillade, and Waltz (1995); Gottman and Krokoff (1989); Gottman and Levenson (1986); Jacobson, Gottman, Waltz, Rushe, Babcock, and Holtzworth-Munroe (1994); Lawrence and Bradbury (2001); Meehan, Holtzworth-Munroe, and Herron (2001); Waltz, Babcock, Jacobson, and Gottman (2000).

General Comments and Recommendations for Researchers and Practitioners

The SPAFF was intended to diverge with systems relying on the *physical features* approach by incorporating an emphasis on the *cultural informants* approach to coding emotion. The physical features approach assesses emotional information by deconstructing emotional messages and using only nonverbal cues; thus important verbal indicators of emotional content are lost. Also, using this method only culturally universal emotions are extracted, even though some emotional communication is culturally specific. In contrast, the cultural informants approach assumes that "emotion in the stream of natural social interaction is conveyed by a nonadditive gestalt of information, which is detectable by competent cultural informants" (Gottman & Levenson, 1986, p. 36). Thus, the SPAFF relies on multiple channels of information in assigning codes, that is, it relies on the gestalt of multiple cues including verbal content, voice tone, body movement, and facial expression.

Further, as one of the extant coding systems that has been used in the assessment of marital violence (e.g., Gottman et al., 1995; Jacobson et al., 1994), this system contains codes such as contempt, belligerence, and defensiveness (which captures fear responses) that particularly pertain to the interactions of aggressive couples and may be considered forms of emotional abuse.

References

Adams, D. (1988). Treatment models of men who batter: A profeminist analysis. In K. Yllo & M. Bograd (Eds.), *Feminist perspectives on wife abuse* (pp. 176–199). Newbury Park, CA: Sage.

Adams, M. M., Shulman, H. B., Bruce, C., Hogue, C., Brogan, D., & the PRAMS Working Group. (1991). The Pregnancy Risk Assessment Monitoring System: Design, questionnaire, data collection and response rates. *Paediatric and Perinatal Epidemiology, 5,* 333–346.

Aguilar, R. J., & Nightingale, N. N. (1994). The impact of specific battering experiences on the self-esteem of abused women. *Journal of Family Violence, 9,* 35–45.

American Psychiatric Association. (1987). *Diagnostic and statistical manual of mental disorders* (3rd ed., Rev.). Washington, DC: Author.

American Psychiatric Association. (1994). *Diagnostic and statistical manual of mental disorders* (4th ed.). Washington, DC: Author.

American Psychological Association. (1997). *Professional, ethical, and legal issues concerning interpersonal violence, maltreatment, and related trauma.* Washington, DC: Author.

Ammerman, R. T., & Hersen, M. (Eds.). (1999). *Assessment of family violence: A clinical and legal sourcebook.* New York: Wiley.

Archer, J. (1999). Assessment of the reliability of the Conflict Tactics Scales: A meta-analytic review. *Journal of Interpersonal Violence, 14,* 1263–1289.

Archer, J. (2000). Sex differences in aggression between heterosexual partners: A meta-analytic review. *Psychological Bulletin, 126,* 651–680.

Archer, J. (2002). Sex differences in physically aggressive acts between heterosexual partners: A meta-analytic review. *Aggression and Violent Behavior, 7,* 313–351.

Arellano, C. M., & Markman, H. J. (1995). The Managing Affect and Differences Scale (MADS): A self-report measure assessing conflict management in couples. *Journal of Family Psychology, 9,* 319–334.

Arias, I., & Beach, S. R. H. (1987). Validity of self reports of marital violence. *Journal of Family Violence, 2,* 139–149.

Arias, I., & Pape, K. T. (1999). Psychological abuse: Implications for adjustment and commitment to leave violent partners. *Violence and Victims, 14,* 55–67.

Ayerle, C. L., & Vivian, D. (1996). *Alcohol use and husbands' violence in couples seeking marital therapy.* Unpublished manuscript, Department of Psychology, State University of New York at Stony Brook.

Babcock, J. C., Waltz, J., Jacobson, N., & Gottman, J. M. (1993). Power and violence: The relation between communication patterns, power discrepancies, and domestic violence. *Journal of Consulting and Clinical Psychology, 61,* 40–50.

Barber, J. P., Connolly, M. B., Crits-Christoph, P., Gladis, L., & Siqueland, L. (2000). Alliance predicts patients' outcome beyond in-treatment change in symptoms. *Journal of Consulting and Clinical Psychology, 68,* 1027–1032.

Barbour, K. A., Eckhardt, C. I., Davison, G. C., & Kassinove, H. (1998). The experience and expression of anger in maritally violent and maritally discordant-nonviolent men. *Behavior Therapy, 29,* 173–191.

Barling, J., O'Leary, K. D., Jouriles, E., Vivian, D., & MacEwen, K. E. (1987). Factor similarity of the Conflict Tactics Scales across samples, spouses, and sites: Issues and implications. *Journal of Family Violence, 2,* 37–53.

Basco, M. R., Birchler, G. R., Kalal, B., Talbott, R., & Slater, M. (1991). The Clinician Rating of Adult Communication (CRAC): A clinician's guide to the assessment of interpersonal communication. *Journal of Clinical Psychology, 47,* 368–380.

Baucom, D. H., & Adams, A. N. (1987). Assessing communication in marital interaction. In K. D. O'Leary (Ed.), *Assessment of marital discord* (pp. 139–182). Hillsdale, NJ: Erlbaum.

Baucom, D. H., & Lester, G. W. (1986). The usefulness of cognitive restructuring as an adjunct to behavioral marital therapy. *Behavior Therapy, 17,* 385–403.

Beck, A. T., Ward, C. H., Mendelson, M., Mock, J., & Erbaugh, J. (1961). An inventory for measuring depression. *Archives of General Psychiatry, 4,* 53–63.

Beere, C. A., King, D., Beere, D. B., & King, L. A. (1984). The Sex Role Egalitarianism Scale: A measure of attitudes toward equality between the sexes. *Sex Roles, 10,* 563–576.

Begun, A. L., Murphy, L. M., Bolt, D., Weinstein, B., Strodhoff, T., Short, L., & Shelley, G. (2003).Characteristics of the Safe at Home Instrument for assessing readiness to change intimate partner violence. *Research on Social Work Practice, 13,* 80–70.

Bellack, A., & Hersen, M. (1998). *Behavioral assessment: A practical handbook* (4th ed.). Boston: Allyn & Bacon.

Bergen, R. K. (1998). *Wife rape: Understanding the response of survivors and service providers.* Thousand Oaks, CA: Sage.

Berk, R. A., Berk, S. F., Loseke, D. R., & Rauma, D. (1983). Mutual combat and other family violence myths. In D. Finkelhor, R. J. Gelles, G. T. Hotaling, & M. A. Straus (Eds.), *The dark side of families: Current family violence research* (pp. 197–212). Beverly Hills, CA: Sage.

Berry, J. W. (1994). An ecological perspective on cultural and ethic psychology. In E. J. Trickett, R. J. Watts, & D. Birman (Eds.) *Human diversity* (pp. 115–141). San Francisco: Jossey-Bass.

Bersani, S. W., & Chen, H. T. (1988). Sociological perspectives in family violence. In V. B. Van Hasselt, R. L. Morrison, A. S. Bellack, & M. Hersen (Eds.), *Handbook of family violence* (pp. 57–86). New York: Plenum.

Biaggio, M. K. (1980). Assessment of anger arousal. *Journal of Personality Assessment, 44,* 289–298.

Biaggio, M. K., Supplee, K., & Curtis, N. (1981). Reliability and validity of four anger scales. *Journal of Personality Assessment, 45,* 639–648.

Birchler, G. R., Weiss, R. L., & Vincent, J. P. (1975). A multimethod analysis of social reinforcement exchange between maritally distressed and nondistressed spouse and stranger dyads. *Journal of Personality and Social Psychology, 31,* 349–360.

Bograd, M. (1984). Family systems approaches to wife battering: A feminist critique. *American Journal of Orthopsychiatry, 54,* 558–568.

Bograd, M. (1988). Feminist perspectives on wife abuse: An introduction. In K. Yllo and M. Bograd (Eds.), *Feminist perspectives on wife abuse* (pp. 11–26). Newbury Park, CA: Sage.

Bograd, M. (1990). Why we need gender to understand human violence. *Journal of Interpersonal Violence, 5,* 132–135.

Bohannon, J. R., Dosser, D. A., & Lindley, S. E. (1995). Using couple data to determine domestic violence rates: An attempt to replicate previous work. *Violence and Victims, 10,* 133–141.

Bordin, E. S. (1979). The generalizability of the psychoanalytic concept of the working alliance. *Psychotherapy: Theory, Research, and Practice, 16,* 252–260.

Borum, R. (1996). Improving the clinical practice of violence risk assessment. *American Psychologist, 51,* 945–956.

Boyle, D. J., & Vivian, D. (1996). Generalized versus spouse-specific anger/hostility and men's violence against intimates. *Violence and Victims, 11,* 293–317.

Breines, W., & Gordon, L. (1983). The new scholarship on family violence. *Signs: Journal of Women in Culture and Society, 8,* 490–531.

Breslin, F. C., Riggs, D. S., O'Leary, K. D., & Arias, I. (1990). Family precursors, expected and actual consequences of dating aggression. *Journal of Interpersonal Violence, 5,* 247–258.

Briere, J. (1996). Treatment outcome research with abused children: Methodological considerations in three studies. *Child Maltreatment, 1,* 348–352.

Briere, J., & Runtz, M. (1989). The Trauma Symptom Checklist (TSC-33): Early data on a new scale. *Journal of Interpersonal Violence, 4,* 151–162.

Brown, P. C., & Smith, T. W. (1992). Social influence, marriage, and the heart: Cardiovascular consequences of interpersonal control in husbands and wives. *Health Psychology, 11,* 88–96.

Brown, P. D., & O'Leary, K. D. (2000). Therapeutic alliance: Predicting continuance and success in a group treatment for spouse abuse. *Journal of Consulting and Clinical Psychology, 68,* 340–345.

Browne, A. (1987). *When battered women kill.* New York: Macmillan/Free Press.

Browne, A. (1993). Violence against women by male partners: Prevalence, outcomes, and policy implications. *American Psychologist, 48,* 1077–1087.

Browning, J., & Dutton, D. (1986). Assessment of wife assault with the Conflict Tactics Scale: Using couple data to quantify the differential reporting effect. *Journal of Marriage and the Family, 48,* 375–379.

Buchlman, K., & Gottman, J. (1996). The oral history interview and the oral history coding system. In J. M. Gottman (Ed.), *What predicts divorce? The measures* (pp. OHI1–OHI118). Mahwah, NJ: Erlbaum.

Buehlman, K., Gottman, J. M., & Katz, L. (1992). How a couple views their past predicts their future: Predicting divorce from an oral history interview. *Journal of Family Psychology, 5,* 295–318.

Burt, M. R. (1980). Cultural myths and supports for rape. *Journal of Personality and Social Psychology, 38,* 217–230.

Busby, D., Christensen, C., Crane, D. R., & Larson, J. H. (1995). A revision of the Dyadic Adjustment Scale for use with distressed and nondistressed couples: Construct hierarchy and multidimensional scales. *Journal of Marital and Family Therapy, 21,* 289–308.

Buss, A. H., & Durkee, A. (1957). An inventory for assessing different kinds of hostility. *Journal of Consulting Psychology, 21,* 343–349.

Buss, A. H., & Perry, M. (1992). The aggression questionnaire. *Journal of Personality and Social Psychology, 63,* 452–459.

Campbell, D. T., & Fiske, D. W. (1959). Convergent and discriminant validation by the multitrait–multimethod matrix. *Psychological Bulletin, 56,* 81–105.

Campbell, D. W., Campbell, J., King, C., Parker, B., & Ryan, J. (1994). The reliability and factor structure of the Index of Spouse Abuse with African American women. *Violence and Victims, 9,* 259–274.

Campbell, J. C. (1986). Nursing assessment of risk of homicide with battered women. *Advances in Nursing Science, 8*(4), 36–51.

Campbell, J. C. (Ed.). (1995a). *Assessing dangerousness: Violence by sexual offenders, batterers, and child abusers.* Thousand Oaks, CA: Sage.

Campbell, J. C (1995b). Prediction of homicide of and by battered women. In J. Campbell (Ed.), *Assessing dangerousness: Violence by sexual offenders, batterers, and child abusers* (pp. 96–113). Thousand Oaks, CA: Sage.

Campbell, J. C. (2000). Promise and perils of surveillance in addressing violence against women. *Violence Against Women, 6,* 705–727.

Cantos, A., Neidig, P., & O'Leary, K. D. (1994). Injuries of women and men in a treatment program for domestic violence. *Journal of Family Violence, 9,* 113–124.

Carey, M. P., Spector, I. P., Lantinga, L. J., & Krauss, D. J. (1993). Reliability of the Dyadic Adjustment Scale. *Psychological Assessment, 5,* 238–240.

Cascardi, M., Langhinrichsen, J., & Vivian, D. (1992). Marital aggression: Impact, injury, and health correlates for husbands and wives. *Archives of Internal Medicine, 152,* 1178–1184.

Cascardi, M., O'Leary, K. D., Lawrence, E. E., & Schlee, K. A. (1995). Characteristics of women physically abused by their spouses and who seek treatment regarding marital conflict. *Journal of Consulting and Clinical Psychology, 63,* 616–623.

Cascardi, M., & Vivian, D. (1995). Context for specific episodes of marital violence: Gender and severity of violence differences. *Journal of Family Violence, 10,* 265–293.

Cascardi, M., Vivian, D., & Meyer, S. L. (1991, November). *Context and attributions for marital violence in discordant couples.* Poster presented at the meeting of the Association for the Advancement of Behavior Therapy, New York, NY.

Chase, K. A., Treboux, D., O'Leary, K. D., & Strassberg, Z. (1998). Specificity of dating aggression and its justification among high-risk adolescents. *Journal of Abnormal Child Psychology, 26,* 467–473.

Check, J. (1998). Hostility toward women: Some theoretical considerations. In L. Russell & W. Gordon (Eds.), *Violence in intimate relationships* (pp. 27–42). Costa Mesa, CA: PMA Publishing Corp.

Christensen, A., & Jacobson, N. S. (1996, November). *Acceptance in marriage.* Paper presented at the meeting of the Association for the Advancement of Behavior Therapy, New York, NY.

Coccaro, E. F., Harvey, P. D., Kupsaw-Lawrence, E., Herbert, J. L., & Bernstein, D. P. (1991). Development of neuropharmacologically based behavioral assessments of impulsive aggressive behavior. *Journal of Neuropsychiatry, 3,* S44–S51.

Coccaro, E. F., Siever, L. J., Klar, H. M., Maurer, G., Cochrane, K., Cooper, T. B., et al. (1989). Serotonergic studies in affective and personality disorder patients: Correlates with suicidal and impulsive aggressive behavior. *Archives of General Psychiatry, 46,* 587–599.

Cohen, J. (1960). A coefficient of agreement for nominal scales. *Educational and Psychological Measurement, 20,* 37–46.

Coleman, D., & Straus, M. A. (1986). Marital power, conflict, and violence in a nationally representative sample of American couples. *Violence and Victims, 1,* 141–157.

Collins, N. L., & Read, S. J. (1990). Adult attachment, working models, and relationship quality in dating couples. *Journal of Personality and Social Psychology, 58,* 644–663.

Conner, K. R., & Ackerly, G. D. (1994). Alcohol-related battering: Developing treatment strategies. *Journal of Family Violence, 9,* 143–155.

Cordova, J. V., Jacobson, N. S., Gottman, J. M., Rushe, R., & Cox, G. (1993). Negative reciprocity and communication in couples with a violent husband. *Journal of Abnormal Psychology, 102,* 559–564.

Costello, A. J., Edelbrock, C. S., Dulcan, M. K., Kalas, R., & Klaric, S. H. (1984). *Report to NIMH on the NIMH Diagnostic Interview Schedule for Children (DISC)*. Washington, DC: National Institute of Mental Health.

Crocker, L., & Algina, J. (1986). *Introduction to classical and modern test theory*. New York: Holt, Rinehart, & Winston.

Cronbach, L. J. (1951). Coefficient alpha and the internal structure of tests. *Psychometrika, 16*, 297–334.

Crossman, R. K., Stith, S. M., & Bender, M. M. (1990). Sex role egalitarianism and marital violence. *Sex Roles, 22*, 293–304.

Crowne, D. P., & Marlowe, D. (1960). A new scale of social desirability independent of psychopathology. *Journal of Consulting Psychology, 24*, 349–354.

Cunradi, C. B., Caetano, R., & Schafer, J. (2002). Socioeconomic predictors of intimate partner violence among White, Black, and Hispanic couples in the United States. *Journal of Family Violence, 17*, 377–389.

Dahlstrom, W. G., Brooks, J. D., & Peterson, C. D. (1990). The Beck Depression Inventory: Item order and the impact of response sets. *Journal of Personality Assessment, 55*, 224–233.

Daniels, J. W., & Murphy, C. M. (1997). Stages and processes of change in batterers' treatment. *Cognitive and Behavioral Practice, 4*, 123–145.

Davison, G. C., Navarre, S. G., & Vogel, R. S. (1995). The Articulated Thoughts in Simulated Situations paradigm: A think-aloud approach to cognitive assessment. *Current Directions in Psychological Science, 4*, 29–33.

Davison, G. C., Robins, C., & Johnson, M. K. (1983). Articulated thoughts during simulated situations: A paradigm for studying cognition in emotion and behavior. *Cognitive Therapy and Research, 7*, 17–40.

Davison, G. C., Vogel, R. S., & Coffman, S. G. (1997). Think-aloud approaches to cognitive assessment and the Articulated Thoughts in Simulated Situations paradigm. *Journal of Consulting and Clinical Psychology, 65*, 950–958.

Deffenbacher, J. L., Oetting, E. R., Thwaites, G. A., Lynch, R. S., Baker, D. A., Stark, R. S., et al. (1996). State–trait anger theory and the utility of the Trait Anger Scale. *Journal of Counseling Psychology, 43*, 131–148.

DeKeserdy, W. S. (2000). Current controversies on defining nonlethal violence against women in intimate heterosexual relationships. *Violence Against Women, 6*, 728–746.

Dobash, R. E., & Dobash, R. (1979). *Violence against wives: A case against the patriarchy*. New York: Free Press.

Dobash, R. E., & Dobash, R. P. (1984). The nature and antecedents of violent events. *British Journal of Criminology, 24*, 269–288.

Dobash, R. P., Dobash, R. E., Daly, M., & Wilson, M. (1992). The myth of sexual symmetry in marital violence. *Social Problems, 39*, 71–91.

Dunford, F. W. (2000). The San Diego Navy Experiment: An assessment of interventions for men who assault their wives. *Journal of Consulting and Clinical Psychology, 68*, 468–476.

Dutton, D. G. (1986). Wife assaulters' explanations for assault: The neutralization of self-punishment. *Canadian Journal of Behavioral Science, 18*, 381–390.

Dutton, D. G. (1995). Propensity for Abusiveness Scale (PAS). *Journal of Family Violence, 10*, 203–221.

Dutton, D. G., & Browning, J. J. (1988). Power struggles and intimacy anxieties as causative factors of wife assault. In G. W. Russel (Ed.), *Violence in intimate relationships* (pp. 163–175). Costa Mesa, CA: PMA.

Dutton, D. G., & Hemphill, K. S. (1992). Patterns of socially desirable responding among perpetrators and victims of wife assault. *Violence and Victims, 7*, 29–39.

Dutton, D. G., & Kropp, P. R. (2000). A review of domestic violence risk instruments. *Trauma, Violence, and Abuse, 1,* 171–181.

Dutton, D. G., & Painter, S. L. (1993). Emotional attachments in abusive relationships: A test of traumatic bonding theory. *Violence and Victims, 8,* 105–120.

Dutton, D. G., & Starzomski, A. J. (1993). Borderline personality in perpetrators of psychological and physical abuse. *Violence and Victims, 8,* 327–337.

Dutton, D. G., & Starzomski, A. J. (1994). Psychological differences between court-referred and self-referred wife assaulters. *Criminal Justice and Behavior, 21,* 203–222.

Dutton, D., vanGinkel, C., & Landolt, M. A. (1996). Jealousy, intimate abusiveness, and intrusiveness. *Journal of Family Violence, 11,* 411–423.

Dutton, M. A. (1992a). Assessment and treatment of posttraumatic stress disorder among battered women. In D. W. Foy (Ed.), *Treating PTSD: Cognitive–behavioral strategies* (pp. 69–98). New York: Guilford Press.

Dutton, M. A. (1992b). *Empowering and healing the battered woman.* New York: Springer.

Eckhardt, C. I., Barbour, K. A., & Davison, G. C. (1998). Articulated thoughts of maritally violent and nonviolent men during anger arousal. *Journal of Consulting and Clinical Psychology, 66,* 259–269.

Eckhardt, C. I., Barbour, K. A., & Stuart, G. L. (1997). Anger and hostility in maritally violent men: Conceptual distinctions, measurement issues, and literature review. *Clinical Psychology Review, 17,* 333–358.

Eckhardt, C. I., & Kassinove, H. (1998). Articulated cognitive distortions and cognitive deficiencies in maritally violent men. *Journal of Cognitive Psychotherapy, 12,* 231–250.

Eddy, J. M., Heyman, R. E., & Weiss, R. L. (1991). An empirical evaluation of the Dyadic Adjustment Scale: Exploring the differences between marital "satisfaction" and "adjustment." *Behavioral Assessment, 13,* 199–220.

Edleson, J. L., & Brygger, M. P. (1986). Gender differences in self-reporting of battering incidences. *Family Relations, 35,* 377–382.

Ehrensaft, M. K., Langhinrichsen-Rohling, J., Heyman, R. E., O'Leary, K. D., & Lawrence, E. (1999). Feeling controlled in marriage: A phenomenon specific to physically aggressive couples? *Journal of Family Psychology, 13,* 20–32.

Ehrensaft, M. K., & Vivian, D. (1996). Spouse's reasons for not reporting existing marital aggression as a marital problem. *Journal of Family Psychology, 10,* 443–453.

Ehrensaft, M. K., & Vivian, D. (1999). Is partner aggression related to appraisals of coercive control by a partner? *Journal of Family Violence, 14,* 251–266.

Ekman, P., & Friesen, W. V. (1978). *Facial Action Coding System.* Palo Alto, CA: Consulting Psychologists Press.

Ewart, C. K., Taylor, C. B., Kraemer, H. C., & Agras, W. S. (1991). High blood pressure and marital discord: Not being nasty matters more than being nice. *Health Psychology, 10,* 155–163.

Fals-Stewart, W. (2003). The occurrence of partner violence on days of alcohol consumption: A longitudinal diary study. *Journal of Consulting and Clinical Psychology, 71,* 41–52.

Fals-Stewart, W., Birchler, G. R., & Kelley, M. (2003). The Timeline Followback Spousal Violence Interview to assess physical aggression between intimate partners: Reliability and validity. *Journal of Family Violence, 18,* 131–142.

Fals-Stewart, W., O'Farrell, T., Freitas, T. T., McFarlin, S. K., & Rutigliano, P. (2000). The Timeline Followback reports of psychoactive substance use by drug-abusing patients: Psychometric properties. *Journal of Consulting and Clinical Psychology, 68,* 134–144.

Feindler, E. L., Rathus, J. H., & Silver, L. B. (2003). *Assessment of family violence: A handbook for researchers and practitioners.* Washington, DC: American Psychological Association.

Feldbau-Kohn, S. R., Heyman, R. E., & O'Leary, K. D. (1998). Major depressive disorder and depressive symptomatology as predictors of husband to wife physical aggression. *Violence and Victims, 13,* 347–360.

Ferraro, K. J. (1983). Rationalizing violence: How battered women stay. *Victimology, 8,* 203–212.

Fincham, F. D., & Bradbury, T. N. (1992). Assessing attributions in marriage: The relationship attribution measure. *Journal of Personality and Social Psychology, 62,* 457–468.

Finkelhor, D., & Berliner, L. (1995). Research on the treatment of sexually abused children: A review and recommendations. *Journal of the American Academy of Child and Adolescent Psychiatry, 34,* 1408–1423.

Finn, J. (1986). The relationship between sex role attitudes and attitudes supporting marital violence. *Sex Roles, 14,* 1986.

First, M. B., Gibbon, M., Spitzer, R. L., & Williams, J. B. W. (1995). *User's guide for the Structured Clinical Interview for DSM–IV Axis I Disorders.* New York: Biometrics Research.

First, M. B., Gibbon, M., Spitzer, R. L., & Williams, J. B. W. (1997). *Structured Clinical Interview for DSM–IV Axis I Disorders—Clinician version.* Washington, DC: American Psychiatric Press.

First, M. B., Spitzer, R. L., Gibbon, M., & Williams, J. B. W. (1995a). *Structured Clinical Interview for DSM–IV Axis I Disorders—Clinician version administration booklet* (and Clinician Version Scoresheet). New York: New York State Psychiatric Institute, Biometrics Research Department.

First, M. B., Spitzer, R. L., Gibbon, M., & Williams, J. B. W. (1995b). *Structured Clinical Interview for DSM–IV Axis I Disorders—Patient edition* (SCID I/P, Version 2.0). New York: New York State Psychiatric Institute, Biometrics Research Department.

First, M. B., Spitzer, R. L., Gibbon, M., Williams, J. B. W., & Benjamin, L. (1994). *Structured Clinical Interview for DSM–IV Axis II Personality Disorders—Patient edition* (SCID-II, Version 2.0). New York: New York State Psychiatric Institute, Biometrics Research Department.

Fischer, G. J., & Chen, J. (1994). The Attitudes Toward Forcible Date Rape scale: Development of a measurement model. *Journal of Psychopathology and Behavioral Assessment, 16,* 33–50.

Foa, E. B, Cashman, L., Jaycox, L., & Perry, K. (1997). The validation of a self-report measure of posttraumatic stress disorder: The Posttraumatic Diagnostic Scale. *Psychological Assessment, 9,* 445–451.

Follette, V. M., & Alexander, P. C. (1992). Dating violence: Current and historical correlates. *Behavioral Assessment, 14,* 39–52.

Follingstad, D. R., Hause, E. S., Rutledge, L. L., & Poleck, D. S. (1992). Effects of battered women's early responses on later abuse patterns. *Violence and Victims, 7,* 109–128.

Follingstad, D. R., Rutledge, L. L., Berg, B. J., Hause, E. F., & Polek, C. F. (1990). The role of emotional abuse in physically abusive relationships. *Journal of Family Violence, 5,* 107–120.

Fraser, I. M., McNutt, L., Clark, C., Williams-Muhammed, D., & Lee, R. (2002). Social support choices for help with abusive relationships: Perceptions of African American women. *Journal of Family Violence, 17,* 363–376.

Fruzzetti, A. E., Saedi, N. N., Wilson, M. E., & Rubio, A. (1998). *Assessing the function of violence using the Domestic Violence Interview: Coding manual.* Reno: University of Nevada Press.

Gaston, L. (1990). The concept of alliance and its role in psychotherapy: Theoretical and empirical considerations. *Psychotherapy, 27,* 143–153.

Gelles, R. J. (1974). *The violent home: A study of physical aggression between husbands and wives.* Beverly Hills, CA: Sage.

Gelles, R. J. (1978). Methods for studying sensitive family topics. *American Journal of Orthopsychiatry, 48,* 408–424.

Gelles, R. J., & Straus, M. A. (1988). *Intimate violence.* New York: Simon & Schuster.

Golden, C. J., Sawicki, R. F., & Franzen, M. D. (1984). Test construction. In G. Golden & M. Hersen (Eds.), *Handbook of psychological assessment* (pp. 19–37). New York: Pergamon Press.

Gondolf, E. W. (1997). Patterns of reassault in batterer programs. *Violence and Victims, 12,* 373–387.

Gondolf, E., & Russel, D. (1986). The case against anger control treatment for batterers. *Response, 10,* 31–34.

Gordon, M. (2000). Definitional issues in violence against women. *Violence Against Women, 6,* 747–783.

Gottman, J. M. (1979). *Marital interaction: Experimental investigations.* New York: Academic Press.

Gottman, J. M. (1993). The roles of conflict engagement, escalation, and avoidance in marital interaction: A longitudinal view of five types of couples. *Journal of Consulting and Clinical Psychology, 61,* 6–15.

Gottman, J. M. (1994). *What predicts divorce? The relationship between marital processes and marital outcomes.* Hillsdale, NJ: Erlbaum.

Gottman, J. M. (1996). *What predicts divorce? The measures.* Hillsdale, NJ: Erlbaum.

Gottman, J. M., Jacobson, N. S., Rushe, R., Shortt, J. W., Babcock, J., La Taillade, J. J., & Waltz, J. (1995). The relationship between heart rate reactivity, emotionally aggressive behavior, and general violence in batterers. *Journal of Family Violence, 9,* 227–248.

Gottman, J. M., & Krokoff, L. J. (1989). The relationship between marital interaction and marital satisfaction: A longitudinal view. *Journal of Consulting and Clinical Psychology, 57,* 47–52.

Gottman, J. M., & Levenson, R. W. (1985). A valid procedure for obtaining self-report of affect in marital interaction. *Journal of Consulting and Clinical Psychology, 53,* 151–160.

Gottman, J. M., & Levenson, R. W. (1986). Assessing the role of emotion in marriage. *Behavioral Assessment, 8,* 31–48.

Gottman, J. M., & Levenson, R. W. (1992). Marital processes predictive of later dissolution: Behavior, physiology, and health. *Journal of Personality and Social Psychology, 63,* 221–233.

Gottman, J. M., Markman, H., & Notarius, C. (1977). The topography of marital conflict: A study of verbal and nonverbal behavior. *Journal of Marriage and the Family, 39,* 461–477.

Gottman, J., Notarius, C., Gonso, J., & Markman, H. (1976). *A couple's guide to communication.* Champaign, IL: Research Press.

Gottman, J., Notarius, C., Markman, H., Bank, S., Yoppi, B., & Rubin, M. E. (1976). Behavior exchange theory and marital decision making. *Journal of Personality and Social Psychology, 34,* 14–23.

Grann, M., & Wedin, I. (2002). Risk factors for recidivism among spousal assault and spousal homicide offenders. *Psychology, Crime, & Law, 8,* 5–23.

Greene, A. F., Coles, C. J., & Johnson, E. H. (1994). Psychopathology and anger in interpersonal violence offenders. *Journal of Clinical Psychology, 50,* 906–912.

Griffen, D., & Bartholomew, K. (1994). Models of self and other: Fundamental dimensions underlying measures of adult attachment. *Journal of Personality and Social Psychology, 67,* 430–445.

Gunn, J., & Gristwood, J. (1975). Use of the Buss–Durkee Hostility Inventory among British prisoners. *Journal of Consulting and Clinical Psychology, 43,* 590–599.

Hahlweg, K., Reisner, L., Kohli, G., Vollmer, M., Schindler, L., & Revenstorf, D. (1984). Development and validity of a new system to analyze interpersonal communication (KPI). In K. Hahlweg & N. S. Jacobson (Eds.), *Marital interaction: Analysis and modification* (pp. 182–198). New York: Guilford Press.

Hahlweg, K., Revenstorf, D., & Schindler, L. (1984). The effects of behavioral marital therapy on couples' communication and problem solving skills. *Journal of Consulting and Clinical Psychology, 52,* 553–566.

Haj-Yahia, M. M. (2002). The impact of wife abuse on marital relations as revealed by the second Palestinian National Survey on Violence Against Women. *Journal of Family Psychology, 16,* 273–285.

Hamberger, L. K., & Hastings, J. E. (1988). Characteristics of male spouse abusers consistent with personality disorders. *Hospital and Community Psychiatry, 39,* 763–770.

Hamby, S. L. (1996). The Dominance Scale: Preliminary psychometric properties. *Violence and Victims, 11,* 199–212.

Hansen, M., Harway, M., & Cervantes, N. (1991). Therapists' perceptions of severity in cases of family violence. *Violence and Victims, 6,* 225–234.

Hare, R. D. (1985). Comparison of procedures for the assessment of psychopathy. *Journal of Consulting and Clinical Psychology, 53,* 7–16.

Harvey, P. D., Greenberg, B. R., & Serper, M. R. (1989). The Affective Lability Scales: Development, reliability, and validity. *Journal of Clinical Psychology, 45,* 786–793.

Hathaway, S. R., & McKinley, J. C. (1989). *Minnesota Multiphasic Personality Inventory–2.* Minneapolis: University of Minnesota Press.

Hayes, S. C., Barlow, D. H., & Nelson-Gray, R. O. (1999). *The scientist practitioner: Research and accountability in the age of managed care.* Needham Heights, MA: Allyn & Bacon.

Hayes, S. C., Nelson, R. O., & Jarrett, R. B. (1987). The treatment utility of assessment: A functional approach to evaluating assessment quality. *American Psychologist, 42,* 963–974.

Haynes, S. N., & O'Brien, W. H. (1990). Functional analysis in behavior therapy. *Clinical Psychology Review, 10,* 649–668.

Heyman, R. E. (1993). *Distress and abuse classification interviews.* Unpublished manuscript, State University of New York at Stony Brook.

Heyman, R. E. (2001). Observation of couple conflicts: Clinical assessment applications, stubborn truths, and shaky foundations. *Psychological Assessment, 13,* 5–35.

Heyman, R. E., Brown, P. D., Feldbau-Kohn, S. R., & O'Leary, K. D. (1999). Couples' communication behaviors as predictors of drop-out and treatment response in wife abuse treatment programs. *Behavior Therapy, 30,* 165–189.

Heyman, R. E., Eddy, J. M., Weiss, R. L., & Vivian, D. (1995). Factor analysis of the Marital Interaction Coding System (MICS). *Journal of Family Psychology, 9,* 209–215.

Heyman, R. E., Feldbau-Kohn, S. R., Ehrensaft, M. K., Langhinrichsen-Rohling, J., & O'Leary, K. D. (2001). Can questionnaire reports correctly classify relationship distress and partner physical abuse? *Journal of Family Psychology, 15,* 334–346.

Heyman, R. E., O'Leary, K. D., & Jouriles, E. N. (1995). Alcohol and aggressive personality styles: Potentiators of serious physical aggression against wives? *Journal of Family Psychology, 9,* 44–57.

Heyman, R. E., & Schlee, K. A. (1997). Toward a better estimate of the prevalence of partner abuse: Adjusting rates based on the sensitivity of the Conflict Tactics Scale. *Journal of Family Psychology, 11,* 332–338.

Heyman, R. E., & Vivian, D. (1993). *Rapid Marital Interaction Coding System (RMICS): Training manual for coders.* Retrieved November 6, 2003, from http://www.psy.sunysb.edu/marital

Heyman, R. E., & Vivian, D. (1997a). *Rapid Marital Interaction Coding System (RMICS): Reliability and validity of a category-based observational coding system.* Manuscript submitted for publication.

Heyman, R. E., & Vivian, D. (1997b). *R-MICS coding manual.* Stony Brook: State University of New York at Stony Brook.

Heyman, R. E., Weiss, R. L., & Eddy, J. M. (1995). Marital Interaction Coding System: Revision and empirical evaluation. *Behavioural Research and Therapy, 33,* 737–746.

Hilberman, E. (1980). Overview: The "wife beater's wife" reconsidered. *American Journal of Psychiatry, 11,* 1336–1347.

Holtzworth-Munroe, A., & Anglin, K. (1991). The competency of responses given by maritally violent versus nonviolent men to problematic marital situations. *Violence and Victims, 6,* 257–269.

Holtzworth-Munroe, A., Beatty, S. B., & Anglin, K. (1995). The assessment and treatment of marital violence: An introduction for the marital therapist. In N. S. Jacobson & A. S. Gurman (Eds.), *Clinical handbook of couple therapy* (pp. 317–339). New York: Guilford Press.

Holtzworth-Munroe, A., & Hutchinson, G. (1993). Attributing negative intent to wife behavior: The attributions of maritally violent versus nonviolent men. *Journal of Abnormal Psychology, 2,* 206–211.

Holtzworth-Munroe, A., Meehan, J. C., Herron, K., Rehman, U., & Stuart, G. L. (2000). Testing the Holtzworth-Munroe and Stuart batterer typology. *Journal of Consulting and Clinical Psychology, 68,* 1000–1019.

Holtzworth-Munroe, A., & Stuart, G. L. (1994). Typologies of male batterers: Three subtypes and the differences among them. *Psychological Bulletin, 116,* 476–497.

Holtzworth-Munroe, A., Stuart, G. L., & Hutchinson, G. (1997). Violent versus nonviolent husbands: Differences in attachment patterns, dependency, and jealousy. *Journal of Family Psychology, 11,* 314–331.

Holtzworth-Munroe, A., Waltz, J., Jacobson, N. S., Monaco, V., Fehrenbach, P. A., & Gottman, J. M. (1992). Recruiting nonviolent men as control subjects for research on marital violence: How easily can it be done? *Violence and Victims, 7,* 79–88.

Hops, H., Wills, T. A., Patterson, G. R., & Weiss, R. L. (1972). *Marital Interaction Coding System.* Unpublished manuscript, University of Oregon, Oregon Research Institute.

Hornung, C. B., Mc Cullough, C., & Sugimoto, T. (1981). Status relationships in marriage: Risk factors in spouse abuse. *Journal of Marriage and the Family, 43,* 675–692.

Horowitz, M. J., Wilner, N., & Alvarez, W. (1980). Signs and symptoms of posttraumatic stress disorder. *Archives of General Psychiatry, 37,* 85–92.

Hotaling, G., & Sugarman, D. (1986). An analysis of risk markers in husband and wife violence: The current state of knowledge. *Violence and Victims, 1,* 101–124.

Houskamp, B., & Foy, D. W. (1991). The assessment of PTSD in battered women. *Journal of Interpersonal Violence, 6,* 367–375.

Hudson, W. W., & McIntosh, S. R. (1981). The assessment of spouse abuse: Two quantifiable dimensions. *Journal of Marriage and the Family, 43,* 873–888.

Hughes, D., Seidman, E., & Williams, N. (1993). Cultural phenomena and the research enterprise: Toward a culturally anchored methodology. *American Journal of Community Psychology, 21,* 687–704.

Hutchinson, S. A., Wilson, M. E., & Wilson, H. S. (1994). Benefits of participating in research interviews. *IMAGE: Journal of Nursing Scholarship, 26,* 161–164.

Hysjulien, C., Wood, B., & Benjamin, G. A. H. (1994). Child custody evaluations: A review of methods used in litigation and alternative dispute resolution. *Family and Conciliation Courts Review, 32,* 466–489.

Jackson, D. N. (1970). A sequential system for personality scale development. In C. D. Spielberger (Ed.), *Current topics in clinical and community psychology* (Vol. 2, pp. 61–92). New York: Academic Press.

Jackson, D. N. (1974). *Personality Research Form manual.* Goshen, NY: Research Psychologists Press.

Jacobson, N. S., Gottman, J. M., Gortner, E., Berns, S., & Shortt, J. W. (1996). Psychological factors in the longitudinal course of battering: When do the couples split up? When does the abuse decrease? *Violence and Victims, 11,* 371–392.

Jacobson, N. S., Gottman, J. M., Waltz, J., Rushe, R., Babcock, J., & Holtzworth-Munroe, A. (1994). Affect, verbal content, and psychophysiology in the arguments of couples with a violent husband. *Journal of Consulting and Clinical Psychology, 62,* 982–988.

Jacobson, N. S., & Traux, P. (1991). Clinical significance: A statistical approach to defining meaningful change in psychotherapy research. *Journal of Consulting and Clinical Psychology, 59,* 12–19.

Jaffe, P. G., Sudermann, M., Reitzel, D., & Killip, S. M. (1992). An evaluation of a secondary school primary prevention program on violence in intimate relationships. *Violence and Victims, 7,* 129–146.

Johnson, M. P. (1995). Patriarchal terrorism and common couple violence: Two forms of violence against women. *Journal of Marriage and the Family, 57,* 283–294.

Jorgensen, S. R. (1977). Societal class heterogamy, status striving, and perception of marital conflict: A partial replication and revision of Pearlin's contingency hypothesis. *Journal of Marriage and the Family, 39,* 653–689.

Jouriles, E. N., & O'Leary, K. D. (1985). Interspousal reliability of reports of marital violence. *Journal of Consulting and Clinical Psychology, 53,* 419–421.

Julien, D., Markman, H. J., & Lindahl, K. M. (1989). A comparison of a global and a microanalytic coding system. Implications for future trends in studying interactions. *Behavioral Assessment, 11,* 81–100.

Kantor, G. K., & Straus, M. A. (1990). The drunken bum theory of wife beating. In M. A. Straus & R. A. Gelles (Eds.), *Physical violence in American families* (pp. 203–224). New Brunswick, NJ: Transaction Books.

Kaslow, N. J., Thompson, M. P., Meadows, L. A., Jacobs, D., Chance, S., Gibb, B., et al. (1998). Factors that mediate and moderate the link between partner abuse and suicidal behavior in African American women. *Journal of Consulting and Clinical Psychology, 66,* 533–540.

Kaslow, N. J., Thompson, M. P., Okun, A., Price, A., Young, S., Bender, M., et al. (2002). Risk and protective factors for suicidal behavior in abused African American women. *Journal of Consulting and Clinical Psychology, 70,* 311–319.

Katkin, E. S. (1985). Blood, sweat, and tears: Individual differences in autonomic self-perception. *Psychophysiology, 22,* 125–137.

Kazdin, A. (1998). *Research design in clinical psychology.* Needham Heights, MA: Allyn & Bacon.

Kerig, P. K., & Lindahl, K. M. (2001). (Ed.). *Family Observational Coding Systems: Resources for systematic research.* Mahwah, NJ: Erlbaum.

Kiecolt-Glaser, J. K., Malarkey, W. B., Chee, M. A., Newton, T., Cacioppo, J. T., Mao, H. Y., & Glaser, R. (1993). Negative behavior during marital conflict is associated with immunological down-regulation. *Psychosomatic Medicine, 55,* 395–409.

Kiecolt-Glaser, J. K., Newton, T., Cacioppo, J. T., MacCallum, R. C., Glaser, R., & Malarkey, W. B. (1996). Marital conflict and endocrine function: Are men really more physiologically affected than women? *Journal of Consulting and Clinical Psychology, 64,* 324–332.

Koss, M. P. (1990). The women's mental health research agenda: Violence against women. *American Psychologist, 45,* 374–380.

Koss, M. P., Goodman, L. A., Browne, A., Fitzgerald, L. F., Puryear, G., Keita, G. P., & Russo, N. F. (1994). *No safe haven: Male violence against women at home, at work, and in the community.* Washington, DC: American Psychological Association.

Krokoff, L. (1984). *The anatomy of blue-collar marriages.* Unpublished doctoral dissertation, University of Illinois at Urbana-Champaign.

Krokoff, L. J., Gottman, J. M., & Hass, S. D. (1989). Validation of a global rapid couples interaction scoring system. *Behavioral Assessment, 11,* 65–79.

Kropp, P. R., & Hart, S. D. (1997). Assessing risk of violence in wife assaulters: The Spousal Assault Risk Assessment Guide. In C. D. Webster & M. A. Jackson (Eds.), *Impulsivity: Theory, assessment, and treatment* (pp. 302–325). New York: Guilford Press.

Kropp, P. R., & Hart, S. D. (2000). The Spousal Assault Risk Assessment Guide: Reliability and validity in adult male offenders. *Law and Human Behavior, 24,* 101–118.

Kropp, P. R., Hart, S. D., Webster, C. W., & Eaves, D. (1994). *Manual for the Spousal Assault Risk Assessment Guide.* Vancouver, British Columbia, Canada: British Columbia Institute on Family Violence.

Kropp, P. R., Hart, S. D., Webster, C. W., & Eaves, D. (1995). *Manual for the Spousal Assault Risk Assessment Guide* (2nd ed.). Vancouver, British Columbia, Canada: British Columbia Institute on Family Violence.

Kropp, P. R., Hart, S. D., Webster, C. W., & Eaves, D. (1998). *Spousal Assault Risk Assessment: User's guide.* Toronto, Ontario, Canada: Multi-Health Systems.

Kubany, E. S., Leisen, M. B., Kaplan, A. S., & Kelly, M. P. (2000). Validation of a brief measure of posttraumatic stress disorder: The Distressing Event Questionnaire (DEQ). *Psychological Assessment, 12,* 197–209.

Kubany, E. S., Leisen, M. B., Kaplan, A. S., Watson, S. B., Haynes, S. N., Owens, J. A., & Burns, K. (2000). Development and preliminary validation of a brief broad-spectrum measure of trauma exposure: The Traumatic Life Events Questionnaire. *Psychological Assessment, 12,* 210–224.

Kuhn, C. M. (1989). Adrenocortical and gonadal steroids in behavioral cardiovascular medicine. In N. Schneiderman, S. M. Weiss, & P. G. Kaufman (Eds.), *Handbook of research methods in cardiovascular behavioral medicine* (pp. 185–204). New York: Plenum.

Kurz, D. (1993). Physical assaults by husbands: A major social problem. In R. J. Gelles & D. R. Loseke (Eds.), *Current controversies in family violence* (pp. 88–103). Newbury Park, CA: Sage.

Lambert, M. J. (1992). Psychotherapy outcome research: Implications for integrative and eclectic therapists. In J. C. Norcross & M. R. Goldfried (Eds.), *Handbook of psychotherapy integration* (pp. 94–129). New York: Basic Books.

Langhinrichsen-Rohling, J., & Vivian, D. (1994). The correlates of spouses' incongruent reports of marital aggression. *Journal of Family Violence, 9,* 265–283.

Lawrence, E., & Bradbury, T. (2001). Physical aggression and marital dysfunction: A longitudinal analysis. *Journal of Family Psychology, 15,* 135–154.

Lawrence, E., Heyman, R. E., & O'Leary, K. D. (1995). Correspondence between telephone and written assessments of physical violence in marriage. *Behavior Therapy, 26,* 671–680.

Levenson, R. W., & Gottman, J. M. (1983). Marital interaction: Physiological linkage and affective exchange. *Journal of Personality and Social Psychology, 45,* 587–597.

Lewis, B. V. (1985). The Wife Abuse Inventory: A screening device for the identification of abused women. *Social Work, 30,* 32–36.

Limandri, B. J., & Sheridan, D. J. (1995). Prediction of intentional interpersonal violence: An introduction. In J. C. Campbell (Ed.), *Assessing dangerousness: Violence by sexual offenders, batterers, and child abusers* (pp. 1–19). Thousand Oaks, CA: Sage.

Linehan, M. M. (1980). Content validity: Its relevance to behavioral assessment. *Behavioral Assessment, 2,* 147–159.

Locke, H. J., & Wallace, K. M. (1959). Short marital-adjustment and prediction tests: Their reliability and validity. *Marriage and Family Living, 21,* 251–255.

Lockhart, L. (1985). Methodological issues in comparative racial analyses: The case of wife abuse. *Social Work Research and Abstracts, 21,* 35–41.

Lohr, J. M., Hamberger, L. K., & Bonge, D. (1988). The nature of irrational beliefs in different personality clusters of spouse abusers. *Journal of Rational-Emotive and Cognitive-Behavior Therapy, 6,* 273–285.

Lonner, W. J. (1994). Culture and human diversity. In E. J. Trickett, R. J. Watts, R. D. Birman (Eds.), *Human diversity* (pp. 230–243). San Francisco: Jossey-Bass.

Maffei, C., Fossati, A., Agostoni, I., Barraco, A., Bagnato, M., Deborah, D., et al. (1997). Interrater reliability and internal consistency of the Structured Clinical Interview for DSM–IV Axis II Personality Disorders (SCID II), Version 2.0. *Journal of Personality Disorders, 11,* 279–284.

Maiuro, R. D., Cahn, T. S., Vitaliano, P. P., Wagner, B. C., & Zegree, J. B. (1988). Anger, hostility, and depression in domestically violent versus generally assaultive men and nonviolent control subjects. *Journal of Consulting and Clinical Psychology, 56,* 17–23.

Malarkcy, W., Kiecolt-Glaser, J. K., Pearl, D., & Glaser, R. (1994). Hostile behavior during marital conflict alters pituitary and adrenal hormones. *Psychosomatic Medicine, 56,* 41–51.

Manson, S. M. (1997). Cross-cultural and multiethnic assessment of trauma. In J. P. Wilson and T. M. Keane (Eds.), *Assessing psychological trauma and PTSD* (pp. 239–266). New York: Guilford Press.

Margolin, G. (1987). The multiple forms of aggressiveness between marital partners: How do we identify them? *Journal of Marital and Family Therapy, 1,* 77–84.

Margolin, G., & Burman, B. (1993). Wife abuse versus marital violence: Different terminologies, explanations, and solutions. *Clinical Psychology Review, 13,* 59–73.

Margolin, G., Burman, B., & John, R. S. (1989). Home observations of married couples reenacting naturalistic conflicts. *Behavioral Assessment, 11,* 101–118.

Margolin, G., John, R. S., & Gleberman, L. (1988). Affective responses to conflictual discussions in violent and nonviolent couples. *Journal of Consulting and Clinical Psychology, 56,* 24–33.

Margolin, G., Oliver, P. H., Gordis, E. B., O'Hearn, H. G., Medina, A. M., Ghosh, C. M., & Morland, J. (1998). The nuts and bolts of behavioral observation of marital and family interaction. *Clinical Child and Family Psychology Review, 1,* 195–213.

Markman, H. J., & Floyd, F. (1980). Possibilities for the prevention of marital discord: A behavioral perspective. *American Journal of Family Therapy, 8,* 29–48.

Markman, H. J., & Notarius, C. I. (1987). Coding marital and family interaction: Current status. In T. Jacob (Ed.), *Family interaction and psychopathology: Theories, methods, and findings* (pp. 329–390). New York: Plenum.

Marshall, L. L. (1992a). Development of the Severity of Violence Against Women Scales. *Journal of Family Violence, 7,* 102–121.

Marshall, L. L. (1992b). The Severity of Violence Against Men Scales. *Journal of Family Violence, 7,* 189–203.

Marshall, L. L. (1996). Psychological abuse of women: Six distinct clusters. *Journal of Family Violence, 11,* 379–409.

Marshall, L. L. (1999). Effects of men's subtle and overt psychological abuse on low income women. *Violence and Victims, 14,* 69–88.

Mathes, E. W., Phillips, J. T., Skowran, J., & Dick, W. E., III. (1982). Behavioral correlates of the Interpersonal Jealousy Scale. *Educational and Psychological Measurement, 42,* 1227–1231.

Mathes, E. W., & Severa, N. (1981). Jealousy, romantic love, and liking: Theoretical considerations and preliminary scale development. *Psychological Reports, 49,* 23–31.

Matsumoto, D. (1994). *Cultural influences on research methods and statistics.* Pacific Grove, CA: Brooks Cole.

McFarlane, J., Parker, B., Soeken, K., & Bullock, L. (1992). Assessing for abuse during pregnancy: Severity and frequency of injuries associated with entry into prenatal care. *Journal of the American Medical Association, 267,* 3176–3178.

McHugh, M. C., Frieze, I. H., & Browne, A. (1993). Research on battered women and their assailants. In. M. Paludi & F. Denmark (Eds.), *Handbook on the psychology of women* (pp. 513–552). New York: Greenwood Press.

McMahon, M., & Pence, E. (1996). Replying to Dan O'Leary. *Journal of Interpersonal Violence, 11,* 452–456.

Meehan, J. C., Holtzworth-Munroe, A., & Herron, K. (2001). Maritally violent men's heart rate reactivity to marital interactions: A failure to replicate the Gottman et al. (1995) typology. *Journal of Family Psychology, 15,* 394–408.

Menzies, R. J., & Webster, C. D. (1995). Construction and validation of risk assessments in a six-year follow-up of forensic patients: A tridimensional analysis. *Journal of Consulting and Clinical Psychology, 63,* 766–778.

Miller, W. R., & Rollnick, S. (Eds.). (1991). *Motivational interviewing: Preparing people to change addictive behaviors.* New York: Guilford Press.

Millon, T. (1992). Millon Clinical Multiaxial Inventory: I and II. *Journal of Counseling Development, 70,* 421–426.

Mitchell, S. (1979). Interobserver agreement, reliability, and generalizability of data collected in observational studies. *Psychological Bulletin, 86,* 376–390.

Morrison, R. L., Van Hasselt, V. B., & Bellack, A. S. (1987). Assessment of assertion and problem-solving skills in wife abusers and their spouses. *Journal of Family Violence, 2,* 227–238.

Mossman, D. (1994). Assessing predictions of violence: Being accurate about accuracy. *Journal of Consulting and Clinical Psychology, 62,* 783–792.

Murphy, C. M., & Baxter, V. A (1997). Motivating batterers to change in the treatment context. *Journal of Interpersonal Violence, 12,* 607–619.

Murphy, C. M., & Cascardi, M. (1999). Psychological abuse in marriage and dating relationships. In R. L. Hampton (Ed.), *Family violence prevention and treatment* (2nd ed., pp. 198–226). Beverly Hills, CA: Sage.

Murphy, C. M., & Hoover, S. A. (1999). Measuring emotional abuse in dating relationships as a multifactorial construct. *Violence and Victims, 14,* 39–53.

Murphy, C. M., Meyer, S. L., & O'Leary, K. D. (1994). Dependency characteristics in partner assaultive men. *Journal of Abnormal Psychology, 103,* 729–735.

Murphy, C. M., & O'Leary, K. D. (1994). Research values, paradigms, and spouse abuse. *Journal of Interpersonal Violence, 9,* 207–223.

Muskat, Y. (1997). *Social information processing in batterers: A treatment outcome study.* Unpublished doctoral dissertation, Clinical Psychology Department, CW Post Campus of Long Island University, Brookville, NY.

Nabi, R. L., & Horner, J. R. (2001). Victims with voices: How abused women conceptualize the problem of spousal abuse and implications for intervention and prevention. *Journal of Family Violence, 16,* 237–253.

Nazroo, J. (1995). Uncovering gender differences in the use of marital violence: The effect of methodology. *Sociology, 29,* 475–494.

Neidig, P. H., & Friedman, D. H. (1984). *Spouse abuse: A treatment program for couples.* Champaign, IL: Research Press.

Nezu, A. M., & Nezu, C. M. (1989). *Clinical decision making in behavior therapy: A problem-solving perspective.* Champaign, IL: Research Press.

Notarius, C. I., Markman, H. J., & Gottman, J. M. (1981). The couples interaction scoring system. In E. E. Filsinger & R. A. Lewis (Eds.), *Assessing marriage: New behavioral approaches* (pp. 117–136). Beverly Hills, CA: Sage.

Novaco, R. W. (1975). *Anger control: The development and evaluation of an experimental program.* Lexington, MA: Lexington Books.

Novaco, R. W. (1977). A stress inoculation approach to anger management in training of law enforcement officers. *American Journal of Community Psychology, 5,* 327–346.

Nunnally, J. C. (1978). *Psychometric theory.* New York: McGraw-Hill.

O'Brien, M. O., John, R. S., Margolin, G., & Erel, O. (1994). Reliability and diagnostic efficacy of parents' reports regarding children's exposure to marital aggression. *Violence and Victims, 9,* 45–62.

Oldham, J., Clarkin, J., Appelbaum, A., Carr, A., Kernberg, P., Lotterman, A., & Haas, G. (1985). A self-report instrument for borderline personality organization. In T. H. McGlashan (Ed.), *The borderline: Current empirical research—The Progress in Psychiatry series* (pp. 1–18). Washington, DC: American Psychiatric Press.

O'Leary, K. D. (1987). *Assessment of marital discord.* Hillsdale, NJ: Erlbaum.

O'Leary, K. D. (1988). Physical aggression between spouses: A social learning theory perspective. In V. B. Van Hasselt, R. L. Morrison, A. S. Bellack, & M. Hersen (Eds.), *Handbook of family violence* (pp. 31–55). New York: Plenum.

O'Leary, K. D. (1996). Physical aggression in intimate relationships can be treated within a marital context under certain circumstances. *Journal of Interpersonal Violence, 11,* 450–453.

O'Leary, K. D. (1999). Psychological abuse: A variable deserving critical attention in domestic violence. *Violence and Victims, 14,* 3–23.

O'Leary, K. D. (2000). Are women really more aggressive than men in intimate relationships? Comment on Archer (2000). *Psychological Bulletin, 126,* 685–689.

O'Leary, K. D. (2002). Conjoint therapy for partners who engage in physically aggressive behavior: Rationale and research. *Journal of Aggression, Maltreatment, and Trauma, 5,* 145–164.

O'Leary, K. D., & Arias, I. (1988). Assessing agreement of reports of spouse abuse. In G. Hotaling, D. Finkelhor, J. T. Kirkpatrick, & M. A. Straus (Eds.), *Family abuse and its consequences: New directions in research* (pp. 218–227). Newbury Park, CA: Sage.

O'Leary, K. D., Barling, J., Arias, I., Rosenbaum, A., Malone, J., & Tyree, A. (1989). Prevalence and stability of physical aggression between spouses: A longitudinal analysis. *Journal of Consulting and Clinical Psychology, 57,* 263–268.

O'Leary, K. D., & Curley, A. D. (1986). Assertion and family violence: Correlates of spouse abuse. *Journal of Marital and Family Therapy, 12,* 281–290.

O'Leary, K. D., Heyman, R. E., & Neidig, P. H. (1999). Treatment of wife abuse: A comparison of gender-specific and conjoint approaches. *Behavior Therapy, 30,* 475–505.

O'Leary, K. D., & Jacobson, N. S. (1997). Partner relational problems with physical abuse. *DSM–IV sourcebook* (pp. 673–692). Washington, DC: American Psychiatric Association.

O'Leary, K. D., Malone, J., & Tyree, A. (1994). Physical aggression in early marriage: Prerelationship and relationship effects. *Journal of Consulting and Clinical Psychology, 62,* 594–602.

O'Leary, K. D., & Murphy, C. M. (1999). Clinical issues in the assessment of partner violence. In R. T. Ammerman & M. Hersen (Eds.), *Assessment of family violence: A clinical and legal sourcebook* (pp. 24–47). New York: Wiley.

O'Leary, K. D., Neidig, P. H., & Heyman, R. E. (1995). Assessment and treatment of partner abuse: A synopsis for the legal profession. *Albany Law Review, 58,* 1215–1234.

O'Leary, K. D., Vivian, D., & Malone, J. (1992). Assessment of physical aggression against women in marriage: The need for multimodal assessment. *Behavioral Assessment, 14,* 5–14.

Olson, D. H. (1981). Family typologies: Bridging family research and family therapy. In E. Filsinger & R. A. Lewis (Eds.), *Assessing marriage: New behavioral approaches* (pp. 74–89). Beverly Hills, CA: Sage.

Oregon Marital Studies Center. (1975). *Marital Interaction Coding System (MICS): Training and reference manual for coders.* Eugene: University of Oregon, Oregon Marital Studies Program.

O'Sullivan, M. J., & Jemelka, R. P. (1993). The 3-4/4-3 MMPI code type in an offender population: An update on levels of hostility and violence. *Psychological Assessment, 5,* 493–498.

Otto, R. (1992). The prediction of dangerous behavior: A review and analysis of "second generation" research. *Forensic Reports, 5,* 103–133.

Pan, H. S., Ehrensaft, M. K., Heyman, R. E., O'Leary, K. D., & Schwartz, R. (1997). Evaluation of the criteria for spouse abuse in a sample of patients at a family practice clinic. *Family Medicine, 29,* 492–495.

Pan, H. S., Neidig, P. H., O'Leary, K. D. (1994a). Male–female and aggressor–victim differences in the factor structure of the Modified Conflict Tactics Scale. *Journal of Interpersonal Violence, 9,* 366–382.

Pan, H. S., Neidig, P. H., & O'Leary, K. D. (1994b). Predicting mild and severe husband-to-wife physical aggression. *Journal of Consulting and Clinical Psychology, 62,* 975–981.

Patterson, G. R., Ray, R. S., Shaw, D. A., & Cobb, J. A. (1969). *Manual for coding of family interactions.* Unpublished manuscript, University of Oregon.

Pearlman, L. A. (1996). Review of TSI belief scale. In B. H. Stamm (Ed.), *Measurement of stress, trauma, and adaptation.* Lutherville, MD: Sidran Press.

Pelcovitz, D., Vanderkolk, B., Roth, S., Kaplan, S., Mandel, F., & Resnick, P. (1997). Development and validation of a Structured Interview for Disorders of Extreme Stress (SIDES). *Journal of Traumatic Stress, 10,* 3–16.

Pence, E. (1989). Batterer programs: Shifting from community collusion to community confrontation. In P. L. Caesar & L. K. Hamberger (Eds.), *Treating men who batter: Theory, practice, and programs* (pp. 24–50). New York: Springer.

Pence, E., & Paymar, M. (1985). *Power and control: Tactics of men who batter.* Duluth, MN: Domestic Abuse Intervention Project.

Pence, E., & Paymar, M. (1993). *Education groups for men who batter: The Duluth model.* New York: Springer.

Persons, J. B., & Fresco, D. M. (1998). Assessment of depression. In A. S. Bellack & M. Hersen (Eds.), *Behavioral assessment* (pp. 210–231). Boston: Allyn & Bacon.

Plutchik, R., Climent, C., & Ervin, R. (1976). Research strategies for the study of human violence. In W. L. Smith & A. Kling (Eds.), *Issues in brain/behavior control* (pp. 69–94). New York: Spectrum.

Plutchik, R., & van Praag, H. M. (1990). A self-report measure of violence risk: II. *Comprehensive Psychiatry, 31,* 450–456.

Porter, S. J. (1986). Assessment: A vital process in the treatment of family violence. *Family Therapy, 13,* 105–112.

Prochaska, J. O., & DiClemente, C. C. (1983). Stages and process of self-change of smoking: Toward an integrative model of change. *Journal of Consulting and Clinical Psychology, 51,* 390–395.

Prochaska, J. O., & DiClemente, C. C. (1984). *The transtheoretical approach: Crossing the traditional boundaries of therapy.* Homewood, IL: Dow Jones Irwin.

Prochaska, J. O., Velicer, W. F., Rossi, J. S., Goldstein, M. G., Marcus, B. H., Rakowski, W., et al. (1994). Stages of change and decisional balance for 12 problem behaviors. *Health Psychology, 13,* 39–46.

Ptacek, J. (1988). Why do men batter their wives? In K. Yllo & M. Bograd (Eds.), *Feminist perspectives on wife abuse* (pp. 133–157). Newbury Park, CA: Sage.

Rathus, J. H., Campbell, M. G., Cavuoto, N., Wisely, L., Anzalone, A., & Joyce, P. (2001, November). *Assessing change in a batterers treatment program: The victims' perspective.* Paper presented at the annual meeting of the Association for Advancement of Behavior Therapy, Philadelphia, PA.

Rathus, J. H., & Cavuoto, N. (2001, November). *Dialectical behavior therapy for partner-assaultive husbands*. Paper presented at the annual meeting of the Association for Advancement of Behavior Therapy, Philadelphia, PA.

Rathus, J. H., & Miller, A. L. (2002). Dialectical behavior therapy adapted for suicidal adolescents. *Suicide and Life-Threatening Behavior, 32,* 146–157.

Rathus, J. H., & O'Leary, K. D. (1997). Spouse-specific dependency scale: Scale development. *Journal of Family Violence, 12,* 159–168.

Rathus, S. A. (1973). A 30-item schedule for assessing assertive behavior. *Behavior Therapy, 4,* 398–406.

Raush, H. L., Barry, W. A., Hertel, R. K., & Swain, M. A. (1974). *Communication, conflict, and marriage.* San Francisco: Jossey-Bass.

Riggs, D. S., & Caulfield, M. B. (1997). Expected consequences of male violence against their female dating partners. *Journal of Interpersonal Violence, 12,* 229–240.

Riggs, D. S., Murphy, C. M., & O'Leary, K. D. (1989). Intentional falsification in reports of interpartner aggression. *Journal of Interpersonal Violence, 4,* 220–232.

Rodenburg, F. A., & Fantuzzo, J. W. (1993). The measure of wife abuse: Steps toward the development of a comprehensive assessment technique. *Journal of Family Violence, 8,* 203–228.

Rosenbaum, A., & O'Leary, K. D. (1981). Marital violence: Characteristics of abusive couples. *Journal of Consulting and Clinical Psychology, 49,* 63–71.

Rosenberg, M. (1979). *Conceiving the self.* New York: Basic Books.

Rosewater, L. B. (1985). Schizophrenic, borderline, or battered? In L. B. Rosewater & L. E. Walker (Eds.), *Handbook of feminist therapy: Women's issues in psychotherapy* (pp. 215–225). New York: Springer.

Renzetti, C. (1997). Violence and abuse among same-sex couples. In A. P. Cardarelli (Ed.), *Violence between intimate partners. Patterns, causes, and effects* (pp. 70–89). Boston: Allyn & Bacon.

Russel, J., & Mehrabian, A. (1977). Evidence for a three-factor theory of emotions. *Journal of Research in Personality, 11,* 273–294.

Sabourin, S., Lussier, Y., Laplante, B., & Wright, J. (1990). Unidimensional and multidimensional models of dyadic adjustment: A hierarchical reconciliation. *Psychological Assessment: A Journal of Consulting and Clinical Psychology, 2,* 333–337.

Sackett, L. A., & Saunders, D. G. (1999). The impact of different forms of psychological abuse on battered women. *Violence and Victims, 14,* 105–117.

Saedi, N. N., & Fruzzetti, A. E. (2000). *A functional model of aggression and violence in couples.* Manuscript submitted for publication.

Saedi, N. N., Rubio, A., & Fruzzetti, A. E. (1999, November). *The Domestic Violence Interview: A functional assessment of aggression and violence in couples*. Paper presented at the annual meeting of the Association for the Advancement of Behavior Therapy, Toronto, Ontario, Canada.

Saltzman, L. E., Fanslow, J. L., McMahon, P. M., & Shelley, G. A. (1999). *Intimate partner violence surveillance: Uniform definitions and recommended data elements.* Atlanta, GA: National Center for Injury Prevention and Control, Centers for Disease Control and Prevention.

Sandoval, J., Frisby, C. L., Geisinger, K. F., Scheuneman, J. D., & Grenier, J. R. (1998). *Test interpretation and diversity: Achieving equity in assessment.* Washington, DC: American Psychological Association.

Sattler, J. M. (1997). *Clinical and forensic interviewing of children and families.* San Diego, CA: Jerome Sattler.

Saunders, D. (1988). Wife abuse, husband abuse, or mutual combat? In K. Yllo & M. Bograd (Eds.), *Feminist perspectives on wife abuse* (pp. 90–113). Newbury Park, CA: Sage.

Saunders, D. G. (1991). Procedures for adjusting self-reports of violence for social desirability bias. *Journal of Interpersonal Violence, 6,* 336–344.

Saunders, D. G. (1992). Woman battering. In R. T. Ammerman & M. Hersen (Eds.), *Assessment of family violence: A clinical and legal sourcebook* (pp. 208–235). New York: Wiley.

Saunders, D. G. (1999). Woman battering. In R. T. Ammerman & M. Hersen (Eds.), *Assessment of family violence: A clinical and legal sourcebook* (pp. 243–270). New York: Wiley.

Saunders, D. G., Lynch, A. B., Grayson, M., & Linz, D. (1987). The Inventory of Beliefs About Wife Beating: The construction and initial validation of a measure of beliefs and attitudes. *Violence and Victims, 2,* 39–57.

Schacter, J., & O'Leary, K. D. (1985). Affective intent and impact in marital communication. *American Journal of Family Therapy, 13,* 17–23.

Schafer, J., Caetano, R., & Clark, C. (1998). Rates of intimate partner violence in the United States. *American Journal of Public Health, 88,* 1702–1704.

Schumacher, J. A., Feldbau-Kohn, S., Slep, A. M., & Heyman, R. E. (2001). Risk factors in male-to-female partner physical abuse. *Aggression and Violent Behavior, 6,* 281–352.

Schwartz, M. D., & Mattley, C. L. (1993). The battered woman scale and gender identities. *Journal of Family Violence, 8,* 277–287.

Segal, D. L., & Falk, S. B. (1998). Structured interviews and rating scales. In A. S. Bellack & M. Hersen (Eds.), *Behavioral assessment* (pp. 158–178). Boston: Allyn & Bacon.

Segal, D. L., Hersen, M., & Van Hasselt, V. B. (1994). Reliability of the Structured Clinical Interview for DSM–III–R: An evaluative review. *Comprehensive Psychiatry, 35,* 316–327.

Seidman, E. (1993). Culturally anchored methodology: An introduction to the special issue. *American Journal of Community Psychology, 21,* 683–686.

Selzer, M. L. (1971). The Michigan Alcoholism Screening Test: The quest for a new diagnostic instrument. *American Journal of Psychiatry, 127,* 89–94.

Sharpley, C. F., & Rogers, H. J. (1985). *The abbreviated Spanier Dyadic Adjustment Scale: Some psychometric data regarding a screening test of marital adjustment.* Unpublished manuscript, Department of Education, Monash University, Victoria, Australia.

Shepard, M. F., & Campbell, J. A. (1992). The Abusive Behavior Inventory. *Journal of Interpersonal Violence, 7,* 291–305.

Shepard, M. F., & Pence, E. L. (1999). *Coordinating community responses to domestic violence: Lessons from Duluth and beyond.* Thousand Oaks, CA: Sage.

Shields, N. M., & Hanneke, C. R. (1983). Battered wives' reactions to marital rape. In D. Finkelhor, R. J. Gelles, G. T. Hotaling, & M. A. Straus (Eds.), *The dark side of families: Current family violence research* (pp. 132–148). Beverly Hills, CA: Sage.

Shrout, P. E., & Fleiss, J. L. (1979). Intraclass correlations: Uses in assessing rater reliability. *Psychological Bulletin, 86,* 420–428.

Siegel, J. M. (1985). The measurement of anger as a multidimensional construct. In M. A. Chesney & R. H. Rosenman (Eds.), *Anger and hostility in cardiovascular and behavioral disorders* (pp. 59–82). Washington, DC: Hemisphere.

Siegel, J. M. (1986). The Multidimensional Anger Inventory. *Journal of Personality and Social Psychology, 51,* 191–200.

Skinner, H. A. (1982). The Drug Abuse Screening Test. *Addictive Behaviors, 7,* 363–367.

Smith, P. H., Earp, J. A., & DeVellis, R. (1995). Measuring battering: Development of the Women's Experience With Battering (WEB) Scale. *Women's Health: Research on Gender, Behavior, and Policy, 1,* 273–288.

Snyder, C. R., Crowson, J. J., Houston, B. K., Kurylo, M., & Poirer, J. (1997). Assessing hostile automatic thoughts: Development and validation of the HAT scale. *Cognitive Therapy and Research, 21,* 477–492.

Sobell, L., & Sobell, M. B. (1996). *Timeline Followback user's guide: A calendar method for assessing alcohol and drug use.* Toronto, Ontario, Canada: Addiction Research Foundation.

Sonkin, D. J., Martin, D., & Walker, L. E. A. (1985). *The male batterer: A treatment approach.* New York: Springer.

Spanier, G. B. (1976). Measuring dyadic adjustment: New scales for assessing the quality of marriage and similar dyads. *Journal of Marriage and the Family, 38,* 15–28.

Spanier, G. B., & Filsinger, E. E. (1983). The Dyadic Adjustment Scale. In E. E. Filsinger (Ed.), *Marriage and family assessment: A sourcebook for family therapy* (pp. 155–168). Beverly Hills, CA: Sage.

Spence, J. T., Helmreich, R. L., & Stapp, J. (1974). The personal attributes questionnaire. *JSAS Catalog of Selected Documents in Psychology, 4,* 43.

Spielberger, C. D. (1988). *Manual for the State–Trait Anger Expression Inventory.* Odessa, FL: Psychological Assessment Resources.

Spielberger, C. D., & Sydeman, S. J. (1994). State–Trait Anxiety Inventory and State–Trait Anger Expression Inventory. In M. E. Maruish (Ed.), *The use of psychological tests for treatment planning and outcome assessment* (pp. 292–321). Hillsdale, NJ: Erlbaum.

Spitzer, R. L., & Endicott, J. (1978). *Schedule for Affective Disorders and Schizophrenia.* New York: New York State Psychiatric Institute.

Spitzer, R. L., Williams, J. B., Gibbon, M., & First, M. B. (1988). *Structured Clinical Interview for DSM–III–R—Patient version* (SCID-P 6/1/88). New York: New York State Psychiatric Institute, Biometrics Research Department.

Spitzer, R. L., Williams, J. B., Gibbon, M., & First, M. B. (1992). The Structured Clinical Interview for DSM–III–R (SCID): I. History, rationale, and description. *Archives of General Psychiatry, 49,* 624–629.

Stark, E., & Flitcraft, A. (1983). Social knowledge, social policy, and the abuse of women: The case against patriarchal benevolence. In D. Finkelhor, R. J. Gelles, G. T. Hotaling, & M. A. Straus (Eds.), *The dark side of families: Current family violence research* (pp. 330–348). New York: Sage.

Stets, J. E., & Straus, M. A. (1990). Gender differences in reporting marital violence and its medical and psychological consequences. In M. A. Straus & R. J. Gelles (Eds.), *Physical violence in American families: Risk factors and adaptations to violence in 8,145 families* (pp. 151–164). New Brunswick, NJ: Transaction.

Stith, S. (1986). Police officer response to marital violence predicted from officer's attitude, stress, and marital experience: A path analysis. *Dissertation Abstracts International, 47(7),* 240–252. (University Microfilms No. 86-24671)

Straus, M. A. (1974). Leveling, civility, and violence in the family. *Journal of Marriage and the Family, 36,* 13–29.

Straus, M. A. (1979). Measuring intrafamily conflict and violence. *Journal of Marriage and the Family, 41,* 75–88.

Straus, M. A. (1990a). The Conflict Tactics Scale and its critics. In M. A. Straus & R. J. Gelles (Eds.), *Physical violence in American families: Risk factors and adaptations to violence in 8,145 families* (pp. 49–74). New Brunswick, NJ: Transaction.

Straus, M. A. (1990b). New scoring methods for violence and new norms for the Conflict Tactics Scales. In M. A. Straus & R. J. Gelles (Eds.), *Physical violence in American families: Risk factors and adaptations to violence in 8,145 families* (pp. 535–559). New Brunswick, NJ: Transaction.

Straus, M. A. (1993). Physical assaults by wives: A major social problem. In R. J. Gelles & D. R. Loseke (Eds.), *Current controversies in family violence* (pp. 67–87). Newbury Park, CA: Sage.

Straus, M. A. (1995). *Manual for the Conflict Tactics Scales.* Durham: University of New Hampshire, Family Research Laboratory.

Straus, M. A., & Gelles, R. J. (1986). Societal change and change in family violence from 1975–1985 as revealed by two national studies. *Journal of Marriage and the Family, 48,* 465–479.

Straus, M. A., & Gelles, R. J. (1990). *Physical violence in American families: Risk factors and adaptations to violence in 8,145 families.* New Brunswick, NJ: Transaction.

Straus, M. A., Gelles, R. J., & Steinmetz, S. K. (1980). *Behind closed doors: Violence in the American family.* New York: Anchor/Doubleday.

Straus, M. A., Hamby, S. L., Boney-McCoy, S., & Sugarman, D. B. (1996). The revised Conflict Tactics Scales (CTS2): Development and preliminary psychometric data. *Journal of Family Issues, 17,* 283–316.

Straus, M. A., Hamby, S. L., Boney-McCoy, S., & Sugarman, D. (1999). *The Personal and Relationships Profile (PRP) Form P2.* Durham: University of New Hampshire, Family Research Laboratory.

Straus, M. A., & Mouradian, V. E. (1999). *Preliminary psychometric data for the Personal and Relationships Profile (PRP): A multi-scale tool for clinical screening and research on partner violence.* Durham: University of New Hampshire, Family Research Laboratory.

Straus, M. A., & Ramirez, I. L. (1999, November). *Criminal history and assault of dating partners: The role of gender, age of onset, and type of crime.* Paper presented at the American Society of Criminology, Toronto, Ontario, Canada.

Stuart, E. P., & Campbell, J. C. (1989). Assessment of patterns of dangerousness with battered women. *Issues in Mental Health Nursing, 10,* 245–260.

Sudermann, M., & Jaffe, P. G. (1999). Child witnesses of domestic violence. In R. T. Ammerman & M. Hersen (Eds.), *Assessment of family violence: A clinical and legal sourcebook* (pp. 343–366). New York: Wiley.

Sue, D. W., Bingham, R. P., Porche-Burke, L., & Vasquez, M. (1999). The diversification of psychology: A multicultural revolution. *American Psychologist, 54,* 1061–1069.

Sue, S. (1999). Science, ethnicity, and bias: Where have we gone wrong? *American Psychologist, 54,* 1070–1077.

Sugarman, C. B., & Hotaling, G. T. (1997). Intimate violence and social desirability: A meta-analytic review. *Journal of Interpersonal Violence, 12,* 275–290.

Sugihara, Y., & Warner, J. A. (2002). Dominance and domestic abuse among Mexican Americans: Gender differences in the etiology of violence in intimate relationships. *Journal of Family Violence, 17,* 315–340.

Szinovacz, M. E. (1983). Using couple data as a methodological tool: The case of marital violence. *Journal of Marriage and the Family, 45,* 633–644.

Szinovacz, M. E., & Egley, L. C. (1995). Comparing one-partner and couple data on sensitive marital behaviors: The case of marital violence. *Journal of Marriage and the Family, 57,* 995–1010.

Taft, C. T., Murphy, C. M., King, D. W., Musser, P. H., & DeDeyn, J. M. (2003). Process and treatment adherence factors in group cognitive–behavioral therapy for partner violent men. *Journal of Consulting and Clinical Psychology, 71,* 812–820.

Tarasoff v. Regents of the University of California, 131 Cal. Rptr. 14, 551 P. 2d 334 (1976).

Taylor, S. J., & Bogdan, R. (1998). *Introduction to qualitative research methods: A guidebook and resource.* New York: Wiley.

Thyfault, R. K. (1999). Legal and systems issues in the assessment of family violence involving adults. In R. T. Ammerman & M. Hersen (Eds.), *Assessment of family violence: A clinical and legal sourcebook* (pp. 73–87). New York: Wiley.

Ting-Toomey, S. (1983). An analysis of communication patterns in high and low marital adjustment groups. *Human Communication Research, 9,* 306–319.

Tjaden, P., & Thoennes, N. (2000). Prevalence and consequences of male-to-female intimate partner violence as measured by the National Violence Against Women Survey. *Violence Against Women, 6,* 142–161.

Tolman, R. M. (1989). The development of a measure of psychological maltreatment of women by their male partners. *Violence and Victims, 4,* 159–177.

Tolman, R. M. (1999). The validation of the psychological maltreatment of women inventory. *Violence and Victims, 14,* 25–35.

Tolman, R. M., & Bennet, L. W. (1990). A review of quantitative research on men who batter. *Journal of Interpersonal Violence, 5,* 87–118.

Tolman, R. M., & Bhosley, G. (1991). The outcome of participation in a shelter sponsored program for men who batter. In D. Knudsen & J. Miller (Eds.), *Abused and battered: Social and legal responses to family violence* (pp. 169–190). Springfield, IL: Charles C Thomas.

Tolman, R. M., & Edleson, J. L. (1989). Cognitive behavioral interventions with men who batter. In B. A. Thyer (Ed.), *Behavioral family therapy* (pp. 169–190). Springfield, IL: Charles C Thomas.

Tolman, R. M., & Weisz, A. (1995). Coordinated community intervention for domestic violence: The effects of arrest and prosecution on recidivism of woman abuse perpetrators. *Crime and Delinquency, 41,* 481–495.

Tortu, S., Goldsamt, L. A., & Hamid, R. (2002). *Research and service with hidden populations.* Boston: Allyn & Bacon.

Urquiza, A. J., Wyatt, G. E., & Root, M. P. (1994). Introduction to special section: Violence against women of color. *Violence and Victims, 9,* 203–206.

Varvaro, F. F. (1990). Using a grief response assessment questionnaire in a support group to assist battered women in their recovery. *Response, 13*(4), 17–20.

Velting, D. M., Rathus, J. H., & Asnis, G. M. (1998). Asking adolescents to explain discrepancies in self-reported suicidality. *Suicide and Life-Threatening Behavior, 28,* 187–196.

Vincent, J. P., Friedman, L. C., Nugent, J., & Messerly, L. (1979). Demand characteristics in observations of marital interaction. *Journal of Consulting and Clinical Psychology, 47,* 557–566.

Vivian, D. (1990a). *The Adapted Conflict Tactics Scale.* Unpublished manuscript, Department of Psychology, State University of New York at Stony Brook.

Vivian, D. (1990b). *The Semi-Structured Marital Interview (SMI).* Unpublished manuscript, Department of Psychology, State University of New York at Stony Brook.

Vivian, D., & Heyman, R. (1996). Is there a place for conjoint treatment of couple violence? *In Session: Psychotherapy in Practice, 2,* 25–48.

Vivian, D., & Langhinrichsen-Rohling, J. (1994). Are bi-directionally violent couples mutually victimized? A gender-sensitive comparison. *Violence and Victims, 9,* 107–124.

Walker, E. A., Newman, E., Koss, M., & Bernstein, D. (1997). Does the study of victimization revictimize the victims? *General Hospital Psychiatry, 19,* 403–410.

Walker, L. (1979). *The battered woman.* New York: Harper & Row.

Walker, L. E. (1984). *The battered woman syndrome.* New York: Springer.

Walker, L. E. (1991). Posttraumatic stress disorder in women: Diagnosis and treatment of battered women syndrome. *Psychotherapy, 28,* 21–29.

Walker, L. E. (1999). Psychology and domestic violence around the world. *American Psychologist, 54,* 21–29.

Waltz, J. (1995). The relationship between heart rate reactivity, emotionally aggressive behavior, and general violence in batterers. *Journal of Family Violence, 9,* 227–248.

Waltz, J., Addis, M., Koerner, K., & Jacobson, N. S. (1993). Testing the integrity of a psychotherapy protocol: Assessment of adherence and competence. *Journal of Consulting and Clinical Psychology, 61,* 620–630.

Waltz, J., Babcock, J. C., Jacobson, N. S., & Gottman, J. M. (2000). Testing a typology of batterers. *Journal of Consulting and Clinical Psychology, 68,* 658–669.

Weathers, F. W., Keane, T. M., King, L. A., & King, D. W. (1997). Psychometric theory in the development of Posttraumatic Stress Disorder assessment tools. In J. P. Wilson & T. M. Keane (Eds.), *Assessing psychological trauma and PTSD* (pp. 98–135). New York: Guilford.

Webster, C. D., & Menzies, R. J. (1993). Supervision in the deinstitutionalized community. In S. Hodgins (Ed.), *Mental disorder and crime* (pp. 22–38). Newbury Park, CA: Sage.

Weiss, D. S., & Marmar, C. R. (1997). The Impact of Event Scale—Revised. In J. P. Wilson & T. M. Keane (Eds.), *Assessing psychological trauma and PTSD* (pp. 399–411). New York: Guilford Press.

Weiss, R. L. (1989). The circle of voyeurs: Observing the observers of marital and family interactions. *Behavioral Assessment, 11,* 135–147.

Weiss, R. L., & Cerreto, M. C. (1980). The Marital Status Inventory: Development of a measure of dissolution potential. *American Journal of Family Therapy, 8,* 80–85.

Weiss, R. L., & Heyman, R. E. (1997). Couple interaction. In W. K. Halford & H. J. Markman (Eds.), *Clinical handbook of marriage and couples intervention* (pp. 13–41). New York: Wiley.

Weiss, R. L., & Perry, B. A. (1979). Assessment and treatment of marital dysfunction. Eugene: Oregon Marital Studies Program.

Weiss, R. L., & Summers, K. J. (1983). Marital Interaction Coding System—III. In E. E. Filsinger (Ed.), *Marriage and family assessment: A sourcebook for family therapists* (pp. 85–115). Beverly Hills, CA: Sage.

Weiss, R. L., & Tolman, A. O. (1990). The Marital Interaction Coding System–Global (MICS-G): A global companion to the MICS. *Behavioral Assessment, 12,* 271–294.

Werner, P. D., Rose, T. L., & Yesavage, J. A. (1990). Aspects of consensus in clinical predictions of imminent violence. *Journal of Clinical Psychology, 46,* 534–538.

West, C. M. (1998a). Leaving a second closet: Outing partner violence in same-sex couples. In J. J. Jasinski & L. M. Williams (Eds.), *Partner violence* (pp. 163–183). Thousand Oaks, CA: Sage.

West, C. M. (1998b). Lifting the "political gag order": Breaking the silence around partner violence in ethnic minority families. In J. J. Jasinski & L. M. Williams (Eds.), *Partner violence* (pp. 184–209). Thousand Oaks, CA: Sage.

West, M., Sheldon, A., & Reiffer, L. (1987). An approach to the delineation of adult attachment: Scale development and reliability. *Journal of Nervous and Mental Disease, 175,* 738–741.

White, J. W., Smith, P. H., Koss, M. P., & Figueredo, A. J. (2000). Intimate partner aggression: What have we learned? *Psychological Bulletin, 126,* 690–696.

Whittemore, K. E., & Kropp, P. R. (2002). Spousal assault risk assessment: A guide for clinicians. *Journal of Forensic Psychology Practice, 2,* 53–64.

Wieder, G. B., & Weiss, R. L. (1980). Generalizability theory and the coding of marital interaction. *Journal of Consulting and Clinical Psychology, 48,* 469–477.

Wilson, J. P., & Keane, T. M. (Eds.). (1997). *Assessing psychological trauma and PTSD.* New York: Guilford.

Wilson, M. E., & Fruzzetti, A. E. (2000). *Intimacy and control as predictors of violence severity in batterers.* Unpublished manuscript, University of Nevada, Reno.

Wilson, M. I., & Daly, M. (1993). Spousal homicide risk and estrangement. *Violence and Victims, 8,* 3–16.

Wilson, M. I., & Daly, M. (1996). Male sexual proprietariness and violence against wives. *Current Directions in Psychological Science, 5,* 2–7.

Yllo, K. (1988). Political and methodological debates in wife abuse research. In K. Yllo & M. Bograd (Eds.), *Feminist perspectives on wife abuse* (pp. 28–50). Newbury Park, CA: Sage.

Yoshihama, M., & Horrocks, J. (2002). Posttraumatic stress symptoms and victimization among Japanese American women. *Journal of Consulting and Clinical Psychology, 70,* 205–215.

Yudofsky, S. C., Silver, J. M., Jackson, W., Endicott, J., & Williams, D. (1986). The Overt Aggression Scale for the objective rating of verbal and physical aggression. *American Journal of Psychiatry, 143,* 35–39.

Author Index

Subject Index

About the Authors

Jill H. Rathus, PhD, is associate professor of psychology at Long Island University, C.W. Post Campus (LIU) in Brookville, New York, where she is director of the specialty track in family violence. She received her undergraduate degree from Cornell University and her doctoral degree in clinical psychology from the State University of New York at Stony Brook. At Stony Brook she specialized in the study of marital discord and in the etiology and treatment of spouse abuse. Her clinical internship was at Albert Einstein College of Medicine/Montefiore Medical Center in the Bronx, New York, where she then remained as research coordinator of the Adolescent Depression and Suicide Program until she accepted her faculty position at LIU. In addition to training, consulting, and presenting her research nationally, she has published numerous articles and chapters on marital discord and domestic violence as well as on assessment issues, treatment of adolescent suicidality using dialectical behavior therapy, personality disorders, and anxiety disorders. She has authored several books, including *Marital Distress: Cognitive Behavioral Interventions for Couples.* In her clinical work, she has developed an adaptation of dialectical behavior therapy for the treatment of partner violence and maintains an active private practice specializing in couples, families, and adolescents.

Eva L. Feindler, PhD, is professor of psychology at the Long Island University (LIU) doctoral program in clinical psychology. As a faculty member of the specialty track in family violence department and as director of the Psychological Services Clinic, she is directly involved in programs to help children and families manage their anger and resolve conflict. She received her undergraduate degree in psychology from Mount Holyoke College and her master's and doctoral degrees from West Virginia University. Her clinical internship training was completed at the Children's Psychiatric Center in Eatontown, New Jersey. Before her position at LIU, she was associate professor of psychology at Adelphi University, where she also directed the master's program in applied behavioral technology. She has authored several books, including *Adolescent Anger Control, Cognitive–Behavioral Strategies, Handbook of Adolescent Behavior Therapy, Assessment of Family Violence* as well as numerous articles on parent and child anger and its assessment and treatment, and she has conducted professional training workshops internationally. She has also served an appointed term on the New York State Board for Psychology and a term on the Board of the Nassau County Psychological Association, and she was the program coordinator for the Association for the Advancement of Behavior Therapy Conference in 1995. In addition, she served on the American Psychological Association (APA) Commission on Violence and Youth from 1992 to 1995 and on the APA Task Force on Violence and the Family.